KU-164-447

A HISTORY
OF
THE ENGLISH HOUSE

A HISTORY
of the
ENGLISH HOUSE
from Primitive Times To The Victorian Period
By
NATHANIEL LLOYD

*Officer of the Most Excellent Order of the British Empire,
Fellow of the Society of Antiquaries, Fellow of the
Royal Institute of British Architects, Author of
"A History of English Brickwork," "Prac-
tical Brickwork" in the "Encyclopædia
Britannica," "Building Craftsman-
ship," "Garden Craftsmanship,"
etc., etc.*

The Architectural Press
London

Architectural Book Publishing Co.
New York

This edition published 1975 in Great Britain by the Architectural Press,
9 Queen Anne's Gate, London SW1H 9BY. This book was first
published in 1931 and twice reprinted later. First paperback edition 1976.

ISBN 0 85139 286 5 (cloth)
ISBN 0 85139 285 7 (paper)

First published in the United States 1975 by the Architectural Book
Publishing Co., Inc., 10 East 40th Street, New York, N.Y. 10016.

ISBN 0 8038 0107 6

All rights reserved. No part of this publication may be reproduced, stored
in a retrieval system, or transmitted in any form or by any means—graphic,
electronic or mechanical, including photocopying, recording, taping, or
otherwise—without written permission of the publishers.

Copyright © The Architectural Press, London, 1975

Printed in Great Britain by W & J Mackay Limited, Chatham

PUBLISHER'S NOTE

ALTHOUGH it has long been out of print, the demand for this well-known book still continues. There are three main reasons why this is so. Firstly, the late Nathaniel Lloyd brought to its compilation an intensive scholarship gained from a lifetime spent in studying the buildings of this country. Secondly, the chronological arrangement of the illustration sections, which contain nearly 900 pictures, provide an invaluable way of easily understanding how domestic architecture developed and changed in style through the centuries. Thirdly, it may well be claimed that this book is still without rival in the way that, in a single volume, the subject is covered so comprehensively.

Thus, because there is now an increasing interest in the historical buildings of England, and because both the text and the illustrations are as relevant today as when first published, it has been decided to reprint this book once again.

LONDON, *January,* 1975

PREFACE

THE SCOPE of this history is the development of the English House, illustrated by photographs beginning with the earliest examples that exist. Inasmuch as none of these are anterior to Norman buildings, the Introduction includes illustrations of primitive types and traces the connection between them and medieval dwellings. Instead of assuming (as has usually been done) that architecture, as an art, terminated with the eighteenth century, the theme has been continued into the nineteenth century, but allowed to fade away at that Victorian period which the French have named so aptly " l'époque du mauvais goût." Thus it has been possible to trace the decadence of classic design and to indicate the nature of Gothic revival.

Following the general text, which is arranged in centuries, are the illustrations in sections:

1. Plans and Exteriors.
2. External Wall Treatment.
3. Entrances.
4. Windows.
5. Chimneys.
6. Interiors.
7. Internal Wall Treatment.
8. Ceilings.
9. Fireplaces.
10. Staircases.
11. Metalwork.
12. Various, including constructional drawings, etc.,
    incorporated with the general text.

Each illustration has its descriptive caption, so that the volume may be described as consisting of treatises upon a dozen branches of architecture, each of which is independent of others but is linked up with them by its caption and by the general text.

A photograph of a building necessarily includes alterations and additions, which a drawing might omit, but such a mixture of several periods produces a charm and quality of its own. Usually, alterations are obvious, but in many cases they have been indicated in the captions or, alternatively, reference has been made only to the details, for which the illustration is given.

In writing this History, three classes of readers have been considered:

1. The student of architecture, who wishes to inform himself respecting a particular period or to obtain definite knowledge of house design.

2. The general reader, who finds architecture an attractive subject but so complex as to be difficult to grasp.

3. The reader who wishes to identify or to date a Building, Staircase, Chimneypiece, Doorway or other detail.

The illustrations, arranged chronologically, with their descriptive captions are complete in themselves and should render reference quick and easy.

As a preface to each section (Doorways, Windows, etc.), references are made to other pages where further illustrations of Doorways, Windows, etc., are to be found.

Notwithstanding the number of illustrations (which is more than four times as many as in any other work covering similar ground) it would be easy to indicate omissions. Yet a choice had to be made. It is hoped this choice may be found to have included the most typical subjects with special prominence given to those which are most important.

As attaching dates to buildings and their details inevitably produces inconsistencies (real or apparent), it may be mentioned that dates have been determined (i) by documentary evidence, (ii) by comparison with examples not illustrated here (the dates of which were known) and (iii) by illustrations of details in books on architecture (of which many were published in the eighteenth century), which prove when such details were in fashion. Inasmuch as a detail current in London at a certain time may be found repeated in the country twenty, thirty, or forty years later, dating should be regarded only as approximate, and as being introduced for the convenience of the reader and not as irrefutable fact.

The writer of a book of reference must owe much to others for encouragement, for facilities granted and for personal assistance given. The inception of this history is due to the foresight and imagination of Mr. de Cronin Hastings, Editor of the *Architectural Review*, who induced me to undertake the work and who allowed it to run through the pages of the *Review* for three and a half years—probably a record in serials—without suggesting curtailment. That it was curtailed, out of respect for the obvious limitations of space in a journal, will be apparent when it is known that this volume contains 40 per cent. more illustrations and matter than appeared in the *Architectural Review*.

To the owners of houses illustrated, which include the most important and interesting in a country that teems both with great mansions and homely dwellings, I cannot adequately express my gratitude for the opportunities granted me to see and photograph their houses and for the interest and kindness vouchsafed me. They appreciated the educational importance of a history of English Houses, and showed appreciation in that gracious and cordial manner for which English gentlemen and gentlewomen are distinguished.

In acknowledgment of illustrations from photographs or drawings other than my own, I have attached the owners' names, thinking this more adequate than the practice of condensing all acknowledgments into one paragraph. I have to thank that great architectural scholar, Mr. Arthur T. Bolton, F.S.A., F.R.I.B.A., curator of the Soane Museum, for drawing my attention to many matters of interest and for correcting more than one error of fact. To Mr. Maurice A. Regan, of the Architectural Press, my thanks are due for the rare faculty he possesses in ability to scrap old ideas in favour of new ones and for the unflagging energy which he has brought to bear upon the problems of production, by which he has infected everyone concerned with a desire to get right and to get on.

I have been fortunate in having had criticism from that able medieval historian, Mr. T. D. Atkinson, F.R.I.B.A., who read the instalments of the medieval period as they went forward to the *Architectural Review*. The task of correction of proofs has been stupendous, but in this I have had the assistance of my wife, whose knowledge, application and vigilance detected many errors that had escaped others.

One characteristic of English house design is concentration upon essentials both by architects and craftsmen. I have endeavoured to follow their example by eliminating much that might have been included but which was not necessary, and by wording descriptions as concisely as possible. I have tried also to document references sufficiently without irritating the reader.

In presenting *A History of the English House* as I have traced it—which is as it appears to me—I hope I may have been able to make clearer what hitherto has always seemed obscure to the novice. When I began the history, I thought I could make it clearer than I feel I have succeeded in doing, but the theme is complex, the changes in fashions, styles, and methods were slow and involved, and the whole extended over eight hundred years. Perhaps the best method of getting a general view of development and of the relation of one period to another is to turn over the pages of each section of illustrations and to note how, although examples coming close together may seem mixed, illustrations a few pages apart distinctly show the evolution of each new style.

NATHANIEL LLOYD.

GREAT DIXTER,
    NORTHIAM, SUSSEX.
        November, 1931.

CONTENTS

TEXT

ILLUSTRATIONS

INTRODUCTION

IN WRITING of the development of English houses, it is usual to begin with Norman castles, and to refer, perhaps, to buildings showing Norman influence, which were erected shortly before the Conquest ; but the subject cannot properly be understood or the significance of later design appreciated without some reference to the history of this country during Roman and Saxon times, in order to show how far the homes of the dominant inhabitants of the first thousand years affected the developments of the next thousand years.

The Roman occupation of Britain had little permanent effect upon native architecture. At first the Romans enslaved and taxed the conquered people, but gradually assimilated with the inhabitants of the South, East and Midland counties, where Romans and Britons formed a Romano-British stock. In the West and North the occupation was military, and there was little combination of the warring races: indeed, beyond the Trent and in Wales a continuous state of rebellion existed between the inhabitants and the large Roman forces who kept them within bounds. Romanization of the fertile areas of England began before the Roman conquest, so that the inhabitants already had adopted Roman industries, life and manners, including Roman methods of building. After the occupation, colonies and settlements (as at St. Albans and Colchester) were centres from which the surrounding districts became Romanized. Although a considerable measure of independence and self-government was encouraged, the only trained soldiers were those of the regular army, and when the legions were withdrawn early in the fifth century the defenceless and undefended inhabitants were easy prey to every invader. It may seem incredible that a people so long in contact with Roman civilization as to have become thoroughly Romanized should have been effaced so completely that every art, every manufacture, and every custom and habit of living should have disappeared. The explanation lies in the difference between the Romans and those conquerors who succeeded them. The Saxons, Danes and others who invaded the country after Roman evacuation, landed on the east and south coasts. They did not come to rule and take tribute, or to assimilate with the inhabitants, but to supplant and to occupy. Their policy was to destroy the inhabitants, and where they enslaved some, successive waves of immigrants (also from Saxon, Scandinavian and similar sources) treated those who had preceded them just as they had treated the Romanized inhabitants. It is not difficult to realize that such waves of destruction, repeated at frequent intervals during hundreds of years, must inevitably have effaced not only all traces of Roman influence but also those of the inhabitants in those areas where Romanization had been most complete ; for those were precisely the districts assimilated by the Saxons. This view is that adopted by Mr. Trevelyan, who points out that the only tangible results of Roman occupation in England are the roads they made.[1] This is the answer to those who find it difficult to understand how well-established arts could have become extinct in this country between Roman and medieval times. Of these one instance will suffice. If there was one industry which the Romans introduced here that can be said to have been more widely spread than any other, it was that of brickmaking, yet that art died out with their occupation. To those who argue that bricks *may* have been made in the Roman manner by the Saxons, one may reply that as Saxon buildings which contain brick are found only in the neighbourhood of Roman ruins, and where there are no such ruins existing Saxon buildings are constructed of local stone, it is reasonable to infer (until evidence to the contrary is forthcoming) that the Saxons did not make the bricks, and that brick was not made here until about the year 1200, when we find the earliest medieval brick, made in quite different fashion from that of the Romans.

Of Roman houses there were three types, two of which are characteristic. These were the corridor type and the central court type ; practically nothing of these remain but foundations, enabling us only to trace the plans. Large establishments consisted of many buildings, sometimes equal in area and accommodation to a small town. With these we are not concerned, but with typical villas. The corridor type consisted of a series of rooms, often opening one off another and having a corridor on one side, open to the air like a veranda (Fig. 1A). A more developed plan was that where the rooms enclosed a central court (atrium) (Fig. 1B), which was open to the air in sunny climes but may have been roofed over in other latitudes. This central space has been regarded by some as the original of the hall of the medieval manor house, but the central common-room may be traced far back to Greek and Asiatic prototypes, and the English hall is more directly developed from the Saxon *halla* than from the Latin *aula*. There is little resemblance between the medieval hall and the atrium, but close resemblance between the Saxon and Danish hall and our medieval hall.

The Saxon dwelling was of altogether different character from the Roman house (for convenience, the word *Saxon* will be used to include all those invaders and settlers—Scandinavians, Danes, Jutes and Saxons—between the Roman and the Norman invasions), but, unfortunately, no examples remain. It is remarkable that even the earliest invaders after Roman evacuation did not occupy the houses they found, nor do any remains of Roman dwellings show traces of Saxon occupation. There are reasons also for believing that even

[1] *History of England*, by G. M. Trevelyan, London, 1926.

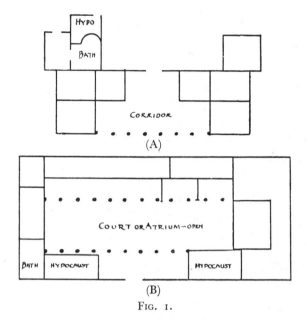

FIG. I.

FIG. I.—*Foundations of Roman houses which have been uncovered reveal many types; two are illustrated : (a) Rooms with a corridor, open to the air on one side; (b) The central court (atrium) surrounded by rooms. Probably the superstructures of most houses, even large ones, were of timber and plaster. Roman houses were heated by hot-air flues from a central furnace, and many had baths, some of which consisted of several rooms, heated to different temperatures, like our " Turkish baths." The Romans do not appear to have used soap, but were scraped and rubbed while in the hot rooms and then rubbed with oil or unguents. The Roman house-plan did not influence later design, nor were its amenities copied by the Saxons.*

Roman villas of the best type had superstructures of wood and plaster, which may account for the total obliteration of everything but their foundations and such details as hot-air flues and bathing arrangements. The Saxons destroyed and killed remorselessly wherever they went, and although they used such building materials as they found, they seem as a rule even to have avoided sites of Roman buildings, preferring fresh ones near at hand; whether superstition was the reason for this abstention, we do not know.

There are Saxon churches, as that at Earl's Barton (Fig. 2), built of stone, but they are of late date and do not materially help us to form any idea of contemporary dwelling-houses. Illustrations of houses in manuscripts and

FIG. 2.—*Though not strictly within the province of this history the Saxon tower of Earl's Barton Church, Northants, is illustrated to show how persons accustomed to build with timber (as the Saxons were) employed the same methods when they had to use stone. The strips of stone, vertical and horizontal like posts and beams, are strutted diagonally with further strips just as the builder would have strutted with oak. The quoins of the tower have alternate upright and horizontal stones, which are examples of the well-known " long and short work," a distinctive feature of Saxon stone buildings. This tower is an interesting survival—even the arches and turned balusters look as if they were made of wood.*

Photo: Valentine and Sons, Ltd.

FIG. 2.

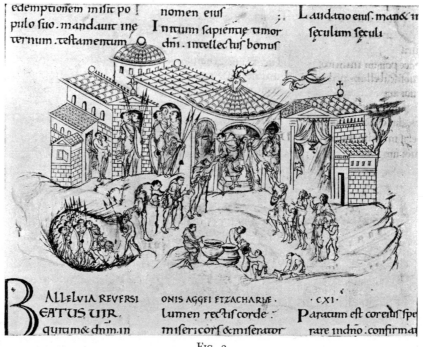

edemptionem misit po
pulo suo. mandauit ine
ternum testamentum

nomen eius
I nitium sapientiæ timor
dñi. intellectus bonus

L audatio eius. manet ii
seculum seculi

ALLELVIA REVERSI
BEATUS UIR
quium & dñm. in

ONIS AGGEI ETZACHARIÆ.
lumen rectis corde:
misericors & miserator

· CXI·
Paratum est cor eius spe
rare indño. confirmat

FIG. 3.

FIGS. 3 AND 4.—*These ninth-century drawings, illustrating Saxon houses, are Byzantine in character, are drawn to represent benevolent actions rather than exact buildings, and must not be accepted too literally. They are free pictures, but the usual elements of hall, bowers, and chapel are there. The Thane's house might consist of separate buildings, enclosed by a stockade, or might combine all three apartments under one roof. Serfs and those who did not share the accommodation of the hall dwelt in huts.*

descriptions of them in Saxon literature must not be taken too literally. References to heroes are often more legendary and mythological than historical, and the Saxon's tendency to boasting, both when in and out of liquor, is apparent. There are illustrations (Figs. 3 and 4) in the Harleian MSS.[1] which at least are interesting. One (Fig. 3) shows a group of Saxon buildings, partly of stone, partly of timber, and represents a lord and his lady in the act of distributing food and clothing to the poor. The building with the antlered head as a ridge finial is the hall, at the entrance to which the benefactors are handing out loaves of bread. On the extreme left is a bower, from which an attendant is bringing clothing for the naked. Between this and the hall is another building, from which armed men are issuing. On the extreme right is the chapel, surmounted by a cross; the lean-to adjoining is probably another sleeping-place. The other illustration (Fig. 4) represents a man and woman, crowned (each with knife in hand), at table, where they are being served by three attendants. Curtains are drawn aside to give a view of the interior, and from contemporary references it appears that a curtain often took the place of a door. The bower is a lean-to structure, also with curtained entrance. In the foreground another crowned man is distributing alms, and on the left is a chapel where foot-washing is in progress.

[1] No. 603, fols. 57 and 67.

FIG. 4.

These drawings are ninth-century illustrations of Psalms cxi and cxxv—Vulgate version. As authorities for contemporary buildings they must be viewed with caution. The draughtsman's details seem to have been inspired by Southern European architecture, and it is quite possible that he himself may have come from the Mediterranean. It is clear that the establishments represented are those of exceptional persons, and certainly show the limited nature of the accommodation enjoyed by, possibly, an earl, who exercised lordship over a large district, whose pursuits were war, hunting, and drinking, and who was maintained by the labours of husbandmen, whom he protected. It should be remembered that the Saxons were agriculturists, that they and their families lived in intimate association with servants and retainers (hearth-men), with whom they shared the home. Under the same roof also cattle were lodged, together with the produce of the land.[1] To find examples of such an establishment we must go to those lands from which the Saxons came, where there survive homesteads of some antiquity and where there are modern ones still built upon the same plan. Fig. 5 shows such a homestead in Friesland; Fig. 6 the plan and section of another at Edam, in Holland, which is only twelve miles from Amsterdam. Long after this type of building was abandoned in England, farm servants continued to share lodgings with cattle, and even sixteenth-century inventories record sheets, blankets, and other bedding in the ox-houses. Recently, until horses were supplanted by motor-cars, it was common practice for the coachman, his wife and family, to be lodged over the stables.

[1] Medieval timber buildings usually were built in bays or half bays, the bay being the space required to stable a yoke of oxen—about 16½ ft. or one rod, a measurement which is still employed in measuring land.

FIG. 5.

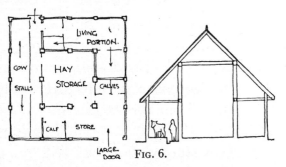

FIGS. 5 AND 6.—*When not warriors the Saxons were agriculturists : the lord living under the same roof as his retainers, his servants, his cattle, and the produce of his land. The " lofty hall " like a barn, with sleeping chambers (bowers) attached, has its modern prototype in the lands (like Friesland) from which the Saxons came. Fig. 5 is a comparatively modern Friesland homestead, where barn, cattle-stalls, stables, and dwelling-house are covered by one roof. Fig. 6 shows the plan and section of another homestead at Edam, only twelve miles from Amsterdam, which marks the divisions of the interior and the timber framing, all similar in character to the Saxon timber house of 1,100 years ago, to the medieval barn (Fig. 18), and to the stone-pillared hall at Oakham (Fig. 581).*

Reference has been made to Saxon churches built of stone. These are all late and possess features such as "long and short work," posts, beams and even struts: all being timber details which were imitated with strips of stone and are reminiscent of timber construction. Timber, which was plentiful everywhere, was the Saxon's building material; indeed, an instance of it remains at Greensted Church, Essex (Fig. 7), a building which

> " is formed of split trunks of oak trees, the top part being cut to a thin edge, which is let into a deep groove in the plate and pinned. The bottoms of these upright timbers were mortised into the sill. Their sides were grooved with tongues of oak let in between them."[1]

The joints between the logs now are covered inside by modern wood fillets pinned to the flat sides of the logs. At the angles a three-quarter log (rebated

[1] *Essex Arch. Soc.*, vol. ii, N.S., p. 397, Colchester, 1884, article by Rev. R. W. Ray, on " Restoration of the Church." Other writers say the sills are later than the uprights, and do not mention grooves and tongues.

FIG. 7.

FIGS. 7 AND 8.—*There is one building, the Saxon church of Greensted, Essex, which provides first-hand evidence of Saxon building methods. Though not now intact it was originally built entirely of timber, and there still remain palisade walls of split logs. It is not unlike the log hut of the backwoods. The plan shows how at the angles a three-quarter section log was ingeniously used.*

SAXON LOG WALL
AS AT GREENSTED CHURCH.

FIG. 8.

inside) was placed (Fig. 8).[1] Such construction is akin to other primitive work, like colonial pioneers' blockhouses, which, however, were usually constructed of logs laid horizontally. That the Saxon's building material was timber is further indicated by his word for building being " timbriam," literally " timber," while " getimbriam " (to build) meant to construct of timber; hence the scanty architectural remains of this period, the paucity of which contrasts with the multitude of buildings left by the stone-working Normans, who succeeded the Saxons.

Fully to establish the origins of the medieval house, it will be convenient now to consider some primitive dwellings and to see how they developed into those of which examples are still extant.

Scientists tell us that an animal's first instinct is to seek shelter, its second

---

[1] *The Arts in Early England*, by G. Baldwin Brown, London, 1905, vol. ii, pp. 41-2.

to obtain food. Such shelters as caves, pits roofed with branches, screens of interlaced boughs, huts formed of a framework of branches arched by sticking the ends into the ground, and others of similarly slight design, scarcely come within the definition of house. It is, however, necessary that allusion should be made to primitive types of dwellings, because the later and more complex house is often a development of these simple forms. It must also be remembered that, up to the close of the medieval period, artisans, labourers, and other humble folk occupied dwellings of flimsy character, constructed of such materials as timber (in small sizes), faggot-wood, mud, reed, and straw. These have long since disappeared; such small buildings as remain being more substantial structures, either the houses of the great, of their servants or of prosperous persons. The circular hut, of whatever materials constructed, is probably the earliest type. Remains have been found not only in this country, but all over the world. At East Tilbury,[1] on the foreshore of the Thames, below the present high-water level, are remains of four circular huts, varying in diameter from $11\frac{1}{2}$ to 20 ft. The circles consist of three rings of pointed stakes, each $1\frac{1}{2}$ to 2 in. in diameter, which form a framework for wattles (interlaced branches), some of which are preserved in the mud as they were made. These huts are of pre-Conquest origin, and were provided with planked floors and burnt roof-tiles; details which earlier huts would not have had.

The occupants of such late Celtic huts as these and of the lake dwellings (c. 300 B.C.) at Glastonbury, had attained a certain standard of civilization. They practised the arts of spinning and weaving, had iron tools and lathes; they also made and used highly decorated pottery of native type. They had rings of jet, amber, and bronze, and glass beads. They grew their own corn, which they ground in querns, and were no mean carvers of wood.[2]

Although early huts have perished, and we can only learn their nature from foundations and scanty remains, the art of constructing them and their very forms and details have been handed down to our own times. As is often the case, survivals from very early periods persist in some vocation or trade. The circular hut, formed of stakes thrust into the ground, forked or tied together at the top and covered with turves or other convenient material, is still built all over Europe, including Yorkshire, by charcoal burners for temporary shelter, but is scarcely capable of affording comfortable housing for longer periods than a few months. A more highly developed construction in the same materials is still built (or was up to the war) by bark-peelers in the Lake District—High Furness. These have been described by Mr. H. S. Cowper, whose photograph of one is shown here (Fig. 9). Four poles are stuck into the ground and their upper ends tied to a short ridge pole. The feet of the four poles enclose a space

---

[1] *Hist. Mon. Com. Essex*, iv, p. 38.
[2] *Evolution of the English House*, by S. O. Addy, London, 1905, p. 8.

Photo by courtesy of H. S. Cowper, F.S.A.

FIG. 9.

FIGS. 9 AND 10.—*In many ways the poor man's house is the most important of all, for it is more interesting to know how ordinary folk were lodged than how kings and lords built castles and fortresses. Unfortunately, the poor man's hut was built of flimsy materials ; it did not last him very long, and, naturally, none have survived to modern times. However, tradition, which often preserves ancient customs and ways in some trade or vocation which is practised in remote country districts, once more furnishes a wonderful illustration. The barkpeeler's hut is an archaic type which is still built for use; just as charcoal burners in Yorkshire and in most European countries still build similar huts of poles and turves, but circular in plan and looking like wigwams. In the bark-peeler's hut here illustrated four men live for months at a time in the summer. The floor of the hut measures about thirteen feet by eight feet. There is a hearth and a stone chimney. Turf huts similar to Fig. 9 are built and occupied in Lapland at the present day.*

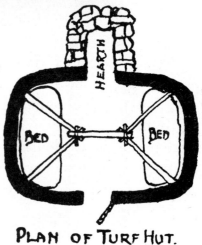

PLAN OF TURF HUT.
FIG. 10.

of 13 ft. by 8 ft. Double side walls, 2 ft. high, are constructed of wattles, and the space between packed tightly with earth. On these dwarf walls lighter poles are set, with their smaller ends supported by the ridge pole, and these are covered with overlapping turves, having the grassy sides turned inwards. The doorway consists of two posts bearing a lintel and with a closing door of wattle. Opposite this is a stone-built hearth with rough chimney, also of stone (see plan, Fig. 10). Such a hut accommodates four men for several months, and there can be no doubt that its construction has been handed down through countless generations from primitive times (Fig. 11 shows a similar hut in Lapland). These are the prototype of the booth, the humble dwelling of medieval times. So firmly was this form of building established that it was retained when other and quite unsuitable materials were employed. It is a remarkable characteristic of builders of all ages to adhere to an established form of design, devised for certain

Photo by courtesy of R. R. Gordon-Barrett.

FIG. 11.—In LAPLAND. A Lapp hut on the edge of LAKE TORNETRASK.

FIG. 11.—*Stake and turf-clad huts of the same form as Fig. 9 are still constructed and occupied by Lapps.   On the right of the illustration is the primitive outdoor cooking apparatus.*

materials, long after those materials have been superseded by others for which the traditional form is quite unsuited. Instances might be quoted from every age, but two will suffice. One, the continuance by the Greeks of principles of timber construction after timber had been abandoned for stone—*e.g.*, the triglyphs of the Doric frieze are stone ornaments representing the ends of wooden beams. A more modern example is that of steel construction, where the same process of evolution is now proceeding, the evolution being from stone forms to new forms of its own. Fig. 12 is of a stone hut at Dingle, County Kerry, known as the Gallerus Oratory, of which other examples exist in the West of Ireland and in the West of Scotland. This is a stone edition of the stakes-and-turves hut of Fig. 9. The builder, having neither imagination nor feeling for construction, followed closely the old type of hut design, although this was unsuited to stone. This building possesses especial interest as having been erected *c.* A.D. 700—1,200 years ago. It is 15 ft. 3 in. in length, 10 ft. 2 in. in width, and 16 ft. high. It is built of flat greenstone rubble, and only the doorway dressings are wrought. No mortar is used. The east window is round-headed and is splayed on all sides. It is only 3 ft. 4 in. high. The doorway is 5 ft. 7 in. high.[1] This building is believed to have been occupied by a priest, but no doubt it was of a type current at that time and was built of stone because stone happened to be plentiful : local material being a determining factor applicable to buildings in days when transport was slow and difficult.

Another structure of the booth type, the ground covered by which, as Mr. Addy points out, is almost identical with the dimensions (20 ft. by 18 ft.) re-

---

[1] *Notes on Irish Architecture*, by the third Earl of Dunraven, London, 1875.

Photo: W. Lawrence, Dublin.

Fig. 12.

FIG. 12.—*So strong was tradition and so general the turf hut that even in stone districts, and amongst comparatively advanced people, established forms lingered on, and the turf hut construction was retained, though unsuited to stone into which it was translated. The Gallerus Oratory, a priest's cell at Dingle, Ireland, is only one of many similar structures.*

corded in the middle of the fourteenth century as those of a booth, still stands at Dalderby, in Lincolnshire. It is known locally as Tea-Pot Hall, and described as:

> Tea-Pot Hall,
> All roof, no wall.

This couplet is actually a description of most early buildings, for the development of the house was the development of the simple, protective roof, consisting, as at Tea-Pot Hall, of two pairs of straight timbers supporting a ridge pole. Such timbers have been called, at various times and in various localities, forks, gavels (hence gable), couples of syles, and crucks, the last term being of wide distribution. Smaller timbers between the pairs of crucks serve as rafters, which in this building are thatched for three-quarters of their length and covered with stone slates near the ground. At the back (not to be confused either with the pantiled building or with the detached thatched building) is a short extension, commonly known as the outshot, which served as scullery, pantry, and to accommodate the step ladder, which gave access to the bedroom above. The thatched roof of this extension can just be discerned in Fig. 13, which also shows the dormer window. Fig. 14 shows the stone chimney, and both illustrations exhibit clearly the crucks at the entrance end. An obvious objection to this type of building is the scanty headroom, particularly in the

Photo: H. Carlton, Horncastle.

FIG. 13.

Photo: H. Carlton.

FIGS. 13 AND 14.—*Tea-pot Hall. Another survival of an early type of building, which in this instance is itself ancient, stands at Dalderby, near Spalding, Lincolnshire. It closely resembles written descriptions that we have of the medieval booth or home of humble folk, and is merely a later stage of development of the " all-roof" type of building. Like the turf hut, it is formed of inclined timbers, supporting a ridge, covered (in this case) partly with thatch and partly with slates. Fig. 14 shows the other side of the house with its stone chimney, and both views clearly indicate the crucks supporting the roof at the entrance end although they have been white-washed. At the back of the house is a short extension called the outshot, which serves as a scullery and pantry.*

FIG. 14.

bedroom. This brought forth devices to secure upright walls, the transition to which is clearly to be seen in the view of a cottage at Didbrook, Gloucestershire (Fig. 15), which is typical of many others even now remaining in the midland and northern counties; though those in the latter, often being cased with stone, are not so easily detected. The gable end of the Didbrook cottage shows the pair of crucks as in the wall-less house called Tea-Pot Hall, but at the feet of these are upright posts, set on horizontal timbers (sills), raised slightly from the ground on stones. These posts are tied to the crucks by short hori-zontal pieces of oak, and on top of the posts are the horizontal timbers called wall-plates, on which the feet of the common rafters, covered by tiles, rest. The wall-plates cannot be seen in the illustration, being concealed by the eaves, but the common rafters are exposed to view. Between these and the crucks are rudimentary principal rafters. The illustration of the interior of a barn at Tirley, Gloucestershire (Fig. 17), shows cruck construction where the effort

FIG. 15.—A cottage at DIDBROOK, GLOUCESTERSHIRE.

FIG. 15.—*The great defect of the preceding buildings illustrated was lack of headroom. Here this is rectified by the addition of upright posts set on timber sills, which support and raise the roof timbers away from the inclined crucks, which may be seen in the exposed gable wall, and which correspond with the roof of Tea-pot Hall.*

FIG. 16.—LINK FARM, EGERTON, KENT.

FIG. 16.—*The inclined crucks as used in the house at Didbrook (Fig. 15) were no longer required after posts and wall-plates had been adopted, so, presently, were omitted. Thus the true medieval hall-in-the-centre house was ultimately evolved from the primitive hut type. The windows are later insertions.*

to make upright walls is less advanced than at Didbrook. In course of time crucks were omitted from such timber construction and the framing carried out with upright and horizontal timbers, the only sloping timbers being the rafters, and perhaps short curved or straight braces as at Link Farm, Egerton, Kent (Fig. 16).

Fig. 18 shows the interior of a late medieval barn (probably fifteenth century) at Godmersham, Kent, which is typical of timber construction whether applied to church or hall or barn. This has a central nave with aisles on either side, formed by extension of the roof beyond the great posts on each side of the nave. We are prone to regard such structures as peculiar to ecclesiastical buildings, but up to and during

Photo by courtesy of W. L. Mellersh, Esq.

FIG. 17.—The interior of a barn at TIRLEY, GLOUCESTERSHIRE, built with couples of crucks and showing a timid effort to form upright walls.

FIG. 18.—The interior of a barn at GODMERSHAM, KENT.

Photo: Valentine and Sons, Ltd.

FIG. 19.—ST. MARY'S HOSPITAL, CHICHESTER.

FIGS. 18 AND 19.—*Elementary problems of roof construction having been overcome, their development and application to the building of church or house proceeded simultaneously ; the medieval
builder not having one style for God's house and another for man's house.   The barn at Godmersham,
Kent (Fig. 18), is thus a type of construction common to barns, churches, and halls during the
Middle Ages.   St. Mary's Hospital, Chichester, which is similar to the Godmersham barn, was
built first to house the sick and later to house pensioners, who used the nave as a hall, the aisles as
lodgings, and the nave extension as a chapel.   Here we have domestic and ecclesiastical architecture,
all one style, all under one roof.*

the medieval period the distinctions which we associate with domestic and church
architecture did not exist.   This is exhibited clearly in the interior of St. Mary's
Hospital, Chichester (Fig. 19), built in the late thirteenth century, but including
later alterations.   It consists of a nave 84 ft. long, with aisles on either side,
like the Godmersham barn.   The side walls are only 6 ft. high, and originally
were pierced with sixteen small windows, while at the west end was a
large window.   At a later date the aisles were partitioned into cubicles—the
private apartments of the pensioners, who used the nave as a common-room.
The nave (but not the aisles) is continued a further 47 ft. eastwards, the extension
forming the chapel, divided from the nave by a screen.   The east window of
the chapel is a restoration.   In these two illustrations we have interiors of similar
buildings used respectively for agricultural, domestic, and religious purposes.

Readers will have noticed that all the buildings illustrated thus far have more or less the form of inverted boats or ships, which is particularly striking in these two interiors.   In this relation it is, therefore, interesting to note that the word *nave* is derived from the Latin *navis*, while the German word for the nave of a church is *schiff*, a ship.[1]

Tracing the development of timber construction has carried us too far; we must revert to earlier times, and next take up the study of buildings in chronological order, beginning with the Normans.

[1] *Evolution of the English House*, by S. O. Addy, p. 29.

Chapter I

THE CONQUEST TO THE END OF THE TWELFTH CENTURY

WILLIAM I, 1066-87; WILLIAM II, 1087-1100; HENRY I, 1100-35; STEPHEN, 1135-54; HENRY II, 1154-89; RICHARD I, 1189-99; JOHN, 1199-1216

THE SAXON and Norman invasions were the greatest events in English history, and of these the Saxon was the more important.

"It has given us the blood that flows in our veins, the greater portion of our language, territorial divisions, names of places (each with a few exceptions) and those of the days of the week. No subsequent foreign admixture has so deeply affected it. The Norman Conquest has been the most influential event in our history since the Saxon invasion. It gave us, for many generations, French sovereigns and a French aristocracy, and it modified profoundly our laws and language, without essentially changing the life-blood of the nation."[1]

Following the Conquest, three languages were current in England: French, spoken by the Norman aristocracy; English, spoken by the people they had conquered and held in subjection; and Latin, the language of the Church and of literature and learning. At the end of five hundred years, English was the only language. True, time had modified it from the Saxon-English and it had absorbed much from French and Latin, but neither of these was spoken nor was in daily use by any class of society.

Similarly, the Normans changed the manner of building. They substituted stone for timber; but when the castle-building period of the purely fortress type began to be superseded, towards the close of the reign of Henry II (1154-89), by manor-houses, fortified by walls and moats, the Saxon hall (extending the whole height of the building from ground to roof) gradually took the place of the Norman type of a hall on an upper floor over a vaulted ground-floor chamber. For a time we find both types being built, then only the Saxon; until it, in its turn, merged into houses in that new manner which became general in the seventeenth century.

It took the Normans many years to consolidate their conquest of England, and effectually to do this it was necessary they should establish themselves in fortresses sufficiently strong to resist attacks by any insurrection of Saxons. So far as we know, the Saxons had no stone fortresses, and defensive works were usually confined to a stockade built round their dwellings. It is doubtful

---

[1] G. Warde Norman, in *Arch. Cantiana*, xiii, 97.

whether even so important a place as Dover Castle had stone defences. For many years after the Conquest the Normans (by forced labour) constructed their castles of timber, erecting them on mounds, thrown up to considerable height, the excavations forming a deep ditch all round. The earliest stone castle was the Tower of London, the Keep (White Tower) of which was completed before the death of the Conqueror in 1087. Rochester Castle (Figs. 43 and 578), which commanded the important crossing of the Medway on the road to Dover, was built c. 1130, and Castle Hedingham (Figs. 41, 42, 579) about the same time. These are early examples and each still has many features in good preservation, whilst Castle Rising (Fig. 44) (built a little later) retains the forebuilding which the other two have lost. The nucleus of these fortresses was the square keep, which stood in a court or bailey (seldom in the centre, however), and round the bailey was a wall, having a gatehouse and towers at salient points. Many had also an outer bailey encircled by a similar and more strongly fortified wall. Minor buildings were contained within the walls. Rochester Castle was 300 ft. square within the walls and was capable of holding a garrison strong enough to defy the king himself. There was a trestle bridge 431 ft. long over the river; repairs to it are mentioned in the reign of Henry I, the nature of which shows it must then have been an old bridge. So important was the situation of the castle that it had been the site of other fortresses long before the Conquest. The keep is 70 ft. square at the base, the walls 12 ft. thick, and the height to the summit of the turrets is 125 ft. Each floor consists of two rooms, each 46 ft. by 21 ft.; but the third floor occupied by the Great Hall has arches pierced in the partition wall, and is therefore 46 ft. square and has a height of 30 ft. Further description is given under the illustrations. It will be seen how cold, draughty, and comfortless this type of building must have been. In the reign of Stephen (1135-54) castle-building passed all bounds. Great numbers of castles sprang up all over the country built by minor members of the new aristocracy (without licence of the king, and so termed adulterine castles), who gathered round them forces with which they harassed and plundered the countryside. Perhaps there has never been a time when the inhabitants of England were in such a miserable plight as when at the mercy of these men who knew no mercy. On the accession of Henry II (1154-89) many of these castles, as well as those of the more important nobles, were destroyed or were used by the king to strengthen his own position; but at the end of his reign it has been estimated that there were over a thousand castles in England and Wales. By this time fortified manor-houses, to which reference has been made, were becoming established, but even these required a licence from the king to permit the licensee to " embattle, crenellate, and machicolate " the building contemplated. Castles of the Edwardian type were actually large fortresses pushed forward into hostile country like Wales. They consisted of concentric rings of walls (having towers at frequent intervals), the inner court formed by which contained inhabited buildings. There was no longer a square stone keep of Norman type.[1]

There are a few town houses of this period of which sufficient remain for us to form an accurate idea of the dwelling of a well-to-do person. The Jews' houses at Lincoln (Fig. 45) and that at Bury St. Edmunds consisted only of two rooms: that entered from the street, which was used for storage; and the apartment on the first floor, probably open to the roof, which was the only living-room of the household and probably was partitioned off at one end with a slight division or curtain. This room had a fireplace and chimney. It may seem strange that Jews, from whom kings and barons were accustomed to extort money to enable them to carry on their feuds, should occupy houses of such relative importance and prominence as these certainly were in the twelfth century; the more so when the plunder and extortion of Stephen's reign is remembered. In such a state of society, how could Jews have prospered? The explanation is that until their expulsion in 1290, by Edward I, the Jews were under the protection of successive kings, who drew funds from them, just as they by usury squeezed money from the people.

> " Henry II amerced Jurnet, the Jew of Norwich, in MM marcs, and in 1185 he stood amerced in MMMMMDXXV marcs and a half, for which debt the whole body of the Jews were chargeable and they were to have Jurnet's effects and chattels to enable them to pay it. Jurnet afterwards gave Richard MDCCC marcs that he might reside in England, with the king's goodwill."

Ecclesiastical property was frequently pledged to the Jews. At one time

> " the sacred vessels and jewels of Lincoln Minster were pledged to Aaron, a rich Jew of that city, for seven years or more before Geoffrey, Bishop-elect, redeemed them in 1173."[2]

Aaron the Jew's house stands on Steep Hill, Lincoln, near that illustrated in Fig. 45, which it resembles.

Neither the ecclesiastics nor the laymen of the twelfth century seem to have been good men of business, for the Jews exacted grossly exorbitant interest upon loans; 2d. in the pound interest per week if collected annually amounts to a little over 40 per cent. per annum, but if collected weekly works out at a much higher rate of interest, which simple people might not realize.

When Royal protection was temporarily withdrawn, as happened from time to time, massacres of the Jews ensued. Their houses, however, were sufficiently strong to resist for some time an attack by the mob. The ground-floor rooms had small openings in the walls, while narrow and winding stairs were easily defended by occupants of the upper floor.

Of common houses, none remain; they were still wood and clay hovels or

---

[1] An excellent condensed description of castles may be found in *A Glossary of English Architecture*, by T. D. Atkinson.

[2] *Chronicles of Jocelyn de Brakelond*, edited by Sir Ernest Clarke, London, 1907, p. 223.

rough timber structures, roofed with thatch, reed, rush, and litter. They consisted of one apartment, often shared with domestic beast and fowl. The flimsy nature of these dwellings is made apparent in contemporary references to provision for pulling them down by means of a hook and rope (provided for the purpose) in case of fire. In 1135 a terrible fire spread from London Bridge to St. Clement Danes, following which some citizens abandoned the use of wood and built themselves houses of stone covered with tiles. It was found, not only that such houses resisted fire, but that they frequently arrested the progress of what would have been serious conflagrations. The public benefit arising from such buildings was recognized in 1189, when special privileges were granted to persons willing to build in stone and tile. The encouragement seems to have been inadequate, for in 1212 further regulations as to town buildings were issued, which required the whitewashing of thatched roofs as protection from fire,

> " that cookshops be plastered within and without and all chambers and hostelries be removed so that there may remain only the house and bedroom "—

" house " = houseplace or hall.

When tracing the development of the roof into a house with walls, allusion was made to the fact that ecclesiastical and domestic forms of architecture were identical. In these illustrations of dwellings built since the Conquest, the similarity of ornament to familiar but more ornate church and cathedral details must be obvious; so obvious, indeed, that no one can doubt their having emanated from the same sources. An ornament freely used by the Normans was the chevron or zigzag moulding (of which there is a good example in the doorway at Castle Hedingham, Fig. 387). This was employed in an immense variety of forms, yet one may find an identical variation in a cathedral, in a parish church, and in a domestic building, though these buildings may be in different counties. One naturally asks who was the author. Two explanations have long been current. One, that some monk or other educated person designed the proposed building and instructed crafts-men who were allowed considerable freedom in executing details, and who produced those remarkable carvings, from a chevron moulding to a gargoyle, or from an oak chest to a canopied stall, which are marvels of spontaneity and skill. The other theory is that bands of craftsmen (as freemasons) travelled the country, passing from one building to another where they found employment. Both explanations are untrue, yet both contain certain elements of truth. We will inquire first as to the gifted monk-architect.

Two things are equally noticeable in medieval works—their similarity and their diversity—similarity of plan, similarity of construction, often exact repetition of detail, but even more frequently variation of detail in mouldings and ornament, particularly those associated with windows and doorways. If medieval buildings or even portions of large buildings had been designed by an educated artist having a thorough knowledge of the trade processes involved, one would certainly expect to find greater differences in plans and general appearance, yet, with an occasional exception (such as the lantern at Ely Cathedral), these buildings resemble one another. In contemporary records it is frequently stated that a certain cathedral was built under the direction of some prelate. Occasionally this may have been so, but no clear case of authorship is recorded, and the verb *fecit* cannot be regarded as meaning more than " caused to be made." A case which has been quoted to show actual connection with building operations by a great cleric who carried materials on his own back, really proves the contrary, for evidently the wish to take personal part in operations could only find outlet in common labourer's work for which alone he was suited. It was natural that a cleric who recorded current events should flatter his superior by giving him the credit of designing works which he only instigated (that has been known to be done in more recent times); and even now architects of buildings are seldom remembered, though the names of patrons who caused the work to be done may be recorded on the structures themselves. When, however, such claims are scrutinized, the clerical architect quickly fades away from a designer of works into a promoter of operations. Many instances might be quoted, but two will suffice. In 1179, five years after the fire which worked such havoc at Canterbury Cathedral, there were wide differences of opinion as to how far remaining work could be retained or whether it should be pulled down and rebuilt before proceeding with the superstructure. Who was consulted? Not a superior churchman, responsible for the works, nor a conference of great cleric-architects of wide experience and reputation summoned from afar, but just English and French master-workmen. Even they could not agree; and ultimately one of them, William de Sens, " a strong man and a subtle artificer in wood and stone," was appointed " *because of his experience and reputation in such work.*"[1] Could any words be more significant than this explanation of the chronicler? Where we should have called in and entrusted the works to a leading architect, they committed them to this artificer with a reputation for such work.

A later instance occurred at Lichfield Cathedral in 1337. The new buildings were two feet less in width than the Early English choir, three bays of which were to be retained. The junction of the two portions proved a problem which neither the Dean and Chapter nor any others concerned were able to solve. Did they call in a churchman, wise, experienced, and famous as an architect? No, they sent for Master William de Ramessey, *mason*, to direct operations; and it was he who so harmoniously combined the two portions of the choir. He received 20s. fee for each visit, with travelling allowance of 6s. 8d. for himself and staff for the journey to and from London, four days each way, very much in the same way as architects would now be paid. As

---

[1] *Chron. Gervase of Canterbury*, Rolls Series, 1879, pp. 20-1.

I believe it has not been published previously, I give the text of the entry as transcribed by the Dean (Savage) of Lichfield from the Lichfield Chapter Acts Book.[1]

What has clouded the scrutiny of authorship of buildings is the part not infrequently played by ecclesiastics in building operations: that of clerk of the works, a position filled by a responsible member of a monastery who paid workmen, bought materials, and looked after the commercial and clerical side of the enterprise. Such men when working for the king often had power to impress labour—a power also given to master-craftsmen in many instances. Investigation of many records of clerics furnishes no evidence of their having designed; on the contrary, there are frequently indications that the designing was in the hands of laymen. The confusion arising from the variety of designations and overlapping of duties of superintendents of building operations is natural. Forty years ago Wyatt Papworth[2] traced the names of 400 such men in the Middle Ages, described as Ingeniator, Supervisor, Disposer, Surveyor, Master of the Works, Keeper of the Works, etc.

Whatever the origin of the trade guilds, they certainly were in active existence in the medieval period, and such crafts as the masons' and carpenters' were regulated strictly by their respective lodges as to wages, hours, and conduct. How far these earlier men were influenced in their work by religious emotions, and how far by personal considerations, must be a matter of opinion; but it is certain that by the fourteenth century the objects of the lodges were similar to those of modern trade unions: to obtain as much as they could for the least possible effort. John Wycliff (d. 1384) wrote of fraternities and guilds:

> " They conspire to support each other, yea even in the wrong, and, by their wit and power, oppress other men who are in the right. . . . Also skilled crafts-men as freemasons and others . . . conspire together that no man practising their craft shall take less payment daily than they have agreed amongst themselves, though his conscience may tell him he should accept much less and that none of them shall do such steady true work as might reduce the earnings of other men of his craft, and that none of them shall do ought than hew stone, though he might profit his master twenty pounds by one day's work by laying stones in mortar on a wall, without harm or hurt to himself."[3]

Wycliff's remarks are not couched in language to convince the reader of his impartiality, but the facts of combination and restriction for profit emerge from his opinions. There is no evidence and there are no reasons for supposing

[1] Eodem die (vj. feria x. kal. Jun. ii) conuentum erat inter Decanum et Capitulum et Magistrum Willelmum de Ramessey, Mason, quod ad premunicionem Decani et Capituli idem Willelmus veniet ad superuidendam fabricam ecclesie sue Lych. et quod daret sanum consilium suum circa emendacionem defectuum et ordinacionem suam et informacionem alijs cementarijs circa instruccionem noui operis ejusdem et precipiet in omni aduentu suo de Lond. pro labore XXs. Et pro expensis dimidiam marcam. presentibus Dec(ano), Ley(cestre), Hol(bech), Chel(msford), Clop(ton), Dep(ing), Pa(trica), canonicis. *Lich. Chap. Acts Bk. Ashm. MS.* 794, fol. 57.

[2] *R.I.B.A. Trans.* 1887, vol. xxviii, pp. 89-138.

[3] Quoted in G. G. Coulton's *Social Life in Britain*, p. 491, but here rendered into intelligible modern English.

that human nature in the Middle Ages differed from what it is now or has been at any other period.

The following from W. Forrest's *History of Grisild the Second* shows also how sixteenth-century workmen behaved, if not properly supervised. It refers to the works by Cardinal Wolsey at Christ Church, Oxford:

> " Moste cunnynge woorkemen theare weare prepared,
> Withe spediest ordynaunce for eauery thynge,
> Nothynge expedyent was theare oughtis spared
> That to the purpose myght bee assistynge;
> One thynge (chieflye) this was the hynderynge,
> The woorkefolke for lack of goode ouerseers
> Loytered the tyme, like false tryfelers.

> " Thye weare thus manye, a thousande (at the leaste),
> That thearon weare woorkeynge still daye by daye,
> Their paymentes contynued, their labours decreaste,
> For welneare one haulfe did noughtis els but playe.
> If they had trulye done that in them laye
> By so long space as they weare tryfelynge
> At his fall had been lyttle to dooynge "[1]

—the last line meaning that had work gone on as it should, the buildings would have been completed instead of being far from finished at the time of Wolsey's fall.

From the twelfth century, and more especially from the middle of the fourteenth century, many attempts were made to regulate wages, hours, and guilds—some necessary, some oppressive, all ultimately unsuccessful.

Guilds have always been jealous of any person performing the functions of a trade who was not a fully qualified member bound by oath to keep the secrets of the craft—an oath strictly observed in the Middle Ages, and which survives in the phraseology of modern articles of apprenticeship, which require the apprentice to keep his master's secrets, to refrain from card-playing, fornication, etc.: conditions which are no longer enforceable. The laws of guilds were strictly enforced in the Middle Ages, and breaches of them rendered the offender liable to ruthless expulsion, which involved loss of livelihood. It is difficult to imagine how a cleric-architect could have evaded them.

In the York Fabric Rolls, sixteenth century,[2] we find:

> " Noe mason make moulds nor noe square nor no rule to any rough lyers within the Lodge nor without to hew nor mould stones of his own making."

And in the seventeenth century:

> " You shall not make any mould, square or rule to mould stone withal but such as is allowed by the fraternity."[3]

[1] Quoted by W. D. Caröe in *Wren and Tom Tower*, Oxford, 1923, p. 12.
[2] Quoted in an excellent work by Francis B. Andrews, entitled *The Medieval Builder and His Methods*, Oxford, 1925, p. 41.
[3] Francis B. Andrews, *The Medieval Builder and His Methods*, Oxford, 1925, p. 41.

c

While evidence from contemporary sources negatives the cleric-architect theory and affords little support to the supposed travelling bands of craftsmen, it does show that the master-mason and master-carpenter took sole responsibility for the design and conduct of works, often acting also as contractor supplying materials at agreed rates. Many of these men enjoyed high reputations beyond mere craftsmanship. Sometimes instructions were given that a roof should be "after the manner of" one existing in a building perhaps in a distant county, or indications were furnished as to the employer's general requirements and a contract made in which the dimensions of the building, of walls, or apartments were named, together with positions of rooms, doorways, fireplaces, etc., with stipulations regarding quality of materials and workmanship; but such references as we have to plans or drawings of any kind having been provided for the guidance of the contractors clearly refer to rough drafts, and, at most, a very rough plan might have been furnished. That drawings were prepared by the master-workmen for the guidance of craftsmen is certain, but work must usually have been set out on the job, and drafts on wood or stone would disappear with the execution of the work. Occasionally drawings of details have been preserved,[1] but these were little more than sketches and must have been supplemented by greater detail. No doubt, also, plans and general drawings would be submitted in the course of work. In some instances models were prepared, and there are constant references to "wainscot and boards" provided for patterns and moulds, and more than once to a "tracing house" on the job, which was probably the same building as that elsewhere styled the "loge."

The records of the re-roofing of Westminster Hall (completed c. 1397) give the names of persons in charge of various works and show how responsibility was divided. They were collected in the *Blue Book*[2] reporting the condition of the roof timbers, following survey by H.M. Office of Works. This book gives detailed references to the documents from which the information was derived. It states:

> "In 1394 John Godmeston, Clerk, was appointed to cause the Great Hall in the Palace of Westminster to be repaired, taking the necessary masons, carpenters and labourers, wherever found, except in the fee of the Church, with power to arrest and imprison contrariants until further order, and also to take stone, timber, tiles and other materials and carriage for the same at the King's charges and to sell branches, bark and other remnants of trees . . . accounting for the monies as received and receiving in that office wages and fees at the discretion of the Treasurer of England.
>
> "John Godmeston had been Vicar of Brampton, Prebend of Moreton Parva in Hereford Cathedral, had a third portion of the church of Bromyard in 1387, was Prebend of Wydyngton Parva in Hereford Cathedral in 1389. In 1387 he was granted the chancellorship of St. Paul's Cathedral, and in 1398 the Church of Ross in Hereford diocese. In 1399 the reversion of the first vacant prebend in the college of St. Stephen, Westminster, was a Prebend of Chichester, who

---

[1] Francis B. Andrews, *The Medieval Builder and His Methods*, Plates III, IV, V, of French details.
[2] *Blue Book*, C.D., 7436, pub. 1914.

was made Chamberlain of the Exchequer." [It is evident that he was appointed as a good man of business and to control expenditure.]

"At the same time Hugh Herland, Carpenter, was appointed Controller to John Godmeston in respect of this work.

"Hugh Herland was one of the King's master carpenters, ' verging on old age.' He advised on the repairs of Winchester Castle 1390. In 1396 as Keeper of the King's Carpentry Works he was granted a little house in the Palace at Westminster for keeping his tools and for making his models (formæ, formulæ) and moulds for his carpentry work. . . . In 1397 he is called King's Esquire, Chief Carpenter, Controller and Surveyor of the Works."

The works, being chiefly carpenter's works, were placed in charge of the carpenter who designed the new roof.

Various persons were appointed to collect lead and other materials, to arrest carts, carters and horses and ships for transport.

In 1395 a contract was made with two masons, Richard Washbourn and John Swallow, for carrying the side walls (which were those built by William II) two feet higher and forming tables thereon " to a pattern and mould made by the advice of Henry Yeveley." Corbels were to be made of stone and inset in the walls to a pattern to be shown them by the Treasurer. This suggests a drawing provided by Godmeston, but the paragraph next following provides that these corbels and the spandrels springing from them are to be to the satisfaction of Henry Yeveley and of Watkyn his warden. Yeveley was an aged man, highly respected, King's Mason and Surveyor of Works at Westminster, the Tower of London, and the Castle of Canterbury. In his trade he occupied a position similar to that of Herland in carpentry, and had mason's work predominated would have had control of the works.

So far as evidence at present available shows, it would appear that medieval buildings were projected by ecclesiastical or lay patrons who indicated their requirements, that the designing was done by master-workmen (each in his own trade), and that what may be termed general design and responsibility fell upon the master-mason where the works were chiefly in stone, or upon the master-carpenter if mainly of wood. Further, that for large works a clerk was often appointed to do business in connection with obtaining and paying for labour and materials, and that details were executed by the rules and patterns of the lodges, as modified at their annual meetings. How far craftsmen were permitted to design details themselves is difficult to determine; certainly carvers in wood and stone were allowed some freedom.

The fact that much of the evidence respecting master masons, master carpenters, etc., is derived from the accounts of large works, where they were paid wages, is liable to obscure the certainty that these men were small contractors also. Although capitalists, their capital was limited and inadequate for them to undertake contracts for the larger enterprises: hence they worked and superintended on a wage basis.

Chapter **II**

THE THIRTEENTH CENTURY

JOHN, 1199-1216; HENRY III, 1216-72; EDWARD I, 1272-1307

IN THIS century there were attached to every large establishment tradesmen (such as masons and smiths) whose position was little better than
that of serfs. Freedom was acquired slowly but free men existed in every
age, and, of these, skilled artisans were able to move about the country wherever
work was to be had, while the serf who was unable to produce a licence to
travel was liable to arrest, punishment, and to be returned to his manor. The
term *journeyman* now used to designate a craftsman out of his apprenticeship,
but who is not a master, was once applied to any hired artisan who worked
away from his native place. Some authorities, however, regard a *journeyman* as
one receiving a daily wage.

What has been said already about masons applies also to carpenters and
joiners, but it is interesting to observe how the carpenter's craft first developed
through that of the mason. This, though apparent in design, is particularly

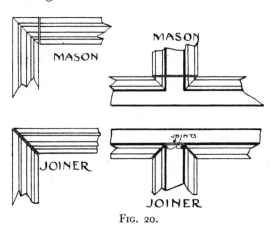

FIG. 20.

noticeable in joints which up to the end
of the fifteenth century were made after
the manner of mason's work—woodwork
of early date almost always being in
imitation of mason's methods. A conspicuous instance is the treatment of
mitres. The mason returns his mouldings
at the mitre so that the joint comes at
right angles to the mouldings. In this
the early carpenters followed his example.
The later carpenters found it saved much
time to cut the joint at an angle of 45°—that is, at the mitre itself. It is obvious
that by doing this the mouldings could often be run in long strips, and when
cut at an angle of 45° two lengths would form a perfect mitre in which, if
carefully done, the joint would be almost imperceptible. It is interesting to
examine medieval benches, stalls, screens, etc., where the carpenter's jointing
is done mason-fashion, and to trace in later work the many methods which
the joiner devised for himself (as applied mouldings for framing and panelling),
always contrived with a view to saving labour; but no applied mouldings ever
equal in interest those earlier ones cut out of the solid.

A list of thirteenth-century tools comprised:

> "Hachet, brode-ax, twybyl, ax, wimble, wedges and pins, celt, plane, mason's line, reule, squyre, hevy plomet."[1]

Of these, by far the most important was the axe, which was the medieval carpenter's "tool of all work." With it he could square and smooth timber, almost equal to work done with a plane. A tool omitted from this list is the adze, which had been in use long before this period. It is significant that the saw also is omitted from the list, for several kinds of saws were in use in the Middle Ages; but men highly skilled in the use of the axe are known to have despised the saw as being

> "a contemptible innovation fit only for those unskilful in the handling of the nobler instrument."[2]

Certainly, had the saw been in more general use it is conceivable that structural timbers of slighter scantlings might have been employed. With a pit saw a large tree could be cut easily into many spars, where a man who worked with the axe would naturally choose logs requiring the minimum of labour merely to square them. In early buildings even the faces of timbers not exposed to view do not show saw marks.[3] Had they been sawn, it is not probable that such marks (being out of sight) would have been dressed off with an axe, and one may reasonably infer that they took their form under the axe alone. Also, timber was squared in the wood where felled, to reduce the weight to be removed.

In this relation a writer on timber roofs in Cyprus mentions that

> "the timber used in these roofs of little churches is always split, not sawn. It is merely shaped roughly with an adze: the beams are carefully squared and sometimes moulded or chamfered. Young pines have been sacrificed without number to form the rafters, and the older stems, which required greater efforts to fell and shape, have been reserved for the tie-beams."[4]

These methods were still practised in Cyprus during the last quarter of the nineteenth century.

A fifteenth-century list of tools is more comprehensive, as might be expected, having regard to the wealth of splendid roofs, church furniture, etc., then produced. It included:[5]

> "Twybylle, compas, groping iren, saw, whetstone, shypax, belte, wryght, adys, fyle, chesyl, lyne and chalke, prykynge-knife, persore, skantyllyon, crow, rewle, brode-ax, pleyn, twyvete, polyff, wyndas, rewle-stone, gowge, gabulle rope, squyre, draught-nayle, ax, wymbulle."

[1] John de Garlande (c. 1230), quoted by C. F. Innocent in *The Development of English Building Construction*, p. 97.

[2] Alex. Beazeley in *R.I.B.A.*, trans. 1882-83, quoted in *The Development of English Building Construction*, p. 97.

[3] There may be exceptions to this experience, but generally it is as stated.

[4] *Byzantine Timber-Building in Cyprus*, by George Jeffery, *R.I.B.A. Journal*, xiv, No. 16, p. 578.

[5] The Debate in "The Carpenter's Tools," M.S. Ashmole, 61, fols. 23-6, as quoted by W. C. Hazlitt in *Early Popular Poetry of England*, vol. i., pp. 79-90.

Twybylle—Twybill: a pickaxe with chisel-pointed ends 2½ in. wide, one blade being in a line with the handle, the other set at right angles.
Wimble—Auger.
Groping iren—Grooving iron.
Persore—Piercer.
Skantyllyon—A gauge for measuring thicknesses: hence scantling.
Twyvete—Used for cutting mortises after boring with an auger.
Polyff—Pulley.
Wyndas—Windlass.
Gabulle rope—Cable rope.

The earliest reference by name that we have to the chisel is by Wycliff in 1382.[1] Yet masons used it in the twelfth century.

The " restwymbyll " was a long auger supported by a grooved rest when making long borings as for water pipes. Neither hammer nor mallet is included in these lists, which cannot be regarded as completely representative.

The wages paid to tradesmen in the year 1292 are recorded[2] as:

					A day.
Mason	..	..	..	..	5d.
Apparitor or foreman	..	..	..	..	7d.
Rob, the carpenter	..	..	..	..	4½d.
Two boys	..	..	..	..	2½d.
William de Haspel	..	..	..	..	2d.
Jacob of Lensham, a smith	..	..	..	..	6d.
					A week.
Other smiths	..	..	..	..	2s.
„	..	..	..	..	1s. 6d.

These wages would be those paid without diet, and when food was provided the payments would be 1½d. *per diem* less. At this time wheat was at 16s. the quarter, having risen in price from 6s. the quarter in 1289, owing to a succession of bad seasons—hail, rains, and storms being recorded;[3] but wages did not increase with the cost of living, which had risen 140 per cent.

A medieval preacher, Berthold of Ratisbon (1230-72), admonished tradesmen that they

> " should all be true and trustworthy in their office, whether they work by the day or the piece, as many carpenters and masons do. When they labour by the day, they should not stand all the more idle that they may multiply the days at their work. If thou labourest by the piece, then thou shouldest not hasten too soon therefrom that thou mayest be rid of the work as quickly as possible and that the house may fall down in a year or two: thou shouldest work at it truly, even as if it were thine own."[4]

The Court Rolls of the Manor of Hales (1272-1307)[5] record particulars of a house provided for the widow of a copyholder, whom other records show to have been a well-to-do man. The floor area was to be 30 ft. by 14 ft. within the walls, which were to be timber framework filled with plastered wattles.

---

[1] *New English Dictionary*, Oxford, 1893, *s.v.* chisel.   [2] *Antiq. Westr.*, p. 77.
[3] *Chroniclon Preciosum*, London, 1707, pp. 81-2.
[4] Pred. I, 146, 285, 478. Quoted in *A Medieval Garner*, by G. G. Coulton.
[5] p. xliv.

Possibly it was partitioned into two rooms, for two windows are specified and three doors—presumably front, back, and partition. No upper floor is mentioned nor any chimney, but the son was to provide five cartloads of sea-coal each All Saints' Day for his mother.

In Bolden Buke, Co. Durham,[1] amongst the services recorded is that

" at the fairs of St. Cuthbert, every two villans make one booth,"

and further that

" the villans (22) ought to make every year in their work, if there shall be need, one house of the length of 40 ft. and of the width of 15 ft., and then, when they make it, each one is quit of 4d. of averpennies ";

averpennies being money paid in commutation of service.

An instance of moving a house from one place to another is recorded on the Court Rolls of the Manor of Wakefield:[2]

" 1297: Sandale . . . Peter the shepherd gives 6d. for leave (of the lord) to buy a house from Geppe Strok, and to put it up (edificandi illam) at Miln-thorpe."

Clearly a timber house.

The thirteenth century saw the dawn of comfort, of which fortunately we are able definitely to learn from contemporary records, which are more abundant than in the preceding centuries. In every age, in every country, one finds that improved conditions of life began at the top of the social scale, and what was a luxury of the king, in course of time becomes a common necessary even of the poor subject, so that comforts enjoyed now by humble persons are immeasurably greater than those which a " dread lord " or sovereign commanded a few hundred years ago.

What the king did in the thirteenth century is recorded in his own orders to custodians of his residences, often sheriffs of the county in which they were situated. These are embodied in the Liberate and Close Rolls, from which the following are drawn.[3] The practice of the king, or indeed, of any great medieval lord, was to move from one residence to another when the resources of a locality had been consumed by his establishment. Amongst the residences of Henry III were: The Tower of London, Winchester Castle, Woodstock, Rochester, Kennington, Newcastle-on-Tyne, Clarendon, Windsor, Nottingham, Marlborough, Reading, Brill, Bristol, Havering, Guildford, Southampton, Gillingham, Westminster. What emerges most clearly from these records (where they do not chronicle mere repairs), is the inadequate and primitive nature of the accommodation afforded by Royal residences before large sums were expended in improving them. They demonstrate not merely what Henry III did for the comfort of himself, his queen, the prince and those

---

[1] *Surtees Society Pub.*, vol. xxv, p. 45.   [2] Vol. ii, p. 12.
[3] Translations of those which refer to building may be found in Parker's *Domestic Architecture of the Middle Ages*, ii, pp. 181-263.

around him, but what elementary comforts and bare necessaries *were not enjoyed*, even by kings, prior, say, to 1233, when these records commence. Henry seems to have added buildings within the encircling walls of his castles, like the hall, buttery, chapel, etc., the foundations of which have been traced outside the Norman keep but within the bailey at Castle Hedingham. The draughtiness even of the king's hall is indicated by the orders "everywhere to repair the crevices in the same hall"—Winchester Castle.

Instructions regarding windows occur more frequently than any other orders, and to these are added comments such as for those to be made in the king's painted chamber at Winchester, "which is too dark"—and to "make two glass windows to shut and open, in our chamber, opposite our bed." At Clarendon, to make windows "cleft through the middle that they may be shut or opened when necessary." At Bristol, "double iron ties to be made for the windows (of the king's wardrobe), with new wooden shutters," and at Clarendon, in the King's Chapel, "to put iron kevils (pegs) with chains to shut the glass windows."

The king's great hall at Northampton was to have

"the windows on the north side glazed with white glass."

I have not found any twelfth-century records of the use of glass in houses; and judging by the frequency with which Henry III ordered it to be inserted in existing windows of his own apartments, it must have been a new luxury. The illustrations of windows of this period make interesting the order to put into the queen's chamber at Marlborough

"four great sitting windows with pillars"

(see Fig. 588), and in her chamber at Reading

"to make a window with two marble pillars and close it with glass windows between the pillars, with panels which may be opened and shut, and large wooden shutters internally, to close over the glass windows."

A glazed window is ordered for the queen's wardrobe at Westminster,

"so that chamber *may not be so windy as it used to be*."

The haphazard way in which chambers were added, either adjoining or detached from existing buildings, is brought out by frequent references to the provision of connecting alleys, passages, stairs, penthouses over external stairs, and penthouse-passages, such as those between hall and kitchen. At Winchester, a chamber was to be built between the hall and kitchen "for the use of the King's seneschals." Buildings were also put up temporarily to meet emergencies, as an apartment consisting of a lean-to roof and chimney of plaster, built up against the wall of a tower at Windsor by Henry III, in which to lodge the Bishop of Laodicea. Like the majority of buildings of this period, these consisted of timber and plaster. Stone was used for structures of greater importance, and only where stone was used for small houses have they survived.

Little Wenham Hall is our only domestic brick building built in the thirteenth century, for brick was not extensively made and used in England until the fifteenth century.

Roofs were covered with thatch, slate, tiles, and lead.   Chimneys and fireplaces were continually ordered to be added to existing apartments as well as to be provided in new ones, and most often for the queen's chambers, which suggest that earlier queens must have lived in very rigorous conditions.   The wardrobes were required not only for storage of clothes and materials, but for accommodation of persons who made garments, of which quantities were required not only for the king's household, but for persons for whom the provision at stated times of a robe was part of their pay.   Henry III found the chambers of his residences with bare plaster-rendered walls; some decorated with paintings, which he occasionally renewed, but which he generally lined with wainscot, consisting of plain boarding which could be painted (see Fig. 674).   There is no suggestion of framing or panelling.   Green was the favourite colouring, either plain, as in the king's painted chamber at Winchester, or in the great chamber there, where the

> " green colour was to be starred with gold; and circles to be made on the same wainscote, in which are to be painted ' histories ' of the Old and New Testament."

The queen's chamber in the Tower of London was to be

> " whitewashed and pointed, and within those pointings to be painted with flowers."

This may imply pointing an unplastered wall or refer to the practice of marking out the wall into rectangles, in each of which a rose or other flower was painted. A year later, orders were given to wainscot the same chamber, which was then to be

> " thoroughly whitened internally and newly painted with roses."

At Westminster, the chimney (breast) of the queen's chamber was to be painted,

> " and on it to be pourtrayed a figure of Winter, which as well by its sad countenance as by other miserable distortions of the body may be deservedly likened to Winter itself."

The development of the king's requirements is shown a few years later, when he orders that his lower chamber at Clarendon shall be wainscoted—

> " And to paint that wainscot of a green colour, and to put a border to it, and to cause the heads of Kings and Queens to be painted on the borders and to paint on the walls of the King's upper chamber the story of St. Margaret Virgin and the four Evangelists, and to paint the wainscote of the same chamber of a green colour, spotted with gold, and to paint on it heads of men and women, and all those paintings are to be done with good and exquisite colours."

At the upper end of the hall was a dais, raised a few inches above the general floor level of the hall.   The wall behind this was wainscoted and painted and a carved chair provided for the king.

The provision of a louvre over a hall shows the fire to have been on an open hearth, as at Stokesay Castle hall, and as at Penshurst (Figs. 594 and 769); the use of chimneys and wall fireplaces usually being confined to first-floor chambers.

Sanitation was still primitive, as is shown by the significant instruction to

> " provide double doors to all the privy chambers "

and

> " a drain from our private chamber to be made in the fashion of a hollow column."

A garderobe at Stokesay Castle is illustrated (Figs. 875 and 876). In 1260 the Treasurer of the Exchequer is ordered to pay for

> " the conduit of water which is carried underground to the King's lavatory (washing place), and to other places there, and for making a certain conduit (drain) through which the refuse of the King's kitchen at Westminster flows into the Thames; which conduit the King ordered to be made on account of the stink of the dirty water, which was carried through his halls, which was wont to affect the health of the people frequenting the same halls."

An earlier entry in the Close Rolls (1246) reads:

> " The King to Edward Fitz-Otho. Since the privy chamber in our wardrobe at London is situated in an undue and improper place, wherefore it smells badly, we command you on the faith and love by which you are bounden unto us, that you in no wise omit to cause another privy chamber to be made in the same wardrobe in such more fitting and proper place as you may select there, even though it should cost a hundred pounds. So that it may be made before the feast of the Translation of St. Edward, before we shall come thither. This however we leave to be done at your discretion."

A hundred pounds would equal fifteen hundred pounds in our money. As an order for new sanitation this would be difficult to surpass; it certainly would delight the modern plumber, though, perhaps, it should not be taken too literally, but only as an emphatic order to " get on."

That sometimes time was the essence of the contract seems to have been the case even in the thirteenth century, for in 1246

> " the Sheriff of Wiltshire is ordered as he loveth his life and chattels, to take diligent care that the queen's new chamber at Clarendon be finished before Whitsuntide, whencesoever monies for the completion of it may be procured."

Light is thrown upon personal habits by an order in 1256 as to pictorial decorations in the wardrobe at Westminster;

> " Where the King is wont to wash his head."

From a mass of instances which cannot be quoted here, it is clear that these manor-houses and castles of the king were not built on any regular plan, but were added to in accordance with the requirements of the moment.

There can be no doubt that, during the Middle Ages, buildings were coloured and even decorated externally—indeed, having regard to acquaintance with

Byzantine buildings which must have been acquired by Crusaders, it would be surprising had this not been the case; but no example remains. In the thirteenth century whitewashing and plastering the exteriors of stone buildings was common practice; and in 1241 instructions were given:

> " To cause all the leaden gutters of the great Tower (of London), through which rain water should fall from the summit of the same Tower, to be carried down to the ground, so that the wall of the said Tower, which has been newly whitewashed, may be in no wise injured by the dropping of rain water nor be easily weakened . . . and whitewash all the old wall around our aforesaid Tower."

The accounts of Windsor Castle, *temp*. Edward III, include details of colours supplied for painting the Round Tower, which was known as the Rose Tower and coloured accordingly.

Of town houses there is little to be said beyond the account given of the flimsiness of their structures in the preceding century, and no progress can be recorded in respect of the dwellings of the working classes.

ROOFS

ROOF TYPES

COUPLE ROOFS	A	Coupled rafters (Fig. 21).
	B	Do. do. embryo braces and wall posts (Fig. 22).
	C	Do. do. with braces and pendent king-post (Fig. 23).
COUPLE CLOSE ROOFS	D	Tie beam—queen-posts and collar beam (Fig. 24).
	E	„ „ braced, king-post and braced collar beam (Fig. 25).
COLLAR-BEAM BRACED ROOFS	F	Collar beam with arch braces and queen-post braces (Fig. 26).
	G	Scissors beams, with braces (Fig. 27).
	H	Trussed rafters, sole piece and ashlar piece (Fig. 28).
HAMMER-BEAM BRACED ROOFS	I	Hammer beam (extended sole piece), ashlar piece and hammer post (Fig. 29).
	J	Hammer beam, wall posts and braces, arch braces to pendent king-post (Fig. 30).
	K	False hammer beam, two collars and arch braces (Fig. 31).
	L	Double hammer-beam, arch-braced (Fig. 32).
	M	Hammer beam and braces, hammer post, lower collar braced by hammer beam braces, and arch rib springing from wall posts to collar beam (Fig. 33).

The English open-timbered roof, whether it covered church, hall, or barn, is a national building development unparalleled on the Continent, or, indeed, in any country in the world.

Evolution from the primitive to the medieval roof has been traced, but it has still to be shown how crude forms were gradually superseded by ingenious roofs in which constructional genius combined strength with beauty. We have not now to consider vaults where timber was used as a substitute for, and after the manner associated with, stone (like the crude work at Warmington Church, Northamptonshire, and the beautifully finished vaulting over cloisters at Lincoln), nor are we concerned with flat roofs or those inclined in one direction, but with roofs consisting of pairs of rafters pitching against one another.

Norman roofs were of several types, often having tie beams with king-posts, but it is difficult to name any Norman roof remaining on a domestic building. The roof of St. Mary's Hospital, Chichester, is recorded as having been built in 1229, and that of the chapel (now ceiled in) in 1290.

Certainly the roof of the main building illustrated in Fig. 19 is of that characteristically rough type associated with its period; indeed, this simple form of tie-beam roof continued to be used for barns until the end of the medieval period. The roof of Stokesay Castle (1240, Figs. 583, 585) is of the arch-braced collar-beam type, and that of the Pilgrims' Hall, Winchester (Figs. 589, 590), c. 1300, is an early and remarkably interesting hammer-beam roof. These roofs show three out of the four main types into which authorities have classed medieval open roofs, the fourth (actually the earliest) being the simple coupled rafter form. The four types of roofs have many subdivisions; indeed, one of the charms and surprises found in their study is the variety produced by roof carpenters in meeting and overcoming special problems. The subject has been exhaustively treated by R. and J. A. Brandon,[1] and more recently by F. E. Howard,[2] who illustrate many roofs. The *Blue Book*, by Sir F. Baines, on Westminster Hall[3] is an able treatise upon this finest of all timber roofs. The following examples should enable observers correctly to class any roofs and intelligently to appreciate the niceties of their construction even where two types are combined in the same roof. To simplify the diagrams, mouldings and tracery have been omitted.

Each pair of rafters may meet by:

1. Being halved and pinned.
2. Being tenoned and pinned.
3. Being pinned or nailed to a ridge-piece (Fig. 22), or tenoned into a pendent king-post (Fig. 23).

Although there are notable instances of the use of ridge-pieces, most medieval rafters were halved or tenoned and pinned.

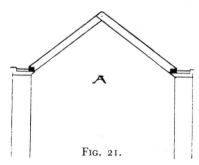

FIG. 21.

The diagram A shows the most simple form of roof, where rafters in pairs span the space they cover, without supports or stiffening of any kind. It is obvious that the outward thrust such a roof exerts upon the walls will vary with the weight of the roof covering, and that, except for very narrow spans, any saving effected by simplicity of roof design would be more than set off by the cost of having to build walls so thick as to avoid danger of overturning.

[1] *The Open Timber Roofs of the Middle Ages*, 1849.
[2] *English Church Woodwork*, Howard and Crossley, Batsford, 1917.
[3] Cd. 7436, H.M. Stationery Office, 1914.

The diagram B is a couple roof where slight braces stiffen the rafters and transfer some of the roof weight in a vertical direction to the wall posts, which stand on stone corbels. This is more interesting as a stage of development than as a practical solution of the problem of transferring the thrust of the roof from an outward to a downward direction.

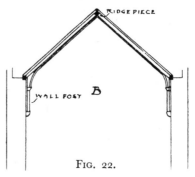

FIG. 22.

In diagram C we have a couple roof to which several features have been added, the most important being the arch braces which spring from points some distance below the tops of the walls and meet in a short pendent king-post.

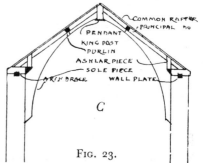

FIG. 23.

The roof is double-framed, inasmuch as the stouter rafters stiffened by the arch braces occur at intervals of about 16 ft. and are connected longitudinally by purlins on which the common (lighter) rafters rest. The stouter, braced rafters are called " principals," and they, combined with the arch braces, etc., form what are termed " trusses," though, as there are no tensional members, they are not really trusses in the full modern sense of the word. In this roof, also, the feet of the common rafters rest on sole pieces, on the inner ends of which are ornamental cornices from which short upright ashlar pieces transfer some of the weight of the roof in a vertical direction.

In diagram D we have a very different construction, called a couple close roof, inasmuch as the feet of the rafters are tied together by a tie beam which is jointed to the wall plates on which the rafter feet rest. It has been suggested that this is a modification of the old Norse roof, the king-post (" roof-tree ") supporting which stood on the floor; by setting it on the tie beam the floor was left clear. The rafters (this is a single-framed roof, having common rafters only) are stiffened by a collar beam to each pair, and where one of these comes over a tie beam it is supported by two queen-posts. The collar beams are tenoned into the rafters and pinned.

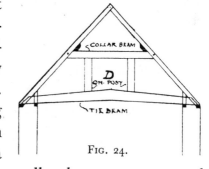

FIG. 24.

Diagram E is of a tie-beam and king-post roof. The tie beam is dovetailed to the posts and notched over the wall plates (or vice versa), the walls being of timber. The tie beam is braced by two braces. The king-post is octagonal in section with moulded base and cap. From the cap four braces spring: two being tenoned into a collar beam and two into the collar-beam purlin which runs longitudinally under the collars, one of which is tenoned into each pair of rafters (see Fig. 607). This also is a single-framed roof, but the tie beams occur at intervals

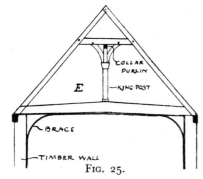

FIG. 25.

of 12 ft. Even for spans of 20 ft. large timbers were required for tie beams, and although these were cut with a camber, as shown in the diagrams D and E, there was often a tendency to sag. By bridging an apartment they reduced the clear height, and for spans of more than 25-30 ft. the weight and size of timbers were very great, and suitable ones were difficult to find. Accordingly, the medieval carpenter was stimulated to devise the arch-braced collar beam, a variety of which is shown in—

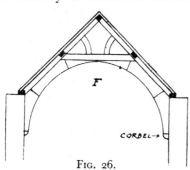

FIG. 26.

Diagram F. Unlike diagram E, these (principal) rafters meet on a ridge piece. One finds ridge pieces in very early roofs, then they are omitted and later reintroduced. The collar beam is tenoned into the rafters about half-way down, and short curved braces (actually curved queen-posts in this instance) further stiffen the upper ends. The collar beam itself is braced by large braces springing from stout corbels some distance down the walls; these braces support the principal rafters into which they are mortised and pinned: they are in three pieces (see Fig. 598).

Such a roof in appearance and in spaciousness was a great advance upon the couple close roof.

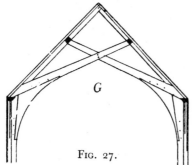

FIG. 27.

Diagram G shows an uncommon but interesting scissors-beam roof, which in principle is actually an arch-braced collar beam roof. The rafters are supported by the upper ends of the scissors beams at about half-way up. The scissors beams themselves are braced, and are also tenoned into the posts of the timber walls.

In diagram H we have one form of trussed rafter roof where the collar beam is stiffened by diagonal struts instead of by arch braces; the inner ends of the sole pieces are tenoned into inner wall plates from which vertical ashlar pieces rise to support the rafters. Such

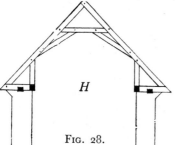

FIG. 28.

roofs were often ceiled; indeed, this construction was seldom designed to be left open.

Diagram I marks an important departure, which is actually the first step in the development of the hammer-beam roof, for it shows the sole piece extended inwards and braced by a curved brace, tenoned to a wall post forming a complete bracket,

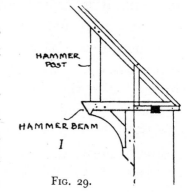

FIG. 29.

which would take considerable weight from the hammer post standing on its inner end. By this extension of the sole piece not only was a very broad base secured for the rafters, but also support at a considerable distance up the rafter.

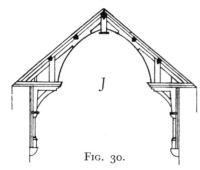

FIG. 30.

In diagram J the same principle is extended by the addition of wall posts standing on stone corbels, which transmit the weight lower down. From the hammer beam the arch brace is in three sections: the middle one being the principal rafter itself and the uppermost sections meeting at a pendent king-post somewhat as those did in diagram C. It will be seen that the hammer post stands on the inner end of the hammer beam, the rafter foot rests on the outer end. If these are constructed rightly they share the weight equally, and the hammer beam becomes a cantilever.

Diagram K is of the arch-braced hammer-beam roof at Eltham Palace (Fig. 606), where the hammer post (instead of standing on the hammer beam) has the hammer-beam end tenoned into it— a weak form of construction which has been termed a "false hammer-beam roof." Owing to the design of the roof and the low pitch of the four-centred arch, this joint is not called upon to bear the compression which would have been required had the arch been as high or the span as wide as that at Westminster Hall, shown in diagram M.

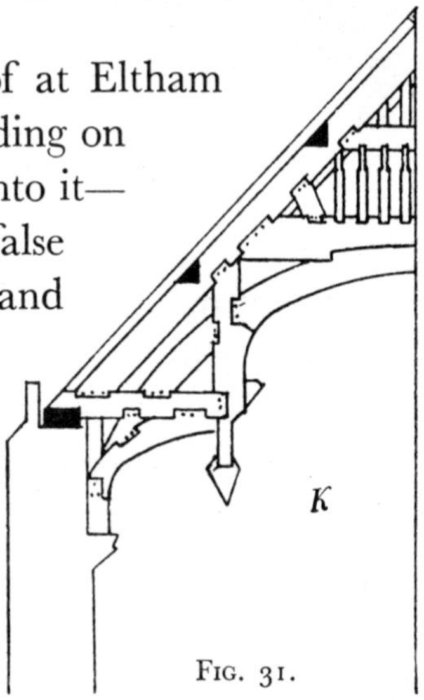

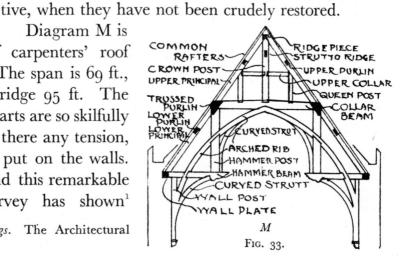

K

FIG. 31.

Diagram L shows the principle of the double hammer-beam roof, such as those in East Anglian churches, where they are treated with much elaboration of tracery and mouldings, the whole being richly coloured in red, green, and gold. Such roofs are highly decorative, when they have not been crudely restored.

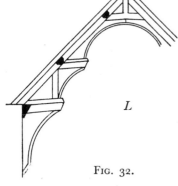

L

FIG. 32.

Diagram M is the high-water mark of carpenters' roof construction (Fig. 599). The span is 69 ft., the height from floor to ridge 95 ft. The design and balancing of parts are so skilfully done that at no point is there any tension, and no outward thrust is put on the walls. The better to comprehend this remarkable roof, Mr. William Harvey has shown[1]

[1] Harvey, *Models of Buildings*. The Architectural Press, London.

COMMON RAFTERS
RIDGE PIECE
STRUT TO RIDGE
CROWN POST
UPPER PURLIN
UPPER PRINCIPAL
UPPER COLLAR
QUEEN POST
TRUSSED PURLIN
COLLAR BEAM
LOWER PURLIN
LOWER PRINCIPAL
CURVED STRUT
ARCHED RIB
HAMMER POST
HAMMER BEAM
CURVED STRUT
WALL POST
WALL PLATE

M

FIG. 33.

FIG. 34.

how the principle can be carried out with loose wooden blocks built up on the same method as this roof but without tenons or pins, yet which is absolutely self-supporting. In this form the adequacy of the design is so obvious as to leave no room for doubt.

Fig. 34 shows such an arrangement of a child's wood blocks as a roof truss to demonstrate the principle upon which the hammer-beam roof was constructed. The members are all under compression, and there are no tensional members as in a modern steel roof. The disposition of the weight of the roof itself, and of the covering with which it would be finished, is such that the weight is transferred to the walls (in the illustration the lowest blocks) in a downward direction, and outward thrust is entirely eliminated. Accordingly, the tenons and pins with which a medieval hammer-beam roof was put together were not subjected to any tensional strain.

There is one type of roof, diagram N, which the student will be unable to identify from the diagrams —the false timber roof, a notable instance of which is that of Crosby Hall, a city merchant's house, built about 1470. Seen from below, this does not correspond with any of the roofs described. The roof one sees from below is only a timber ceiling, having flattened arches, pendants, etc., of wood. The real roof above this is of the scissors-beam type and is

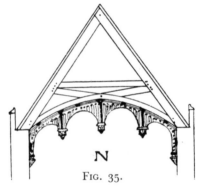

N

FIG. 35.

of steep pitch, whereas the roof seen has little pitch, and performs no structural functions; it is, in fact, merely decorative, and is the prototype of those pendent plaster ceilings which came into fashion in the sixteenth century.

CHAPTER III

THE FOURTEENTH CENTURY

EDWARD I, 1272-1307; EDWARD II, 1307-27; EDWARD III, 1327-77;
RICHARD II, 1377-99

THAT PHASE of Gothic architecture with which we are all familiar, as seen in churches, and which, for convenience (more perhaps than for accuracy), has been styled the Decorative period, prevailed approximately during the reigns of the three Edwards, and during the last quarter of the fourteenth century passed gradually into its ultimate development, which we call the Perpendicular, a term also open to criticism, but which has become firmly established because it is more descriptive than any other that has been coined. Few are unfamiliar with the appearance of decorated architecture— its large windows, filled, first with geometrical, and later with flowing tracery; its greater richness and delicacy of detail as compared with the Early English style, and its profusion of ornament, crockets, foliage, ballflower, etc., all of which we find used (with greater restraint than in churches and cathedrals) in domestic buildings. The Decorated period is regarded by many as the summit of achievement in Gothic architecture, and certainly the houses we can illustrate surpass anything that preceded them. This progress, however, was more in the direction of beautifying than in change of the nature of accommodation, which was affected little; although houses varied, just as requirements varied with geographical position and with the factors of safety or danger. In the north, and particularly in the Border counties, the house was primarily a castle. It might be a mere tower, not very different in accommodation from a Norman keep, as Yanwath Tower (Figs. 74, 75), which consists of one room only on each floor; or like Langley Castle (Figs. 88, 89), where the tower has large turrets at its four angles, providing apartments opening off the large chamber of which each floor of the central tower consists. In such buildings, though domestically developed from the Norman keep, defence against attack was the first and chief consideration, and, though typical of the districts in which they were built, they were not typical of the English house of the fourteenth century. Really typical houses are shown in the illustrations of Penshurst Place, Kent (Figs. 79-81), the palace of a city merchant; in Markenfield Hall (Figs. 69-73), a Yorkshire manor house, occupying one angle of a court, surrounded by a moat; in Martock Manor (Fig. 83), a typical manor-house like others which were springing up in peaceful corners of the land; the gatehouse of Battle Abbey

39

D

(Fig. 327); the great kitchen and the great barn at Glastonbury Abbey (Figs. 77, 78)—evidences of the importance of those spiritual lords who rivalled the greatest of the nobility and even the king himself. Such examples might be multiplied by illustrations of existing remains (such as at Salmestone Grange, Kent, where the frater and chapel buildings stand side by side, inviting comparison of their details), for in each century the choice of subjects available becomes greater.

Edwardian castles were really fortifications, containing dwellings for their garrisons, so scarcely come within the category of " houses." They are subjects for separate study, which have been ably treated by specialists,[1] who point out that all are more or less of concentric character—an arrangement supposed to have been introduced by Prince Edward from Syria, but which existed in this country before the death of his father, Henry III, and before Edward returned from the East. An instance is Caerphilly Castle, which is a complete example of this type, but which was built, not by the king, but by one of his subjects. However, the term " Edwardian " has become attached to them, not only as indicating castles built during the Decorated period, but to fortifications the essential development of which was the abandonment of the keep and the building of towers (connected by curtain walls), from which attacking forces could be enfiladed. They also included second and even third lines of defence—all concentric—with dwellings built against the curtain walls for the lodging of defenders. Notwithstanding the number of these castles, none remain in good condition. Some are a conglomeration of buildings of several periods, most are ruinous, none are complete. Perhaps Bodiam Castle, Sussex (Figs. 85-87), gives the best idea of the type, though it was not commenced until 1386 and has a quadrangular instead of a concentric plan; but its architecture certainly belongs to the Perpendicular period, and must be described with others of the fifteenth century, when it will be convenient also to revert to its Edwardian characteristics of curtain, drum towers, etc.

Leaving the subject of Border castles and towers, we may consider the normal medieval house plan, which consisted of a hall, open to the roof timbers, sometimes with a large open fireplace and chimney, but usually having a central hearth on the floor and an opening in the roof covered by a louvre, through which the smoke escaped. At the lower end of the hall there was an entrance door at each side in houses of any importance; these were connected by a passage, formed by the partition called the screens, through which two doorways gave into the hall. The passage was called the entry, and over it (in the fully developed plan) was the gallery, access to which was by a step-ladder or by a small staircase as at Penshurst (Fig. 80). This gallery led to a room or rooms over the pantry and buttery. From the entry, doors led to pantry, buttery, and, frequently, to the kitchen, but the latter was often a separate

[1] *Medieval Military Architecture in England.* G. and T. Clark, London, 1884.

building, sometimes of permanent character, as the Abbot's Kitchen, Glaston-bury (Fig. 77), and the outbuilding at Martock Manor House (Fig. 83), or it might be a timber and plaster structure such as that which still stood at Stokesay Castle in the first half of the nineteenth century. At the upper end of the hall was the dais, raised only a few inches above the hall-floor level. At one side of the dais was a window, which in the fifteenth century developed into a large bay. At the other side of, or beyond, the dais was a door leading to the room on the same level as the hall, called by such names as the bour, chamber, parlour, or cellar. In the king's house it might be a chamber for audiences, but usually it was a private and sleeping apartment, often for the women of the household. A stairway led from the dais up to the solar, which was always an apartment on an upper floor, having an open roof. The name solar, or sollar, originally applied to an open chamber in the roof, which received much sunlight—e.g., such as places in which the ancient Greeks and Romans took sun-baths—was applied in the Middle Ages indiscriminately to any upper chamber or loft or garret. We have (13 Edward III) in Norfolk a record of—

> " A rent of 10/-, payable yearly out of 12 shops (seldis) with rooms over them (solariis) in the northern corner of Lenne, adjoining Helmynggistance and the great wharf (ripam)."[1]

An interesting application of the names Solar and Bour to the chambers at the upper end of a hall is dated 1394, in an assignment to a widow of—

> " A chamber under the solar, west of the hall, called 'le Bour,' with the easement of the hall and kitchen, with free ingress and egress at pleasure; the grange of the said tenement with gardens thereto belonging, &c."[2]

Such provision by a testator for his widow was common, the eldest son usually having possession of the remainder of the house. That such an arrangement worked fairly satisfactorily is proved by the absence of records of litigation. Although the typical medieval house is correctly described as consisting of hall, with upper-end and lower-end chambers, establishments were not confined to these, nor, on the other hand, did all houses include the whole of them; further, town houses, though often strictly adhering to this accommodation, more frequently departed from the plan, to meet the necessities of restricted or irregular sites.

In ancient times the word hall was applied to any extensive roofed space, and in the medieval period not only to the principal apartment of a large house, but equally to that of one so small as scarcely to be more than a cabin. In this respect the line from Chaucer, c. 1386,

> " Fful sooty was hir bour and eek hire halle,"[3]

---

[1] *A Descriptive Catalogue of Ancient Deeds in the Public Record Office*, vol. vi., No. C 6464.
[2] *Ibid.*, No. C 4950.
[3] *Nonne Prestes*, T. 12.

refers to the humble home of a widow, consisting only of two apartments—the living-room or hall and the sleeping-room or bower, both grimy from the smoke of the fire which burned on the hall floor. The smoke filled such a house before passing out through a hole in the roof, and the discomfort must have been considerable, for we know that women who occupied these houses suffered from red and inflamed eyes. The provision for disposal of smoke by louvres in the roof of the hall of a nobleman is indicated in the undertaking given by a tradesman in the fourteenth century:

> " Adam le Plasterer to find plaster of Paris at my own proper charge good and sufficient . . . proper for the hall of the Earl of Richmond and that I will competently plaster and complete the said hall and will repair the walls of the same with the said plaster and well befittingly within and without ; as also the tewels (louvres or flues for smoke) to the summit, &c."[1]

The plan of the hall at Penshurst Place, Fig. 80, is that of the medieval type. It is of a large house, but almost identical arrangements are found in small houses of this period, and (with slight modifications) the same plan continued in use for almost all houses until well into the seventeenth century; though by that date it was no longer necessary to surround them with moat, wall or palisade, entered by a gatehouse. It cannot be said that the cottage of the fourteenth century was substantially better than its predecessors. All records of small houses show that they were built for persons of substance or, like the Fish House at Meare (Figs. 82, 597), by some lord or prelate or other person of importance. The labourer's and inferior class of artisan's dwelling was primitive, and in remoter districts was of that flimsy character which is referred to by Froissart in his Chronicle when relating how the Scots, on returning from a foray in England, found that in their absence their country had been laid waste by an English expedition. This the Scots took philosophically, saying

> " that with six or eight stakes they would soon have new houses and obtain cattle enough from the forests, whither they had been driven for security."

In towns, however, a middle class consisting principally of traders and merchants had attained some measure of prosperity. This comes out clearly in a contemporary contract made between a carpenter and a pelterer for building a house for the latter, and, as the details of the accommodation to be provided and the form of payment are of interest, it seems worthy of being quoted in full. The words in brackets are comments not in the deed, or giving the Latin words of the deed.

> " Simon de Canterbury, carpenter, came before the Mayor and Aldermen (of the City of London) on the Saturday next after the feast of St. Martin the Bishop (11th November), in the second year of the reign of King Edward, son of King Edward (1308), and acknowledged that he would make at his own proper charges down to the locks for William Haningtone, pelterer, before the

---

[1] *Memorials of London*, by H. T. Riley, London, 1868.

Feast of Easter, then next coming, a hall and a room with a chimney (camino) and one larder between the said hall and room, and one sollar over the room and larder: also, one oriole (probably a recess with a window) at the end of the hall, beyond the high bench (summum scamnum) and one step with an oriole (possibly a porch in this instance) from the ground to the door of the hall aforesaid, outside of that hall: and two enclosures as cellars, opposite to each other, beneath the hall: and one enclosure for a sewer, with two pipes leading to the said sewer: and one stable (the figure is not given) in length between the said hall and the old kitchen and twelve feet in width, with a sollar above such stable, and a garret above the sollar aforesaid: and at one end of such sollar there is to be a kitchen with a chimney: and there is to be an oriole (this may mean a room or more probably—the width only being given—a passage) between the said hall and the old chamber, eight feet in width. And if he shall not do so then he admits, &c. And the said William Haningtone acknowledged that he was bound to pay to Simon before-mentioned, for the work aforesaid, the sum of £9 5s. 4d., half a hundred of Eastern marten skins, fur for a woman's hood, value five shillings, and fur for a robe for him the said Simon, &c."[1]

The complete building would conform with the usual plan. There was to be a hall (with a porch?) with cellars under, the hall floor one step from ground level.[2] At the end of the hall there was to be a room with a chimney (the bower) and a larder. Above these was the sollar. Whether the old chamber to which reference was made was at the other end of the hall is not certain, but this would be in accordance with common practice. The stable with sollar over and garret may well have been a separate structure. The hall was to be provided with a porch, and there was to be a privy, with drains. It will be noted that the stable was to be situated " between the said hall and the old kitchen "—the kitchen, therefore, was a detached building. Provision also is made for a kitchen with a chimney at the end of the sollar over the stable. The nature of the " oriole between the said hall and the old chamber " cannot be determined; the word oriole, as will be shown later, had many applications.

Of large establishments it need only be said that they had the hall, upper-end and lower-end chambers as a nucleus, and that other buildings were added haphazard to meet the requirements of the moment, as to lodge a special guest or to accommodate an increasing retinue. Such buildings were often of less substantial nature than the hall, etc.

The ravages of fire, improvements, and the ordinary course of rebuilding have destroyed town houses to a greater extent than those in country places. Restricted space and narrow frontages naturally produced houses having one gable end facing the street, and whilst familiar names (associated with their uses) were applied to apartments their disposition varied with the requirements of sites. Timber construction lent itself to projecting upper stories (frequently found also in country houses), an easy way of obtaining greater floor space than

[1] Translated in *Memorials of London*, etc., by H. T. Riley, London, 1868.
[2] Frequently this step was down (not up) as the doorways at Thornbury Castle, Glos., and at Penshurst Place, Kent.

the actual site afforded after headroom had been left for passengers along the street. Such buildings may still be seen in country towns, which, though greatly spoiled by the improver and faker, still retain the general appearance of medieval buildings. In Scotland, in the older streets of Edinburgh, Glasgow, and St. Andrews, are houses, built of stone, having crow-stepped gables (Fig. 113) similar to those in towns in the Low Countries. Although these are not of such early date as the fourteenth century, they are characteristic of what we built through foreign influence; indeed, perhaps the best impression now to be obtained of the appearance of an English medieval street is from those existing in continental towns, as Bruges in Belgium, which retains its medieval character in its later gables of varying heights and forms, or in Rothenburg-on-Tauber, in Bavaria, which is, perhaps, the most perfect medieval town in Europe.

The word "oriel" has troubled etymologists, who have sought to trace its derivation, as much as it has others who have tried to determine its application. Now applied to a type of *window*, also called a bay, it seems in medieval times also to have been an *apartment*; but records show the word to have been applied very loosely. One writer[1] has traced six applications, for each of which he quotes several instances. To give all would occupy too much space, so one only of each is quoted here:

1. As a penthouse or covered passage.

> 1338. "Congie et licence de fair un Oriel . . . entre le manoir du dit Massieu ouquel il demeure à present . . . et le manoir, qui est audit Massieu, qui est à l'opposite d'y cellui manoir."

2. A porch attached to any edifice.

> 1235. "In uno magno Oriello pulchro et competenti, ante ostium magne camere Regis castro de Kenilworth faciendo £6 16s. 4d."

3. A detached gatehouse.

> 1251. "Atrium nobilissium in introitu, quod Porticus, vel Oriolum, appellatur."

4. An upper storey.

> 1448. "Cum le ovyrstorye vocat an oriell."

5. A loft.

> 1449. "Pro uno Oriell supra stabulam ibidem."

6. A place for minstrels. (The quotation, the only one, says nothing of "gallery," but indicates a *place* only.)

> 1452. "Pro novo Oreyell pro Trumpetes Domini in Aula ibidem."

[1] W. Hamper in *Archæologia*, xxiii., pp. 105-6.

In Cornwall, a porch or balcony at the head of an outside stair leading to the occupied upper storey of a fisherman's cottage is called an orrell. A deed dated 1341 granted

> " Licence to build an oriole adjoining a tavern . . . so that the three posts of the said oriole shall be on the grantor's waste and on his soil, and that persons on horse and on foot and carts (charz et charettes) may pass beneath without disturbance."[1]

Whether the oriole in question was a balcony, a window or a room is not clear, but it certainly was on an upper floor, and the word " adjoining " suggests an upper chamber standing on posts.

Another record of the year 1269 instructs " to repair without delay the aisles, windows and oriels of the same hall."[2]

Used in the sense of a room in 1246:

> "Make also a door and windows in the oriol beyond the porch of our hall there . . . at Ludgershall."[3]

Used in the modern application as a window, also employed indiscriminately with the word " bay," we have in 1655:

> " Sure I am that small excursion out of gentlemen's halls in Dorsetshire (respect it east or west) is commonly called an Órial."[4]

The plan of Unstone Hall, Derbyshire (Fig. 156), shows an oriel which corresponds with this description.

Recently some writers have applied the term " oriel " to a projecting window of an upper floor, supported by brackets or corbelling, and have employed the word " bay " only when the window started from ground level, whether continued above the first floor or not. For convenience, the same distinction will be observed in this history.

It has been suggested that the true original of the oriel was the reader's pulpit at the dais end of the monastic frater-house, from which one of the brethren read aloud at meal-times. This was universal by the end of the twelfth century, and was generally enclosed in a square projection at the upper end of the frater (hall) to which access was obtained by a stair in the thickness of the wall.[5]

In ancient documents relating to domestic buildings constant references are made to chapels, and we find that even in small houses one room was set apart as a chapel. In the instructions given by Henry III for repair of his houses chapels are almost always mentioned, sometimes a special chapel being provided

---

[1] *Descriptive Catalogue of Ancient Deeds in Public Rolls Office*, vol. vi, No. C 7448.
[2] *Liberate Rolls*, Henry III. Quoted by Parker, ii, p. 84.   [3] *Ibid.*, 83.
[4] Fuller, *Ch. History*, vi, ii (1840), iii, 305. *New English Dictionary*, s.v. Oriel.
[5] *Some Famous Buildings and their Story*, by Clapham and Godfrey, F.F.S.A.

for his queen. Those who have visited the Tower of London will recollect the beautiful Norman chapel to St. John, in the White Tower or Keep. Fig. 587 illustrates the chapel at Little Wenham Hall, *c.* 1260-80, and the plan of Old Soar Manor House, *c.* 1300 (Fig. 60), shows that of three apartments on the first or inhabited floor one was the chapel. Both these chapels were fitted with piscinæ, and that at Little Wenham Hall had sedilia. The piscina at Old Soar is illustrated (Fig. 877). It seems to be of later date than the building itself (though the date of this is difficult exactly to decide), and has a decorated hood over a cinquefoil arch, while the bowl is hexagonal in plan. The chapel of St. Mary's Hospital, Chichester, *c.* 1280 (Fig. 19), is only separated from the hall by an openwork screen. Indeed, there was no common practice observed in placing the chapel, which was frequently an addition to existing buildings. In 1237 (Henry III) the Liberate Rolls record:

> " We command that you cause to be made at Kennington, on the spot where our chapel which is roofed with thatch is situated, a chapel with a stair-case of plaster, which shall be thirty feet long and twelve feet wide ; in such a manner that in the upper part there be made a chapel for the use of our queen, so that she may enter that chapel from her chamber ; and in the lower part let there be a chapel for the use of our family."[1]

At Bodiam Castle, *c.* 1386 (plan, Fig. 86), there is a small room opening off the chapel for use of the priest. The devotion of one room to a chapel even in so small a house as Old Soar (Figs. 58-60, 818) is remarkable, but in no way exceptional. It must not be assumed, however, that the chapel was devoted entirely to religious observances. Turner has pointed out that in the chronicles of the twelfth and thirteenth centuries there are not infrequent notices of the transaction of secular business in the domestic chapel, and that the sovereign used the chapel for giving audiences when for any reason the hall or chamber was not used for the purpose. It will be remembered that churches were used for many purposes during the feudal period, and even up to the eighteenth century manorial courts were held in them. Deeds were drawn up and signed, wills made, and property assigned in churches as being the proper places for such formalities. The desecration of churches was frequent. In the thirteenth century Ely Cathedral contained permanent stalls for merchandise, which were rented to holders for terms of years. St. Paul's Cathedral was used as a market so late as 1554, when an Act in Council was passed to stop this, but it proved ineffectual, and the traffic in the cathedral continued even during service.[2] Produce was habitually stored in[3] churches, as at Chesterfield in 1265 and Tideswell in 1251. Feasting and drinking in churches were forbidden by an injunction of Henry VIII, whilst many records exist of entertainments in churches

[1] Parker, *Domestic Arch.*, ii, p. 80.
[2] *Church and Manor*, by S. O. Addy, London, 1913, pp. 325, 326.
[3] *Ibid.*, p. 329.

(other than sacred plays), as when the Corporation of Rye paid players from Romney for playing in the church.[1]

The fourteenth-century chapel at Salmestone Grange, near Margate, Kent, stands beside the refectory building. The remaining original timbers of the chapel roof are soot-stained from the fires of a hearth which must have been in the middle of the floor, just as that at Penshurst Hall (Figs. 594, 769).

At Heybridge, Essex, c. 1271, there was " solarium cum capella da construction Herveii de Borham cum duobus caminis de plastro Paris."[2] Here we have record, not only of the fireplace in a chapel, but that the chimney was constructed of plaster (see Figs. 558, 763).

The medieval period was one of primitive manners and habits. The indiscriminate use of the hall for eating, amusement, and sleeping by both sexes, herded together in promiscuous fashion, is continually recorded in contemporary records, and to maintain that domestic chapels were devoted entirely to religious purposes is not only contrary to the spirit of the times, but is inconceivable if regarded merely from the standpoint of probability.

Though woven hangings (called " wall clothes ") were used by the Saxons in their halls, the treatment of walls in the twelfth and thirteenth centuries was by rendering with plaster and by wainscoting, and both plastered and boarded surfaces were painted with formal decoration or with pictorial subjects.

Towards the close of the thirteenth century tapestry was being made and freely used in England, so that by the fourteenth century the use of woollen wall hangings and tapestry was firmly established, and before the end of that century every person of importance had hangings of Arras or Paris or London manufacture, which were carried from house to house. The popularity of this wall treatment continued to increase, until we find in the inventories of Henry VIII and Wolsey immense quantities of such hangings, and not until late in the eighteenth century did they pass out of fashion.

The increased comfort as compared with plastered walls is as obvious as is the decorative value of hangings. Persons unable to afford tapestry hung woollen cloths on their walls, and even painted canvas, showing how the new treatment was appreciated and continued in favour long after the medieval period. Shakespeare records this at a later date :

" Good traders in the flesh, set this in your painted cloths."[3]

The furniture and equipment of the medieval house was scanty. In the hall boards on trestles, which could be removed easily, served as tables. At the head of the hall, behind the high table, was a bench seat fixed to the wall, and in the middle of its length a chair (fixed or removable) for the lord. Forms were the best sitting accommodation for other persons; " joyned " tables (joiners' work),

[1] *Church and Manor*, by S. O. Addy, London, 1913, pp. 331, 333.
[2] *The Evolution of the English House*, by S. O. Addy, London, 1913, quoting *Domesday of St. Paul's*, Camden Soc., p. cxix.
[3] *Troilus and Cressida*, V, x.

stools, and chairs did not become general until the sixteenth century. Thus we have in 1397 the items of an inventory,

" iij Mensae mobiles cum tristellis, et j stans,"[1]

the latter probably only differing from the others in being fixed, possibly behind the high table. With these were two chairs, three forms, and three stools

(" ij Cathedrae, et iij formulæ, et iij scabella ").[2]

These, with two or three pots, a few bowls and andirons, formed the equipment of the hall of an ecclesiastic. Beds, even for princes, were rough-planked pieces of furniture, with or without hangings.

The intimate relations which existed in the medieval period between the lord and members of his household, and to a still greater degree between a knight or squire such as occupied houses like Little Wenham Hall and Old Soar and his people, is difficult for us fully to realize, but the limited accommodation would indicate this even if no written records existed. The gradual breaking down of this intimacy and increasing aloofness of the householder are apparent in the following extracts, one written, approximately, 130 years after the other.

Robert Grosstête, who became Bishop of Lincoln in 1235, wrote:

" As muche as ye may, withoute peril of sykenes and weryneys, eat ye in the halle afore youre meyny (household) for that schal be to youre profyte and worschippe."[3]

The other extract is from *The Vision of Piers Ploughman, c.* 1362:

" Elynge is the halle eche day in the wyke,
There the lord ne the ladye lyketh noughte to sytte.
Now hath each riche a reule to eten by hym-selve
In a pryve-parloure, for pore mennes sake
Or in a chambre with a chymneye and leve the chief halle
That was made for meles, men to eten inne
And al to spare to spende, that spille shall another."[4]

This tendency to retire to private apartments increased, notwithstanding influential efforts to check the practice (Henry VIII expressed himself strongly against it) and became the chief stimulus in reducing the size and increasing the number of apartments in a house. In the Elizabethan period the tendency was for small houses to be built without a three-storeyed hall, and the abandonment of the hall as the chief apartment may be said to have culminated in widespread conversion of existing hall houses into apartment houses during the closing years of the sixteenth and the early years of the seventeenth century. In Kent, Sussex, and Surrey, as in other counties, are hundreds of hall houses (as that in Fig. 16), which have been divided thus by insertion of two floors into the open-roofed hall and one floor into the solar, and dividing these again by vertical

[1] *Surtees Society, Status Domus,* 1397, quoted by Parker, ii, p. 32.
[2] MS. Lansdowne, No. 86, fol. 102, quoted by Parker, iii, 75.
[3] *Ibid.*
[4] Ed. by Rev. Walter Skeat, Oxford, 1886. Text B, x, 94.

partitions into bedrooms. By the experienced eye these hall houses are easily recognized, and examination frequently shows that they retain most of their medieval features—ancient windows and doorways being only blocked up, not destroyed. In small houses this proved the final elimination of the hall—once the chief apartment—but in great houses it survived almost until the middle of the seventeenth century, though in its final phases (as we shall see later) it was ceiled, as at Knole (Fig. 625), and not open to the roof.

In the thirteenth century we saw the dawn of *comfort* in increased amenities in the houses of the king and great lords. In this, the fourteenth century, we can perceive the dawn of *freedom* of the people. It is only the dawn; but as ultimately it had far-reaching effects upon the condition of the people, and especially upon their housing, allusion should be made to it.

It will be remembered that in France all children of the *seigneur* inherited his titles, despised any form of work, and entered only the professions of Church and Army; the result being the multiplication of a parasitic class without parallel in England, where families and individuals rose and fell in the social scale. Here, elder sons inherited estates; the younger members who did not espouse the Church or adopt the Army as careers engaged in trade or became yeomen cultivators of land. Such association naturally gave the landed gentry and nobility an interest in trade, in manufacture and in agriculture, and brought them into close connection with burghers to a degree which contrasts markedly with the dissimilar relations of French *seigneurs*. So in England we have the upper classes merging into those below them, whilst on the other hand traders and others recruited the ranks of smaller landholders and frequently also of the nobility. Improved conditions and the prosperity of these middle classes were reflected in the houses they built for themselves in the reign of Edward II, when

> " peaceful stone manor-houses could rise in quiet corners of the land, the export of wool could increase, the population could go up, all classes could grow less poor and less ill-fed because all the while the king's peace was indifferently well enforced."[1]

This progress persisted and swelled with succeeding centuries, always being reflected in the comfortable homes of which every county has abundant examples.

The condition of the majority of the people was feudal. Land was held in large areas by the nobility from the king in return for services and payments. This was divided amongst smaller holders of manors upon an infinite variety of terms, of which one instance may suffice.

In a deed of the third year of Edward I, 1274 :

> " The Earl of Pembroke undertook to enfeoff John Darey of the fords of the Trent, &c., value 20 marks rent in return for which the said John Darey . . . was to take up knighthood and during his life serve the Earl in peace, war, at home or abroad, and to go to the Holy Land, if required."[2]

[1] *A History of England*, G. M. Trevelyan, 1927, p. 199.   [2] *Catalogue of Ancient Deeds in P.R.O.*, vol. iv, p. 35.

On similar and on many other terms manors were held, but—

> " Manorial property was a possession differing in many respects from what is now called landed estate. It was not a breadth of land, which the lord might cultivate or not as he pleased, suffer it to be inhabited or reduce it to solitude or waste; but it was a dominion or empire within which the lord was the superior over subjects of different ranks, his power over them not being absolute but limited by law and custom. The lord of a manor, who had received by grant from the Crown, saca and soca, tol and team, &c., was not merely a proprietor but a prince, and his courts were not only courts of law but frequently of communal justice. The demesne, the assized and the waste lands were his; but the usufruct of the assized lands belonged, on conditions, to the tenants, and the waste lands were not so entirely his that he could exclude the tenants from the use of them. . . . MANORS WERE PETTY ROYALTIES."[1]

The tenants of a manor might be freemen or villains, the free tenant paying rent in cash or kind, the villain also in services.

> " The villain (cotman, bond tenant, farmer) was not a slave, but holding under the lord some small portion of land, had neither a permanent interest in the land nor could he be called a freeman. . . . He could not leave the lord's estate, nor, indeed, give up the land held by him; he was a servant for life, receiving as wages enough land to support himself and family. If he left his lord he could be recovered as a stray, unless he had lived meantime for a year and a day in a privileged town or borough, in which case he received his freedom. He could accumulate no property, everything he possessed was his lord's."

(Notwithstanding this legal position, countless villains did acquire property with which they purchased privileges and often their own freedom.)

> " His services consisted in servile work done by himself and his household on the lord's demesne land . . . which in the end became quite regular and stated in quantity and time. . . .
>
> " All the children inherited the father's condition . . . a bastard was free: being *filius nullius*, and as such unable to have any inheritance, he at all events got his natural freedom by it. The villain, in course of time, became the copyholder."[2]
>
> " The villain of Bolden held 30 acres, worked 144 days annually for his lord, besides extra work in ploughing, harrowing, and reaping. He also paid $\frac{3}{10}$d. and gave 2 hens and 20 eggs. This fairly represents the usual services in Co. Durham."[3]

> " In 1278 Adam Underwood held of the Earl of Warwick one yard of land " (a yard or virgate varied in different counties from 15 to 40 acres) " paying for the same seven bushels of oats yearly and a hen, being to work for the lord from the feast of St. Michael the Archangel to Lammas every other day except Saturday, vizt. mowing as long as that time should last, for which he was to have as much grass as he could carry away with his scythe, and at the end of the hay harvest he and his fellow mowers to have the lord's best mutton, except one, or 16s. in money; with the best cheese, saving one, or 6d. in money; and the cheese vat wherein the said cheese was made full of salt."[4]

The medieval village was small, having a population of 50, 70, or even 100 persons, whose vocabulary did not exceed 600 words. All but freemen were

[1] *Camden Society*, vol. lxix. Introduction by W. H. Hale, p. xxxii.
[2] *Bolden Buke* (twelfth century), lxx. Glossary by the Rev. W. Greenwell.   [3] *Ibid*.
[4] Dugdale's *Warwickshire*, p. 426, quoted in Eden's *State of the Poor*, London, 1797, pp. 13-14.

tied to the spot, and each village was practically self-supporting, for, generally, communications were exceedingly bad, and only necessaries, such as iron, were imported from other districts. For the same reason supplies of produce did not flow into centres of population, and, as has already been stated, the king or any noble or churchman having a large retinue had to move from one residence to another when local supplies were exhausted. Such was the position up to the middle of the fourteenth century, when (in 1349) the Black Death destroyed more than one-third of the population: other visitations in 1361 and 1369 still further reduced numbers so that there were not sufficient hands left to cultivate the land. The demand for labour resulted in less vigilance in returning " strays " to their manors and increased the numbers of wage payments for services. In 1389 a Statute of Labourers ordered that:

> " No servant nor labourer . . . shall depart . . . out of the hundred . . . where he is dwelling to serve or dwell elsewhere or by colour to go from thence in pilgrimage unless he bring a letter patent containing the cause of his going and the time of his returning, if he ought to return, under the King's seale. . . . If found wandering without such a letter he shall be maintenant taken by the said manors, bailiffs . . . and put in the stocks. . . . None to receive a servant . . . without a letter."

Wages were also fixed by the Statute.[1]

This statute was a repressive measure following the peasant rising in 1381, a rebellion which was the expression of a new and general consciousness of freedom and personal rights. Like all similar measures, the Statute of Labourers was ineffectual, the independence of the individual continued to increase; but it is not until three centuries later that we see marked improvement in the housing of the lowest class of labourer; that improvement reaching him through comforts long enjoyed by the yeoman and small farmer class which sprang from his class—the villain (" Pour folke in cotes, charged with children and chef lordes rente ")—existing examples of whose dwellings we shall not find much before the end of the fifteenth and the beginning of the sixteenth centuries.

[1] *Statute of Labourers*, 12, p. 2. Rot. Parl. II, quoted in Eden's *State of the Poor*, III, p. cl.

Chapter IV

THE FIFTEENTH CENTURY

HENRY IV, 1399-1413; HENRY V, 1413-22; HENRY VI, 1422-61; EDWARD IV,
1461-83; EDWARD V, 1483; RICHARD III, 1483-5; HENRY VII, 1485-1509

IT WILL be remembered that during the Hundred Years War English forces penetrated far into France; indeed, at one time, one-half of that country was in English occupation. Such penetration was not confined to the years of war between the English and French kings, but was continued by English noblemen and knights of fortune during periods when the sovereigns were nominally at peace. These knights established themselves in French castles, from which they raided the country far and wide, capturing and holding to ransom, indiscriminately, both men and women. On returning to England the marauders often built castles here for themselves on the lines of those they had occupied in France. The reintroduction of brick into England was partly due to this fashion of copying French castles,[1] notable examples, amongst many others, being Tattershall in Lincolnshire and Hurstmonceaux in Sussex—both built in the second quarter of the fifteenth century, and both upon French models. An earlier instance is Bodiam Castle, in Sussex, licence to build which was granted to Sir Edward Dalyngrigge in 1386 in the following terms:

> "That he may strengthen with a wall of stone and lime, and crenellate and may construct and make into a castle his manor house of Bodyham, near the sea, in the county of Sussex, for the defence of the adjacent country and the resistance of our enemies," etc.

Bodiam Castle is now twelve miles from the sea, but in the fourteenth century the River Rother, near which it stands, was tidal, and the whole valley became an inlet of the sea at high water. The French sent expeditions which sailed up to Bodiam, landed and ravaged the country; hence the allusion in the licence to "resistance of our enemies." Sir Edward liberally interpreted this licence "to strengthen his manor house" by building the entirely new fortress of Bodiam Castle. Amongst the marauding knights who devastated France was Sir John Knollys, who established himself in the Castle of Derval, near Chateaubriant, and Sir Edward Dalyngrigge who entered his service. The latter went to France in 1367 and returned before 1380, when he was head of the king's household. Bodiam Castle[2] is an early example of the French type of castle, built to a

[1] *A History of English Brickwork*, by Nathaniel Lloyd, pp. 7-8.
[2] A detailed description of Bodiam Castle appeared in *The Architectural Review* of October, 1919, and has been ably described, historically and architecturally, by Lord Curzon in his monograph published by Messrs. Jonathan Cape in 1926.

quadrangular plan, which superseded the Edwardian irregular concentric plan. It is an early instance of a dwelling in the Perpendicular style of architecture, and actually belongs to the fifteenth century rather than to the date of its licence, the fourteenth. The influence of the introduction of the quadrangular plan is seen also in the building of unfortified or only slightly fortified types of houses; thus the fifteenth-century house may be divided into two classes: those which had the gatehouse as part of the main structure—as Bodiam, 1386 (Figs. 85-87, 328); Hurstmonceaux, 1446 (Figs. 92, 329), Oxburgh Castle, Norfolk, 1482 (Fig. 331); and those where the gatehouse was a detached building—as at Cothay, Somerset, c. 1480 (Figs. 96, 98), and many other manor-houses, which were only protected by a moat and by the wall which enclosed the square court. The gatehouse of Bodiam (Fig. 328) is a formidable obstacle to entry of the court. Originally approached by an oak trestle bridge (see plan, Fig. 86), which extended from the west bank of the moat to the octagon, persons crossing it were subject to flank attack from the towers. On reaching the octagon, the barbican had to be passed, and then a watery gap of 10 ft. intervened (when the drawbridge was removed) between the causeway and the gatehouse itself. Fig. 328 shows the ancient portcullis raised. Within the doors was a passage or chamber, then another portcullis, a second chamber, and then a third portcullis. The vaulted ceilings of these chambers were pierced with holes, the purpose of which is not known for certain. They are believed to have been contrived for defence, some say by the lowering of posts partially to block the passage of attackers; others think they were for scattering powdered quicklime or for pouring down boiling water or molten lead on their heads; but it is difficult to imagine how sufficient quantities of the latter, to be effectual, could have been provided, or, indeed, handled in the apartments above. It may be pointed out, however, that such practices were adopted for defence in the fifteenth and sixteenth centuries; reference to them is made in *Don Quixote*, when one of a defending force cries:

" This way, brave boys ! . . . guard that postern ! shut yon gate ! . . . this way with your cauldrons of resin, pitch, and boiling oil !"

The author adds:

" In short, he named in the utmost hurry all the necessary implements and engines of war used in the defence of a city assaulted."[1]

Having passed the gatehouse, the doorway into the great hall is seen directly opposite, on the other side of the court (Fig. 87). Sometimes the hall was on the left of such a doorway, sometimes it was placed on the right, but the doorway was almost always exactly opposite the gatehouse entrance (Fig. 86). It may be seen also in the illustration of Oxburgh Castle (Fig. 331), and in the plan of Cothay (Fig. 98). Attention should also be drawn to the fact that the nucleus of the house—hall, upper-end and lower-end chambers—is retained, as usual,

[1] *Don Quixote*, ii, cap. liii, quoted by Lord Curzon, p. 127.

and that the other buildings are added to these. As time passed, the number of additional apartments increased, but this nucleus is to be observed in many houses until the late seventeenth century.

Although the hall, upper-end and lower-end chambers still constituted the accommodation of the manor-house and formed the nucleus of large establishments, smaller houses existed which boasted of only one apartment or, more frequently, of two, often divided by the chimney and fireplaces. If entry was into the kitchen, the inner room would be the bedroom; these were known as the *but* and the *ben*. Where there were three rooms (a rarer provision) the outer would be the kitchen, the room opening off it the parlour, and the room beyond the parlour the bedroom, and these were respectively styled the *but*, the *ben*, and the *farben*. The open-roofed kitchen was, in fact, the hall; the other rooms might be ceiled off to provide storage in their lofts. Such houses still exist in the northern counties and in Scotland.

The chapel was an important feature of the fifteenth-century castle, and, as might be expected, that at Bodiam was conveniently placed (Fig. 86) and furnished with a window that rivalled that of the great hall. The chapel measured approximately 30 ft. by 19 ft., and had a sanctuary at slightly higher level than the nave floor. There was a crypt below, and the roof was high pitched, like that of the great hall; other roofs were almost flat and were covered with lead. Opening off the south wall of the chapel was the sacristy, 13 ft. by 6 ft., which Lord Curzon suggests was also the priests' living-room. Above this was a room communicating with the private apartment over that which I suggest was the bower. Lord Curzon follows the popular attribution of bower to the upper room, but, however that may be, they were both family apartments. The little room over the sacristy had a two-light window looking down into the chapel, and such a room may be regarded as coming within the term " oriel." There was no rule for placing chapels—that at Caerphilly opened off the lower end of the hall. Elsewhere we find chapels occupying towers or opening off the gatehouse or other part of the castle, as at Winchester, where one opened off the Queen's chamber—somewhat like that at Bodiam.

The unsettled state of northern counties is reflected in the maintenance of fortified towers, to which additions were made, as at Yanwath Tower (Fig. 74), where hall and other buildings were added in this century, the whole enclosing a court, which the exigencies of the site caused to depart slightly from strictly quadrangular form. Such protected buildings also served as refuges for the inhabitants of the locality, when threatened by raids of predatory neighbours.

In the fifteenth century the kitchen, once a flimsy and often a temporary structure, had become an important one in all large establishments. The principal kitchen at Bodiam had two large fireplaces and an oven. On the west side of the court was another kitchen, provided for retainers and men-at-arms.

Castles similar in plan to Bodiam were built throughout the fifteenth and well into the sixteenth century.

The alure was a walk or way behind a parapet, provided to accommodate defenders and allow free movement from tower to tower; often it was covered and used as a promenade. Ambulatories were more particularly designed to give access to apartments which opened off them, and to provide covered ways in which to take exercise in foul weather—

> " Deambulatories, men to walke togithers, twaine and twaine to kepe them drye, when it happed to rayne."[1]

Fig. 360 shows a type of ambulatory at Abingdon, Fig. 361 one at St. Cross, both having some likeness to medieval cloisters.

The hall was still the most important apartment of the castle and of the manor-house. Whereas it used to have a floor of beaten earth, paving had now become general, and tiles (imported from Flanders and mentioned in deeds as having been imported for this purpose and for the hearths of fireplaces) were used. The quantities recorded are small, and, like bricks, they were manufactured in increasingly large quantities in this country, at first by Flemings and Dutchmen—who were brought over here for the purpose— and later by English labour. The story of the reintroduction of the art of brick-making into England and of its popularization here is most interesting, for recent research has cleared away misapprehensions long current as to im-portations of brick from the Low Countries; but the story is too full to be related here.[2]

The upper end of the hall floor was not always raised as a dais; but some-times the bay window, which became a feature of the upper end of the hall in this century, had its floor raised slightly above the hall-floor level. Fig. 601 shows the dais at Cothay, and Fig. 603 the raised floor in the bay at Ockwells; and although these are not necessarily the original levels, they illustrate them sufficiently well. At the opposite end of the dais from the bay, but sometimes in the bay recess, would stand the cupboard—a table on which cups were set. This was what we should call a sideboard or court cupboard of a later date. It was provided with shelves in the form of steps for the display of plate. On the Continent the number of steps was regulated according to the rank of the master or mistress of the house—two for a knight, three for a count, four for a prince, and five for the king. English illustrations do not show such fine grada-tions, and three seems to have been the number of steps provided for the king. While the usual covering for the cupboard and for the high table was white linen, the quality of this was defined strictly in accordance with rank. At earlier dates fabrics varied, and rules regulated who might use cloth of gold,

[1] Lydgate, *Boke of Troye.*
[2] This, with other matters relating to brick architecture, is fully treated in *A History of English Brick-work*, second edition, London, 1928.

E

velvet, and even the colours of these. Frequently inventories mention carpets for coverings or cloths laid over such shelves (" cupboards ") as :

"Item, one olde cupporde carpett of frame work, sore worne and moth eten."[1]

While every hall had entrance doorways opposite each other at the lower end, small halls often lacked the screens with gallery over, as the Kentish hall, a plan of which is given in Fig. 101.

Although most halls in the fifteenth century were on ground level, some had wall fireplaces with chimneys, as Ockwells (Fig. 771), and others central hearths as most of the Kentish yeomen's halls (Fig. 101), Penshurst Place (Fig. 594), and the King's great hall at Eltham Place (Fig. 94). Crosby Hall, built in 1466, in the City of London, also had a central hearth. The hall of the Manor House, Liddington (Fig. 614), being on the first floor, had a wall fireplace with chimney.

Some halls which, originally, had central hearths, had fireplaces with chimneys added later, as probably was the case at Cothay (Fig. 602) and at Rufford Hall (Fig. 609).

The solar, on the other hand, always had a wall fireplace, as, indeed, might be expected for an upper chamber.

Walls were hung with woven pictorial tapestries and painted cloths called "hallings," a term which indicates also the apartment in which they were hung. Thus, in 1427, we have reference to

"unum pannum pinctum vocatum hawling."[2]

The term "wainscot" was applied both to boarding of walls and to rough panelling as the screens at Haddon Hall (Fig. 593), at Cothay (Fig. 602), and at Ockwells (Figs. 356, 604). Such panels were boards filling the spaces between studs. Though the studs were often grooved or rebated to take the panels, sometimes the studs were in two halves, one each side of the panel as in Fig. 36.

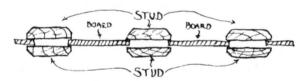

FIG. 36.—Section of studs and panel boards.

Towards the end of the fifteenth century leather stamped with decorative designs was often used in place of tapestry, but the popularity of the latter seems not to have been affected, and large sums were expended by Henry VI, Edward IV, and Henry VII upon arras, cloth of gold, velvets, and stuffs of rich materials and workmanship with which to cover their walls.

Notwithstanding the popularity of hangings, the practice of decorating walls by painting in tempera continued. The subjects were generally decorative ornament and scriptural "stories," and fragments of contemporary work remain, as well as numbers of complete paintings, some of which (like those in Figs. 695, 696, 699) are in fairly good condition.

One form of decoration which prevailed in the fifteenth century was the use

[1] MS. Harl. 1, 419, fol. 194, quoted by Parker, *Domestic Arch.*, iii, 133.
[2] Mem. Ripon (Surtees), i, 329.

of stained glass in windows—sometimes pictorially, generally heraldically. The most notable surviving examples of such glass are those at Ockwells Manor, which occupy their original positions in the windows of the great hall, though, as a matter of fact, they were removed and stored at Taplow Court for many years during which the house was in a semi-ruinous condition, and there can be no doubt that, but for this care, they would have been destroyed. The illustrations of the hall (Figs. 603, 604) and the detail (Fig. 510) give a fair idea of the designs, though they cannot convey any impression of the beauty of colouring in red, yellow, blue, and black. Fragments of similar glass remain, here and there, in contemporary manor-houses; sometimes a roundel or two may have been preserved—often only a coloured quarry. Not many years ago a considerable quantity of glass like that at Ockwells was found stored away at a farmhouse in Sussex. It was removed and sold and has completely disappeared. The importance of such glass resulted in its being willed as a separate property, and so late as the end of the sixteenth century Francis Smallman (who died in 1599) bequeathed to his nephew, Stephen, " the glass in the windows of the house in which I dwell at Wilderhope."[1] Removal from the windows for which it was designed would not often secure the preservation of glass as has happened at Ockwells. Although many manor-houses had glazed windows, others had not, and protection from weather was secured by shutters of wood. In halls like that of which the plan is given in Fig. 101 windows were in both external walls, and the shutters of those on the exposed side were closed in rough weather, leaving open for light and escape of smoke from the central hearth those on the leeward side.

The amenities of life, which we find increasing in the provision of additional chambers under various names—the name *camera* was applied loosely to several not always easy to identify with the apartments—was reflected also in the equipment of houses and in the manners of their occupants. Men who live like brutes naturally have brutish manners. Women especially were treated with courtesy by contrast with the attitude of the Norman baron towards his wife, whom he beat, dragged about by the hair, or disfigured facially when angered. But courtesy was not confined to women; it was the attitude of all gentlefolk, and numerous textbooks exist which give minute directions respecting the conduct of children, servants, and of the household, in all of which courtesy is the keynote and manners the refrain. They were written for the instruction and guidance of young persons domiciled in the houses of strangers, for in the fifteenth century it was common practice (as now amongst the middle and upper classes) to send children away from home to be educated. Amongst tradesmen, children were sent from home at seven or eight years of age and apprenticed for periods

[1] Trans. Salop Arch. and Nat. Hist. Soc., 1896, quoted by Garner and Stratton in *Domestic Arch. of the Tudor Period*, ii, 170.

of from seven to nine years, remaining and lodging with their masters during the whole time. Parents, having so disposed of their children, took those of others into their own households as apprentices. This practice was commented upon by contemporary Continental writers as being evidence of lack of natural affection and of the parsimony of the English, who lodged and fed other people's children worse than it would have been possible to treat their own offspring, and, also, because they could extract more work from them than they could have obtained from their own. Amongst the nobility, children were exchanged between families of similar social standing for the purpose of education, and these performed the duties of personal attendants and servants to their masters. Familiar instances are a lady's maidens who worked tapestries under her guidance and a queen's maids of honour; but these were only a small proportion of the children taken to perform the duties of a household and to be educated therein. Contemporary references and the nature of the instructions given in the books on manners seem to indicate that parents brought up their children without discipline and that they did not begin to learn manners until sent amongst strangers. However, the same remarks might well be applied to many children who are sent to preparatory schools at the present day, and parents may not have been less efficient in the fifteenth century than they are in the twentieth.

Education in letters was in the hands of churchmen, and boys of gentle birth were received into the monasteries and ate at the abbot's table. Richard Whiting, Abbot of Glastonbury, c. 1525, had no less than three hundred youths under his care, whom he treated as members of his family. The founding of Winchester College by William de Wykeham, 1373, marked a new departure in education, but the older channels persisted until the middle of the sixteenth century.

The question naturally arises of how far the substitution of children of strangers to perform personal and household services, for the upbringing of children at home may have been accountable for the slow development of house design and the tardiness shown in the multiplication of chambers and the desire for privacy. It is certain that householders have always lodged servitors and dependents less handsomely than members of their own families, and the limited accommodation provided in an important establishment, even as amplified in the fifteenth century, is remarkable.

The minute instructions as to cleanliness of person, of utensils, and of apartments, contained in the *Books of Nurture*, indicate the habits of slightly earlier times, as well as those of contemporaries of less gentle birth, rather than those for whom they were intended as guides; indeed, even the king (Edward IV) does not appear to have been scrupulously clean in his person, for, in his black household book it is provided that:

> "This barbour shall have . . . every Saturday nyght, if it please the Kinge to cleanse his head, legges, or feet, etc."[1]

[1] Quoted in *The Babees Book*, E. Eng. Text Soc., vol. xxxii.

and the usher of the chamber was to decide whether the "barbour's" allowance was to be provided or not; from which one gathers that frequently it was not. Many lavatories and drains exist of this period, frequently resembling the piscinæ of chapels, and affording what we should regard as scanty washing accommodation. Illustrations of the period show the washing of hands merely by pouring water over them whilst held over a basin, and the use of soap seems to have been confined to the washing of clothes.

The development of sanitary conveniences in the fifteenth century was more in the direction of increased accommodation than in improved methods. Bodiam Castle was provided with more than twenty garderobes, the outlets of which passed down through the thickness of the walls to discharge in the moat some distance below the surface of the water. In the north, where tower houses were not always surrounded by water, garderobes were contrived in a projecting turret or bartizan, from which the soil dropped into a barrel set below, which could be removed from time to time. Where a stream ran under a house, it was used to cleanse the outlets of garderobes, but all these contrivances were so imperfect as certainly to have been offensive.

The garderobe chambers at Langley Castle are described and shown in Fig. 88, and similar conveniences are referred to in a roll of the rites of Durham, about the year 1600, where apartments attached to the Dorter are detailed:

> "Also there was a faire large house and a most decent place adioyninge to the west syd of the said Dortre, towards ye water for ye mounckes and nouices to resort vnto, called the prvies wch was maide with two greate pillers of stone that did beare vp the whole floore thereof and every seate and pticiõ was of wainscott close of either syde verie decent so that one of them could not see one another, when they weare in that place, there was as many seates of prvies on either syde as there is little wyndowes in ye wall, wch. wyndowes was to give leighte to every one of the saide seates wch. afterward was walled up . . . over ye saide seates is an other faire glasse wyndowe."[1]

From amongst the multitude of guides to conduct published in the fifteenth century, the following may serve as a sample:[2]

> Aryse erly
> Serue god devowtely
> And the Worlde beseley
> Do thy worke wisely
> Yeue thyne almes secretely
> Goo by the waye sadly
> Answer the people demuerly
> Go to thy mete apetitely
> Sit thereat discretely
> Of thy tunge be not to liberally
> Arise therefrom temperally
> Go to thy supper soberly
> And to thy bed merely
> Be in thine Inne iocundly
> Plese thy loue duely
> And slepe suerly.

---

[1] Surtees Society, vol. cvii, pp. 85-6.
[2] MSS. Lansdowne, 762, fol. 16b. Printed in *Reliquiæ Antiquiæ*, vi, p. 233.

CHAPTER V

THE SIXTEENTH CENTURY

HENRY VIII, 1509-47; EDWARD VI, 1547-53; MARY, 1553-58;
ELIZABETH, 1558-1603

TO SAY that the dawn of the sixteenth century coincided with the advent of a new stimulus to architecture is inadequately to express what happened. It was the dawn of a new architectural era—nothing less. The change may be likened to an ocean wave, having origin so small as at first to be almost imperceptible, but gradually gaining volume and strength until it rises to its highest crest; then breaking and dying away, itself to disappear just as it had obliterated what it overwhelmed. The period of this wave may be said to cover the whole of the sixteenth, seventeenth and eighteenth centuries. Its inception was Italian influence, and, although the pure stream of this was cut off for a time, so that new ideas came to us polluted, it flowed again with renewed volume and purity, which continued for a further hundred years before it died away and was dispersed. Let us outline the sequence of events.

Until the end of the fifteenth century, English art and English architecture had been uninfluenced, practically, by that great movement which began in Italy and spread over Europe, which we call the Renaissance. The country had been unsettled, the Wars of the Roses had been composed and peace established in the reign of Henry VII; a parsimonious prince, who did not launch out into new enterprises or fashions involving expenditure. His son, Henry VIII, was otherwise. Young, gifted, the successor to a firmly established throne and to riches accumulated by his father, he plunged into life with zest. Immense sums were spent upon luxurious living; the richest fabrics and finest products were imported from the Continent; and foreign workmen, including artist-artisans of the greatest ability, were tempted to come to England to work in the King's service. These, however, could not undertake a fraction of the enterprises of the King, his Cardinal, and nobles of the Court. Consequently, we find the foreigners' work confined to the production of ornamental details, or of decorative units; complete in themselves, but of no great magnitude. The major works—chapels, houses, and the like—were built by Englishmen; tombs, decorations, and accessories were supplied by foreign workmen. Instances which can be quoted are familiar—Henry VII's tomb in the Perpendicular chapel at Westminster is a conspicuous example. Elsewhere are tombs in Gothic churches: two at Layer Marney to the Marneys; two at Oxburgh, Norfolk, to Bedingfelds; one at Norwich, in the church of St. George's, Colegate, to Robert Jannys—all of terra-cotta, the manufacture of which was previously unknown in England—and another of marble at Battle Church to Sir Anthony Browne, the King's Master of Horse. These are typical examples of works by Italians, the list of which might be indefinitely extended. The same limited influence is found applied to houses. At Hampton Court Palace, the English Tudor buildings erected by Wolsey include little Italian work besides the roundels containing heads of Roman Emperors, and one tablet of Wolsey's own arms—all in terra-cotta. At Sutton Place, near Guildford (Fig. 108), there is greater concession to the foreigner than is to be found in other contemporary buildings, inasmuch as the positions of the entrances to the hall have been changed from the lower end to the centres of the side walls, in order that the elevation to the court may be symmetrical. We also find here variety of Italian ornament (Fig. 403), sometimes in units, as tablets, or employed in the decoration of Tudor forms, or as the arabesques in the hollows of Perpendicular mouldings of windows; but the windows retain their English forms, mouldings and character—the ornament is merely accessory. At Layer Marney Hall, Essex, several windows are entirely Italian in design, material, and workmanship, as, also, are the decorative parapets of the towers. The structure itself and its other details are purely English (Fig. 107). Further instances are unnecessary; the Italian "influence" of the first half of the sixteenth century was no real influence—it was confined to the importation of a few workmen by the King and certain of his nobility for the production of tombs and toys. The divorce of Catherine of Aragon, the fall of Wolsey, the dissolution of the monasteries, the resulting break with Rome, were events not tending to encourage the importation of Italians; and, in fact, by the end of Henry's reign, there seem to have been few left in England. Edward VI, unlike his father, inherited debts; the reign of Mary was short and unprogressive; whilst the estrangement from Rome became intensified when Elizabeth ascended the throne. During this reign, England more than recovered prosperity, her trade increased, her merchants became peers and built themselves great houses, as, indeed, did every prosperous man of this thriving age. Trade relations with the Low Countries were intimate, and, accordingly, the arts and architecture of the Renaissance came to us through Holland, Germany, and Flanders. It was not an inspired Renaissance, but, on the whole, clumsy, ignorant, and often grotesque. No building was the creation of an able and reasoning mind, but rather the grafting of new details on old forms; extended and modified gradually to meet changing requirements, but seldom conceived as a whole. Not only did the Low Countries produce workmen who came here; they also provided pattern books, of which that entitled *Architectura* by De Vriese of Antwerp, issued in 1577, is an instance. These pattern books included designs for frames, columns, chimneypieces, and ornamental units in great variety, which were extracted, combined, and modified by English craftsmen. At Charlton

House, Kent, is an overmantel of early seventeenth-century date (Fig. 786), the design of which is copied from a panel design published by Abraham de Bruyn, c. 1575. The results, in some cases, were improvements effected by English hands, but on the whole were poor in conception and coarse in execution. The same may be said of works executed by imported craftsmen, though amongst these were several men of ability, as Ghiles de Witt (Fig. 778), who worked at Cobham Hall, Kent, towards the close of the sixteenth century. Instances might be multiplied, but perhaps enough has been said to show that the Elizabethan period, though a period during which many great houses were built, was not one of great or fine architecture; indeed, Sir Reginald Blomfield refers to the imported designs so freely copied as " the imbecilities of the Germans," while another architect is said contemptuously to have condensed a description of the work of the period 1560 to 1625 into the compound word " Jacobethan." These indictments ignore the good qualities of Elizabethan architecture. The late fifteenth and early sixteenth-century buildings are sometimes styled early Tudor, and the Elizabethan late Tudor; certainly the latter is in many respects a logical development of the early Tudor, as modified by the influence of the Low Countries. The early Tudor houses—not the castles, but houses like the Tribunal House, Glastonbury, and Abbot's Lodgings, Thame Park (Figs. 104 and 103)—are some of the most reasonable and successful ever designed to meet domestic requirements. No conventional symmetry of façades restricted the development or variation of plans to meet individual needs or the exigencies of restricted sites. Their fenestration was the most flexible that has ever been devised, and enabled additional window areas to be provided as and where required without injury to the elevations. Symmetry was not insisted upon whilst balance was easily secured. Such architecture was the last phase of the Gothic, and embodied nothing of that new manner which was shortly to be combined with and ultimately to supplant it. But there was no violent wrench. The coming of the new manner was gradual, the passing of the old was slow. In districts where traditional building methods have proved to be strongest (as in the Cotswolds), small houses, having doorways and windows substantially the same as those at Thame Park and Glastonbury, continued to be built for more than a hundred years—that is, far into the seventeenth century. The medieval plan was equally persistent, and buildings, far removed in character and external appearance from the Gothic, retain in their plans (even after the middle of the seventeenth century) the ancient disposition of hall, upper-end and lower-end chambers.

The beginning of Elizabeth's reign was marked by the publication of the earliest book on Architecture in English. The author, John Shute, is described on the title-page as " Paynter and Archytecte." The book, which is a rare one, was not printed until 1563,[1] although the author had gained his experience

---

[1] A facsimile of the first edition, with an introduction by Sir Lawrence Weaver, was published by *Country Life* in 1912.

during a journey to Italy, at the cost of the Duke of Northumberland, in 1550. Shute's visit enabled him personally to meet and to see works being carried out by Vignola, Michelangelo, and Palladio. He seems to have observed buildings himself, though his book is based upon those of Vitruvius, Serlio, and Philander, whose proportions for drawing the Orders are qualified by Shute's own views. In a section entitled

"What the Office and Duetie is of him that wil be a perfecte Architecte or Mayster of buyldings"

he insists that knowledge of the building crafts is not adequate equipment for an architect, who needs, also, to have understanding of the sciences and arts, which he then enumerates and shows their bearing upon the practice of architecture. In fact, he insists that the competent architect must be educated and not a mere tradesman, however skilled. No building in England can be assigned to John Shute, but students of detail recognize his influence, if not his hand, in contemporary buildings, and no doubt he prepared the way to that fuller appreciation of Italian Renaissance architecture which developed here in the seventeenth century.

It is in houses erected during the latter half of the sixteenth century that we see the hands of the English builders—at their worst (Fig. 370), loading their buildings with details borrowed from the Low Countries; at their best, in such houses as Lake House, near Salisbury (Fig. 127), Montacute, Yeovil (Figs. 128-131), and Kirby Hall, Northants (Fig. 122); though it is true that in the last two instances such eccentricities as chimneys formed as columns are incorporated. At Kirby Hall the gables of the south front (Fig. 522) are fantastic, and in the entrance to the great hall from the court (Fig. 122) the designer (in this case John Thorpe) has indulged in a riot of useless columns; but, on the whole, such buildings (and fortunately many remain) testify to the sober common sense and good taste of their English architect-builders. This was recognized by no less an authority than Sir Christopher Wren, who, in remarks addressed to the committee of Christ's Hospital on November 24, 1692, said:

"It was observed by somebody that our English artists are dull enough at invention, but when once a foreign pattern is set they imitate it so well, that commonly they exceed the original—I confess this observation is generally true." [1]

He then proceeds to say that, when they fail, it is not for lack of genius, but for want of education (a view which seems equally applicable to architects at the present day). Of these men much has been written; little is definitely known, but their names occasionally appear as surveyors, as architects, or as being responsible for the conduct of building works.

[1] Quoted by Martin A. Buckmaster, in an address to the Conference of Public School Head Masters, December 21, 1928.

In the accounts for the building of Hengrave Hall, Suffolk, two of the contracts refer to drawings. The mason's contract, with John Eastawe, specifies that the work shall be

" according to a frame, which the said Iohn has seen at Comby."

In the plasterer's contract (1538) reference is made to

" Robert Watson, ruler of his (Sir Thomas Kytson's) building in Hengrave."

This work was to be done

" substantially, without deycete,"

but no further mention is made of Watson.[1]

In the accounts of Bess of Hardwick's buildings the entry appears:

" 24.12.1551. Item given Roger Worde, my masters mason for drawing my masters platt xxs."[2]

This was the plan of Chatsworth and is interesting as a record of a special payment made for a particular service rendered by a (chief) mason. It could only have been a general plan, and seems to have been a complete transaction.

The subject is an attractive one, which has been pursued by several investigators, amongst whom Mr. J. A. Gotch, Sir R. E. Blomfield, and Mr. M. S. Briggs are authorities.[3] The last named quotes from records of Hampton Court accounts,[4] and suggests that Henry Williams may have been the designer of Wolsey's works there. He is described as " priest, surveyor of the works," and payments were made in respect of the building operations in his presence each month. It is pointed out that the similarity of Wolsey's two great buildings —Hampton Court Palace and Christ Church, Oxford, the halls of which are almost identical—indicate their having had the same designer, but there does not seem to be any direct evidence which would justify the attribution of these works to Mr. Henry Williams.

Another alleged architect, using the word in its modern sense, was John Thorpe (practised *c.* 1570-1610), for whom a stronger case has been made out, but the extent of whose activities is uncertain. Kirby Hall, Northants, is generally ascribed to him, and in a book of drawings which belonged to him (now preserved in the Soane Museum) is a plan of Kirby (Fig. 121), which approximates to the building as erected, less a loggia and other portions which were never carried out and the later additions attributed to Inigo Jones.

Wollaton Hall (Figs. 123, 124) has also been regarded as having been designed by Thorpe, because a plan of it is amongst those in his book of drawings. All the drawings, however, are not of his own works, and Wollaton may be more securely attached to the name of Robert Smithson, whose tomb in Wollaton Church describes him as

[1] Hist. and Antiq., *Hengrave in Suffolk*, by John Gage, London, 1822, pp. 41, 42.
[2] *Bess of Hardwick's Buildings and Building Accounts*, by Basil Stalybrass, *Archæologia*, lxiv, p. 35.
[3] *Renaissance Architecture in England*, J. A. Gotch, London, 1901; *A History of Renaissance Architecture in England*, R. Blomfield, London, 1897 ; *The Architect in History*, M. S. Briggs, Oxford, 1927.
[4] *History of Hampton Court*, Ernest Law, 1924, p. 28.

" gent., architector, and surveyor unto the most worthy House of Wollaton, with divers others of great account."[1]

He was also employed as " Free master-mason " at Longleat, begun 1567—a designation which students of the subject may think more correct as describing the scope of his practice than that of the epitaph on his tomb. Another Smithson, John, and his son, Huntingdon Smithson, superintended the building of Bolsover Castle in the early seventeenth century. The former is stated to have been sent to Italy to collect designs; he regularly visited the works, and his charges of 4d. for refreshment for himself and 2d. for his horse appear in the accounts. There is no evidence to show how much detailing was done by these designers of the general fabric and how far this was still left to each trade. The inscription on Huntingdon Smithson's tomb in Bolsover Church states that his

" skill in architecture did deserve a fairer tombe his mem'ry to preserve."[2]

Fig. 135 shows the plan of Beaufort House, Chelsea, as standing, drawn by J. Symonds, c. 1595. The whole of the south front conforms with the medieval plan. The porch gives into the entry, under the gallery of the great hall, at the upper end of which is the dais and beyond this the chamber. The lower-end chambers are more numerous and extensive. This front is symmetrical, the porch in the middle, on each side of it are bays (one being the hall bay window, the other containing a circular staircase), wider and less projecting bay windows flank these, so that we have five projections symmetrically arranged on this front. The other elevations show no similar Renaissance influence; they are irregular and there is no tendency to repeat features.

Fig. 136 shows a plan, drawn by Spicer, c. 1595, for rebuilding the same house. He aims at more complete symmetry. In the south elevation the porch is still in the centre, and the apartments at the S.E. and S.W. angles of the building have been brought forward as deep projecting wings. The hall has been moved westwards, and the hall bay and stair bay have been eliminated altogether. The north elevation has been made symmetrical—boldly projecting wings, with a low wall on the north side forming a court. It is interesting to note how the N.E. bay is repeated by one on the N.W., which encloses the ovens and has blind windows, for such devices to secure absolute symmetry are continually found in subsequent architecture. No effort has been made in this plan to make east and west elevations the same.

Whether Spicer's plan for alterations was carried out in its entirety or partially we do not know, but the house was rebuilt after the plan by John Thorpe, c. 1620 (Fig. 137). In this we have absolute symmetry of front and back elevations. The porch, which has classic columns, is the most prominent feature of the south elevation; on either side of it are slightly projecting bay windows, one of the great hall, the other of a room beyond the buttery, which is called a " lodging." The S.E. and S.W. angles, which Spicer projected as wings, are

[1] Quoted by Louis Ambler, in a note in *The Builder*, December 1, 1911, p. 650.   [2] *Ibid.*

only brought forward slightly as bays, each furnished with angle turrets.   A new and interesting feature of this plan is the central corridor, called

" a longe entry through all,"

which we should regard as essential for access to apartments, without passing through one to reach another, but which was not generally adopted by house-planners until the eighteenth century.   Not only is the medieval plan of hall, upper-end and lower-end chambers clearly to be seen, but the draughtsman has added lettering to identify the chambers. The chamber is called the " p'loure," the buttery is identified, as is the pantry across the " longe entry."   The " chaple," with east window, is next to the parlour, whilst the kitchen and other offices are placed in the N.W. angle.   The terrace is called " a back walke," and other apartments are named " lodgings."   In front is the " large terrace," from which six steps lead down to " the inner greene court," entrance to which is between two square lodges, set diamond-wise.

These three plans are extraordinarily interesting.[1]   The first (Fig. 135) as of a house existing in 1595, the second (Fig. 136) as a suggestion for rebuilding which embodied current taste, and the third (Fig. 137) as of a house built c. 1620, which embodied later ideas in house design.   The persistence of the medieval nucleus in all is remarkable; indeed, the only progress made is in a more orderly and convenient disposition of apartments additional to a medieval plan.   Kip's view of the house (1699) shows the south front to have had classic pediments over the upper storeys of the porch, and of the four bays; the main roof behind the latter being carried up in steep gables, connected by a balustraded parapet—a curious mixture of old and new styles.

In every period, house designers have broken away from conventional design and have indulged in eccentricities.   As the object of this history is to illustrate *types*, such variations have usually been omitted, but towards the close of the sixteenth and in the early seventeenth century numbers of buildings were erected to triangular, hexagonal, and other geometrical plans.   Fig. 133 combines both, yet embodies the medieval hall with upper-end and lower-end rooms.   The plan of Chilham Castle, Kent, dated 1616 (Fig. 134), being of a building which was not only erected but still stands substantially unaltered, possesses especial interest, and in it also we can trace the same medieval nucleus, though more faintly. John Thorpe went so far as to plan (but not to build) a house for himself, the plan of which was in the form of the initials of his own name I—T, the connecting link being an open passage (Figs. 138, 139).   On the drawing he wrote:

" These 2 letters I and T
ioyned together as you see
Is ment for a dwelling howse for mee
John Thorpe."

[1] Taken from *Some Famous Buildings and their Story—The Great House, Chelsea*, by courtesy of the authors, A. W. Clapham, F.S.A., and W. H. Godfrey, F.S.A.   The Architectural Press, London.

His perspective view (Fig. 138) of the proposed house shows the building contemplated, which has marked Dutch characteristics. Although this design never seems to have reached fruition, one of triangular plan which he designed for Longford Castle was followed, with slight variations. The chief novelties are the round towers at the angles and the converging of the wings to an apex, so that they enclose a small triangular court instead of the larger and conventional rectangular one, but the base of the triangle, which is the normal entrance front of the building, virtually conforms to the medieval plan.

Another freak house is Wollaton Hall, Notts (Figs. 123, 124), c. 1580, where the hall occupies the position of a court, the inner walls of which are carried up as a central tower. The only lighting of the hall, therefore, is from the high windows of this central tower. At the four main angles of the building are smaller towers. The entrance to the hall is now straight through the central entrance doorways, but originally a turn to the left or right of these had to be taken on entering, to enter the hall behind the screens in the usual way.

Sixteenth-century contracts to build are purely between the employer and the contractor—usually they contain no stipulation that the works are to satisfy any third person, nor are the drawings mentioned as being the work of a third party, as an architect. In addition to specifying that materials and workmanship are to be what we call " the best of their respective kinds," the results to be achieved are sometimes stated as to be like or in the same manner or of the same measurements as another building which is named. The second party to the contract was a carpenter if the structure was to be chiefly of wood, and a mason if of stone and brick. Thus we have the contract for building the Fortune Theatre, London,[1] which begins:

> " This Indenture made the eighte daie of January 1599 . . . between . . . and Peeter Streete cittizein and carpenter on th' other parte."

Many dimensions are given, and materials to be used for each portion of the structure are specified. The stage and staircases are to be

> " sett . . . in such sorte as is prefigured in a plott thereof drawen."

This is the only reference to any plan, and the contract seems to have depended upon the measurements of the parts, which are enumerated.

Another more detailed and interesting contract was for the building of kitchen, brewhouse, larders, and other offices to an existing house at Woolavington, Sussex (which, however, had not long been built). The contract refers to four " plotts," two of which have been preserved. These drawings, which in various places in the contract are referred to as plotts, platts, pattornes, and samples, are rough drawings of two floors, approximately to scale of $\frac{1}{8}$ in. to the

---

[1] *Some Famous Buildings and their Story*, by A. W. Clapham, F.S.A., and W. H. Godfrey, F.S.A. The Architectural Press, London.

foot.   The walls in the plan of the first floor come fairly accurately upon those of the ground floor, but the dimensions figured in (as they are for all rooms) have several obvious inaccuracies: so obvious, indeed, that their author could scarcely defend an accusation of carelessness.   As the structure was to be of stone, the contractor was a mason, but as no mention is made of joinery, there must have been another contract made for this.   Indeed, the contractor's obligations are summarized in one paragraph as

> " all other thinges and workes what soever belonginge to the handes of a mason and brycklayer according to the saide Pattornes."

The contract[1] for the stone structure is dated 1595, and is between Giles Garton, citizen and ironmonger of London, and Henry Hobbes, alias Hunt, of Arundel, Freemason, who is

> " To buylde make & set upp at Woollavington in the saide Countie of Sussex in the place nexte adjoyninge to the new buyldinge there of the saide Giles latlie buylte by the saide Henry in good substantiall fayre & wokenmanlyke manner and order one good substancyall comlie & fayre Capitall messuage or mansyon house of Stone of good substanciall sounde & artifyciall workenman-shippe; & stuffe accordinge to Foure pattornes or samples Indented drawne for the purpose and annexed to these p͠ntes . . . and all other thinges in good sounde substanciall coninge comelie decent fayre & substancyall manner and Fasshion in all thinges & after the best sorte & manner as it is set downe in the saide plott with such and so many romes stories chymneys and wyndowes & all other thinges and buyldinges as by the saide patornes is portrayed drawne & set downe . . . the stones to be wrought hewen laid placed and builded in moste durable manner to contynue in the saide buyldinge."

This clause as to proper bedding of stone is so important that it is strange it should not have been specified in many later works.

Certain works are to be executed " lyke and in such manner as " the existing building.

One " pryvie " is specified, with a drain to be carried to a point indicated. The kitchen is to be paved with Purbeck stone, the larders with tiles.   The floors of the other offices are to be made " level and even in good and decent manner " —i.e., floors of beaten earth.   Certain materials and plant and tools are specified as to be provided by the employer.   The contract price for the works is £130, of which the sum of £40 is to be paid on signing of the contract, a further £10 on starting the works, and other sums on dates named.   There is a maintenance clause for one year, a balance of £10 being kept back for that time. Apparently the work was done to the satisfaction of the employer, for in his notes of payment on the back of the document he refers to the contractor as " good man Hunt " up to and including the last payment, which he might not have done had matters gone unsatisfactorily.

[1] *An Elizabethan Builder's Contract*, now in the possession of Sir Charles Thomas Stanford, Bart., F.S.A., by W. H. Godfrey, F.S.A.   *Sussex Archæological Collections*, vol. lxv, pp. 210-23, 1924.

An Indenture dated November 16, 1597, provided that a lessor was:

> " To build a house containing two bays of sawn timber with a solar over one of them ready to be thatched and clayed within three years."[1]

This would be a half-timbered house, " clayed " being the filling of panels between the timbers.

Although conditions of labour in the mid-sixteenth century had developed far in the direction of greater freedom of the employed, they were regulated with considerable restriction and severity. In the opening years of Elizabeth's reign an Act of Parliament[2] was passed, which embodied " Orders for Artificers . . . Servants and Apprentices." The minimum term of an engagement was for one year, and a quarter's notice was required to terminate. Employees might not leave the neighbourhood without a testimonial from the employer. The hours of labour were regulated. Wages were to be assessed by justices and proclaimed. Employers giving higher wages and servants accepting them were liable to imprisonment, and servants assaulting employers were liable to severe punishment. Women between the ages of twelve and forty were compelled to work. At Maidstone, Kent, in 1563, wages were fixed according to the statute as follows:

> " Artificers, Brycklayers, the Chief Brycklayer, Tyler, and Sawyer, from Easter till Michaelmas, with meate and drynke, (daily) 6d. and without meate and drynke 10d. and in wynter season with vittells 5d. and without vittells 9d. Master Ploughwrytes to be paid at the same rates as the Carpenters.
> " Of the seconde sorte, every seconde of all the said Artificers from Easter to Michaelmas with vittells 5d. and without vittells 9d. and in wynter season with vittells 4d. and without vittells 8d."[3]

Long hours were worked in summer, hence the higher daily wage.

In man's age-long struggle with the elements he has been more successful in his roof construction than in his walls, for even the thickest walls built of stone or of brick are permeable by wind and rain when in exposed situations.

During the medieval period this was remedied by plastering and whitewashing walls externally. In the thirteenth century the Close Rolls of Henry III contain repeated instructions by him to his Constables, Sheriffs, Keepers of Manors, and other persons having charge of the king's buildings to

> " repair the walls outside with plaster and to whitewash them "

or

> " to plaster the walls all over, with plaster,"

the outer wall surfaces being indicated. This covering with a thin coat of plaster is still practised in the Northern Counties and in Scotland, where it is called " harling "; the plaster being thrown forcibly against the wall from a wooden

---

[1] Cat. Ancient Deeds in P. Record Office, vol. vi, p. 561 (c. 8051).
[2] 5 Eliz., c. 4, &c.
[3] *Arch. Cantiana*, xxii, p. 317. London, 1897.

trowel, shaped like a housemaid's dustpan. So skilfully is this done that it is scarcely possible to distinguish where one trowel charge of plaster ends and the next begins. In other districts, plaster is applied with a trowel of ordinary pattern, and probably this suggested the application of plaster or mortar over brickwork to simulate stone. Fig. 305 shows a small garden-house (*c.* 1530) where columns, the string-course, the mouldings of the doorway and windows have been rendered with a thin coating of plaster to make them look like stone dressings. The composition of this kind of plaster varied in different localities. Often it was of sand and lime—coarse sea sand containing pebbles was used for the building illustrated.

Although, as might be expected, we learn that the use of glass increased in the sixteenth century, its introduction into house windows was far from universal, as may be gathered from the remarks of contemporary writers. W. Horman, in his *Vulgaria*, printed in 1519, wrote:

> "Glasen wyndowis let in the lyght, and kepe out the winde; paper or lyn clothe straked accrosse with losenges make fenestrals in stede of glasen wyndowes. Wyndowe leuys of tymbre be made of bourdis joyned to gether with keys of tree let into them. I will have a latesse before the glasse, for brekynge . . . I have many prety windowes shette with leuys goynge up and downe."[1]

Horman's preference for paper stretched across a window, with sticks placed diagonally, was based upon unfortunate experience of glass breaking. His description of the folding shutters of wood is clear, but the leaves going up and down suggest some form of sash in grooves.

Taverns (for distinction) were furnished with red lattices. Fastolfe's page describes Bardolph looking through a red lattice thus:

> "A' calls me e'en now, my lord, through a red lattice, and I could discern no part of his face from the window: at last, I spied his eyes; and, methought, he had made two holes in the ale-wife's new petticoat and so peeped through."[2]

In Harrison's *Description of England* (1584), referring to the early sixteenth century, he writes:

> "Of old time, our countrie houses, instead of glasse, did use much latisse and that made either of wicker or fine rifts of oake in chekerwise."

He goes on to say:

> "I read also that some of the better sort in and before the time of the Saxons did make panels of horne insted of glasse and fix them in wooden calmes . . . now glass is become so plentiful &c."[3]

Eden adds (1797):

> "Glass is at length introduced into windows of most cottages."

[1] Quoted in Parker's *Glossary of Architecture*, p. 205.
[2] *Second Part of Henry IV*, Act II, Scene 2, ll. 85-9.
[3] Quoted in Eden's *State of the Poor*, vol. i, p. 78, 1797.

That casements were regarded as separate pieces of furniture at one time and not part of the structure of a house is shown in the will of B. Coksedge (*d.* 1467), in which he leaves part of his dwelling-house and certain casements to his wife.[1]

In a Survey of Alnwick Castle, 1567:

> " And because throwe extreme winds the glass of the windowes of this and other of my lord's castles and houses here in the country doth decay and waste, yt were good the whole leights of everie windowe at the departure of his lord-shippe from lyings at any of his said castles and houses and dowring the time of his lordshippes absence, or others lying in them, were taken downe and lade up in safety &c."[2]

In 1579 a legal decision was given on the point whether glass in removable frames was furniture or a fixture. As a previous decision was reversed, it has special interest:

> " Glass fixed by nails to windows or in any other manner cannot be moved, for without glass is no perfect house."[3]

Whereas in 1439 English glass was of little repute, in 1589 there were fifteen glass-houses (factories) in England.

In leaded lights remarkable variety of quarry shapes are found. At Moreton Old Hall this is particularly noticeable, and it is said that no two lights amongst the large number in the gallery (Fig. 621) have the same design of leadwork. A book published in 1615 entitled *A Booke of Sundry Draughtes, Principally serving for glasiers* contains over one hundred designs for lead glazing.

The introduction of roundels of stained glass designed in the form of coats of arms, to which allusion was made in writing of fifteenth-century windows, continued during the sixteenth century. Until lately the windows at Gilling Castle, Yorks (Fig. 616), made in 1585 by a German named Dininckhoff, contained a profusion of such armorial devices.

Henry VIII was an insatiable purchaser of tapestries to hang on walls, and at his death an inventory made included over 2,000 pieces.

> " Neither Queen Mary nor Queen Elizabeth evinced much liking for woven tapestries. . . . Queen Elizabeth, as far as present knowledge takes us, lent little encouragement to the weaving of tapestries, and in her extreme age used to thrust a sword through wall hangings in case they harboured ' murtherers.' "[4]

William Harrison, in his *Description of England*, published in 1577, refers to " the great amendment of lodging " in his day. He proceeds as follows:

> " The walls of our houses on the inner sides be either hanged with tapestries, arras work or painted cloths, wherein either divers histories, or herbs, beasts, knots and suchlike are stained, or else they are seeled with oak."[5]

---

[1] Camden Soc., 49, 1850.
[2] Eden, i, 77, quoting *Northumberland Household Book*, pref., p. xvii.
[3] Lord Coke's Reports, p. 63b. 41-42 Elizabeth, 1579.
[4] *Tapestry Weaving in England*, by W. G. Thomson. Batsford, 1914, p. 32.
[5] Quoted by A. F. Kendrick in *The Connoisseur*, March, 1927, p. 144.

Also Harrison saw that many small farmers

> " garnished their beds with tapestry and silk hangings and their tables with carpets and fine napery."[1]

Paul Henzner, in *Travels in England*, saw, in 1598, at Windsor, the state beds of Henry VII, Henry VIII, and Edward VI, all eleven feet square and covered with quilts shining in gold and silver.[2]

The description of Imogen's chamber is of a room of this period:

> " First, her bedchamber, . . . it was hanged
> With tapestry of silk and silver; the story
> Proud Cleopatra, when she met her Roman,
> And Cydnus swell'd above the banks, or for
> The press of boats or pride: a piece of work
> So bravely done, so rich, that it did strive
> In workmanship and value; which I wonder'd
> Could be so rarely and exactly wrought,
> Since the true life on't was—
>   . . . The chimney
> Is south the chamber; and the chimney-piece,
> Chaste Dian bathing; never saw I figures so likely to report
>   themselves:
>   . . . The roof o' the chamber
> With golden cherubins is fretted: her andirons—
> I had forgot them—were two winking Cupids
> Of silver, each on one foot standing, nicely
> Depending on their brands."[3]

From time to time reference has been made to the lining or seeling of rooms with wainscot, and instances have been quoted from contemporary records. The practice seems, however, not to have been general until the sixteenth century, when it became so popular as, ultimately, to supersede wall hangings.

The term " wainscot " is of obscure origin, and the reason for its application to oak timber is still more difficult to determine. We find its earliest use in reference to boards, planks, and balks of timber (usually oak of good quality) imported into England from the Baltic countries, but the term was also applied to soft woods. In 1253, Henry III gave orders

> " to buy in our town of Southampton, for our use, two hundred Norway boards of fir and deliver them without delay to our sheriff of Southampton to wainscot therewith the chamber of our beloved son Edward, in our castle of Winchester."

In this order, the word " wainscot " is used to describe the purpose to which the boards were to be applied, for by this date the wall lining had become known by the term which was first used to describe the wood itself. Unfortunately, no wainscoting of this early date remains, but records show that such boarding

---

[1] Quoted by A. F. Kendrick in *The Connoisseur*, March, 1927, p. 144.
[2] *Ibid.*
[3] *Cymbeline*, Act II, Scene 4.

or wainscoting of the walls of rooms was often painted, the favourite colour being green.   In 1233 Henry III ordered

> " the wainscoting (*lambreschuram*) of the king's great chamber to be painted in green colour."[1]

Sometimes we read that the green colour was to be

> " studded with stars "

or directions were given to add more elaborate pictorial decoration.   In one instance only is mention made of any special treatment of the boards themselves, when, in 1244, the king directed that the wainscoting was to be done

> " with radiated and coloured boards."[2]

The practice of lining rooms with boarding was firmly established in the thirteenth century.   In the Court Rolls of the Manor of Wakefield are several references to thefts of such boarding from unoccupied houses of no great importance.   In 1297 we read that at Holne

> " A certain house has been left empty by William Yoil, the boards of the inner walls (*de parietibus*) have been carried away by persons unknown.   An inquisition is to be held thereon at the next court."
> " It is found by the inquisition that Robert de Harop carried away (boards) from the inner wall of a certain house . . . to the value of 2d.   He is therefore fined 2d."[3]

Although no thirteenth-century wainscot exists, later medieval examples of early types are still to be found in contemporary houses, of which those illustrated in Fig. 37 and Fig. 673 are instances.   Fig. 673 is of wainscoting frequently found in fifteenth-century and sixteenth-century houses in Kent. The boards are set up vertically and overlap one another in the fashion called clapboarding from

FIG. 37.—Section of clapboarding shown in Fig. 673; one side flush boarding, the other (clinker or clapboard) overlapping.

medieval times and still so termed (when used horizontally) in the United States.   In this example of wainscoting the joint is not a mere overlapping of one board by another (as in weatherboarding, used to protect walls from the weather) but is accurately tongued and grooved.   Reference to Fig. 37 will show that this medieval tongueing and grooving is quite different from modern practice.   It presents two fair faces—one of overlapping boards, the other perfectly flush, the joints of which remain fine and accurate after the lapse of over 450 years.   The workmen grooved one edge of a board and then cut one side of the groove to a knife-edge.   One edge of the adjoining board was then planed to a feather edge so as to fit tightly into the groove of its neighbour and fade away just at the knife-edge of the groove.   Where used for a partition

[1] Calendar of the Liberate Rolls, Henry III, 1226-40.
[2] *Ibid.*
[3] *Court Rolls of the Manor of Wakefield*, vol. i, p. 261.

or where the boarding was to be visible on both sides, the flush side presented a beautifully even surface, broken only by the fine lines of the vertical joints: so fine were these that they could easily be stopped with paint or plaster, and were admirably adapted as a ground upon which to apply painted decoration in colours. In some instances no paint was applied, but the wood was left to show the figure and beauty of grain possessed by boards picked out for the purpose. In this state the wainscoting of the Council Chamber at Compton Wynyates has been left (Fig. 674). It is tongued and grooved, as in Fig. 37, but both tongue and groove have slight shoulders, more like modern work. In the surfaces presented by the two sides of such boardings we have survivals of joiners' methods which originated in earlier medieval times.

Another medieval treatment of partitions was to groove a narrow board into thick upright timbers or posts (Figs. 356, 359, 593). This is found in screens, and such boards actually form tall, narrow panels of primitive type, grooved or rebated into framing timbers or studs. An instance of the treatment is shown in Fig. 676, where the upright timbers are tenoned into the cill and extend up to the moulded beam, into which also they are tenoned. The sides of these timbers are grooved or rebated (the precise treatment cannot be seen, but grooving, being less laborious than rebating, is probably the method adopted). As, also, it is less laborious to plough a narrow groove than a wide one, it was usual to thin the edges of the panel board to fit into the grooves, leaving the centre of the board its full thickness. This seems to have suggested using the greater thickness out of which to mould a vertical rib, as seen upon the boards in Fig. 676, the rib being stopped at its ends by the cill and beam. Such ribs seem to have developed a treatment of vertical clapboarding (like that in Fig. 673) by moulding the boards with vertical ribs (also stopped by cill and beam), as in the wainscoting in Fig. 675, and this method was also used contemporaneously for doors moulded with rounds, quirks and hollows. In some fifteenth-century doors one finds simple ribs, like those worked on the boards in Fig. 675, the ribs running out at the top and bottom of the door (Figs. 406, 479).

It was natural that the joiner should not be contented with such unfinished treatment, but that some form of stop should be devised to finish the ends of the vertical ribbed mouldings. A simple form of stop is that adopted in the panels of an early oak chest, a portion of which is illustrated in Fig. 677, where the moulded ribs of the framing are unstopped, but those of the panels are stopped by a semicircle across each hollow. The simple semicircular stops in Fig. 677 are developed further in Fig. 679, though they have not yet assumed any likeness to linenfolds. The panels at Paycockes, Great Coggeshall (Fig. 678), have the ribs set more closely; the three panels showing two forms of ribbing and three of stopping. Today, these would be called linenfold panels, but it is doubtful whether, had the treatment halted at this stage, any resemblance to folds of cloth would ever have been traced.

Fig. 680 shows the fine workmanship of the hall screens at Compton Wynyates, Warwickshire. Here the cutting of ribs and hollows and the method of stopping the ends produce distinctly the appearance of folds of cloth and, though not yet fully elaborated, it is an indisputable example of linenfold panelling.

Fig. 682 is of a well-developed linenfold panel; the folds are natural and cloth-like, the ends of the ribs are stopped to represent the margin of a piece of cloth. In Figs. 681, 683 the imitation of linen reaches its fullest development, for a stitched, embroidered border is successfully counterfeited by use of punches.

Reference should here be made to a form of panel, kindred of the linenfold, in which the rib branches to the four corners and, in some instances, resembles the curling up of the corners of a piece of parchment. Modern writers have named this "parchemin" pattern. In its most elementary form the rib is stopped by ogival curves, as in Fig. 38.

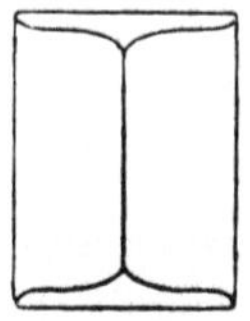

FIG. 38.

Many fifteenth-century MSS. have illustrations of furniture fitted with panels having this simple rib and ogival terminations, but soon this was elaborated by increasing the number of ribs and by addition of cusps, vine stems, fruit, etc., as illustrated in the panels of Fig. 684.

"Linenfold" and "Parchemin" are modern words (the former of nineteenth-century, the latter of recent origin) not used by the fifteenth- and sixteenth-century panel makers. "Wavy woodwork" (*lignum undulatum*) was probably their term. Joscelin (*c.* 1529-1603) describing chambers of Corpus Christi College, as they existed in his own time, records works done in the past by college benefactors, apparently drawing his information from lists now lost. He mentions the wainscoting of the old library, next the Master's Lodge, by John Botwright (master, 1443-74), as made of wavy wood (*lignis undulatis facta*).[1] This has been interpreted as linenfold panelling, but it more probably describes ribbed boards like those in Fig. 675.

Writing of a partition erected by William Sowoode (1523-44) Joscelin uses the words *septum undulatum*[2] (a wavy partition). These also appear to have been copied from earlier records, as other passages in Joscelin certainly are, and we shall probably be right in concluding that *lignis undulatis* was the fifteenth-century name for such mouldings as those in Figs. 675 and 679, which was applied later to the linenfold panelling into which it developed.

The earliest instance of the word "wainscot" given in the New English Dictionary is 1352. The word "clapboard" (still used in America, but almost obsolete in England) is found as early as 1520, associated with wainscot, while in 1725 we have mention of "clapboards for wainscot," and in 1833 they were defined (in an Act of Parliament[3]) as not exceeding "sixty-three inches in length," and

---

[1] *Architectural History of Cambridge.* Willis and Clark, vol. i, p. 253.
[2] *Ibid.*, p. 256.   [3] 3-4 William IV, c. 26.

in 1641 in the U.S.A. is record of " clabords of five foot in length," applied to overlapping weather-boarding.

The evidences of existing examples of wainscot and panelling, together with those afforded by contemporary and earlier documents, seem to indicate that medieval rooms were lined with boards of oak or fir, sometimes overlapping one another, sometimes presenting a flush surface, but grooved into each other (Figs. 37, 673, and 674); that the prototype of the panel was a narrow board, fitted into grooved posts (Figs. 356, 359, 393); that the thinning of these boards at the edges suggested moulding the centre with a rib (Fig. 676), and that such ribbing was extended to clapboarding (Fig. 675); that the natural way of finishing such ribbing was to stop the ends, as done in simple form (Fig. 677); that this treatment was carried further as in Fig. 679, and developed as in Fig. 678, until it suggested folds of cloth and the counterfeiting of these, as in Fig. 680; the likeness to cloth being continued until it reached the faithful representations of Figs. 681, 682, and 683; that the development of the rib varied much when once the idea of imitating materials occurred to joiners—one variant being the representation of sheets of parchment, curled at the corners, often ornamented, as in Fig. 684.

Contemporary with the linenfold and parchemin panels (late fifteenth and early sixteenth centuries) was the panel having a roundel in the middle, the roundel being furnished with a head in profile, with a shield of arms or with other device or decoration, as in the upper range of panels at Thame Park in the Abbot's Chamber (Fig. 613), and in the detail panels (Fig. 686). Such panels were usually of Italian origin, French transmission, and Renaissance in character. The panels in Cardinal Wolsey's Closet, Hampton Court Palace (Fig. 39) are tall and narrow, and the framing is simply moulded (a somewhat similar mould is used at Thame Park, Fig. 613). In the second half of the sixteenth century this developed into a great number of moulds all small in scale (Figs. 697, 698), and although the elements were restricted to bead, fillet, hollow, ovolo and ogee, these were varied to an infinite extent without the general character being altered. Fig. 39 shows two of these types from Moreton Old Hall, which, with Figs. 617, 691, 773, represent panelling introduced into large and small houses during the reigns of Elizabeth and James I.

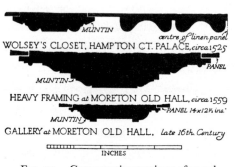

FIG. 39.—Comparative sections of panel moulds.

Early panelling—approximately up to the middle of the sixteenth century and some, of course, much later—was often made in sections four, five, six or more panels wide, no attempt being made to cover the joints where sections butted one against another. Often at this point the stiles were halved, the joint coming down the middle line of the complete stile; but in other cases the stile was double width—i.e., there were two stiles together where sections joined—a clumsy piece of workmanship. To hide this, strips of wood in the form of pilasters were applied—a Renaissance feature which ultimately became general. At first, the divisions of the pilasters bore no relation to those of the panelling, as at Sandwich (Fig. 774), where the only division of the pilaster that corresponds with the panelling is the cap, and that only approximately. At Burton Agnes Hall (Fig. 693), the mouldings of the pedestal cap are carried round the room as a horizontal division of the panelling, but the pilaster, its cap, and the entablature of the doorcase bear no relation to the wall panelling. The designer of the unscholarly but interesting room from Sizergh Castle (Fig. 690) was more precise, though he bungled over the relation of his pilaster caps to the frieze, owing to his arcaded panels being too tall for the cap mouldings to be carried round the room in the same way as those of the pedestal cap and base. The fact is that all these examples were efforts of men who were handling unfamiliar motifs based upon imperfect appreciation of the designs of foreigners or copied from pattern-books by bad designers. They are the lisping adventures of children attempting a new language, and should be regarded as such and not criticized as if they were mature works. Another detail which was developed imperfectly during the last quarter of the sixteenth century was arcading, of which Figs. 411, 690, 693 furnish illustrations. The rectangular centre panel surrounded by four L-shaped panels formed by applied mouldings is seen in Figs. 411, 690. Several forms of raised centres to panels appear at this time; as those over the mantel at Sandwich (Fig. 774), which are inlaid with exploits of Samson. Much panelling during the sixteenth century and afterwards was coloured with pigments, and this taste for colour was shown also in inlays of light and dark woods. Poplar and dark oak were commonly used, but fruit-tree woods (especially later) were frequently employed. Amongst the subjects illustrated where inlay was employed are those of Gilling Castle (Fig. 616), Sizergh Castle (Fig. 690), and the important fireplace at Sandwich (Fig. 774), where, in addition to the figures to which reference has been made, there is floral inlay and in the lower frieze spirited representations of hounds in motion. An uncommon practice in England, but a popular one at this time in Flanders, was the use of spiral shavings embedded in glue, out of which the three columns in the middle of this overmantel are turned. They reflect light, so that the spirals within do not come out in photographs.

In some mid-sixteenth-century rooms the panelling has framing of massive character, as that in the parlour at Moreton Old Hall (Figs. 39, 615). Panelling in the same house (as that in the gallery, Fig. 691), put in later in the century, has the contemporary slighter framing.

The following contract for joinery—piece work, c. 1580—illustrates the methods of the period:

"Xpopher Saydgfeld hath tayken by great the parloure floure at the upper end of the hall pfectly to finish and laye (to mak and set upp the portall workmanly to the height in every respect) and to seall the same parloure rond about wth frenche panell foure foot and tene ynches hye according to a patterne drawne for the same with base and arketrave and to set a cornish uppon the topp of the (flour) rom foure ynches in breadth dounward or mor and to mak a portall of the same frenche panell to the hyght of the flour to be set upp and workmanly finished in everye respect and to mak for the topp of the same arketrav frisse and cornishe and tow dores on for the portall and on other for the lytle wayneschot chambr the steapts that fall into the portall and the steapts for the window and to mak towe dores (and hang thē up) for the (dores) turrit at the bridg end the one to be hong upp to shut and the other to stand and a (playn) coberd at the great chambr dore with arkatrave frisse and cornish as himself shall think fytte for yt plac and me the doing hearof to hav in money VII^li XIII^s IIII^d wth meat drink and lodging for himself and his folkes tembr naylles glew (or any other things to be fond) and tene groats to by him candles all at yor la charges but only his work to be payd at thrye sondyr tymes vizd &c. &c."[1]

It will be seen that references are made to three descriptions of woodwork— " frenche panel," which, it has been suggested, was panelling with mitred joints, instead of with masons' joints, but may equally probably have been panelling of some new fashion; " wayneschot " in a " lytle chambr," probably boarding such as illustrated in Fig. 673; and a " coberd," the design for the details of which was to be " as himself shall think fytte." This is a clear instance of detailing being left to the craftsman.

Medieval roofs and ceilings were of three main types: (1) The vault (usually of stone) divided into panels and carved with bosses and devices in the manner of the fan-vault of the porch at Cowdray House (Fig. 735); (2) the open roof, the principal timbers of which were moulded and even carved (but seldom the rafters) as Fig. 606 and most of the open-roofed halls and solars already illustrated; (3) the flat beams and joists of an upper floor, seen from the room below, the timbers of which were usually chamfered or moulded with stops (Figs. 879, 880). The late fifteenth century and especially the early sixteenth century brought great changes. Where beams and joists were exposed we frequently find them moulded with bold rounds and shallow hollows, as at Moreton Old Hall (Fig. 615), at Smarden (Fig. 620), and the moulded and carved beams at Coggeshall (Fig. 731). These are carved out of the solid oak; but in the Abbot's Chamber at Thame Park (Fig. 736) the beams are moulded on the chamfers and the soffits decorated with arabesque ornament fretted and applied, as also is the decoration of the frieze, all being the work of Italian workmen, and forming a remarkable contrast in design and methods with the work at Coggeshall (Fig. 731), which is Gothic in character. The four ceiling spaces at Thame Park, which are formed by the decorated beams, are divided into smaller squares by applied mouldings of wood. Another instance of the use of applied wood mouldings is shown in illustrations of boarded ceilings at Compton Wynyates (Fig. 733) and Liddington

---

[1] *Archæologia*, vol. 64, p. 357. " Bess of Hardwick's Buildings and Building Accounts," by Basil Stallybrass.

(Fig. 614), which, similarly, have been divided into rectangles by moulded strips. In other instances the intersections of such mouldings were enriched with cusps or flower ornament or bosses, all in wood. The intersection of the beams at Thame Park is furnished with a pendant made of wood. The tendency towards carved pendants appears in those of the hammer-posts of the open roof of Eltham Palace, *c.* 1479 (Fig. 606), and in Crosby Hall, *c.* 1470, false roof construction, of which a section is shown in Fig. 35, p. 38. The later chapel at Hampton Court Palace has a richly decorated fan-vault and pendent roof—a mixture of Gothic and Renaissance details—of carved wood; all forerunners of the papier-mâché and plaster ceilings which came in shortly afterwards.

Plaster and papier-mâché work was introduced into England by Italian workmen, but soon the processes were learned by Englishmen, who, as was their way, adapted and modified these to their own practice.

An early ceiling is that at Hampton Court Palace, in the room known as Wolsey's closet (Fig. 734). The divisions formed by wood mouldings are of simple geometrical shapes, filled with papier-mâché ornament painted and gilded; the bosses at the intersections are carved from wood and applied over the lead leaves, which are bent into the panels to cover the joints of the strips of wood moulding.

The Watching Chamber at Hampton Court Palace, *c.* 1535, like that at Gilling Castle (Fig. 616), *c.* 1575, is divided by slight mouldings into geometrical panels, occasionally converging as pendants. Another treatment represented beams sometimes in shallow relief, as at Upper Swell Manor (Fig. 779), and often actual structural timbers plastered over, as at Sandwich (Fig. 738). The two illustrations also show two treatments of the ceiling spaces: at Upper Swell by occasional interpolation of ornament, badges, etc.; at Sandwich by division into many panels having floral ornaments and a central panel with a larger device.

The illustrations of ceilings show how their treatment was continued to the frieze, generally in character similar to that of its ceiling, but in other instances (as a frieze at Hardwick Hall, in the Presence Chamber, Figs. 623 and 694) it is given full pictorial treatment of scenes and figures in relief. Another wall treatment in plaster is that at Moreton Old Hall (Fig. 691). Such sententious subjects in plaster and in flat colouring are found in north country and Scotch houses of the second half of the sixteenth century. A story of different character is set forth in a frieze in the hall at Montacute (Fig. 692).

Although wall and ceiling treatments with panelling and plaster developed during Elizabeth's reign, the practice of painting on plaster continued even in houses of importance. One at Barhams Manor (Fig. 696) is a formal design applied over an old timber and plaster wall, like the more ambitious one at Oxford (Fig. 695). Many of these designs were poor, but that at West Stow Hall (Fig. 699) is an interesting example and reaches a higher decorative standard.

We do not find many surviving instances of early external decoration; that of the plaster-rendered brickwork of the gatehouse at Beckingham Hall, *c.* 1546 (Fig. 306), being a rare exception. The formal decoration is done with precision, though, as the enlarged detail shows, it demanded accuracy on the part of the workmen.

There is no doubt that our ancestors liked bright, even showy, exteriors. We, who may have perception of more subtle qualities, appreciate the silvery tones assumed by oak timbers as the result of exposure to sun and rain, and we, rightly, deprecate the painting in strong black and white of the fronts of old half-timbered buildings. That the Elizabethan householder had no such scruples is proved by the household accounts of Sir Thomas Kytson, Aug.- Sept., 1574, where the clerk entered the following:

> " For plastering and whitening the fore front of my Mr. his house in Coleman Street and the courte, with the blacking of the timber work, xlijs, vjd."[1]

The progress or decadence of domestic manners is best ascertained from the works of contemporary writers, and these vary with the social status or affluence of the owners of the houses to which reference is made. The first half of the sixteenth century is characterized by the increasing tendency of the master and his family to leave the great hall to dependents and to eat and live in the parlour and the solar in a small establishment, as the great lord did in his private apartments in a large one.

Erasmus, in a letter to Francis, physician to Cardinal Wolsey, wrote (prior to 1530) of English houses:

> " The floors are commonly of clay, strewed with rushes, under which lies unmolested an ancient collection of beer, grease, fragments, bones, spittle, excrements of dogs and cats, and everything that is nasty."

This is a mild translation of the Latin original, which ran as follows:

> " Tum sola fere sunt argilla, tum scirpis palustribus, qui subinde sic reno- vantur, ut fundamentum maneat aliquoties, annos viginti, sub se fovens sputa, vomitus, mictum canum et hominum, projectam cervisiam, et piscium reliquias, aliasque sordes non nominandas. Hinc mutato cœlo vapor quidam exhalatur, mea sententia minime salubris humano corpori."

Although floors of halls and other apartments frequently were paved with stone or tiles, the practice of strewing them with rushes continued even in large establishments. In 1573 the household accounts of Hengrave have the entry:

> " For a houseload of rushes from Lackford to Hengrave, vjd ";[2]

but it is possible these were for making rushlights, no purpose being mentioned.

[1] *History and Antiquities of Hengrave in Suffolk.* John Gage, London, 1822, p. 44.
[2] Gage's *Hengrave*, p. 194.

Instructions from Elizabeth Cavendish:

> " To my servante Francys Wytfelde—Cause the flore of my bedchamber to be made even either with plaster claye or lyme."[1]

In the King's Ordinances, 1526, it is ordered to:

> " Prouide and sufficiently furnish the said kitchens (the King's) of such scolyons as shall not go naked or in garments of such vileness as they now do, nor lie in the nights and days in the kitchen or round by the fireside."[2]

In Capulet's house the scene opens with a meal (supper) nearly finished in the chamber, or parlour, which opened off the hall, from which Capulet and his party enter the hall, where musicians were awaiting them (no mention is made of their being in a gallery), and cries:

> " Come, musicians, play.
> A hall, a hall ! give room ! and foot it, girls.
> More light, you knaves; and turn the tables up,[3]
> And quench the fire, the room is grown too hot."[4]

From this quotation we may infer that the state of the hall floor was better at the end of the century than that described by Erasmus in Wolsey's time.

Historians and students of the Elizabethan period have speculated upon the uses to which the long galleries of contemporary houses were put, without arriving at any definite conclusion. They are believed to have been used for dancing and for exercise in wet weather, but, having regard to the number of persons attached to large establishments, it is probable that they served also as dormitories. There were two long galleries (one each side of the court) at Cowdray House; and in the *Book of Household Rules*, drawn up by Lord Montague in 1595 for the regulation of the large staff, instructions to " the Yeoman of my wardroppe " are:

> " I will that he see the galleryes and all lodginges reserved for strangers cleanly and sweetly kepte, with herbes, flowers and bowes in their seasons and the beddes of such as shall hither resorte att their firste cominge to be mayde and the better sortes of quiltes of beddes at any tyme to be used at nightes taken off, and Yrish Rugges layd in their places . . . and in the morning to be agayne laid on."[5]

Rule 20 instructs the " Yeoman of my Chamber ":

> " Everye morning they doe ryse att a convenient hower to remove the pallettes (if there be any) out of my said withdrawinge chamber."[6]

Although not definitely stated, it may be inferred from these rules that the galleries were used as dormitories and the bedding left there during the day. In the withdrawing chamber the use as a sleeping apartment was occasional and bedding was cleared away early each morning.

---

[1] *Archæologia*, vol. 64, p. 357.   [2] *Babees Book*, E. E. Text Soc., vol. 32, p. lxvi.
[3] The tables to be turned up were boards on trestles.   [4] *Romeo and Juliet*, I, 5, 26.
[5] *Cowdray*, by Mrs. C. Roundell, 1884, p. 66.
[6] *Cowdray*, by St. John Hope. London, 1919, p. 129.

The number of persons attached to a large house was excessive. The same book of rules enumerates thirty-seven offices, at the head of whom was the steward. They were:

" My Stewarde of Household.
My Comptroller.
My High Stewarde of Courtes.
My Auditor.
My General Receaver.
My Solliciter.
My Other Principal Officers.
My Secretarye.
My Gentleman Ushers.
My Carver.
My Server (who set and removed dishes, tasted them, &c.).
The Gentleman of My Chamber.
The Gentlemen of My Horse.
The Gentlemen Wayters.
The Marshall of My Hall.
The Clarke of My Kitchen.
The Yeomen of My Great Chamber.
The Usher of My Halle.
The Chiefe Cooke.
The Yeoman of My Chamber.
The Clarke of My Officers' Chamber.
The Yeomen of My Horse.
The Yeomen of My Seller.
The Yeomen of Myne Ewrye (cared for table linen, laid cloth, served water in silver ewers after dinner).
The Yeomen of My Pantrye.
The Yeomen of My Butterye.
The Yeomen of My Wardroppe.
The Yeomen Wayters.
The Seconde Cooke and the Reste.
The Porter.
The Granator (in charge of the granary).
The Bayliffe.
The Baker.
The Brewer.
The Grooms of the Great Chamber.
The Almoner.
The Scullery Man."

There was no chaplain (unless the almoner performed his duties), but housekeeper, footmen, " boyes of the kytchen " and others are mentioned. None of the large staff might lodge abroad, and tradition is that 200 persons slept in the house. The only women of the house were gentlewomen in Lady Montague's service. There were no women servants. Yeomen of the chamber acted as housemaids; the " boyes of the kytchen " had to

" keepe it with all things therein cleane and sweete."

Lord and Lady Montague dined in the parlour; the gentlewomen's service was at a separate table in the same room. The officers dined at four tables in the Great Hall, and after their meal was " a second service " in the hall for the rest of the establishment. Dinner was at 10 a.m., supper at 5 p.m.

The improvement in the state of great men's and yeomen's houses does not seem yet to have affected the condition of those of the poor, as it did ultimately. Where chroniclers do mention such humble dwellings, the evidence is conflicting; possibly because they wrote at different times and of different parts of the country. William Harrison, writing c. 1577, says:

> " In times past men were contented to dwell in houses built of sallow, willow, plum-tree, hardbeam and elm, so that the use of oak was in manner dedicated wholly unto churches, religious houses, princes' palaces, noblemen's lodgings, and navigation; but now all these are rejected and nothing but oak in any whit regarded."[1]

Ancient records show that small houses were constantly built of oak throughout the medieval period wherever oak was plentiful; but Harrison may have had in mind mere cots, in the construction of which turf was the common covering.

Another writer, 1555, mentions

> " cottages made with bouwes of trees plastered with chauke."[2]

Notwithstanding the progress made in development of comforts and conveniences in great houses, sanitation lagged behind, and references to the offensiveness of garderobes and privies are frequently found in current literature. One, in the thirteenth century, is given on page 32, and another, c. 1600, on page 59, describes what evidently was regarded as a model arrangement of privies. Four years earlier than this (1596) Sir John Harington published a book entitled *The Metamorphosis of Ajax; a Cloacinean Satire*, in which he described a water-closet of his invention, erected at his seat at Kelston, near Bath, and afterwards copied at the Queen's Palace at Richmond. His illustration of the completed contrivance is given here (Fig. 40, p. 84), together with his key to the parts. It comprises a seat with pan, a cistern (in which are shown water and fish swimming) at a higher level, an overflow pipe from the cistern, a flushing pipe and a waste. To prevent waste of water provision is made

> " That children and busy folk disorder it not, or open the sluice with putting in their hands without a key, you should have a little button or scallop shell, to bind it down with a vice pin, so as without the key it will not be opened."

Further, Sir John says:

> " If water be plenty, the oftener it is used and opened, the sweeter; but if it be scant, once a day is enough, for a need, though twenty persons should use it."

[1] *Description of England.* Quoted by W. B. Sanders in *Half-Timbered Houses.* London, 1884.
[2] Eden, *Decades*, p. 344.

The cost of each item of the mechanism is given, the total being £1 10s. 8d., and the author sums up by saying:

" And this being well done, and orderly kept, your worst privy may be as sweet as your best chamber."

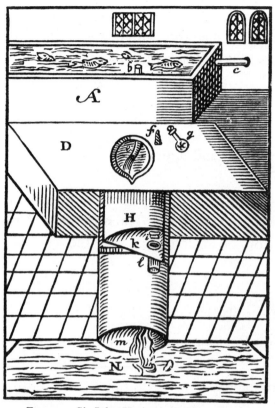

FIG. 40.—Sir John Harington's Water-closet.

KEY TO FIG. 40.

"*A*, the cistern.
b, the little washer.
c, the waste pipe.
D, the seat board.
e, the pipe that comes from the cistern.
f, the screw.
g, the scallop shell, to cover it when it is shut down.
H, the stool pot.
i, the stopple.
k, the current.
l, the sluice.
m, *N*, the vault into which it falls : always remember that at noon and at night empty it, and leave it half a foot deep in fair water."

Sir John Harington's invention embodies all the features of the modern water-closet, even to the water seal, but its coming into general use was long delayed and few could have been made before the nineteenth century.

The Elizabethan period was one of strong contrasts. Interiors of houses were sparsely furnished (much of the furniture still being primitive), but walls and beds might be hung with rich and costly fabrics. The extent of furnishings is exposed by contemporary inventories, from two of which (one that of a great house, the other that of a farmer's goods) the following are extracted:

" *INVENTORY* made in 1603 at Hengrave, in Suffolk.
In the HALL.

Items—
Three square boards, with fast frames to them.
Two joyned coobards, made fast to the wainskote.
One long table for a sholven borde, with a fast frame to it.
One other longe table, with tressels to it.
One piece of wood craved with the Queen's arms.
Ten joyned formes for the square borde.
One long forme not of joyner's work.

One great branch of copper which hangs in the midst of the hall to serve
for lights.
Four copper-plate candlesticks, iii of them being great and one little, which
hangs upon the skreine by ye pantrye.
One cradle of iron for the chimnye to borne seacole with.
One fier sholve made like a grate to sift the seacole with.
One other fier sholve and one payer of tongues.
Two payr of tables."

The square boards were the steward's table: the master's table was in the
chamber.

The seacole was bought and brought from Lynne.

" In ye GREAT CHAMBER.

Arras.
Carpets.
Cushions.
Thirty-two stools, joyned.
Four chayers.
Curtains.
One joyned coobard.
One square borde.
Longe joyned borde and extension piece.
Two longe footstools under above.
One payer of tables.
One sevenfold and one fourfold skreenes.
One great copper sesteurne to stand at the coobard.
Two payer andyrones.
Two payer creepers (small andirons placed within the larger ones).
Four copper branches for lights.
Two fier sholves, two payer tongues and one fier forke.

In ye GALLERYE at ye TOWER.

One billiarde borde with two staves to it of bone and two of wood and
4 balls."[1]

" INVENTORY of the goods and chattels of John Andrews, of Bepton,
Sussex, taken 1577.

In the HALL.

One tabell a forme and a cubberd a round tabell a chayre vi joyned stoles
a banker (chair-seat covering) and iii cusshens with the stayne clothes
(coloured cloths) praysed at XXs.

In the PARLOR.

One joyned bedsted a fether bed a bolster a coberleyght (coverlet) one
payre of blanketts a quelte and fower pyllowes praysed at XLs.
One presse for clothes one tabell with a frame a carpet a coffer a chest with
the stayne clothes of the same parlor praysed at XXs."[2]

Carpets were used to cover seats as well as tables and cupboards.

[1] Gage's *Hengrave*, pp. 22 *et seq.*
[2] *Sussex Notes and Queries*, vol. i, No. 4, p. 120.

There were no chairs in the hall at Hengrave, and only four in the Great Chamber. In the farmer's hall at Bepton there was only one chair. Whereas our houses have many more chairs than any other piece of furniture, in the sixteenth century forms (fixed to the walls or movable) and stools were commonly used; chairs only being provided for distinguished persons, as the master or lord, who presided at meals and upon other occasions—a practice which is preserved in our modern expression

" to take the chair."

Chapter VI

THE SEVENTEENTH CENTURY

JAMES I, 1603-25; CHARLES I, 1625-49

JACOBEAN

AS ALREADY mentioned, the Jacobean period was the culmination of the Elizabethan; indeed, the two can scarcely be separated. In this relation the period may be said to extend to the end of the first quarter of the seventeenth century, before which, however, the new influences derived directly from Italy began to affect designs for certain important buildings. The coming of the new was very gradual, and completely Jacobean work, as well as isolated fragments of it, are frequently to be found in houses built even up to the end of the seventeenth century.

In 1611, Robert Peake, of Holborne, published *The First Book of Architecture made by Sebastian Serly, translated out of Italian into Dutch and out of Dutch into English.* Serly, or Serlio, was born at Bologna. Study of Vitruvius and the measuring of ancient buildings preceded the publication at Venice of Books iii, 1537, and iv, 1540. The other three books were published in France: i and ii, 1545; v, 1547. The volume consisted of: 1st Book, *Geometrie*; 2nd Book, *Perspective*; 3rd Book, *Excellent Antiquities*; 4th Book, *Five Orders, with ceilings, doors, panels, etc.*; 5th Book, *Temples*. Books iii and iv are made up largely of drawings and comments by Peruzzi.[1] The English edition of 1611 was dedicated to Prince Henry, and was a folio of over 400 pages of elevations, sections, and detail drawings of ancient buildings, with minute instructions for drawing. Such a work could not fail to influence English designers and to pave the way towards that full development of Italian design which we owe to Inigo Jones. Serlio's authority as an exponent of the Orders cannot be doubted; so firmly established was it, that his proportions for drawing them are shown (together with those of other authorities) by Batty Langley over a hundred years later,[2] and the effect upon English designs of the early seventeenth century in popularizing the Italian manner was profound.

Another apostle of the Italian manner was Sir Henry Wotton, who regarded Vitruvius as " our principall master " and Alberti as

" the most learned architect beyond the Alps."

Wotton was born 1568, travelled in France, Geneva, Germany, and Italy, 1589-98; was knighted and sent to Venice as ambassador, 1603; was sent on

---

[1] *Dic. Archtre.*, iv, 57.   [2] *A Sure Guide to Builders*, Batty Langley, London, 1729.

87

G

a mission to the United Provinces and Venice, 1615; again to Venice, returning 1619; and died 1639. His travels enabled him to study architecture by comparison of the productions of the best designers in each country, and his preference for the Italian is clearly expressed in his *Elements of Architecture*, the first edition of which was published in 1624 in London. Although somewhat wordy, this treatise attracted much attention, being reprinted many times; indeed, under the title

> "The Ground Rules of Architecture . . . by that learned and ingenious Gentleman Sir Henry Wotton, in his *Elements of Architecture*, Now corrected for Public Benefit"

it was republished with Scamozzi's *Mirror of Architecture* and Leyburn's *Compendium of the Art of Building* as late as 1734.

Wotton's *Elements of Architecture*, in which he only claims to have

> "collected from the best authors and examples,"

is not illustrated. He approaches the subject from a practical building standpoint, beginning:

> "In *Architecture* as in all other *Operative* Arts, the *end* must direct the *Operation*.
> "The *end* is to build well.
> "Well, building hath three Conditions:
> "*COMMODITIE, FIRMENESS*, and *DELIGHT*." [1]

In these words Wotton seizes upon essentials as unerringly as would any modern exponent; absolutely discarding Dutch, German, and other Low Country methods of loading with ornament, the introduction of useless detail, and all the monstrosities by which our native designers had been influenced for the last seventy years. He divides his subject into general heads—

> "the *Seate* and the *Worke*" [2]

—*i.e.*, situation and aspect, and materials and the use of them. Although there is much to be said for his selection of an easterly aspect for the principal chambers and living-rooms, few will support his selection of a southern aspect for

> "Offices that require heat, *Kitchens, stillatories, stoves*, rooms for *Baking*, Brewing, Washing or the like." [3]

However, he chooses the north for

> "all that need a coole and fresh temper, as *Cellers, Pantries, Butteries, Granaries*." [4]

The same aspect is recommended for chambers

> "that are appointed for gentle Motion, as *Galleries*, especially in warme Climes, or that otherwise require a steady and unvariable light . . . as certaine *Repositories* for workes of rarity in Picture or other Arts." [5]

Here we have indication of two uses for galleries.

[1] p. 1.　　[2] p. 2.　　[3] p. 8.　　[4] *Ibid.*　　[5] *Ibid.*

Although he divides consideration of the " Workes " into

" Principall parts,
" Accessorie or *Ornaments*,"

he proceeds to instance the Church of Santa Giustina in Padoua as

" in truth a sound piece of good Art, where the *Materials* being but ordinarie stone, without any garnishment of sculpture, doe yet ravish the Beholder, (and hee knows not how) by a secret *Harmony* in the *Proportions*. And this indeede is that end, at which in some degree, we should ayme even in the privatest workes."[1]

He recognizes " two opposite affectations " in Architecture,

" *Uniformitie* and *Varietie*, which yet will very well suffer a good reconcilement,"[2]

and instances the human form as an illustration. Amongst other points that are emphasized in planning, he advocates the offices being placed on the basement floor, but that the principal floor should be raised fifteen feet above the ground level to provide convenient space for these and to

" adde to the *Majestie* of the whole *Aspect*."[3]

He pleads for

" a more spacious and luminous *Kitchen* . . . with a more competent neereness likewise to the *Dyning Roome* ; or else, besides other inconveniences, perhaps some of the Dishes may straggle by the way . . . and for a Place properly appointed, to conserve the meate that is taken from the Table, till the *Waiters* eate, which with us by an old fashion, is more unseemly set by, in the meanwhile."[4]

Another weak point in current planning is attacked by him vigorously in

" that they (designers) do so cast their *partitions* as when all *Doors* are open a man may see through the whole *House*, which doth necessariely put an intollerable servitude upon all the *Chambers* save the Inmost, where none can arrive, but through the rest; or else the Walles must be extreame thicke for secret passages. And yet this also will not serve the turne, without at least *Three* doores to every Roome : a thing most insufferable. . . . I cannot commend the direct opposition of such *Overtures*, being indeede merely grounded upon the fond ambition of displaying to a *Stranger* all our *Furniture* at one *Sight*."[5]

He points out at length the inconveniences of such planning and repudiates a supposed suggestion that he should furnish plans to illustrate this, as other writers have published designs, by saying that

" speculative *Writers* (as I am) are not bound to comprise all particular Cases within the Latitude of the *Subject*, which they handle ; Generall Lights and *Directions* and pointings at some faults, is sufficient. The rest must be committed to the sagacitie of the *Architect*, who will bee often put to divers ingenious shifts, when hee is to wrestle with scarsitie of *Ground*."[6]

[1] *Elements of Architecture*, by Sir Henry Wotton, printed by John Bill, London, 1624, p. 12.
[2] *Ibid.*, p. 20. [3] *Ibid.*, p. 70. [4] *Ibid.*, p. 71. [5] *Ibid.*, p. 72.
[6] *Ibid.*, p. 74.

In describing the design for a great room

"for *Feastes* and other *Jollities*,"[1]

which shall be in the centre of the house, surrounded by chambers and its interior furnished with a colonnade on three sides, he expresses his own preference for an Egyptian house and is not describing any fashion in England, although the hall at Wollaton (Figs. 123, 124) to some extent answers to his description.

His remarks regarding the use of painting and sculpture outside and inside buildings are admirable. Of the practice by the Germans of painting the outsides of their houses in colours he disapproves, saying that

> "various colours on the *Out-walles* of *Buildings*, have always in them more *Delight* then *Dignity*; Therfore I would there admit no *Paintings* but in *Blacke* and *White*, nor even in that kinde any *Figures* (if the roome be capable) under *Nine* or *Ten* foot high, which will require no ordinary *Artizan*; because the faults are more *visible* than in small *Designes*."[2]

This suggestion of a scale which shall ensure only the employment of skilled men shows considerable astuteness on the part of the writer. It also implies the prevalence of decorating exteriors in colours at the time he writes.

He observes that the difference between a plasterer who models and a carver is that one works by adding material to his object whilst the other takes away material. He says:

> "Of this *Plastique Art*, the chief use with us is in the gracefull *fretting* of roofes: but the *Italians* applie it, to the *manteling* of *Chimneys*, with great Figures. A cheape piece of *Magnificence* and as durable almost within doores, as harder *Forms* in the weather."[3]

Plaster ceilings and plaster chimneypieces had been popular in England for years before this was written.

He proceeds then to express his admiration of the Italian

> "manner of disguising the shaftes of *Chimneys* in various fashions, whereof the noblest is the *Pyramidall*."[4]

One wonders how far he had Low Country builders in mind when he wrote this. On the whole, however, Sir Henry Wotton's book is the work of an intelligent, travelled, and observant man, who was endowed with taste and discrimination, and who set out to expound practical and reasonable architecture, to discountenance current eccentricities of ornament and design, and to establish rules and principles (some trivial, some foolish, but mostly admirable) which were not known to his untravelled fellow-countrymen. The vogue of his book (to which allusion has been made) is in itself proof that he achieved his object.

Although during the late sixteenth and early seventeenth centuries the

---

[1] *Ibid.*, p. 78.　　　[2] *Ibid.*, p. 96.　　　[3] *Ibid.*, p. 108.　　　[4] *Ibid.*

publication of books on architecture in English was in its infancy, it must not be supposed that Dutch books on the Orders and of designs (of which so much use was made by designer-craftsmen) were the only sources of knowledge. Peers, who built great palaces, took intelligent interest in these works and qualified themselves to an extent that few building owners at the present day would contemplate doing. Thus—

> " In 1568, Lord Burghley had written to Elizabeth's ambassador at Paris, asking him to procure a certain book ' concerning architecture.' That this was one of Philibert de Lorme's works is made clear by Lord Burghley asking for another book on architecture, and stating : 'The book I most desire is made by the same author and is entitled *Novels institutions per bien baster et à petits frais*, par Philibert de Lorme,' Paris, 1576."[1]

That the designing and controlling architect, as we know him, had not yet developed is made clear in the Hatfield Papers, concerning the building of Hatfield House by the Earl of Salisbury, *c.* 1607-11.

The charge of these works was in the hands of Thomas Wilson, who is described as "my servant," and who was general supervisor and paymaster. He was assisted by Simon Basil (Surveyor of the Royal Works prior to Inigo Jones), whose special duty appears to have been to appraise the extent and value of works done. These two men were instructed by the Earl to

> " repair to my said building and diligently note and consider how much of the work estimated to cost £8,500 is completed, whether the money has been rightly expended and what is still necessary to be done and spent."[2]

In August, 1607, Wilson had been at Hatfield with Sir Walter Cope (who built Holland House) for three days, and the two

> " had beaton the rates with the workmen as low as we can get them."[3]

It was arranged that Simon Basil was to sign the workmen's sheets before Wilson paid them.

As might be expected, there is no direct attribution in the papers of the authorship of the design, the building or its details to any man, but records made during progress of the works clearly show the procedure.

In Wilson's letters he refers, August 12, 1607, to

> " the estimate which Lyminge and we have made for Hatfield,"

and in a letter written on August 21, 1607, which Mr. Tipping thinks may refer to work at Salisbury House and not to Hatfield, Wilson writes:

> " Lymming is confident in his platt for the point of the great chamber where he designed it which we will dispute when Your Lordship comes to Windsor. In the meantime the foundations may go forward for all the rest and that (as a thing standing apart from all) may be added at any time if Your Lordship may so please."[4]

---

[1] Quoted by H. Avray Tipping (from the Hatfield Papers) in *Country Life*, lxi, p. 429.
[2] *Ibid.*, p. 433.   [3] *Ibid.*, p. 433.   [4] *Ibid.*, p. 433.

In 1609, a letter by Robert Lyminge contains the following passage:

> "I am about the drawing of an upright for the front of the gallery, which I can do but little to but in the evenings by reason of giving orders to the workmen and following them for the despatch of it."[1]

Uprights were elevations. Lyminge was a carpenter by trade, who took prominent part in building other great houses, including Blickling in Norfolk. His name appears in the church register of deaths at Blickling, where he is described as

> "the architect and builder of Blickling Hall,"

date January 8, 1628. His own words show that he was foreman at Hatfield, and that he was responsible for the preparation of drawings, which, no doubt, embodied general instructions given him by his employer. Another interesting and illuminating reference is to Jenever, a joiner, in a letter written by Lyminge to Wilson on January 18, 1610. He writes:

> "Mr. Jenever, the joiner, hath been down at Hatfield and we have had some conference about ceiling the rooms with wainscot, and he hath taken measure of certain chimney-pieces to be made, and saith he will draw some plotts of the manner of them and show my Lord and you, and between this and Saturday I will write you at large my opinion what rooms are fittest to be ceiled with wainscot and the manner of them, that your worship may take the joiner with you and confer with my Lord."[2]

These extracts from contemporary records of the building of a great house for a powerful and wealthy peer in the neighbourhood of London may be regarded as fairly representing the extent to which architectural practice had developed at this date, but persons who proposed to build seem frequently to have protected themselves by having a model made of the building contemplated. Shakespeare describes the course pursued with some minuteness, *c.* 1597. The passage is well known, but in this relation will bear being quoted once more:

> "When we mean to build,
> We first survey the plot, then draw the model :
> And when we see the figure of the house,
> Then must we rate the cost of the erection ;
> Which if we find outweighs ability,
> What do we then but draw anew the model
> In fewer offices, or at least desist
> To build at all ? . . .
> Like one that draws the model of a house
> Beyond his power to build it ; who, half through,
> Gives o'er and leaves his part-created cost
> A naked subject to the weeping clouds,
> And waste for churlish winter's tyranny."[3]

The last line alluded to great houses of the period which stood unfinished and derelict.

[1] *Ibid.*, p. 434.   [2] *Ibid.*, p. 462.   [3] *Henry IV*, Part II, act i, sc. 3.

The word *model* seems here to mean *plan*, but Sir Henry Wotton, *c.* 1624, goes farther by recommending that a model should be constructed. His injunctions are:

> " First therefore, Let no man that intendeth to build, setle his Fancie upon a draught of the *Worke* in *paper*, how exactly soever measured, or neatly set off in *perspective* ; And much lesse upon a bare *Plant* thereof, as they call the *Schiographia* or *Ground lines* ; without a *Modell* or *Type* of the whole *Structure*, and of every parcell and Partition in *Pastboord* or *Wood*.
> " Next that the said Modell bee as plaine as may be, without colours or other beautifying, lest the pleasure of the *Eye* pre-occupate the *Judgement*; which advise omited by the *Italian Architects*, I finde in *Philippe de l'Orme*. . . . Lastly, the bigger that this *Type* be, it is still the better . . . in a *Fabrique* of some 40 or 50 thousand pounds charge, I wish 30 pounds at least layd out before hand in an exact *Modell* ; for a little misery in the *Premises*, may easily breed some absurdity of greater charge, in the *Conclusion*."[1]

Some idea of the class of perspective to which reference is made may be obtained by reference to John Thorpe's drawing (Fig. 138).

House-plans of the first quarter of the seventeenth century tended towards greater symmetry, as that of the Great House, Chelsea, *c.* 1620 (Fig. 137), and that of Hatfield House, *c.* 1607-11 (Fig. 143), where, however, we have the unusual feature of wings more than one room wide.

Contemporary writers give us some idea of those humble dwellings of this period, which have long since perished. Bishop Hall gives a minute but painful description of such a hut, *c.* 1610:

> " Of one baye's[2] breadth, God wot ! a silly cote,
> Whose thatched sparres are furr'd with sluttish soot
> A whole inch thick, shining like black-moor's brows,
> Through smok that down the head-les barrel blows :
> At his bed's-feete feeden his stalled teme ;
> His swine beneath, his pullen ore the beame :
> A starved tenement, such as I gesse
> Stands stragling in the wasts of Holdernesse ;
> Or such as shiver on a Peake-hill side,
> When March's lungs beate on their turfe-cladhide."[3]

Evidence of the same kind, but softened by its application, is given by Milton, *c.* 1634, when he refers to

> " . . . . honest-offer'd courtesie,
> Which oft is sooner found in lowly sheds
> With smoky rafters, than in tap'stry Halls
> And Courts of Princes. . . ."[4]

Both these quotations refer to houses without chimneys, where the hearth was in the middle of the floor—in each case a hall only, without rooms adjoining.

[1] *The Elements of Architecture*, pp. 64-6.
[2] One baye=16½ feet. The body of a barrel built into the turf roof formed the chimney. " Turf-clad hide " indicates a roof covering, if not also walls of turf.
[3] *Bishop Hall's Satires*, Bk. v, satire i.   [4] *Comus, a Mask*, by John Milton.

That the poor and their housing were a serious problem in the reign of Elizabeth, as since, is brought out in an Act, which, *inter alia*, provided that:

> "Justices of the Peace . . . to erect, build and set up in fit and convenient places of habitation in such waste or common at the general charges of the parish . . . convenient houses of dwelling for the said impotent poor; and also to place inmates or more families than one in one cottage or house."[1]

In *A Survey of Lands belonging to the Mannor of Sheffield*, 1611, the accommodation of each holding is given, of which the following are typical:

> "JAMES HILL. One dwellinge house 2 baies, 2 chambers, one barne 2 baies, one parler with a chimney, one kytchen, one warehouse.
> "SIMON HEATHCOTE FARME. One house 2 baies, one parler, one chamber, one houell to set beast in, corne barne made of poules very badd.
> "THOM. UNWIN FARME. One house 3 baies, 2 parlers, one chamber, one cowe house 2 baies, one barne 2 baies, one outshutt, one turffe house 2 baies."[2]

These houses do not represent the latest type of dwelling that was being built at the date of the survey, but they do indicate the extent of accommodation enjoyed by such middle-class householders as farmers and tradesmen in Yorkshire. A room with a chimney is sufficiently exceptional as to merit notice; on the other hand, more primitive structures, as a barn made of poles and a house 33 ft. long which was built of turf, are sufficiently important to be included.

---

[1] An Act for the Relief of the Poor, 43 Eliz., c. 2 (1601), quoted in Eden's *State of the Poor*, III, clxvii, 1797.

[2] Quoted by S. O. Addy in *The Evolution of the English House*, London, 1905, pp. 207-9.

Chapter VII

THE SEVENTEENTH CENTURY (Continued)

James I, 1603-1625; Charles I, 1625-1649; Commonwealth, 1649-1660; Charles II, 1660-1684

INIGO JONES

To UNDERSTAND the great change now to take place in house planning and design, it is necessary clearly to appreciate the difference between Gothic and Renaissance buildings.

Gothic architecture developed from:

(*a*) The plan, which followed requirements. A rough plan was first made, which was modified as work progressed. Detailing was done by master men in each trade. Supervision was by the master tradesman whose trade was most involved, and by a clerk or surveyor who ordered materials, kept accounts, etc. ;

e.g. (1) The similarity of church and cathedral planning ; (2) the persistence of the nucleus of the house plan—hall, upper end and lower end chambers—from which extensions were made.

(*b*) The materials used, the natures of which suggested forms and details. It was the flexibility of the materials that produced variety of forms, which were conditioned by the natures of the materials ;

e.g. (1) The development from the ponderous Norman arch to the soaring Gothic roof was the result, not so much of preconceived design, as of greater skill in building with stone and an understanding of its possibilities ; (2) the development of church woodwork in the fifteenth century followed the emancipation of joiners from masons' methods of construction (from which they started) and consequent development of skill in using wood.

In short, the results were obtained adventitiously through the practice of building, and not by application of, or in accordance with, reasoned rules.

In Renaissance architecture:

(*a*) The building and all its details were the conception of one man's mind.

(*b*) The designer worked to certain formal canons of art, to which his building conformed.

(*c*) These canons were purely arbitrary and bore no relation to the peculiarities of materials to be used ; the materials had to be shaped to the forms, instead of the forms arising out of the peculiarities of the materials.

(*d*) Designing was done in orderly fashion, according to rules, which were laid down strictly and departure from which would usually prove disastrous. The essentials were—ORDER—PROPORTION.

The difference, therefore, between Gothic and Renaissance methods was the difference between a product of many minds, freely exercised in developing forms suggested by the materials with which they worked, and a product of one highly trained and organized mind, working to rules, which imposed forms upon the building. For convenience, we speak of the Gothic and of the Renaissance styles; but the essential difference was not one of style (there were many styles during the Gothic period), but the difference of method. This the Elizabethan and Jacobean builders failed to realize; they simply took new forms and applied them to their works. It was Inigo Jones who led into the clear light of the new day those who had been groping in twilight for a century and a half, during which they exhibited remarkable aptitude in combining incongruous elements to produce works—at their worst, ridiculous; at their best, possessing beauty and interest, but without achieving any great distinction as works of art.

Notwithstanding centuries of building enterprise (during which immense numbers of ecclesiastical and domestic buildings were erected), at no time had any man yet risen so much above his fellows, by his exceptional ability in designing, as to cause any revolution in style or in methods. Yet these had changed. In the course of seven hundred years such marked styles as Saxon, Norman, Early English, Decorated, Perpendicular, Tudor, Elizabethan, and Jacobean had come, left their impress upon those which succeeded them, and then ceased to be living architecture. The subdivision of duties and control amongst the considerable number of persons engaged upon any large building enterprise, together with the fidelity with which these adhered to traditional forms (modified by variations suggested by patterns from the Continent), were factors which must persist until the advent of a man of wider knowledge and greater ability, who should cut adrift from tradition and really give effect to the principles of that Renaissance which had been filtering in diluted forms into England for a hundred and fifty years.

As we look into the succession of periods, of styles, and of buildings, we see, now and again, but indistinctly, the forms of their authors pass across the scene. Now a greater form looms into view out of the confusion and obscurity of architectural practice, as a giant might out of a misty landscape. The mist is Time and, like other mists, distorts the forms partially enveloped—often by magnifying parts or even the whole of them. Such has frequently proved the case with great men, and is what has happened to Inigo Jones. Thirty years ago the number of existing buildings attributed to him was considerable. Most are now discredited; even those notable instances, affirmed by tradition, confirmed by men who wrote of him not many years after his death,[1] and used by modern authorities as illustrations of his stupendous ability, recently have been proved to be, not his own work, but works " of his school." Reference to two such attributions will suffice. Raynham Hall, Norfolk, shows no record in its minute building

[1] Conspicuous amongst these are the attributions in *Vitruvius Britannicus*, by Colen Campbell, who credits to Inigo Jones the plans for Whitehall Palace (now known to be Webb's) and the centre block of Cobham Hall, which is so unworthy as to be incredible as an example of his work. In other attributions Campbell has proved equally incorrect.

accounts to connect the design with Inigo Jones, but contains many references to designing by craftsmen such as have been quoted in these pages in connection with other houses. Coleshill House, Berkshire, seemed more securely fixed to Inigo Jones as his design than almost any other existing building; yet the note-books[1] of Sir Roger Pratt (his friend) prove that Pratt was the designer, architect, and superintendent of the whole.

Although few buildings can be stated, definitely, to have been designed by Inigo Jones, two remain of which there is no doubt: the Banqueting House, Whitehall, and the Queen's House, Greenwich. The Banqueting House (Fig. 162), finished in 1622, was the first building of its kind to be erected in England. Although in the manner of Italian palaces, it is no copy, but an original and vigorous composition, such as has seldom been surpassed in any country. The Queen's House (Figs. 163, 164, 165), finished in 1635, is equally Italian in inspiration, equally original in its conception, and just as distinct from other buildings in England at that time. Notwithstanding the promise of its exterior, the Banqueting House is not a building of two storeys, but a large hall, the whole height of the building, with a gallery round, at first-floor level. The Queen's House, however, was planned as a dwelling, and its internal plan and divisions correspond with its exterior. Both these buildings were remarkable at the time they were erected, but their qualities are such that they remain examples of outstanding merit for all time. There can be no doubt that they attracted attention, gained approval, and set a fashion, but it is doubtful whether these and perhaps a few other buildings (some destroyed, some of doubtful authorship) alone would have brought about the great changes in house design and planning which occurred.

In Inigo Jones's sketchbook are two references to architectural principles,[2] both dated January, 1614. In these he says that first the plan must be designed, consideration being given to utility, and that then this may be varied and adorned. He then expresses his opinion that elaboration in details and ornaments should be reserved for interiors and that exteriors should incline towards severity, or, as he terms it, " graviti," concluding with the words:

> " In architecture ye outward ornaments oft (ought) to be sollid, proporsionable according to the rulles, masculine and unaffected."

The last phrase has been quoted frequently but always divorced from its contextual reference to " outward ornaments."

In the second paragraph of remarks on architecture he instances the study of parts of the human body before drawing the whole figure, and applies this method to architectural design by saying that:

[1] *The Architecture of Sir Roger Pratt*, edited by R. T. Gunther, Oxford, 1928.
[2] Quoted in full in *Inigo Jones*, by J. Alfred Gotch, pp. 81-2.

> " One must studdy the Parts as loges Entrances Haales chambers staires doures windowes and then addorne them with Colloms cornishes sfondati, stattues, paintings, compartiments, quadratues, Cartochi, tearmi, festoni, armes," etc.

It is unnecessary to quote the long list of parts which he names, but both extracts from the sketchbook are interesting as records of his own system of working at that date.

Inigo Jones was born in 1573 ;[1] his father was a cloth-worker in a small way of business, and the son received scanty education. There is no evidence as to his having been apprenticed (as has been stated) to a joiner, though subsequent events suggest this is possible, but he showed early ability as a draughtsman and painter. After the death of his father in 1597 (perhaps two or three years later) he went to Italy, and remained on the Continent until 1603, when he was again in England, for in contemporary records a payment is mentioned,

> " To Henygo Jones, a picture maker, x, li."[2]

In 1605 he was (probably) in Italy again. In 1611 he was appointed Surveyor to Prince Henry, who died in 1612. In 1613 he went to Italy once more, returning in 1615, when he was appointed Surveyor to the King. Between 1619 and 1622 the Banqueting House was built. The Queen's House, Greenwich, commenced 1618, was not completed until 1635. In 1634 he was appointed Surveyor to undertake the restoration of Old St. Paul's Cathedral, which he furnished with classic details (including a Corinthian portico to the west front) all out of keeping with the Gothic structure, but the novelty and new fashion of which brought him unstinted praise. He died in 1652, aged 79.

The fragmentary records of Inigo Jones include references to his connection with other architectural enterprises, to most of which his claim to be the designer is slenderly supported. There are more records of his duties as surveyor, such as reports on existing buildings, highways, and matters so incongruous as a report as to the dearth of grain and an appointment to examine the King's coins. The fact is that the duties of the King's Surveyor were multifarious, and designing buildings was a small part of those duties. An instance of the scope of his obligations is furnished in a petition dated June 27, 1646:

> " Petition of the Officers of His Majesties Works, who complain that Arthur Cundall, of Westminster, carpenter, has brought a suit against them for the timberwork of the court for the trial of the late Earl of Strafford in Westminster Hall, which he pretends was taken from him after the trial by the Earl of Lindsay, &c. &c., whereas Cundall was to find the workmanship and have his stuff again. As the suit is likely to become a precedent to others who have money owing to them from his Majesty in the said office, to the Petitioners utter ruin, they pray that some course may be taken for their protection."[3]

The Petition is signed by Inigo Jones and Henry Wicks.

---

[1] For this and the following dates I have followed the " Chronology " in *Inigo Jones*, by J. Alfred Gotch, London, 1928.   [2] Rutland Papers.   [3] L.J. viii, 397. Hist. Commn., pt. 3, 1877 (C. 1745).

It seems, sometimes, to be forgotten that books like those of Serlio and Sir Henry Wotton prepared the way and that both public taste and public inclination (that is, inclination of the influential public) were disposed to adopt architecture in the Italian manner in place of a second-hand renaissance derived from the Netherlands, so that Inigo Jones was not so completely a pioneer entering unknown territory as has been represented.

Up to his appointment as the King's Surveyor in 1615, Inigo Jones's name is not associated with any building, but he had long established a reputation as a designer of scenery for masques, beginning with " The Masque of Blackness " in 1605 and concluding the long series with " The Masque of Salmacida Spolia " in 1640. Of drawings by him which have been preserved, upwards of 450 relate to masques, 70 or 80 to architecture. His copy of *Palladio*, which he bought in Italy and which he studied assiduously, has many notes upon architecture, together with others such as are usually associated with a commonplace book. His sketchbook is filled with drawings other than architectural—studies of human figures, heads and limbs, drapery—all with copious notes. The impression conveyed is that these occupied him more than his architectural studies. Inigo Jones's appointments as surveyor to prince and to king, together with his ingenuity in devising stage scenery of more elaborate nature than anything yet seen (the scenery of the Elizabethan stage was negligible) and carrying stage mechanism to a high point of development, are indirect confirmations of the supposition that he was engaged in one of the building trades in his youth, for that would have given him valuable insight into the practical side of construction. The elaboration of the large number of masques which he produced must have occupied the greater part of his time, and the opportunities which they afforded, when designing scenery, for the presentation of Italian architecture and the popularizing of it are obvious. Had his architectural practice been immensely larger than it was, it could not have exercised so much influence upon current taste as the repeated presentation of architectural scenery, after the manner of Italian buildings, before the king and court. In considering the factors which enabled Inigo Jones to revolutionize architectural design in England it will probably be right to allow at least as much influence to his introduction of the new manner through stage scenery as to the effect produced by actual buildings which he designed; added to this is the force of a personality of which little direct evidence exists, but which is so potent as to be felt by every student.

John Webb (1611-72), who was Inigo Jones's nephew by marriage, became his pupil at the age of seventeen and afterwards his assistant. Several records exist of his testimony to the abilities of his master, and, without having pretensions to the latter's brilliant abilities, he certainly was a sound architect. Recent investigations have shown that he was author of the drawings for the immense palace at Whitehall which never materialized. It has been customary to regard these and other drawings, which undoubtedly were made by him, as having been inspired by Inigo Jones's sketches, but it now seems that this view scarcely does Webb justice. Thorpe Hall is generally attached to him, as author, though not by any documentary evidence. Its elevations (Figs. 168, 169), as we should expect, are in the full Italian manner, as is the detailing. The ground plan (Fig. 170) takes the form of two passages crossing, so that the house is divided into four equal quarters, but the surprising feature of this plan is that the whole width of the entrance front (shaded in the drawing, Fig. 170) conforms to the medieval plan, so far as hall and lower-end chambers—yet another instance of the persistence of that plan in buildings of altogether different character.

Sir Balthazar Gerbier, Baron D'Ouvilly, usually known as Sir Balthazar Gerbier, Knight, was born at Middleburg about 1591, educated in France, returned to Holland and formed friendship with the Duke of Buckingham, who first employed him as his architect. He had many accomplishments, including painting, designing masques and engines of war. He busied himself in politics and religion, from which politics were inseparable. In 1662 and again in 1664 was published *A Brief Discourse concerning the Three Chief Principles of Magnificent Building, vizt., Solidity, Convenience and Ornament*, in which he discussed sites, planning, the Orders, and practical details of building. In 1663 and in 1664 he published *Counsel and Advice to All Builders*, which was the first book published of measurements and prices of works. By " Builders " Gerbier meant persons proposing to build or what are styled " building owners," to whom he offers much shrewd and amusing advice, as:

" Let all owners be prepared to repent, whether they build or not, for it is likewise the fate of many that marry or marry not."[1]

Another of his aphorisms referring to the rambling Jacobean houses is:

" Too many stairs and back doors make thieves and whores."

Gerbier had the promise of Inigo Jones's post as Surveyor-General, but never received the appointment. He died 1667. As a courtier he was knighted in 1629. None of his architectural works remain; Hempstead Marshall, with which he was associated, no longer exists. This was not free from Jacobean details, so Gerbier cannot fully have adopted Italian design.

Hugh May (1622-84) was an able architect of this school, whose name has been rescued from comparative oblivion and established as author of works attributed to better-known men. He was

" Comptroller of the Works to King Charles the Second, Comptroller of the Castle of Windsor, and by his Maytie appointed to be sole Architect in Contriving and Governing the Works in the Great alterations made by his Maytie in that Castle."

Evelyn states that he was a commissioner for the repair of St. Paul's and employed Grinling Gibbons extensively at Windsor and at Cassiobury, finishing the latter

[1] *Dic. Architectural Pub. Soc.*, London, 1553, *cf.* Gerbier.

before Evelyn visited it in 1680. May was also paymaster of the King's works, being appointed in 1660. Eltham Lodge, a beautiful building (Fig. 174), which was once assigned to Wren's school, is now proved to have been designed by May and finished in 1664. Wren only commenced architectural practice in 1661 and could scarcely have "founded a school" by 1664. That May was the designer is definitely stated by Sir Roger Pratt in his notebooks, in one of which he refers to "Sir John Shawe's house at Eltham designed by Mr. May,"[1] and in July, 1664, John Evelyn went "to Eltham to see Sir John Shaw's new house now building," which he criticizes. This quiet, homely type of house, built of red brick (once furnished with mullioned and transomed window frames) and having a hipped roof swept out over a handsome cornice, was destined to become popular later in the seventeenth century. The plan (Fig. 175) does not conform to the practice of filling the centre third of the house with a spacious staircase hall, with large salon beyond, as at Coleshill (Fig. 171). The front and back are divided into apartments and separated by a wide, central corridor which contains both principal and subsidiary stairs. The plan resembles that of Thorpe Hall (Fig. 170), but is free from any trace of the medieval plan. The interior contains contemporary woodwork (Figs. 702, 703), and several rooms have plaster ceilings of fine workmanship (Fig. 749).

Allusion has been made to recent investigations which have brought to light documentary evidence requiring that we should readjust our ideas as to the relative importance of architects of the Inigo Jones school. The effect of these is to deprive Inigo Jones of much work which, hitherto, has been credited to him, to credit John Webb with the authorship of important designs hitherto ascribed to Inigo Jones, and to show that a forgotten genius—Sir Roger Pratt—was one of the most able architects of his time and the real designer of Coleshill House, so long regarded as a masterpiece of Inigo Jones.

Until 1919, the name of Sir Roger Pratt (1620-84) was connected only with Clarendon House, London, and Horseheath, Cambs. (both destroyed long since), and with the commission to survey St. Paul's after the Great Fire. He is now found to have been the architect who designed and conducted the building operations at Coleshill House, Berks. (which still stands unmutilated); of Kingston Lacy Hall, Wimborne, Dorset (since altered by casing with stone, etc.), hitherto attributed to John Webb; and of Ryston Hall, Norfolk (since mutilated). He had something to do with Raynham Hall, Norfolk, also, but at least the shell of this house had been completed long before he began practice.

The evidence for confidently associating these buildings with Sir Roger Pratt's name is the minute records of his own notebooks[2] which contain immense

[1] *The Architecture of Sir Roger Pratt*, R. T. Gunther, Oxford, 1928, p. 232.
[2] *The Architecture of Sir Roger Pratt.* Now printed for the first time from his notebooks, edited by R. T. Gunther, Oxford, 1928. This volume, from which the following extracts are drawn, is a mine of information respecting mid-seventeenth-century building and architectural practice, of which it is the most important and valuable record yet published.

quantities of information respecting building details, methods of construction, and prices; some being records of work done, others of work started, and others, again, of matters upon which the writer wished definitely to inform himself. Architectural principles and design are discussed, and most of the records of details are associated with the actual houses to which they related—viz.: Coleshill, Kingston Lacy, Horseheath, Clarendon House, and Ryston Hall.

Perhaps the chief impression derived from the study of Sir Roger Pratt's notebooks is the thoroughness of the man, who set down his views upon architectural design and the fruits of his experience of minute building details as no man had ever done before. Sir Balthazar Gerbier's *Counsel and Advice to all Builders* is an insignificant treatise by comparison with Pratt's notes. Pratt spent the period April, 1643, to August, 1649, travelling in France, Italy, Flanders, Holland, etc., as he says,

> " to avoid the storm (of the Civil War) and to give myself some convenient education."

During 1644-45 he was in Rome with John Evelyn. On his return to England he lived in London as any other young man of fashion and had many discussions with his kinsman, Sir George Pratt, who had begun to build himself a house at Coleshill, Berkshire. This, Roger persuaded him to alter; in fact, to abandon it and use the materials for a house of Roger's design which was commenced in 1650. Inigo Jones accompanied Pratt to Coleshill more than once, when they discussed the proposed changes with Sir George Pratt. Further than this friendly interest, there is no evidence that Inigo Jones had any part in the designing of the house; indeed, he died a year after it was begun, aged seventy-nine, and in poverty. On the other hand, the evidence that Pratt was competent to be the author of the work is the record of his own notebooks. There is no reason to suppose, as has been alleged, that John Webb had anything to do with Coleshill. It is necessary thus to clear away all fog as to the authorship of Coleshill (Figs. 172, 420, 833), because it is the most remarkable building of its period; it is the best work of Sir Roger Pratt (notwithstanding the praise[1] heaped upon Clarendon House); and it, alone, establishes him as a great architect.

The opinions expressed by authorities writing of Coleshill, whilst supposed to be the design of Inigo Jones, must now be transferred to the credit of Sir Roger Pratt.

Lord Burlington commissioned Ware to make drawings of the house

> " that he might be able to study them continually."

It has been described as:

> " Inigo Jones's most perfect work. The finest specimen of Jones's taste and talent."

---

[1] In 1665, Evelyn writing to Lord Coventry after visiting Clarendon House, then incomplete, said: " Nothing abroad pleases me better, nothing at home approaches it. . . . I pronounce it the finest palace of England, deserving all I have said of it, and a better encomiast."—Pratt, p. 10.

Indeed, every architectural writer and authority has confirmed Jones's author-ship and praised the building as a transcendent example of his genius.

Pratt acquired a library of foreign architectural books which he proceeded to master and to compare. No detail of building construction was too insignifi-cant for him to explore, consider, and record. He set down (1660) *Certain Short Notes Concerning Architecture*, in which he deals with the appearance and character of several types of buildings, measurements of quantities, prices of materials, etc. Then follow *Notes as to Building Country Houses*, in which he considers situation and sets forth the advantages of

" the raising with steps to a House after my manner "

in prospect, improved servants' accommodation in basement and less deep excavations; but he cannot be allowed the credit he claims for introducing this practice, to which reference was made in the Jacobean section of this history, when it was quoted from Sir Henry Wotton,[1] 1624. In other chapters he advocates that having decided to build a house, if unable

" handsomely to contrive it yourself, you should get some ingenious gentle-man, who has seen much of that kind abroad and been somewhat versed in the best authors of architecture: viz. Palladio, Scamozzi, Serlio, etc., to do it for you, and to give you a design of it on paper, though but roughly drawn (which will generally fall out better than one by a home-bred architect for want of his better experience as is daily seen)."

He then recommends a model to be made of wood and says that a double build-ing is " most commodious." This in another place he speaks of as the " double pile," by which he means one planned with a central corridor having rooms back and front as distinguished from " single pile " in which plans were all one room deep, such as hitherto had been the fashion. Guidance as to building details is followed by *Rules for the Guidance of Architects* (1665), in which he deals with super-vision, bargains, and the trades employed. In respect of bargains, he begins:

" If workmen be employed by the day, they will make but small haste to finish the building. If agreed with all by the great as to all particulars . . . the difficulty is very much in making the bargain, which they will still be trying to break either in the matter or manner of their working,"[2]

and proceeds to tell how such contracts should be made and enforced. He even adds:

" Mem. : That £200 to £300 will be saved in a great building, if we agree with workmen to find their own nails, etc."[3]

In this chapter the directions as to supervision include:

" To determine anything without due premeditation, is rashness. Not to come to any determination in a convenient time, is an effect either of ignorance or sloth.

[1] *The Elements of Architecture*, p. 70.   [2] Pratt, p. 87.   [3] *Ibid.*, p. 88.

" To be so forward in his premeditation as to make no trade at a stand for want of his directions, which will cause great repining, &c., and to be careful to see them all exactly performed, for otherwise all trades will be at catch with him.

" An able Architect ought perfectly to understand these things :

" 1. To be able to design all sorts of buildings after the most useful, strong, and beautiful manner. . . .

" 2. To perfectly understand the natures and qualities of all the most useful sort of materials. . . .

" 3. To know the best manner of working in all kinds of materials, the just dimensions, distances, and the whole method of them, the usual frauds, or errors in it, the true value of it, which must proceed not from any guess but from a most clear demonstration of the progress of every particular in it, all proved by a most diligent, and reiterated observation of how much of each can be done by a sufficient workman per diem, at such wages as most usually is given to them. . . .

" 4. To contrive all things with the most orderly thrift, and longest duration.

" 5. Somewhat nearly to calculate the expense of any designed building. . . .

" To put rarely into any building what does not as well add to the strength or safeguard as to the beauty of it.

" When we are in doubt . . . not to trust . . . to the bare force of our imagination or reason . . . but in things of small cost there to make trial first of some little part of it ; in greater, by some model of it."[1]

Directions are given for setting out a building and points to watch in relation to each trade, and as to measuring up works.[2]

The windows at Coleshill are an example of Pratt's pains in recording particulars of details. Exact measurements are given; a note to put

" a little piece of iron over the rebate of the casements to keep out the wind . . . a border of lead at bottom and sides . . . a strip of lead over the heads,"[3]

and everything carefully thought out to secure perfect efficiency.

The wainscot moulds are described:

" The moulds of the panels, first a bottle, then a great ogee with a Gola roversica. Then the moulds of a capital. The panels raised with an ogee. In some panels a fascia about 3 in. broad with an ogee besides the moulds aforesaid."[4]

Certain workmen's names are mentioned (as that of Richard Cleave, whose bill for carver's work exists), but though sometimes consulted on points of construction, in no instance is mention made of tradesmen designing. Apparently Pratt directed tradesmen as to the nature of details (as in the particulars of mouldings given above), approved a pattern and bargained for certain areas or feet run of work; as, indeed, labours would be reckoned today.

Horseheath, near Cambridge (long attributed to John Webb), was also by Pratt, and details respecting it appear in his notebooks. The front of the house as drawn by Colen Campbell was eleven windows wide and in many respects like Coleshill, but the centre (three windows wide) projected slightly and was finished with a triangular pediment. It was destroyed in 1777.

[1] Pratt, pp. 83-5.   [2] Ibid., pp. 86-9.   [3] Ibid., p. 95.   [4] Ibid.

Directions for the carver of roses for the cornice show Pratt's forethought and method:

"Roses are to lye at 13 inches distance from ye proiecture of ye capo, first they are to have a margent of 3 inches. Theire whole holoweing ought to bee 5 inches, inpr : 1 in. for a fillet, 2½ for ye ouvolo, 1½ for ye square edge above. Ye whole deepth of ye rose is to be 5 ins., its breadth 6 in. Ye whole Plank is to bee thick 6 in., & to rest upon each modiglion about 3 in. on a side soe yt these peeces must be about 2 ft. in length & 6 in. broad, 20 in. at ye least. It : how they are cutt, what time each in doing."[1]

There seems to have been friction in settling accounts with tradesmen on conclusion of the works, and Edward Pearce, writing from Horseheath in April, 1665, advises having forwarded to Pratt

"ye Molds of ye great and lesser scroles : those for Modelions cannot be found."[2]

He adds measurements of each (square and raking) for the pediments, evidently for Pratt's information.

The building for which Sir Roger Pratt received greatest credit during his own lifetime was Clarendon House, Piccadilly, built for the Earl of Clarendon, 1664-67, who was suspected of having obtained the necessary funds by foreign bribes, as recorded in the lines:

"Upon Clarendon House built by the Lord Chancellor Hyde, anno 1665, on the Hill against St. James's.[3]

"Here lye the consecrated bones
Of Paules, late gelded of his stones,[4]
Here lyes the golden Briberies,
The price of ruin'd Families
The Caviliers debenter wall
    Built in th' excentrick Basis,
Heer's Dunkirk Towne and Tangier Hall
    The Dutchman's *Templum pacis*."

A contemporary illustration of Clarendon House shows it to have been similar in style to Coleshill, but to have the centre slightly advanced and crowned by a triangular pediment (like Horseheath); it also had the Elizabethan feature of wings projecting one-third of the width of the centre—in fact, the elevation was, in plan, a letter ⊓. The entrance, fenestration, dormers, roof, balustrade, chimneys, and cupola were in the same manner as those at Coleshill and Horseheath. Undoubtedly, it was a fine house which earned the praises of Lord Clarendon's friends and the envy and hatred of his enemies.

Pepys, after viewing it before completion (1665), said:

"Indeed it is the finest pile I ever did see in my life and will be a glorious house."

---

[1] *Pratt*, p. 124.   [2] *Ibid.*, p. 130.
[3] MS. Ashmole 36, fol. 117, quoted by R. T. Gunther in *The Architecture of Sir Roger Pratt*, London, 1928.
[4] "The stones designed for repair of St. Pauls, he borrowed to use in his building—they were duly paid for."

In 1666, he commended the view from the roof, adding:

> " In everything it is a beautiful house and most strongly built."

Evelyn (1666) went to see the house which:

> " now almost finished, is a goodly pile to see but has many defects as to architecture, yet placed most gracefully."

In 1665, Evelyn had written of Clarendon House to Lord Cornbury:

> " It is, without hyperbolies, the best contriv'd, the most usefull, gracefull and magnificent house in England. I except not Audley-end which though larger and full of gaudy and barbarous ornaments, does not gratifie judicious spectators."[1]

No doubt Pratt's success with Clarendon House brought him into the first rank amongst contemporary architects; he was commissioned to design a house for the prince (? the Duke of York, married to Lord Clarendon's daughter Anne), which, however, was not built, and he was appointed a commissioner for the repair of St. Paul's, after the Great Fire. Amongst his fellow-commissioners were: Dr. Wren, John Evelyn, Hugh May, Thomas Chicheley, Slingsby, the Bishop of London, and the Dean of St. Paul's.

Amongst a multitude of details specified for Clarendon House by Pratt is one addressed to

> " Kinnard ye Joyner
> " Lett his men proceede to finish ye other sides & end of ye chappell according to ye designe in their handes, only ye Frontispeece of ye doore there is to bee circular & not angular.
> " Then lett him provide & sett up three Frontispeeces over ye doores in my Ladyes Lobby, two whereof to be Angular. . . ."[2]

A carver's bill " for strings of flowers " is certified by Hugh May.[3]

That Pratt drew his own details appears from time to time, by inference, in the notes—

> " 1663, Mem. that a cornice is much easier drawn after the way of Scamozzi than of Palladio.[4]
> " The cornice . . . at Kingston Hall was about 3 ft. in depth and as much in projecture, all of which will most clearly appear by the draft."[5]

But (? at Kingston) in a memorandum for Mr. Taylor, carpenter—

> " Let the grand cornice of the house be drawn out for me on paper, as it is to be set up, as likeways the framing of the roof, that I may, at leasure and by myself consider of them. Consider in the framing of the roof how all the walls of the house lie below, &c."[6]

Then follow many queries on structural matters, from which it would appear that Pratt depended upon the tradesmen, at least to check his own conclusions.

Of Mouldings, he says:

> " The dimensions of these are to be given them (joiners) most particularly by the architect, according to art, for being left to themselves, they make most

---

[1] *The Architecture of Sir Roger Pratt*, p. 10. [2] *Ibid.*, p. 155.
[3] *Ibid.*, p. 157.   [4] *Ibid.*, p. 264.   [5] *Ibid.*, p. 265.   [6] *Ibid.*, p. 269.

wild proportions, and extravagant orders, applying all things to all places, not considering the reason of them, where perhaps they first saw them juditiously placed, for we are not only to know that such things are, but also to consider why and how well."[1]

Minute notes as to making contracts for each trade conclude:

" Three parts of these articles to be presently drawn up and signed, sealed and delivered, the one to the builder, the other for the architect, the third for the workman, to prevent all losses, excuses, frivolous pretences, &c., and this some competent time before the building,[2] &c., &c."

In *Certain Short Notes concerning Architecture* (1660), Pratt remarks:

" It is most certain, that no man deserves the name of an Architect, who has not been very well versed both in those old ones of Rome, as likewise the more modern of Italy and France, &c., because that with us, having nothing remarkable but the banquetting house at Whitehall and the portico at St. Pauls, it is in no ways probable that any one should be sufficiently furnished with the variety of invention, and of excellent ideas, which upon several occasions it will be necessary for him to have. who has had but so great a scarcity wherein to employ his judgement, neither can it be supposed that anything should be in the Intellect, which was never in the senses.

True it is that a man may receive some helps upon a most diligent study of those excellent, and most exact designs of Palladio, Freart, Scamozzi and some few others, yet never having seen anything in its full proportions it is not to be thought that he can conceive of them as he ought. . . ."[3]

It is significant that Pratt here only allows two buildings (both in London) to be " remarkable," both being by Inigo Jones (in another place he also refers to the Queen's House, Greenwich, as by him), yet, though he was in a position to know all the works of his friend, in none of his notebooks is Inigo Jones's name mentioned as author of other buildings.

These extracts from Sir Roger Pratt's notebooks might be amplified (they are full of most interesting and valuable information), but those given, if considered in conjunction with the architectural qualities of the buildings of which he was the author, show that he was an architect having exceptional natural abilities, sharpened by travel in Italy, France, and Holland, a keen and judicious observer, and an exceptionally close and methodical student of building and of the details of every trade concerned. There is abundant evidence to prove that he was *architect* of the buildings in the modern use of the word; indeed, no English tradesman of his time was capable of designing such houses or of setting out their details, though we shall see later in the century how master tradesmen adapted themselves and even qualified by study as architects in the new manner. Meantime, such tradesmen-designers were superseded, and Architecture, the highly specialized vocation of educated and travelled men, could no longer successfully be practised by mere craftsmen. The change from Old to New—revolutionary and far-reaching, though slow in development— was now complete.

[1] *The Architecture of Sir Roger Pratt*, p. 273.   [2] *Ibid.*, p. 278.   [3] *Ibid.*, p. 23.

Chapter VIII

LATE SEVENTEENTH AND EARLY EIGHTEENTH CENTURIES

CHARLES II, 1660-84; JAMES II, 1684-88; WILLIAM AND MARY, 1688-1702; ANNE, 1702-14

SIR CHRISTOPHER WREN

THE ARCHITECTURAL period from the Great Fire of London (1667) to the early years of the eighteenth century is dominated by the figure of one man—Sir Christopher Wren—whom we are accustomed to regard as our greatest architect, but who we are apt to forget was not only a genius in his own time but one of the greatest intellects of all time. His abilities were not confined to architecture but were manifested in scientific attainments which would have rendered him eminent in any country at any period.

His application of scientific principles was not always well directed, some of his inventions verging upon the trivial (evidence, perhaps, to the wideness of his interests); but things which impress students of his career are his clearness of reasoning, his power of assimilating knowledge, and the ability he displayed in applying it. Naturally, this application is most marked in his architectural work, for that absorbed the energies of his prime. We find evidence of this in the ingenuity he displayed in construction as well as in the development of his powers as a designer—a development which can be traced through successive works. It is these practical and artistic qualities that distinguish him from the mere man of science. The following bare details are drawn from *Parentalia*, by his son Christopher, published in 1750.

Born on October 20, 1632, Wren for a short time was at Westminster School. At the age of thirteen he invented a new astronomical instrument of general use, a pneumatic engine, and an instrument of use in gnomonics. When fourteen years old (1646) he was admitted a Gentleman Commoner at Wadham College, Oxford. Before he attained the age of seventeen he had produced inventions for sowing corn, new astronomical and geometric instruments, a weather clock, and a treatise on spherical trigonometry.

In 1650 he was a Bachelor of Arts.

In 1653 he was Master of Arts and a Fellow of All Souls.

In 1657 he was a Professor of Astronomy at Gresham College, London.

In 1660 he was a Savilian Professor of Astronomy at Oxford University.

In 1661 he was D.C.L. Oxon., later D.C.L. Cantab.

In 1680 he was President of the Royal Society.

"A Catalogue of New Theories, Inventions, Experiments, and Mechanical Improvements exhibited by Mr. Wren at the first assemblies at Wadham College in Oxford" include the following connected with building: "A Pavement harder, fairer, and cheaper than Marble." "New Designs, tending to Strength, Convenience, and Beauty in Building." "Inventions for better making and fortifying Havens, for clearing Sands, and to Sound at Sea." "Some Inventions in Fortification." "To pierce a Rock in Mining." "To perfect Coaches for Ease, Strength, and Lightness, &c."[1] An extract from Dr. Spratt's *History of the Royal Society* (1667) says that whereas conclusions of Des Cartes

> "were only derived from the gross Trials of Balls meeting one another at Tennis and Billiards, Dr. Wren produc'd before the Society, an Instrument to represent the Effects of all Sorts of Impulses, made between two hard globous Bodies . . . of all of which he demonstrated the true theories after they had been confirm'd by many hundreds of Experiments in that Instrument."[2]

In 1665 Wren took a journey to Paris. In a letter to a friend he says:

> "I busied myself in surveying the most esteemed Fabricks of Paris and the Country round; the Louvre for a while was my daily Object, where no less than a thousand Hands were constantly employ'd in the Works . . . which altogether make a School of Architecture, the best probably, at this Day in Europe."[3]

Amongst others he met Colbert, "Surintendant," and Bernini, architect. He remarks that—

> "the Women, as they make here the Language and Fashions, and meddle with Politicks and Philosophy, so they sway also in Architecture; Works of Filgrand, and little Knacks are in great Vogue; but Building certainly ought to have the Attribute of eternal, and therefore the only Thing uncapable of new Fashions."[4]

After enumerating the buildings he has seen and surveyed he remarks:

> "I shall bring you almost all *France* in paper, which I found by some or other ready design'd to my Hand, in which I have spent both Labour and some Money. *Bernini's* Design of the *Louvre* I would have given my skin for, but the old reserv'd *Italian* gave me but a few Minutes View; it was five little Designs in Paper, for which he hath receiv'd as many thousand Pistoles; I had only time to copy it in my Fancy and Memory; I shall be able by Discourse, and a Crayon, to give you a tolerable Account of it. I have purchas'd a great deal of *Taille-douce*, that I might give our *Countrymen* Examples of Ornaments and Grotesks, in which the *Italians* themselves confess the *French* to excel. I hope I shall give you a very good Account of all the best Artists of *France*; my Business now is to pry into Trades and Arts, I put myself into all Shapes to humour them; 'tis a Comedy to me, and tho' sometimes expenceful, I am loth yet to leave it."[5]

He adds that he proposes to return to England at Christmas (1665).

> "1666. Appointed *Surveyor General* and *principal Architect* for rebuilding *the whole City*; the Cathedral Church of *St. Paul*; all the parochial Churches (in Number Fifty-one, enacted by Parliament, in lieu of those that were burnt

[1] *Parentalia*, p. 198.   [2] *Ibid.*, p. 207.   [3] *Ibid.*, p. 261.   [4] *Ibid.*, p. 261.   [5] *Ibid.*, p. 262.

and demolished) with other publick Structures ; and for the Disposition of the Streets. A Charge so great and extensive, incumbent on a single person, disposed him to take to his Assistance *Mr. Robert Hook*, Professor of *Geometry* at *Gresham College*, to whom he assigned chiefly the Business of measuring, adjusting, and setting out the Ground of the private Street-houses to the several Proprietors ; reserving all the publick Works to his own peculiar Care and Direction."[1]

" 1667-8 H.M. Warrant to office of Surveyor-General of the Royal Works.
" 1674 Knighted.
" 1675 Design for St. Paul's finally approved.
" 1671-7 The Monument.
" 1676-93 Trinity College Library, Cambridge.
" 1682 Chelsea Hospital.
" 1684 Appointed ' Comptroller of the Works in the Castle of Winasor . . .
in the Roome of Hugh May, deceas'd.'
" 1689-1702 Hampton Court Palace.
" 1696 Greenwich Hospital begun.
" 1697 Choir of St. Paul's opened for service.
" 1711 St. Paul's ' declared finished.'
" 1718 Superseded in Surveyorship.
" 1723 Died 25th February, aged 91."

He designed fifty-two churches in London.

Having regard to the public buildings which he designed and the multitude of questions which came before him daily in his office of Surveyor-General, it is not surprising that minute investigations have resulted in inability to attribute any domestic building (except official residences) to him as architect. The wonder is that any man could find time to give personal attention to details of all the buildings of which he was the undoubted author, to superintend works, to discharge his multifarious official duties (many of which were only remotely connected with architecture or building), to endure with unfailing tact and patience the caprice and stupidity of employers and the plots of unscrupulous rivals and assistants who hoped to supersede him.

Wren had rivals but no peers. William Talman (a Dutchman), who was comptroller of works at Hampton Court Palace until the appointment of Sir John Vanbrugh in 1702, was architect of several buildings, the most notable of which is Chatsworth. For years he seems to have been troublesome to Wren —constantly scheming and making mischief, apparently with a view to supplanting him as architect at Hampton Court Palace. Talman's own designs were of mediocre quality.

Edward Jerman, the architect of the Royal Exchange (built after the Great Fire and burned in 1838), which was severely criticized by contemporaries, is also credited with the halls of several City companies. Certain responsibility in connection with these would fall upon Wren in his official capacity, and we may suppose that he would not be less thorough in respect of these designs than he showed himself to be in his connection with other buildings, where his editing of plans actually amounted to designing.

[1] *Parentalia*, p. 263.

Captain William Wind, Winde, or Wynne (a Dutchman), was an architect of ability, of whose works only the mutilated Newcastle House, No. 66, Lincoln's Inn Fields, remained until recently. He was a pupil of Sir Balthazar Gerbier. Probably his most notable work was at Hampstead Marshall, Berkshire (c. 1662), which, it is believed, was built by Gerbier and to which Wynne built a new front—destroyed in the eighteenth century. To him the handsome gate piers are credited. He was also the architect of Buckingham House (Figs. 198, 199), since destroyed.

It is worthy of note that, of architects contemporary with Wren, Talman, Wynne, and Vanbrugh were Dutchmen.

Nicholas Hawksmoor (1661-1736), clerk of works at Greenwich Hospital, at Kensington Palace, and other buildings, was assistant to Wren. He also assisted Vanbrugh at Castle Howard and Blenheim Palace. He designed five City churches, of which Christ Church, Spitalfields, is the most distinguished. Often it is difficult to separate his works from those of Wren and Vanbrugh, whom he assisted for years on many buildings. From his youth he worked for Wren, first as a clerk, then as clerk of works and surveyor. Thus he had opportunity of learning both designing and practical building. His work bears evidence of the influence exercised upon him both by Wren and Vanbrugh. Easton Neston, Towcester (Figs. 200-202), is fairly securely attached to him as author. In this building the influence of Vanbrugh, with whom Hawksmoor had become associated, seems to dominate that of Wren, and it should be classed with the school of Palladians.

The great era of building was during the eighteenth century; the latter half of the seventeenth century was still overcast by the wastage of the Civil War, by plague, fire, war with Holland, and the Revolution of 1688, events which retarded even normal building enterprise.

The trend of design in England had been determined before Wren commenced full architectural practice. Domestic buildings like Thorpe Hall (Figs. 168, 169), Coleshill House (Fig. 172), and Eltham Lodge (Fig. 174)—notwithstanding their Italianate features—had established such characteristics of contemporary Dutch dwellings as the hipped roof, the central pediment, the spacing and proportions of windows, the massive, symmetrically disposed chimneys and the cupola which covered the point of access to the flat portion of a roof. The parapet partially (and later completely) masking the roof had been introduced by Inigo Jones in the Queen's House (Figs. 163 and 165) and in the Banqueting House (Fig. 162). Late in the seventeenth century we still find houses built to plan, the wings of which often projected only a little, but which had hipped roofs instead of the gables which were current fifty years earlier. All these Wren used for his domestic buildings, and, although he did not invent any of them, he succeeded in clarifying design and investing it with that quality and grace which distinguishes all his work. So great was this influence that it is to be seen in many houses scattered about the country with which he can have had nothing to do, but the architects of which are generally unknown. Wren was never in Holland nor in Italy. His only Continental journey was that to France, in 1665. The catalogue of his library, sold in 1748, included works of Alberta, Scamozzi, Serlio, and Palladio, to which reference has been made. There were also at his disposal a host of engravings of Italian buildings, published during the second half of the seventeenth century, and Dutch books illustrating the architectural works of such men as Philip Vingboon, Jacob van Campen, and Hendrik de Keyser, or books of views of buildings as those by Schenck, Danckerts, and Dahlberg. In England, William Leybourn produced a book entitled *A Platform for Purchasers—A Guide for Builders—A Mate for Measurers*, in 1668, similar to a work by S. Primatt, published 1667. This is an early textbook of materials, prices, and wage rates, together with tables of measurements and instructions for measuring materials and the labours relating thereto. Joseph Moxon's *Mechanic Exercises*, published 1678, 1682, and 1703, includes information respecting many architectural and building details. Leybourn's book remained a standard work for more than sixty years. As late as 1734 a volume was published[1] containing:

> " Pages 1-16 and 40 plates. 'The Mirror of Architecture or the Ground Rules of the Art of Buildings exactly laid down by Vincent Scamozzi.' "

The plates illustrated the Orders with their proportions and details.

> " Pages 17-40. 'The Description and use of an Ordinary Joynt-Rule . . . for the ready finding of the lengths and angles of Rafters and Hips . . . and the ready drawing of . . . any Order.' &c., by John Brown."

This was illustrated by plates and tables.

> " Pages 41-56. 'The Ground Rules of Architecture,' &c., collected . . . by Sir Henry Wotton in his Elements of Architecture. Now corrected for Public Benefit."

This was substantially a reprint of the edition of 1624.

> " Pages 57-112. 'Architectonice or a Compendium of the Art of Building. Giving a Brief Account of the Names, Natures, Qualities, Quantities and Rates of all the Materials belonging to the Erection of any Edifices. And what Quantity of each sort will be needful for the Building of any House, Great or Small. Whereby Estimates, Valuations and Contracts may be made between Builder and Workman without any great Damage to either,' &c. &c., by William Leyburn."

These were not the only Guides to the Orders and price books published during the late seventeenth and early eighteenth centuries, but probably these four were those widely used and having most influence with master tradesmen throughout the country.

Although Wren's Continental travels were confined to France, his archi-

---

[1] By B. Sprint, London.

tectural studies extended to Italian, Dutch, and Northern European examples. Through these studies, checked by actual examination of the works of Bernini, Mansart, Le Vau, Gobert, and Le Pautre, and by experience which he gained in course of practice, Wren obtained a thorough acquaintance with the principles of classic architecture and grounding in the grammar of design; indeed, a man endowed with his intellectual abilities was certain to set himself thoroughly to master any subject with which he engaged. In a sense, he was an amateur, and because he did not enter the practice of architecture through the customary channels he incurred the enmity of more orthodox surveyors. Such jealousy has always been shown by dull, conventional practitioners who fail to recognize ability, even when far transcending their own, and (like the religious fanatic who acknowledges but one path to heaven) would require genius to enter the profession through the same rut that they themselves have trodden.

Although Wren made himself familiar with the architecture of other climes, he never lost touch with the real problems of building in England. His designing was always sane and practical. Daily requirements were studied, climate was not forgotten. He never subordinated real requirements to the exigencies of the Orders. He showed himself master of the Orders, of proportion, of composition, and did not subordinate necessaries to these. Above all, he had that rare gift of great architects, the power to conceive and visualize a whole scheme in perspective, complete in its relation to its own setting or to other buildings. This enabled him to modify a design whilst work was in progress without that injury to its unity or coherence so often to be seen in buildings designed by less able men. Wren's skill in devising a setting for a building may be seen in the plan of the grounds at Hampton Court Palace: his ability in grouping and developing existing buildings in Greenwich Hospital (Figs. 183, 184), where he had to accept not only the Queen's house by Inigo Jones, but the partially built palace of Charles II. These he combined with new buildings into a noble group comparable with any palace in the world. It has been said that Wren had no successor, that he did not found a " school " in any sense of that elastic word. To some extent this is true. Whilst still associated with him, Hawksmoor and Vanbrugh were heading in another direction. It is in the works of lesser men— of men whose names are forgotten—that we must look for continuance of the Wren influence; in houses built for prosperous traders in country towns and for small squires in every parish. It is in these that we find the Wren influence lingering notwithstanding the vagaries of Time and Fashion.

We have seen how the new architecture produced the architects—men who had architectural education, who had travelled and made acquaintance at first hand with Continental buildings of the Renaissance, artists who made themselves fully acquainted with the building trades but who had not handled tools nor were in any sense tradesmen. Such architects were Inigo Jones, John Webb, Roger Pratt, and Christopher Wren. Skilled tradesmen worked for them to whom was delegated detailing which could not now be entrusted to mere work-men. On large works, contracts were given out to each trade, as is still the prac-tice in the Northern Counties and in Scotland; indeed, frequently the work belonging to a trade was divided between several contractors, but these con-tractors were themselves workmen; not mere employers of labour or men of business having organizing abilities like many modern contractors, who do not work with their own hands and may never have done any manual work. In the absence of a general contractor (as conducting most modern works) the architect had to regulate the activities of each trade; the importance of ability to do which was emphasized by Sir Roger Pratt in a passage already quoted.[1]

The architect provided designs, gave directions, examined accounts, and ap-proved prices. An assistant surveyor measured up work, bought all materials that did not necessitate absence from the job, and kept account of materials brought to the works. The clerk of works and paymaster kept account of materials received, paid for them and assisted the surveyor. Another clerk acted as timekeeper and assisted the clerk of works.

The architect's provision of detail designs was thorough. In writing of the designs for the library at Trinity College, Cambridge, Wren says:

> " I suppose you have good masons, however I would willingly take a farther paines to give all the mouldings in great, wee are scrupulous in small matters and you must pardon us, the Architects are as great pedants as Critics or Heralds. And therefore if you approve the designes, let the mason take his measures as much as is necessary for the present setting out of the worke and be pleased to transmit them to me again and I shall copy out partes of them at large, more proper for the use of the workmen and give you a carefull estimate of the charge, and return you again the originall designes, for in the handes of the workemen they will soon be soe defaced that they will not be able from them to pursue the worke to a conclusion."[2]

It appears also that whilst the architect continued to occupy the originating and directing position which he had attained in Inigo Jones' time, the master-tradesman-architect, though obscured, was not completely obliterated. He set himself to master books on the Orders and to acquaint himself with the principles of design and proportion. Probably the first tradesmen to rise to these new heights were men associated with Wren, in daily execution of works under him, as Thomas Strong, Nicholas Stone, Christopher Kempster, and Robert Grumbold.

The Grumbolds were a family of masons. Thomas, who built the east and south ranges of Clare College, Cambridge, 1638-42, in the Perpendicular manner, was paid 3s. (January 18, 1638-39) for " a draught " of the bridge, upon which also he worked. Robert Grumbold, his successor, directed the works of Trinity College Library, Cambridge, from 1676-82, working to Wren's designs and fre-quently journeying[3] to London to confer with him—there is no record of Wren's visiting the works. Grumbold (a local tradesman) appears to have been chosen and

[1] Page 104. [2] Wren Society, vol. v, p. 33. [3] *Ibid.*, pp. 32-44.

employed by the college authorities. His supervision, journeys to London, weekly wages and payments "by the great" are recorded in the contemporary accounts now in the college library.[1] Another mason—George Grumbold—also was employed.

Robert Grumbold also built part of the west range of Clare College buildings, 1662-76, in Perpendicular manner. The educative effect of his having worked at Trinity College Library under Wren may be seen in the elevation of the north range (hall, kitchen, combination room and library) at Clare, which Grumbold built 1683-93. A payment to him of £2 10s. for designing this and £1 weekly for survey and overseeing the works is recorded in 1682. Here he has designed in classic manner, and whilst he has adopted several features from Wren's designs for Trinity College Library, other details certainly are not by Wren; indeed, there is no reason to suppose that he was consulted. Grumbold's progress in classic designing is further exemplified in the river front of the Master of Clare's Lodge, 1705-7, which is an ambitious composition in the full classic manner and possessed of considerable merit.[2]

Wren's practice of furnishing designs, with or without detail drawings, for provincial buildings and leaving the execution of the works to others, frequently makes it difficult to apportion architectural credit, but enough emerges from scattered and imperfect records to satisfy us that, before the end of the seventeenth century, master tradesmen had gone far to qualify themselves in knowledge of classic architecture and in ability to design not only details but whole works. Wren himself recognizes the progress of such men, referring to them when, following the collapse of buildings at Hampton Court, 1689, he suggests taking

" affidavits of able men, not interested, Bricklayers, Carpenters and Masons that have left off their aprons and are without suspition of being influenced by him."[3]

When we study the second and third quarters of the eighteenth century we shall see how completely the master mason and master carpenter undertook the designing as well as the erection of buildings.

Wren's methods of working are interesting. Pipe Roll No. 1, 1689-91, contains the accounts for the building of Hampton Court Palace for two years, from which the names of superintending " officers " are drawn. Riding charges are allowed for:

Sir Christopher Wren, Knight	Surveyor
Wm. Talman Esq.	Comptroller
John Oliver	Master Mason
Matthew Banckes	,, Carpenter
Nicholas Hawksmoor	Surveyor's Clerk
John Deeplore	Comptroller's Clerk
Thomas Taylor	Paymaster
John Scarborough	Measuring Surveyor
Charles Browne	Clerke Assistant[4] &c. &c.

[1] Wren Society, vol. v, p. 38.
[2] The connection of Robert Grumbold with Cambridge buildings has been ably traced by Geoffrey Webb in *Country Life*, vol. lx, pp. 18-26 and 58-65.
[3] Wren Society, vol. iv, p. 72.   [4] Quoted in Wren Society, vol. iv, p. 22.

An undated letter, *c.* 1676, from Wren, addressed to Isaac Barrow, Master of Trinity College, Cambridge (with drawings for the proposed library, which included plans, elevations, sections, and details even down to the bookshelves), goes into minute descriptive detail. In addition to these Wren gives reasons for his choice where alternatives presented themselves. Of the elevation towards Nevile's Court he says:

> " I chose a double order rather than a single because a single order must either have been mutilated in its members, or have been very expensive, and if performed would not have agreed with the lownesse of the porches, which would have been too darke and the solids too grosse for the openings. I have given the appearance of arches as the order required fair and lofty; but I have layd the floor of the Library upon the impostes, which answer to the pillars in the Cloister, and the levels of the old floores, and have filled the Arches with relieves of stone, of which I have seen the effect abroad in good buildings and I assure you where porches are low with flat cielings is infinitely more gracefull than lowe arches would be, and is much more open and pleasant : nor need the mason feare the performance, because the Arch discharges the weight, and I shall direct him in a firme manner of executing the designe. By this contrivance the windowes of the Library rise high and give place for the deskes against the walls, and being high may be afforded to be large and being wide may have stone mullions and the glasse pointed; which after all inventions is the only durable way in our climate for a public building, where care must be had that snowe drive not in. I have given noe other Frontispiece to the middle than Statues, according to ancient example because in this case I can find any thing else impertinent, the Entrances being endwise, and the roofe not suiting it. This may be done, if you please, you may make the three middle arches with three quarter columnes, and the rest with pilasters of a third of their diameter, which will save some charge of stone, but it is best as it is designed."[1]

When advising the Bishop of Oxford upon the erection of Tom Tower on the gateway of Christ Church, Oxford, Wren shows his knowledge, not only of design, but of construction. In respect of the foundations of new work to supplement the old, he vigorously disputes the advice given the Bishop by his masons and does this in such detail and so convincingly as to induce the Bishop to undo work started and to begin again in Wren's way and to place the works under the control of Christopher Kempster, whom Wren recommended. The letters[2] show an intimacy with building problems, the fruit of extensive experience, beyond that of any " professional " architect of his time.

Wren was a fair draughtsman, whether the drawings were small-scale plans, elevations, sections, larger details, or the working out of structural problems such as were involved in adding new work to fortify old—as at Tom Tower. He used his assistants to set out ground plots and also to develop details, as when Grinling Gibbons filled in the decorative carving and mouldings on one-inch

[1] Wren Society, vol. v, p. 33.
[2] Given in full in *Wren's Tom Tower*, W. D. Caröe, Oxford, 1923, pp. 23-33.

scale details drawn in outline and supplied to him. For greater certainty, Wren also had models[1] made from his drawings.

Where contracts were made with each trade[2] the terms were set out minutely, reference being made to a drawing or a model. Where detail drawings were furnished they were described by Wren as " mouldings in great,"[3] but, in advising Ralph Bathurst, President of Trinity College, Oxford, regarding the chapel which Bathurst was building from designs not made by Wren, he says:

> " I believe your worke is too far advanced to admitt of any advice ; however, I have sent my thoughts which will be of use to the mason to form his mouldings. He will find two sorts of cornice ; he may use either. . . . A little deal box with a drawing in it is sent."

Probably the " mason " was Phips, a builder who was in charge of the building works and whom Bathurst had sent to wait upon Wren to show

> " a scheme of the new building. . . ."

Wages varied with the skill of the tradesmen. At Cambridge (1675-76)[4] a bricklayer, for working foundations, received 1s. 8d. per diem for wages only, his labourer 10d., but Robert Grumbold (who had charge of the works) received 21s. weekly.

At Hampton Court Palace (1691-94) the rates for " Wages and Entertainments " were: Masons 2s. 8d., Carpenters, Joiners, Bricklayers, Plasterers 2s. 6d. per diem, Labourers 1s. 8d. to 2s. per diem, Clerk of the Works 2s. 3d. per diem.[5]

Most of the work, however, was done by price or contract.

At this time the casement window—which had lingered so long in the form illustrated in Fig. 523, but latterly having frame, transom, and mullion of wood, as in Figs. 161, 525, built into the opening of stone or brickwork—was discarded for the sash window, hung with weights and pulleys, which it happened could be exactly proportioned to the window openings hitherto furnished with wooden or iron casements. The origin of the sash window is unknown. The word sash is a corruption of chassis,[6] and in its earliest application denoted a frame of wood as distinguished from a leaded light. Possibly this may be the application in early uses of the word, as the following:

In 1356 King John II of France, who was imprisoned in the Tower of London after being taken prisoner at the battle of Poitiers, paid

> " Denys de Lombart, de Londres, charpentier, pour la façon de 4 fenestres pour la chambre du Roy en la Tour de Londres. Cest assavoir ; pour le bois des 4 chassis, 3s. 2d."[7]

[1] Sir B. Gerbier, in his *Council and Advice to all Builders*, 1663, advises raising " wooden molds to the position the masonry is to occupy that the effect may properly be judged." He uses the terms Architect and Surveyor as synonyms.

[2] *e.g.*, Wren Society, vol. v, pp. 27-29.   [3] *Ibid.*, p. 33.

[4] *Ibid.*, pp. 36 and 39.   [5] *Ibid.*, vol. iv, p. 25.   [6] *New English Dictionary, cf.* Sash.

[7] *Accounts of John of France, whilst a prisoner in London*, preserved in Biblio. Nat., Paris, and printed in Douet d'Arcq, Comptes de l'Argenterie.

In 1393 Ripon Minster paid

> " In wages to two workmen (carpenters) making and fixing saches."[1]

In 1519 William Horman wrote:

> " I have many pretty wyndowes shette with leuys goynge up and downe."[2]

In 1699 Lister, in his *Journal of Paris*, tells how he was shown over a house at Montmartre by the owner, who

> " showed us his great Sash Windows ; how easily they might be lifted up and down, which contrivance he said he had out of England by a small model brought on purpose from thence there being nothing of this poise in windows in France before."[3]

In 1686-88 (Accounts of Windsor Castle) is the entry:

> " Sarah Wyatt for a Sash Window and Frame, with Weights, Lynes and Pulleys."[4]

In the Works Accounts, Whitehall Palace, November, 1685, Charles Hopson's charges for " Joyners " work done in the Vane Room include:

> " 1426 ft. of very strong shasses with their frames and brass pullies and Very Good lines to them, xxii pr. ft., £130 14s. 4d."[5]

The last two are the earliest *records* of sash windows hung with lines and pulleys, but the quantities made for Whitehall Palace imply that the sash was well established in 1685 and we may look for the discovery of still earlier records. It is probable that an earlier type was not hung in this manner (with lines, weights and pulleys), for in decayed houses of the early eighteenth century sash windows are still to be found which never had weights, but were supported when open by an iron quadrant pivoted on one corner so that another corner could be turned into a notch in the bead. In these windows the upper sash was fixed, only the lower one moving up and down. Such windows are referred to by Dr. Johnson as current in Scotland in the late eighteenth century. He says:

> " Their windows do not open upon hinges, but are pushed up and down in grooves, yet they are seldom accommodated with weights and pullies. He that would have the window open, must hold it with his hand, unless, what may be found amongst good contrivers, there be a nail which he may stick into a hole to keep it from falling."[6]

If we ignore occasional medieval windows made to be raised, we may conclude that the modern sash window, whether weighted or not, came into use during the second half of the seventeenth century. Its origin, at present, is unknown, but apparently it was not a French invention, and the suggestion that it was introduced into England from Holland lacks confirmation. Prior to the

[1] *Memorials of Ripon*, Surtees Society, vol. iii, p. 119.
[2] *Vulgaria*, p. 244.
[3] Lister, *Journey to Paris*, 8vo, 1669, p. 191.
[4] *Windsor Castle*, by W. H. St. John Hope, p. 329.
[5] Wren Society, vol. viii, p. 98.
[6] *Johnson's Works*, 1792, vol. viii, p. 231.

last half of the seventeenth century, casement windows were used in England. Unfortunately seventeenth-century and eighteenth-century draughtsmen seldom represented their window openings as furnished with frames, leaving them void, but occasionally frames and glazing are shown. A drawing of a house façade amongst the Wren drawings shows mullion and transom wooden frames, filled with lead lights, which would open as casements,[1] and such seventeenth-century drawings as show window frames are of this type. Once introduced, sash windows rapidly superseded casements, as in the Tudor buildings at Hampton Court Palace when these were altered to provide lodgings for the household of King William and Queen Mary in 1699. Probably what facilitated the alteration was the fact that the proportions of the window openings for the mullion and transom casement frames (2-1 to 2½-1) were admirably adapted for sashes either in equal halves or having a larger upper half that the meeting rails might not be on the eye line. Figs. 187, 525, of Rampyndene, Burwash, show the original type at first floor and the sashes introduced later at ground floor.

At Hampton Court Palace (Fig. 180) it may be noted that Wren varied the sizes of his glass squares to obtain effects of scale. The glass used here was slightly bevelled: some faintly tinted, mauve and pink shades.

The following entry recalls the use of oiled paper instead of glass in medieval times :

> " 5 ream Dutch Demy paper to make sashes before the glass was put up to preserve the lodgings £10: 0: 0."[2]

Occasionally we find records of the practice of filling in the spaces under floorboards between joists with cockleshells, to absorb sound vibrations. In Hampton Court Palace accounts, September, 1691, is the entry:

> " Labourers clearing the floors between the joysts and filling them with cockleshells."[3]

At Pepper Harrow, in 1777:

> " All the floors both on the principal story & attick to be fill'd between the joists with cockle Shells."[4]

In many English counties medieval houses were built of timber; where stone was scarce, most houses were of timber. In other districts where there was

---

[1] B.M. Soane Collection 5238, No. 66. Illustrated in Wren Society, vol. v, plate xxvii.
[2] Wren Society, *Hampton Court Accounts*, vol. iv, p. 49.
[3] Wren Society, vol. iv, p. 50.
[4] " Memorandums relating to the finishing of the House at Pepper Harrow," quoted by H. Avray Tipping in *Country Life*, vol. lviii, p. 1008.

I

stone, some houses were constructed of oak, probably because it was plentiful, and also because carpenters' labour may have been available. Such buildings had the spaces (panels) between the timber filled with plaster. In early work this plaster was applied on hazel sticks wedged between the timbers (Fig. 303), but later on laths, nailed to fillets. The plaster was composed of loam mixed with about half its bulk of reed, both leaf and stem of which were used. Such plaster was known as raddle and daub, wattle and daub or pug. It dried hard, was tough, and only crumbled when removed from its panel. Notwithstanding these good qualities, walls of timber and plaster were draughty and leaky, because the materials were shrunk by the sun and swelled in wet weather. Other panel fillings were of flints in mortar (Fig. 308) and brick nogging (Fig. 304). The seventeenth century was a great period of adapting and reconditioning houses. In the late sixteenth and early seventeenth centuries houses had floors put into the halls, and these were partitioned to provide separate chambers for which there was demand in place of promiscuous huddling of sexes in the hall. No doubt, at the same time, steps were taken to render walls weatherproof, but it is towards the end of the seventeenth century and in the eighteenth century that we find most examples of houses protected by devices to repel wind and wet. These expedients produced pleasing exteriors and improved by weathering, but perhaps the most interesting and attractive of all of them was pargeting. Before describing forms of this it may be well to try to clear away some confusion which exists regarding the nature of the art.

During the medieval period, plasterers are frequently called pargeters, but their work bears no resemblance to the decorative work to which the term pargeting has long been applied.

> " The sheriff of Dorset and Somerset is ordered to cause the tower of the castle of Corfe to be pargeted (perjactari) with mortar where needful, and to whitewash the whole of it externally."[1]

The pargeting has been thought to refer to filling fissures in the walls, but the original Latin suggests harling.

Pointing, in medieval language, meant the simulation of ashlar jointing, as in the illustrations from Trottescliffe and Colchester (Fig. 315 and Fig. 317).

The following dated quotations from references in the *New English Dictionary* (Oxford) show applications of the word pargeting and its variations :

> 1396. " Item pro carecta calcis pro parchetting vjs, viijd."

Evidently lime for plastering.

> 1565. " To parget or to roughcast."

Here the words are used synonymously.

> 1588. " INCRUSTATIO—A laying over, a pargetting . . . a roughcasting."

[1] *Liberate Roll*, 28, Hen. III, 1243-44.

Again roughcasting and pargeting are synonymous.

> 1519. "Some men wyll haue theyr wallys plastered, some pargetted . . . some roughe caste."

Here the terms are distinct, but there is no indication as to the distinction.

> 1538. "The playstrynge or pariettynge of a house."

Again synonymous.

> 1592–3. "BOTTOM : Some man or other must present wall : and let him have some plaster, or some loam, or some rough-cast about him, to signify wall. . . ." [1]

Although no reference is made to pargeting, the materials named (especially loam) are significant.

No early quotation refers to pargeting in its ornamental sense, other than as plaster upon which paintings are to be made, but in 1606 we have—

> "All the Parget carv'd and branched trim
> With Flowrs and Fruits and winged Cherubim." [2]

Contemporary descriptions, *temp*. Henry VIII, of the palace of Nonsuch, record the external panels of plaster, enriched with pictorial subjects in relief, but these were executed by Italian artists in stucco, and with the departure of these men the art ceased to be practised in England.

Judging by remaining examples and by the absence of any which date from the sixteenth and early seventeenth centuries, we may infer that pargeting in the full sense of the term was then practised little and that the many existing examples dating from the third quarter of the seventeenth century indicate that then the art suddenly became fashionable.

It must be remembered that all this time there existed skilled workmen who produced plaster ceilings and plaster overmantels, so that there was no lack of talent when the call came for pargeting. One strange fact is that the late seventeenth-century work burst forth like Minerva, fully equipped, and, further, that the richest work is found at this time, which suggests its having been introduced from the Low Countries after the Restoration.

The materials used for pargeting vary with each county, but loam, lime, and some binding material were the usual constituents. An essential factor was preparation long before use, which, with thorough mixing, may account for the durability of the work.

The illustrations may be divided into four groups:

(*a*) Decorative, floral or pictorial subjects in high relief, as at Ipswich (Fig. 309), Earls Colne (Fig. 311), Newport (Fig. 310), Clare (Fig. 312). It is significant that all these examples belong to the last quarter of the seventeenth century and that they are in East Anglia.

---

[1] *A Midsummer Night's Dream*, Act iii, Sc. 1, 69.   [2] Sylvester, *Du Bartas* II, iv, ii; *Magnificence*, 1162.

(*b*) Combed work, usually in panels, having a slight border. In these the pattern is scratched or impressed upon the final coat of plaster. The undercoat is exposed near a corner of the scale pattern from Newport (Fig. 313). There is considerable variety of these patterns; the scale pattern from Newport being one most in favour. Herringbone and zigzag patterns, one of which is illustrated from Thaxted (Fig. 316), are also widely distributed. This shows, also, a formal panel treatment, with which whole fronts of houses were covered as at Sawbridgeworth (Fig. 318).

(*c*) Sunk patterns, formed with templates of wood, which were fixed to the penultimate coat of plaster and only removed when the final coat had been applied. This treatment was capable of infinite variation, limited only by the number of patterns available or capable of being devised. Two examples are shown, from Mereworth and Sawbridgeworth (Figs. 314 and 318).

(*d*) Imitation of masonry (possibly the " pointing " of the medieval period). The examples show application to two kinds of wall: at Colchester (Fig. 317) it is upon a timber and plaster front, but at Trotterscliffe (Fig. 315) on Elizabethan brickwork.

The development from the pargeting of the house front at Sawbridgeworth (Fig. 318) to that roughcasting[1] and stuccoing which were so prevalent in the late eighteenth and early nineteenth centuries is obvious, and differed chiefly in the composition of the material. The brothers Adam popularized stuccoed walls, Nash made it universal, but to his part allusion is made on page 157.

[1] 1797, " Our cottage is now in the act of being roughcast."—Mme. D'Arblay, *Letters*, 27.7.1797.

CHAPTER IX

THE EIGHTEENTH CENTURY

GEORGE I, 1714-27; GEORGE II, 1727-60

PALLADIAN AND GEORGIAN

THE BEGINNING of the eighteenth century synchronized with an architectural impulse which not only produced palaces built for peers and men of fortune, but materially influenced the character and details of multitudes of smaller houses.

Although not dead, the Gothic vernacular was dying. It persisted in smaller domestic buildings in the provinces, but, gradually, was being transformed by the addition of classic details. It died hard, and even in the twentieth century its influence may be traced, as in the productions of local craftsmen in the Cotswold district and in adjacent stone counties. During the first half of the eighteenth century, though classic architecture prevailed, there were two distinct types: one the Italian mansions of the great, the other a new vernacular of the same character as works by May and Wren, but continually modified by the architecture of the great houses which were being built concurrently.

These may be likened to two streams flowing in the same direction, the larger of which frequently overflowed into and tinged the waters of the smaller, sometimes to such an extent as momentarily to confuse the two, although on the whole they can be distinguished clearly. Naturally, architects specialized as navigators of one stream or the other, but at least one instance will be illustrated of an eminent architect designing a mansion in the grand manner and a country house of moderate dimensions and simple homely character.

A singular feature of the late seventeenth century was the predominance of architects who began as amateurs and only devoted themselves to architecture after they had achieved distinction in other and unallied vocations.

Sir John Denham was a poet who was appointed Surveyor-General of Works in 1660, but Webb's memorial of protest to the king shows this was purely a political appointment:

> "Though Mr. Denham may, as most gentry, have some understanding of the theory of architecture, he can have none in practice, but must employ another, whereas he (Webb) has spent thirty years at it, and worked for most of the nobility."[1]

---

[1] Quoted by E. Beresford Chancellor in *The Lives of British Architects*, London, 1909-11, p. 98.

Sir Roger Pratt was a young man of fashion who varied the ordinary occupations of his position by extensive travel.

Henry Bell, of King's Lynn, was an engraver who designed admirable buildings in his own county of Norfolk.

Sir Christopher Wren, an astronomer and mathematician, did not take up the practice of architecture until he was over thirty years of age.

Sir John Vanbrugh—soldier, dramatist, and herald—embarked upon architecture at the age of thirty-six.

Others, like John Evelyn, author of *The Whole Body of Ancient and Modern Architecture*, 1680, who did not practise architecture, were well informed, had travelled abroad, and exercised their influence as architectural critics as well as in all matters pertaining to the fine arts.

Of the purely professional architects, Nicholas Hawksmoor, pupil and assistant of Wren, showed ability.

The eighteenth century, which has been described as the era of Power, Prestige, and Prosperity, was the heyday of the aristocracy and gentry who recruited, and whose ranks were recruited from, the prosperous commercial community. Trade expansion at home and overseas provided ample funds for patrons of letters, painting, and architecture, which to some proved even more absorbing and interesting than politics, agriculture, or sport. The Grand Tour (a term applied to describe a tour of the principal cities and places of interest on the Continent) was regarded as an essential part of the education of every young man of position and fortune. The trip might extend over a few months or even several years, and afforded opportunities for the study of architecture and for the acquisition of works of art, the possession of which inspired the planning and erection of buildings in which to display them. The rivalry in palace building and the facility with which imposing elevations could be designed by acquaintance with rules for drawing the Orders, and the observance of proportions as published by various authors, resulted in every man being his own architect; or, if anyone should be so dull and incapable as to be unable to master these rudiments, he certainly would have some friend willing and competent to act for him. Such professors of the art did not need to concern themselves with the details of design nor with technicalities of the trades involved —there were numerous surveyors and obsequious professionals willing to do the work and forego the credit. The fact that the latter had seldom travelled and seen buildings by famous foreign architects, and, further, that (at first) the number of good examples built in England was limited, gave a distinct advantage to men of education and ability who had spent considerable time in studying abroad. This, then, was the opportunity of the amateur who could afford to travel, for travel was essential to the acquisition of first-hand knowledge. The majority of these amateurs were impostors, possessed only of a superficial knowledge of the art, and passing off as their own the works of their hirelings; but others were men of different calibre, who entered upon what they undertook seriously and who were determined to master the art they were to profess down to the minutest details. Such a man was Sir Roger Pratt, whose notebooks already have been quoted, showing him to have been fully acquainted with details of all the building trades. Sir Christopher Wren, also, regarded nothing as too small or unimportant for personal investigation. This we notice frequently in his letters, which show the pains he took to inform himself, so that he was able to correct the established practices of tradesmen and demonstrate their errors to third parties.[1]

Sir John Vanbrugh (1664-1726) is, perhaps, the most notable converted amateur of his period. As a soldier, dramatist, and man of fashion, he had attained a high reputation before he appears to have directed his attention to architecture. Except for some small opportunity for the observation of architecture in France, he seems to have plunged into extensive practical work at the age of thirty-six, when the immense structure of Castle Howard was begun. In 1702 he was appointed to the official position of Comptroller of Works, and about the same time became a member of the Board of Directors of Greenwich Hospital, the actual conduct of which works he seems to have taken over from Wren. The minutes of the Board record the labour he expended in revising accounts and otherwise performing the duties of architect. His greatest ability was in his imaginative handling of masses and the production of picturesque effects in which, doubtless, his experience of stage scenery assisted him. His works were on so large a scale as often to be clumsy and detrimental to the proportions of his interiors and to their suitability for practical occupation as dwelling-rooms. However, he learned by experience, and his later works, though no less stately and original, are more practical and restrained than his earlier essays. The ponderous and unpractical nature of some of his most important houses did not escape the criticism of his contemporaries, providing them with an easy butt. Notwithstanding these, he earned the commendation of so distinguished a man as Sir Joshua Reynolds, and was employed to design and build many houses of the first importance. That Vanbrugh was not in agreement with the criticisms of his vast interiors is apparent in a letter which he wrote to Taylor, the official at the Treasury who paid out moneys for Blenheim. The letter is dated October, 1713, and upon this point he says:

> " I am much pleased here[2] (amongst other things) to find Lord Carlisle so thoroughly convinced of the Conveniencys of his new house now he has had a years tryall of it : And I am the more pleas'd with it, because I have now a proof, that the Dutchess of Marlborough must find the same conveniency in Blenheim, if ever She comes to try it (as I still believe she will in spite of all these black Clouds). For my Lord Carlisle was pretty much under the same Apprehensions with her, about long Passages, High Rooms &c. But he finds what I told him to be true. That those Passages wou'd be so far from gathering &

---

[1] Some of these have been quoted in the section of this History devoted to Sir Christopher Wren, pp. 108-119.   [2] At Castle Howard.

drawing wind as he feared, that a Candle wou'd not flare in them of this he has lately had the proof, by bitter stormy nights in which not one Candle wanted to be put into a Lanthorn, not even in the Hall, which is as high (tho not indeed so big) as that at Blenheim. He likewise finds that all his Rooms, with moderate fires Are Ovens, And that this Great House, do's not require above One pound of wax, and two of Tallow Candles a Night to light it, more than his house at London did Nor in Short, is he at any expence more whatsoever than he was in the Remnant of an Old house, but three housemaids and one Man, to keep the whole house and Offices in perfect cleanliness, which is done to such a degree, *that the Kitchen*, and all the Offices and Passages under the Principall floor are as dry as the Drawing room : And yet there is a great deal of Company, and *very good housekeeping*. So that upon the whole (except the keeping of the New Gardens) the expence of living in this Great fine house do's not amount to above a hundred pounds a year, more than was spent in the *Old one*. If you think the knowledge of this, may be of any satisfaction to my Lady Marlborough, pray tell her what you hear."[1]

At the date when this letter was written, however, the west wing of Castle Howard (which included the chapel) had not been built.

Possessed of ability and sparing no pains he, who began as an amateur, qualified by application and experience to a high position amongst serious architects. Important examples of his work are Castle Howard, Yorkshire, 1702-14, Fig. 203; Blenheim Palace, Oxfordshire, 1706-24, Figs. 205, 206, 207, 379; and Seaton Delaval, Northumberland, 1721, Figs. 217, 218. Not only was he the architect of these and many other buildings, but he influenced the designs of lesser men in every county. Blenheim appears to have been Vanbrugh's favourite work, as it was his largest, yet he was not allowed to supervise its finishing. Although Parliament approved its being built, funds were not provided. The Treasury defaulted, the queen herself gave large sums during her lifetime, but debts were piled up as quickly as the buildings. Ultimately, Vanbrugh's quarrels with the Duchess of Marlborough culminated in a permanent rupture, and, when Parliament voted £22,000 a year to her, Vanbrugh ungallantly said that:

" Parliament has allowed the Duchess £10,000 a year to spoil Blenheim and £12,000 a year to keep herself clean and to go to law."

The Duchess's retort is not recorded, but after Vanbrugh's death, her protégé, the Rev. Abel Evans, suggested as his epitaph the couplet:

" Lie heavy on him earth, for he
Laid many a heavy load on thee."

Amongst dilettanti architects, Richard Boyle, Earl of Burlington and Cork (1695-1753), was the most eminent. As a patron of the art, he had no equal either in attainments, devotion, or munificence. His real claims to be the author of designs are obscured by the fulsome flatteries of his admirers and dependents, so that it is impossible to say how far works attributed to him were his own. It is certain that he employed Campbell, Leoni, and Kent. Leoni he brought to

[1] Quoted by H. Avray Tipping in *Country Life*, lxi, p. 956.

England; Kent he befriended and even lodged in his own house. An instance of conflicting testimony is the statement by Walpole that the design of Burlington House was by Lord Burlington, whereas Colen Campbell claims the authorship for himself. It seems certain that Lord Burlington was the great arbiter of architectural taste, that he had some knowledge of draughtsmanship and that he concerned himself chiefly with the appearance of the exterior of a building, to which he sacrificed internal convenience. An instance of this arose in connection with the house he designed for General Wade (Fig. 233), to whose complaint Lord Chesterfield retorted in the callous fashion recorded in the caption. Burlington House, c. 1716, was praised by Gay in the words,

"Beauty within; without proportion reigns";

but Lord Hervey, more wittily, if spitefully, described it as:

"Possessed of one great hall of state
Without a room to sleep or eat."

It has been pointed out that Burlington's designs (or those claimed for him) lack originality; indeed, that they are mostly adaptations or copies of Italian buildings, as was Mereworth Castle (Figs. 221-224) by Colen Campbell. Another adaptation of the same original at Chiswick, which was attributed to Burlington, is, in fact, less successful. Students differ as to Lord Burlington's qualifications to be regarded seriously as an architect. One authority[1] maintains that he was merely a man of taste and travel who influenced and made suggestions to those who were the actual designers, and supports this view by weighty observations upon the complexity of the knowledge necessary for a competent architect and the slight acquaintance with design which will enable an amateur to make a show of knowledge. Others (arguing from the distinction which Lord Burlington enjoyed amongst his contemporaries, and noting that, in an age when criticism was unsparing, no cynic is recorded as doubting his abilities or his claims to authorship) regard his claims more seriously, and it is possible that records may yet come to light which will support this view. Meantime, it is significant that no records are known which show that he had any practical knowledge of the problems of building or of the trades concerned—as had Pratt, Wren, and Vanbrugh. What has been said above regarding Lord Burlington covers, in substance, the claims of other amateurs (Lord Pembroke, Dean Aldrich, etc.), amongst whom he was the most distinguished exemplar.

The difference between Wren and the Palladian school (which regarded Palladio as its master and Inigo Jones as his prophet) was the difference between a fertile, original mind, fully informed, and minds devoid of creative powers, often ignorant, which were content to adapt and copy. Wren absorbed everything and produced new creations. The Palladians designed so slavishly to

[1] *A History of Renaissance Architecture in England*, R. E. Blomfield, vol. ii, p. 223 *et seq.*

rules and drew so freely upon the works of Palladio and other Italian architects, as to stifle any germs of originality they might have possessed. Imitation and copying are seeds of an insidious disease, which atrophies the faculties and which have had as devastating effects upon architecture as they have produced upon any other art or vocation.

Colen Campbell was a Scotsman who came to England early in the eighteenth century and became one of Lord Burlington's protégés. His early history is unknown. He died in 1729. For some time he was Surveyor of Works at Greenwich, but was ousted by Thomas Ripley. This was an age of intrigues, and Campbell himself had taken an active part in that by which Wren had lost the same appointment. Campbell produced the important record of architecture, *Vitruvius Britannicus*, the three volumes for which he was responsible appearing 1715-25. The attributions of buildings to authors in this work are unreliable, and the whole is poisoned by the fulsome flattery Campbell lavished upon patrons. Although the work professes to be representative of the best architecture, the selections are partial. Wren is only represented by two plates of St. Paul's Cathedral and one of the steeple of Bow Church. His work at Greenwich is not mentioned; indeed, the only person referred to in connection with this palace, with which so many architects were concerned, is the decorative painter, Sir James Thornhill. Of Marlborough House, always attributed to Sir Christopher Wren, Campbell says that it was " invented by Christopher Wren, Esquire, 1709." Wren was knighted in 1674, and both " Sir Christopher Wren " and " Mr. Christopher Wren " are mentioned in the Introduction, vol. i, page 2, amongst other architects. As Campbell mentions (page 6) that the design of Marlborough House, which he illustrates, was " given by Mr. Wren," the implication is that the son, Christopher, was an architect also, but there is no other evidence to this effect, whereas on 16th May, 1709, the Revd. Ralph Bridges wrote to Sir William Turnbull:

> " Your friend Sir Chr. Wren is busy building the Duke of Marlborough another new house, to which one half of the Queen's Garden at St. James' are to be laid." [1]

Lord Burlington employed Campbell, and Campbell claims the credit for having designed the greater part of Burlington House. He was also the designer of Houghton Hall, Norfolk, a design altered and completed by Ripley. Another important building by Campbell was Wanstead Hall, Essex, now destroyed, but perhaps that of which he himself was most proud was Mereworth Castle in Kent (Figs. 221-224). This was, admittedly, a copy of a building at Vicenza by Andrea Palladio; and of Mereworth Campbell says:

> " I shall not pretend to say, That I have made any improvements in this Plan from that of Palladio for *Signor Almerico*."

[1] Wren Society, vii, p. 226.

And he continues :

"Here nothing was wanting for Strength, Conveniency or Ornament."[1]

The plans and photographs of this house are worthy of study because they represent a current idea of perfection in house design. To us their unsuitability to English requirements is obvious, yet so obsessed were the Palladians by Italian design as to be incapable of exercising ordinary discrimination and intelligence.

Giacomo Leoni (c. 1686-1746), a Venetian, was brought to England by Lord Burlington to assist in the production of an edition of *The Architecture of A. Palladio*, 1715, for the drawings in which Leoni was responsible. In addition to the assistance he rendered Lord Burlington, he designed several important buildings, including Moor Park, Herts, 1720 (Figs. 219-220); the south front of Lyme Hall, Cheshire, 1726-32, a very indifferent composition; Bold Hall, Warrington, Lancs, 1730; Moulsham Park, Essex; Clandon Park, Surrey; and Argyll House, Chelsea, 1723 (Fig. 225). Probably, also, he designed the colonnade of Burlington House.

That Leoni should have designed buildings of great scale like Moor Park, in the Italian manner, is natural; that he should have designed Argyll House (Figs. 225-6) is surprising, for although the entrance doorway, the window over it, and the entablatures over the first-floor windows all have something of the grand manner (the doorway particularly), the general air, both of exterior and interior, is domestic and homely, without any more pretensions to grandeur than the house, No. 69, The Close, Salisbury (Fig. 216), and certainly less than the house at Burford (Fig. 210). In treatment of small houses, however, we find that the architects of the first half of the eighteenth century showed more discretion than others did later who introduced columns and porticoes out of proportion and out of keeping with the importance of the houses upon which they were imposed.

James Gibbs, an Aberdonian (1682-1754), is best known as the architect of the churches of St. Martin's-in-the-Fields, 1721-26, and St. Mary-le-Strand, 1714-17, the Fellows' buildings, King's College, Cambridge, 1724, and of the Radcliffe Library, Oxford, 1737-47. He studied in Italy, where he was sent by his patron, the Earl of Mar. He was architect of a number of houses, amongst which was the Palladian villa built for another patron, the Duke of Argyll, at Sudbrooke Park, Richmond, Surrey, c. 1726 (Figs. 229, 231). In the dedication of his *Book of Architecture* (published 1728) to the Duke of Argyll and Greenwich Gibbs acknowledges the

"early encouragement received from Your Grace in my Profession on my Return from *Italy*."

The Introduction to this volume not only shows the object the author had in view in preparing it as a guide to amateurs (he also made a profit of £1,900), but reflects certain phases of the practice of architecture at this time to which

[1] *Vitruvius Britannicus*, iii, p. 8.

reference already has been made. Having referred to " Persons of Distinction " by whose direction the work was undertaken, he goes on to say:

> " They were of opinion that such a Work as this would be of use to such Gentlemen as might be concerned in building, especially in the remote parts of the Country, where little or no assistance for Design can be procured. Such may here be furnished with Draughts of useful and convenient Buildings and proper Ornaments which may be executed by any Workman who understands Lines, either as here Design'd, or with some Alteration, which may be easily made by a person of Judgment; without which a variation in Draughts, once well digested, frequently proves a Detriment to the Building, as well as a disparagement to the person that gives them. I mention this to caution Gentlemen from suffering any material change to be made in their Designs, by the Forwardness of unskilful Workmen, or the caprice of ignorant, assuming Pretenders.
>
> Some, for want of better helps, have unfortunately put into the hands of common workmen, the management of Buildings of considerable expense; which, when finished, they have had the mortification to find condemned by persons of Tast, to that degree that sometimes they have been pulled down, at least alter'd at a greater charge than would have procur'd better advice from an able Artist, or if they have stood, they have remained lasting Monuments of the Ignorance or Parsimoniousness of the Owners, or (it may be) of a wrong-judged Profuseness.
>
> What heaps of Stone, or even Marble, are daily seen in Monuments, Chimneys, and other Ornamental pieces of Architecture, without the least Symmetry or Order ? When the same or fewer Materials under the conduct of a skilful Surveyor, would, in less room, and with much less charge, have been equally (if not more) useful, and by Justness of Proportion have had a more grand Appearance and consequently have better answered the Intention of the Expense. For it is not the Bulk of a Fabrick, the Richness and Quantity of the Materials, the Multiplicity of Lines, nor the Gaudiness of the Finishing, that give the Grace or Beauty and Grandeur to a Building, but the Proportion of the Parts to one another and to the Whole, whether entirely plain, or enriched with a few Ornaments properly disposed.

Gibbs's remarks upon the essentials of good architecture are sound and to the point; whilst, incidentally, he gives us vivid pictures of events which actually had taken place.

Gibbs was one of the most able architects who succeeded Wren, of whom, indeed, he confesses he was a protégé.

William Kent (1684-1748) was a Yorkshireman, apprenticed to a coach painter, from whom he ran away to London, where he earned a living by painting portraits and there attracted the attention of a patron who enabled him to study in Italy. Here he secured further patrons, including Lord Burlington, to whom he became closely attached and in whose house he lived and worked for nearly thirty years, dying there and being buried in the Burlington vault at Chiswick.

Kent's painting, whether of portraits, many of which he produced, or of wall decoration, was inferior; but his designs for furniture and decoration are now recognized as reaching a high standard. He was also a pioneer in introducing into England a bad style of scenic gardening, quite unrelated to the house to which it should have been an harmonious setting.

In addition to the assistance he rendered Lord Burlington in architectural designing (which must have been considerable, for his patron cannot be supposed to have lodged him in his own house so many years from motives of esteem alone), he was architect of a number of town and country houses. His most important buildings are the Horse Guards, Whitehall (*c.* 1742), an admirable composition, and Holkham Hall, Norfolk 1734-61 (Figs. 238, 239, 240), where his pupil, Matthew Brettingham, 1699-1769 (once a bricklayer's apprentice in Norwich, and afterwards a successful architect), became clerk of the works, and, after Kent's death, superintended the completion of the building. It is not necessary here to enumerate all the architects who meddled with what was substantially Kent's design. For the design of Holkham, Brettingham took the whole credit in a volume entitled *Plans, Elevations and Sections of Holkham in Norfolk*, which he published in 1761, and in which no mention of Kent is made.

The plan of Holkham (Fig. 240) consists of a large central block and four smaller blocks, symmetrically disposed and connected with the centre by links. The centre block contains the State apartments and reception rooms, designed to receive the collection of works of art brought by the owner from Italy. The subsidiary blocks are assigned to Library, Visitors, Chapel, and Kitchen. The centres of the kitchen and the dining-room are over 200 feet apart, and communication between the two entails crossing the main block.

Holkham is severe and bare to the uninitiated eye (barer looking than it would appear had not the original glazing bars of the windows been replaced by large sheets of plate-glass), but it has fine architectural qualities. The grouping of masses and the proportions are excellent. The architect has relied upon such fundamental factors for his effects; not upon adventitious ornament. The formal setting, fountains (Fig. 241), etc., are in harmony with the house. The whole covers an immense area, and the fine effect may be seen in the illustration (Fig. 238).

Amongst other London architects of this period, mention should be made of: Thomas Archer (*c.* 1680-1743), a pupil of Vanbrugh, who designed Heythrop Hall, Oxfordshire, 1705; Roehampton House, Surrey, 1712; and several churches, the most famous of which are St. Philip's, Birmingham, which has an exceptionally fine tower, and St. John's, Smith Square, Westminster, 1714-28.*

Thomas Ripley, a Yorkshireman, was a carpenter who, in 1721, succeeded Grinling Gibbons as chief carpenter of H.M. Works, and in 1727 became Comptroller-General. He was architect of the Admiralty Buildings, Whitehall, 1724-26, and amongst houses of which he was architect are Houghton Hall, Norfolk, 1722-25, a design by Colen Campbell, in which Ripley substituted domes for pitched roofs on the corner pavilions, and made other alterations of a minor nature. He succeeded Campbell as Surveyor of Greenwich Hospital, part of which he built. Ripley died in 1758.

Henry Flitcroft (1697-1769), who, also, was a carpenter, succeeded Ripley

* See also Fig. 192.

as Comptroller of Works in 1758, having followed Kent as Master Mason in 1748. He made the drawings for all the plates in *The Designs of Inigo Jones*, edited by W. Kent, 1727. He was a protégé of Lord Burlington and a man of some ability, who designed Woburn Abbey for the Duke of Bedford, *c.* 1740, which, afterwards, was considerably altered by Henry Holland.

John Vardy was an assistant of Kent, whose design for the Horse Guards he completed. He was the architect of Spencer House, London, 1762, a distinguished piece of work. He died in 1765.

Isaac Ware (d. 1766) was of humble origin. The story is that he was a sickly boy, apprenticed to a chimney sweep—at a time when such boys had to climb up the flues, many of which were ample, but in some of which a wretched child might get wedged. He had a passion for drawing, and one day, whilst indulging in this by drawing the elevation of the Banqueting House in Whitehall upon the stones of its rusticated ground storey, a gentleman who was passing was struck by his ability, questioned him, bought him off the remainder of his term of apprenticeship, educated him, sent him to Italy and enabled him to become an architect. The patron is reputed to have been Lord Burlington, but this is mere surmise. From the year 1728 and onwards Ware received various official appointments and was concerned in the production of numerous books on architecture, of which *A Complete Body of Architecture*, 1756, was the most important. In the preface to this large folio he justifies its publication by stating that—

> " We propose in this undertaking to collect all that is useful in the works of others, at whatsoever time they may have been written, or in whatsoever language ; and to add the several discoveries and improvements made since that time by the genius of others, or by our own industry. By this means we propose to make our work serve as a library on this subject to the gentleman and the builder ; supplying the place of other books."

He points out that other writers have been so carried away by ideas of grandeur as to have ignored utility, saying:

> " Architecture has been celebrated as a noble science by many who have never regarded its benefits in common life ; we have endeavoured to join these several parts of the subject, nor shall we fear to say that the art of building cannot be more grand than it is useful ; nor its dignity a greater praise than its convenience. From the neglect of this consideration, those who have written to inform others of its excellence, have been too much captivated by its pomp, and have bestowed in a manner all their labour there, leaving the more serviceable part neglected.
>
> This is the character of many of the celebrated books of architecture; and 'tis this has swelled such performances to an expense too great for persons to whom they would be most useful ; while, on the other hand, those of small price are, in general, of less value : most of them indeed useless.
>
> Upon these considerations, we have been induced to undertake the present extensive work: the purpose of which is to instruct rather than to amuse; in which nothing will be omitted that is elegant or great ; but the principal regard will be shown to what is necessary and useful."

As an indictment of fashionable architecture and an exposition of sound principles, this extract from Ware's preface could scarcely be surpassed.

In a later passage he shows independence of thought and sound common sense, which distinguish him from the academism of the Palladians. In a chapter on " Retrenching Errors " he condemns the custom amongst English architects—

> " to transfer the buildings of Italy right or wrong, suited or unsuited to the purpose, into England ; and this, if done exactly, the builder has been taught to consider as merit in his profession." [1]

After further development of this theme he advises that—

> " In studying a design of Palladio's, which we recommend to the young architect as his frequent practice, let him think, as well as measure. Let him consider the general design and purpose of the building, and then examine freely how far, according to his own judgment, the purpose will be answered by that structure. He will thus establish in himself a custom of judging by the whole as well as by parts ; and he will find new beauties in the structure considered in this light.
>
> He will improve his knowledge and correct his taste by such contemplation ; for he will find how greatly the designer thought, and how judiciously he has done many things ; which, but for such an examination, would have passed in his mind unnoticed; or at best not understood.
>
> Possibly, when he has thus made himself a master of the author or designer's idea, he will see wherein it might have been improved. Now that he understands the work, he will have a right to judge thus ; and what would have been absurdity in one who knew not the science, or presumption in such as had not enough considered the building, will be in him the candid and free use of that knowledge he has attained in the art.
>
> . . . Let him commit to paper his thoughts on these subjects ; not in words only, but in lines and figures. He will be able to reconsider them at leisure ; and thence adopting or condemning his first thought, he will either way improve his judgment, and probably introduce new excellences in his practice." [2]

Our most modern professors could not give better advice.

Ware enters into each stage of building construction. Beginning with terms and materials, he passes to the consideration of situation, foundations and drainage, the carcass of the house, ornamental parts, including the use of the Orders, proportions and design, with all the minutiæ of details and decoration. His comprehensiveness is tedious; indeed, he is even more long-winded than his contemporaries, but there are many enlightening passages, which show us the methods of working in vogue, most of which are applicable to building at the present day. Ware's book, and others like it, brought knowledge of architecture into remote counties, where they formed tastes, and inculcated sound principles of design and building.

Batty Langley (1696-1751) was the author of upwards of twenty works of varying merit. As an " architect and surveyor " he had no reputation amongst his contemporaries, by whom he was ridiculed, and as a designer of buildings he

---

[1] *A Complete Body of Architecture*, by Isaac Ware, London, 1756, p. 694. [2] *Ibid.*, p. 695.

seems to have been so incompetent as to have brought his books into the same disrepute as his ventures into practical architecture.   Elmes said that—

" he formed a school of excellent workmen, although his taste as an architect was deservedly derided."[1]

Blomfield mentions Langley's name in a footnote as a

" voluminous writer . . . none of whose works are of sufficient value to warrant a detailed account."[2]

Another historian[3] does him greater justice in respect of the school which he opened, and of his writings.   He tells how Langley was the son of a gardener, and followed that trade in his youth, and that four of his books relate to gardening and cognate pursuits.   His *Gothic Architecture Restored and Improved by Rules and Proportions* had some vogue, but was ridiculed by competent persons, and Walpole (in *Anecdotes of Painting*) remarked that—

" all Langley's books achieved has been to teach carpenters to massacre that venerable species "—

Gothic Architecture.   Later, his name became a byword and " Batty Langley Gothic " a term of architectural opprobrium.   About 1740, Langley set up a school of architecture in Soho, where his brother Thomas, an engraver, assisted him in teaching drawing.   Elmes states that all his pupils were carpenters, and that many skilful artisans were turned out of Langley's Academy.   He also practised as a surveyor and valuer of timber.

It is during the present century that the value of Langley's books has been recognized.   Of these the following may be mentioned:

A Sure Guide to Builders.   1726, 1729.

The Young Builder's Rudiments.   1730-36.

The Builder's Compleat Assistant.   1738.   4th ed. after 1788.

The City and Country Builder's and Workman's Treasury of Designs.   1740, 1741, 1750, 1756.

The Builder's Jewel.   1741.   11th ed. 1787.

The London Prices of Bricklayers' Materials and Works.   1747, 1748, 1749, 1750. 2nd ed. 1818.

Although the matter in one book was often repeated in another, the number of editions sold, and the long period during which these works remained standard textbooks, are testimonies to their value and importance.   *A Sure Guide to Builders* comprised geometry applied to architectural drawing; proportions of the Orders, which included comparative drawings showing the proportions of Vitruvius, Palladio, Scamozzi, Vignola, Serlio, Perrault, Bosse, and Angelo; a summary of Acts of Parliament relating to building; and forty plates of designs

[1] *Dictionary of Architecture*, vol. iii, " L," p. 18; *cf.* Langley.
[2] *A History of Renaissance Architecture in England*, R. E. Blomfield, 1897, vol. ii, p. 316.
[3] E. Beresford Chancellor in *Lives of the British Architects*, 1909 and 1911, pp. 231-3.

for doors, windows and other details, evidently drawn from many sources and of varying merit. *The Young Builder's Rudiments* and *The Builder's Jewel* consisted chiefly of architectural geometry, the drawing of the Orders and (in the latter) some details of mouldings, and of roof trusses. *The Builder's Compleat Assistant* gave instruction in arithmetic, geometry, architecture (which included proportioning the Orders and practical instruction in building, surveying, etc.), mechanics, and hydrostatics. *The Builder's and Workman's Treasury of Designs* displayed the drawing of the details of the Orders " at large " and included plates showing over four hundred details from ceilings to pavements—including chimneypieces and bookcases, some of which are ridiculous, but many of which illustrate forms current at the time.

Like other writers of his period, Langley does not spare rival authors. In the Introduction to *A Sure Guide to Builders* he says:

> " The Great Want of Architectonical Principles has caused many good-natur'd Workmen, such as Halfpenny,[1] Hoar &c. to communicate what little they knew for the Good of their Fellow-Workmen, in as good a manner as they were capable ; but being without Demonstration, they have left Workmen in the dark, and all that they have done, is, therefore, of very little Service ; and the *Builder's Dictionary* (the most surprising, undigested Mess of Medley that yet was ever put together), consists of nothing more than Hear-says, Reports of God knows who, and what, without any real Matters of Fact that either Workman or Master can depend upon.

Batty Langley's works were the most widely used architectural textbooks in the eighteenth century. From them provincial architects, master carpenters and masons, obtained that knowledge of classic design which enabled them to produce the multitude of small and medium-sized houses by which most of our country towns are enriched. Their plans were simple and practical; their rooms were designed for use rather than for show; they were built of local materials and their elevations were conceived in the spirit of the house of Wren's period, modified by elements inspired by the Palladians, but avoiding their extravagances. At first these houses had hipped roofs as those in Figs. 190, 197, but ultimately these were generally superseded by roofs concealed behind parapets (Figs. 213, 216); indeed, this change in fashion was expressed in Walpole's contemptuous reference to houses roofed in the former manner as having " cottage roofs." In considering the relative merits of English house design of different periods, these earlier Georgian houses (Figs. 213, 216, 225) and the later Tudor types (Figs. 104, 127, 132) will be found nearly approximating to modern requirements. Each has its advantages and, equally, its shortcomings. Each is a vernacular. What the Tudor house gains in its flexibility and adaptability, the Georgian house matches in its compactness and reasonableness. Either may better suit a situation or particular requirements; in other cases, both are equally suitable and possess outstanding merits.

[1] William Halfpenny, " carpenter and architect," author of *The Art of Sound Building*, 1725, and other works.

K

A tradesman-architect was Francis Price (d. 1753), whose *British Carpenter*, published 1733, fourth edition, 1759, was long the best textbook on the subject. Price was (1734) clerk of the works and surveyor of Salisbury Cathedral. The frontispiece of the second edition, published 1835, of his book is the representation of a pedimented tablet, on the field of which is a testimonial :

> "June the 28th, 1733
> Having perused this Treatise
> of CARPENTRY compiled
> by Mr. Francis Price, We think
> it a very Useful and Instructive
> Piece, and as such, recommend
> it to everyone concerned in
> Works of that kind.
>   N. Hawksmoor
>   Jno. James
>   Ja. Gibbs."

These architects gave a similar testimonial to *The Builder's Dictionary*, published 1733-34, which was so mercilessly criticized by Batty Langley, as quoted on p. 135.

John Carr, of York (1723-1807), a mason by trade, was architect of many admirable buildings, of which the finest is Harewood House, near Leeds, Yorkshire, 1760, the interior of which was decorated by Robert Adam, who may have contributed the design for the exterior. Carr was architect of Basildon Park, Berkshire (Figs. 265, 266A, 266B, 458, 459, 665), but much of the internal decoration was by J. B. Papworth, 1838-40.

James Smith, of Warwick, built the Court House, Warwick, *c.* 1700, and the south front of Stoneleigh Abbey, *c.* 1720, as well as other houses, many of which are only attached to him by inference.

John Wood, of Bath, was a native of Yorkshire, whose connection with Bath began as Road Surveyor in 1727, but who speedily attained a prominent position in connection with planning those large extensions of the city which have made it what it is. It has been said that Inigo Jones anticipated Wood by combining several houses in one architectural composition, in his designs for the north and south sides of Covent Garden,[1] but Wood also showed himself a town-planner of ability. As a designer of buildings, Wood varied. The great house of Prior Park, built by him for Ralph Allen, the owner of the quarries from which Bath stone was obtained, is one of his best efforts, and, on a smaller scale, the elevation shown in Fig. 237 of Belcombe Brook possesses a distinction which many of his houses in the city itself lack. Wood designed Queen Square, the north side of which, begun 1729, is shown in Fig. 232, and plans of one house in Fig. 234. The illustration of an interior and staircase (Fig. 848) shows the quality of his design and work, but the stucco decoration of the walls was, no doubt, carried out by Italian workmen.

---

[1] *History of Renaissance Architecture in England*, R. E. Blomfield, vol. ii, p. 248.

The names of those architects mentioned far from exhaust the list which could be compiled, but however comprehensive such a list might be, there would still remain a large body of men of local reputation, authors of admirable buildings, whose names are unknown. Few buildings surpass that in the main street of Burford (Fig. 210), yet attempts to trace its author have been fruitless. The same may be said of the front of Compton Beauchamp, illustrated in Fig. 208, the unadorned and basic merits of which appeal more strongly to the observer the longer he regards it. We can only say that the first half of the eighteenth century was a great architectural period, great in its diffusion, in its ideals, and great in its opportunities for the manifestation of native talent.

Much of what has been written here relates to the exteriors of houses. It may, therefore, be convenient shortly to indicate certain characteristics of internal details and decoration.

In the early part of the eighteenth century the practice of wainscoting rooms with oak, and the later one of using painted pine, continued, but presently the heavy bolection panel moulds (with raised panels) of the Wren period (Figs. 422, 708) were superseded by slightly sunk panels, having a small ovolo moulding (Fig. 647). Although panelling was never entirely superseded, after the first quarter of the century the tendency (particularly in large houses) was to substitute stucco decoration (Figs. 650, 654, 848). Decoration itself underwent a radical change about the same time (1735-40), when rococo ornament (consisting of C and S shaped scrolls and other curves terminating in little volutes and flourishes of a vague and straggling kind) was introduced from France (Figs. 653, 718, 804). Other carved and modelled ornament included masks, festoons, and swags (Figs. 800, 844), often remarkably like work designed by Inigo Jones (Figs. 700, 743). Never has the workmanship of this period been excelled. Doorcases and chimneypieces, designed with columns or pilasters, were admirably proportioned and worked (Figs. 639, 646, 648, 649, 851). Mouldings were inclined to be large in scale, often enriched with carving and gilded (Figs. 641, 717, 798).   Some mantelpieces were designed in monumental manner and constructed of marble (Figs. 796, 798, 799). Rooms had massive cornices; mantels and doorcases were furnished with triangular and other pediments, both being continued upwards by decorated frames to contain paintings (Figs. 442, 647, 802, 803).

Some late seventeenth-century and early eighteenth-century doors had two large square raised panels (Fig. 846), or, later, sometimes sunk, with ovolo moulding. At Mereworth are doors having ten panels (Fig. 438), but the six-panel door was most often adopted. At Thame Park (Fig. 441) the doors are of mahogany (which became the favourite wood by the middle of the century), but others were of deal, painted like the panelling.

Types of mantelpieces include:

The monumental, as at Castle Howard and Sudbrooke Park (Figs. 796, 798).

Simple pilasters and shelf on consoles, as at Argyll House, Chelsea (Fig. 647).

More elaborate examples of the same type with stucco ornaments, as at Honington (Fig. 654).

The corner type, carved, enriched, painted and gilded as at Mereworth (Fig. 795).

In coloured marbles and with a tablet breaking the frieze, as at Honington (Fig. 801).

Aurora in carved and painted pine (Fig. 805); also worked in white statuary marble.

Rococo as at Chesterfield House (Fig. 653) and Winchester House (Fig. 804).

The correct decoration

" for a country seat for a small family "

was thus described in 1757:

> " The Parlour story is 13 feet high in the Clear, and the rooms to be wainscotted throughout with plain Marble Slab Chimney Pieces, and the Withdrawing Room to be wainscotted but Chair high, and the remaining Heighth stucco'd in Pannels, with Paper Ornaments, and a plaistered Cornice enriched, the Floors to be of the second best Deal dowell'd. . . . The Chamber Story is 12 Feet high in the Clear, and to be wainscotted for Hangings with neat Plaister Cornices and Marble Slab Chimney Pieces." [1]

Isaac Ware gives three kinds of decorations for the inside of rooms: [2]

1. Stucco, " wrought into ornaments."
2. Wainscot.
3. Walls hung with paper, silk, tapestry, etc.

> " Of the three kinds we have named, the grandest is that in stucco ; the neatest, that in wainscot ; and the most gaudy, that in hangings."
> " For a noble Hall, nothing is as well as stucco ; for a parlour, wainscot seems properest ; and for the apartments of a lady, hangings." [3]

Hangings he defines as

> " comprehending paper, silk, tapestry, and every other decoration of this kind." [4]

Of the chimneypiece, he says:

> " A principal compartment should be raised over it to receive a picture. This will be very happily terminated by a pediment. . . . It may be broken to receive a bust, a shield or other decoration : and as this can reach only to the chimneypiece, which must be a great deal above the height of the pedestal, the compartments, or pannels, on each side being brought within a small space of the pedestal, will give a pleasing variety." [5]

---

[1] *The Modern Builder's Assistant*, by William and John Halfpenny, Architects and Carpenters ; Robert Morris, Surveyor ; T. Lightoler, Carver, London, 1757.

[2] *A Complete Body of Architecture*, Isaac Ware, London, 1756, p. 469.

[3] *Ibid.*, p. 470.　　　　[4] *Ibid.*, p. 469.　　　　[5] *Ibid.*, p. 475.

The chimneypieces at Mereworth, Cadogan House, Lewes and Thame Park (Figs. 794, 797, 800, 803) meet this description.

Of the doorcase, he advises:

> " Over the door there is a space for lower pannels, unless where pediments intercept them. In this latter case the pediment should be opened to receive a figure that will fitly occupy the place ; in the other, the whole is to be ornamented with a compartment in stucco or wainscot, according to the construction of the room ; and if not pictures, festoons should be the ornaments."[1]

(*See* Figs. 438, 442, 449.)

Ware illustrates his remarks with drawings of the staircase hall and salon ceiling at Coleshill, which he ascribes to Inigo Jones, but which we know to have been by Sir Roger Pratt.   In another place he refers to the way

> " the British Palladio, Inigo Jones, conducted himself in these noble ornaments."[2]

The Palladians favoured ceilings divided into compartments, as those at Coleshill (Fig. 748); other ceiling treatments are shown in Figs. 754, 755, 756. Italian stuccoists treated ceilings in harmony with their own wall decorations (Figs. 439, 654).[3]

Having shown his preference for classic details for walls, ceilings, doorcases, and fireplaces, Ware proceeds to speak of decorations in the rococo manner, which he calls French, but he cautions his reader—

> " first to establish in his own mind the great superiority there is in the true and noble ornaments over these petty wildnesses ; but we must advise him also to understand the construction of both : for, unless he can conform himself to fancy, as well as work with judgment, he will do little in an age like this."[4]

In a preceding paragraph, he referred to the need to consult

> " the fancy of the proprietor "

and Ware's own submission to Lord Chesterfield's wishes for such French ornament is illustrated in Figs. 653, 718, of the drawing-room at Chesterfield House, where walls, ceiling, and fireplace are designed in this manner.

Staircases had balustrades of wood or iron; those of wood (or stone) were in the Italian manner (Fig. 850), having large balusters and a wide handrail like that at Coleshill (Fig. 833).   Iron balustrades were furnished with handrails less wide than those of the seventeenth century, and usually started with a twisted volute at the foot of the stairs (Figs. 843, 847-849).   Batty Langley says of these:

> " It was the Custom of the Ancients to begin a Ballustrade of a grand Staircase with a Pedestal, which to a large Stair-case is yet the most grand Manner, but many modern Architects who think themselves wiser, place a twisted Rail at the lowermost Stair instead of a Pedestal.
> In small Buildings a twisted Rail is very proper, but in magnificent Buildings I think them vastly inferior to a noble Pedestal."[5]

[1] *A Complete Body of Architecture*, p. 476.　　　　[2] *Ibid.*, pp. 468, 485.
[3] The connection between plaster treatment of walls and ceilings is thoroughly explored in *English Decorative Plasterwork of the Renaissance*, by M. Jourdain, London, 1926.
[4] *A Complete Body of Architecture*, p. 501.　　　[5] *The Builder's Compleat Assistant*, 2nd ed., p. 166.

Turned wood balusters passed from spirals (of which there was considerable variety) to a diversity of other designs. Newel posts, lately only a thicker barley-sugar spiral (Fig. 836) or a substantial square post panelled on each side (Fig. 837), now usually took the form of columns complete with the cap appropriate to the order chosen (Fig. 838). Metal balustrades, at first heavy and richly designed as at Chesterfield House (Figs. 844, 845) and at Easton Neston (Fig. 841), tended to become lighter—that at Honington Hall (Fig. 851) is exceptionally so— and their handrails, of wood, were narrower, like those of the wooden balustrades. The general tendency of iron balustrades was towards greater simplicity than those in earlier manner at Easton Neston and Chesterfield House; the acanthus leaves were omitted, and the design became a succession of panels filled with straight and scroll work (as that on the left in Fig. 841) sometimes approaching to lyre shape. External balustrades might have these panels at intervals, the intervening spaces being filled with straight vertical bars of square section, pointed or arrow-headed (Fig. 451).

It might be supposed that the only effect of the changes in architectural styles, plans and materials (dictated by fashion and introduced into houses built for wealthy and prosperous persons) was to gratify caprice and pander to luxury. Such a view would be superficial and so far from actual facts as to deceive no impartial person; but contemporary testimony is valuable in showing how the standard of accommodation improved.

Writing in 1749, John Wood the elder comments upon the effect of improvements in Bath, thus:

> " About the Year 1727, the Boards of the Dining Room and other Floors were made of a Brown Colour, with Soot and small Beer, to hide the Dirt, as well as their own Imperfections ; and if the walls of any of the Rooms were covered with Wainscott, it was with such as was mean and never Painted ; the Chimney Pieces, Hearths and Slabbs were all of Free Stone, and they were daily cleaned with a particular White-wash, which, by paying Tribute to every thing that touched it, soon rendered the brown Floors like the Starry Firmament ; the Doors were slight and thin, and the best locks had only Iron Coverings Varnished. . . . Each Chair seldom exceeded three half Crowns in Value ; nor were the Tables or Chests of Drawers, better in their Kind, the chief having been made of Oak ; the Looking Glasses were small, mean and few in Number ; and the Chimney Furniture consisted of a slight Iron Fender, with Tongs, Poker and Shovel, all of no more than three or four Shillings Value. . . . As the new Buildings advanced, Carpets were introduced to cover the Floors, though laid with the finest clean Deals, or Dutch Oak Boards ; the Rooms were all Wainscoted and Painted in a costly handsome Manner ; Marble Slabbs and even Chimney Pieces became common ; the Doors in general were not only made thick and substantial, but they had the best sort of Brass Locks put on them ; Walnut Tree Chairs, some with Leather and some with Damask or Worked Bottoms supplied the place of such as were seated with Cane or Rushes ; the Oak Tables and Chests of Drawers were exchanged, the former for such as were made of Mahoggany, the latter for such as were made either with the same Wood, or with Walnutt Tree ; handsome Glasses were added to the Dressing Tables, nor did the proper Chimneys or Peers or any of the Rooms long remain

without well Framed Mirrours of no inconsiderable Size ; and the Furniture for every chief Chimney was composed of a Brass Fender with Tongs, Poker and Shovel agreeable to it. . . . To make a just Comparison between the public Accommodation of Bath at this time and one and twenty years back, the best chambers for Gentlemen were then just what the Garrets for Servants now are."[1]

Before the middle of the eighteenth century drainage systems had become orderly, though far from sanitary. The cesspool method of disposing of soil was the usual one; indeed, it remains in many country houses and cottages in the twentieth century. Isaac Ware[2] gives a house plan showing the run of drains beneath, including cesspools and " bog-houses," the latter outside the main walls but attached to them. He specially commends drains and sewers (built of brick), the floors of which are inverted arches, as being better than flat floors, with angles, in which soil would lodge, and he mentions that these improved drains had been constructed under the new building of the Horse Guards.[3] The practice of taking soil and waste pipes into drains or cesspools, without intervening traps, would be offensive. Sir John Harington's water closet (Fig. 40, p. 84) was forgotten.

The provision of accommodation for servants is referred to by Ware. In addition to lodging them in the garrets of an " ordinary town house," he suggests supplementing that by beds

" contrived to let down in the kitchen."

As the kitchen already had been provided in the basement, he adds:

" but in this case the necessary care for these peoples healths requires it should be boarded."[4]

In a country house

" there must be in such a piece of building lodging-rooms for several servants of the meaner kind; and these may be much better provided in the out-parts, than in the house.
If some be lodged over the hen-houses, that common thievery of hen-roost robbing will be avoided; and a great deal of mischief of a like kind will be prevented by the same careful disposition in other respects."[5]

House bells were in use by the middle of the eighteenth century, being referred to (in inns) by Fielding;[6] but for entrance doors the knocker, a good early type of which is illustrated (Fig. 874), was usual. This type, no doubt, is that to which Fielding refers in the passage:

" He had scarce finished his story when a most violent Noise shook the whole House. To attempt to describe this Noise to those who have heard it would be vain, and to attempt to give an idea of it to those who have never . . . In short, a Footman knocked. . . ."[7]

[1] Preface to An Essay towards a Description of Bath, by John Wood, Architect., 2nd edition, London, 1749, vol. ii.
[2] A Complete Body of Architecture, 1756, plates 29-30, opposite p. 286.
[3] Ibid., p. 288.   [4] Ibid., p. 347.   [5] Ibid., p. 354.
[6] Tom Jones, by Henry Fielding, 1749, Bk. vii, ch. 2 and ch. 15.   [7] Ibid., Bk. xii, ch. 4.

The burden of certain taxes on houses is well brought out by contemporary references.

Of the Window Tax:

" Landlady of Inn—' For it is a dreadful thing to pay as we do. Why now there is above forty Shillings for Window lights, and yet we have stopped up all we could : we have almost blinded the house, I am sure.' "[1]

The Window Tax continued throughout the eighteenth century; it was instituted in 1695, supplementary to the tax upon inhabited houses (Fig. 540).

The incidence of Chimney Money is brought out in an epitaph which reads:

" A house she hathe, its made
Of such good fashione
The tenant shall ne'er paye
For repparatione.

" Nor will her landlord ever
Raise her rente
Or turne her out of doors
For non paymente.

" From chimney money too
This cell is free,
To such a house who
Would not tenante be ?"[2]

The practice of covering walls with mathematical tiles which closely imitated brickwork (Figs. 271, 326), plain tiles (Figs. 285, 323), ornamental tiles (Fig. 325), slates and weatherboarding (Figs. 274, 322, 324), already well established, was fostered by the taxes on bricks, which were first imposed in 1784, increased from time to time, and finally abolished in 1850.[3] So popular did wall tiling and weatherboarding become that for small houses and cottages they may be said to have been the predominant building materials of the period between 1750 and 1850 in the eastern and southern counties.

Ware refers to " Common Builders " of London houses who

" sell for fourteen years purchase, exclusive of ground rent,"[4]

from which it might be inferred that speculative builders let houses as well as rented them. Speculative building of houses on an extensive scale was going on at an earlier date than this (1747), for Sir John Lowther, writing to Mr. William Gilpin (his agent at Whitehaven), February 19, 1697, after referring to house-building operations in Whitehaven, said of Dr. Nicholas Barbon:

[1] *Tom Jones*, Bk. vii, ch. 13.
[2] Epitaph on a tombstone in Folkestone churchyard, date 1668, In Memory of Rebecca Rogers.
[3] *A History of British Brickwork*, by Nathaniel Lloyd, p. 52.
[4] *A Complete Body of Architecture*, p. 347.

" Dr. Bairbones, has, in this Town (London) not laid out less than £200,000 in ye same manner, for which, in my opinion, he deserves more of ye public than any Subject in England."[1]

That the city merchant whose dwelling and place of business had been combined for so long now tended to reside outside the town is recorded in the following poem, which describes, also, some current fashions in architecture.

THE CIT'S COUNTRY BOX, 1757

Vos ſapere & ſolos aio bene vivere, quorum,
Conſpicitur nitidis fundata pecunia villis.—HOR.

The wealthy Cit, grown old in trade,
Now wiſhes for the rural ſhade,
And buckles to his one-horſe chair,
Old *Dobbin,* or the founder'd mare ;
While wedg'd in cloſely by his ſide,
Sits Madam, his unwieldy bride,
With *Jacky* on a ſtool before 'em,
And out they jog in due decorum.
Scarce paſt the turnpike half a mile,
How all the country ſeems to ſmile !
And as they ſlowly jog together,
The Cit commends the road and weather ;
While Madam doats upon the trees,
And longs for ev'ry houſe ſhe ſees,
Admires its views, its ſituation,
And thus ſhe opens her oration.

What ſignify the loads of wealth,
Without that richeſt jewel, health ?
Excuſe the fondneſs of a wife,
Who doats upon your precious life !
Such eaſeleſs toil, ſuch conſtant care,
Is more than human ſtrength can bear.
One may obſerve it in your face—
Indeed, my dear, you break apace :
And nothing can your health repair,
But exerciſe, and country air.
Sir Traffic has a houſe, you know,
About a mile from *Cheney-Row* :
He's a *good* man, indeed 'tis true,
But not ſo *warm,* my dear, as you :
And folks are always apt to ſneer—
One would not be out-done, my dear !

Sir Traffic's name ſo well apply'd
Awak'd his brother merchant's pride ;
And Thrifty, who had all his life
Paid utmoſt deference to his wife,
Confeſs'd her arguments had reaſon,
And by th' approaching ſummer ſeaſon,
Draws a few hundreds from the ſtocks,
And purchaſes his Country Box.

[1] Extract from the original letter in the office of the Lowther Estates, Whitehaven, communicated by E. L. Nanson, Whitehaven.

Some three or four mile out of town,
(An hour's ride will bring you down,)
He fixes on his choice abode,
Not half a furlong from the road :
And fo convenient does it lay,
The ftages pafs it ev'ry day :
And then fo fnug, fo mighty pretty,
To have an houfe fo near the city !
Take but your places at the Boar
You're fet down at the very door.

Well then, fuppofe them fix'd at laft,
White-wafhing, painting, fcrubbing paft,
Hugging themfelves in eafe and clover,
With all the fufs of moving over ;
Lo, a new heap of whims are bred !
And wanton in my lady's head.

Well, to be fure, it muft be own'd,
It is a charming fpot of ground ;
So fweet a diftance for a ride,
And all about fo *countrified* !
'Twould come to but a trifling price
To make it quite a paradife ;
I cannot bear thofe nafty rails,
Thofe ugly broken mouldy pales :
Suppofe, my dear, inftead of thefe,
We build a railing, all Chinefe.
Although one hates to be expos'd,
'Tis difmal to be thus inclos'd ;
One hardly any object fees—
I wifh you'd fell thofe odious trees.
Objects continual paffing by
Were fomething to amufe the eye,
But to be pent within the walls—
One might as well be at St. Paul's.
Our houfe beholders would adore,
Was there a level lawn before,
Nothing its views to incommode,
But quite laid open to the road ;
While ev'ry trav'ler in amaze,
Should on our little manfion gaze,
And pointing to the choice retreat,
Cry, that's Sir Thrifty's Country Seat.

No doubt her arguments prevail,
For Madam's TASTE can never fail.

Bleft age ! when all men may procure,
The title of a Connoiffeur ;
When noble and ignoble herd,
Are govern'd by a fingle word ;
Though, like the royal German dames,
It bears an hundred Chriftian names ;
As Genius, Fancy, Judgment, Goût,
Whim, Caprice, Je-ne-fcai-quoi, Virtù :
Which appellations all defcribe
TASTE, and the modern *tafteful* tribe.

Now bricklay'rs, carpenters, and joiners,
With Chinefe artifts, and defigners,
Produce their fchemes of alteration,
To work this wond'rous reformation.
The ufeful dome, which fecret ftood,
Embofom'd in the yew-tree's wood,
The trav'ler with amazement fees
A temple, Gothic, or Chinefe,
With many a bell, and tawdry rag on,
And crefted with a fprawling dragon ;
A wooden arch is bent aftride
A ditch of water, four foot wide,
With angles, curves, and zigzag lines,
From Halfpenny's exact defigns,
In front, a level lawn is feen,
Without a fhrub upon the green,
Where Tafte would want its firft great law,
But for the fkulking, fly *ha-ha*,
By whofe miraculous affiftance,
You gain a profpect two fields diftance.
And now from Hyde-Park Corner come
The Gods of Athens, and of Rome,
Here fquabby Cupids take their places,
With Venus, and the clumfy Graces :
Apollo there, with aim fo clever,
Stretches his leaden bow for ever ;
And there, without the pow'r to fly,
Stands fix'd a tip-toe Mercury.

The Villa thus completely grac'd,
All own, that Thrifty has a Tafte ;
And Madam's female friends, and coufins,
With common-council-men, by dozens,
Flock ev'ry Sunday to the Seat,
To ftare about them, and to eat.

From Poems by ROBERT LLOYD, A.M.
LONDON, 1762.

Chapter X

LATER EIGHTEENTH CENTURY: EARLY NINETEENTH CENTURY

GEORGE III, 1760-1820; GEORGE IV, 1820-30; WILLIAM IV, 1830-37

REVIVALS

THE ARCHITECTURAL history of the second half of the eighteenth century and thereafter is a history of Revivals.

The Gothic Revival was no new thing. Gothic design had had its recrudescences in different forms and degrees of intensity from time to time during the preceding two hundred years. It never died out, it merely subsided. It is constantly found in ecclesiastical buildings, it was persistent in the house plan, as shown repeatedly in this History, and it was firmly established in minor domestic architecture in almost every county. Even a classic architect like Wren practised it, as in Tom Tower, Christ Church, Oxford. Its fullest developments in pointed openings and in tracery fascinated some minds. About 1750 Horace Walpole added extensive buildings to a cottage (including chapel, refectory, and picture gallery) in this Gothic manner and even incorporated details from demolished medieval buildings. So notorious were these achievements as to earn the appellation of "Strawberry Hill Gothic." In 1742 Batty Langley published an attempt to improve Gothic architecture by rules and proportions, and took the opportunity of displaying "many grand designs" of his own invention, all "geometrically expressed." That he made himself ridiculous is immaterial, but it *is* material to note that "Batty Langley Gothic" catered for a public want. When the Duke of Buckingham wanted a muniment room for storing his collection of Saxon MSS., Sir John Soane, *c.* 1805, designed a room for him on the ground floor at Stowe (Fig. 668), the tracery, tabernacle work, and ceiling of which were copied from the Henry VII Chapel at Westminster. Eaton Hall, Cheshire, was designed by W. Porden for the Marquess of Westminster in 1803 mainly in the Perpendicular style. Perhaps this architect's chief claim to distinction is for the profuseness of his use of cast-iron in the construction of window tracery and "stone" balustrades which were painted to represent stone. In this, however, he only developed the methods of his early master, Wyatt. Instances might be multiplied. The publication (*c.* 1812 and thereafter) of voluminous illustrated works on English medieval buildings, by John Britton, familiarized the public with ancient Gothic architecture and created a public taste, whilst the publication by Augustus Pugin and E. J. Willson of measured drawings, which included large details from medieval buildings, enabled architects to design in the Gothic manner correctly and with facility. In *Examples of Gothic Architecture* by these authors, second edition, published 1831, the Introductory Remarks indicate this as an object of the work:

> " In the selection of the subjects for this work, a preference has been given to such as appeared most likely to afford useful lessons to the modern artist."[1]

And, later:

> " A selection of such as have appeared best suited for imitation, particularly in domestic architecture."

It is not surprising that with a public interest revived and with material for easy guidance at hand, many domestic buildings were designed in medieval and Elizabethan manner during the remainder of the nineteenth century, and that, notwithstanding their deficiencies, these compared not unfavourably with the debased and clumsy classic revivals and with the nondescript architecture which dominated the second and third quarters of that century. It must not be supposed, however, that houses designed by copyists to meet the vulgar taste were models either of dignity or utility, and their deficiencies proved easy butts for the pen of Ruskin, who spared neither them nor the classic monstrosities with which they competed.

Augustus Welby Northmore Pugin (1812-52), who was as enthusiastic and thorough a medievalist as his father, Augustus Pugin, assisted him in measuring and drawing and in the application of medieval designs to furniture, plate, and decoration, from which he passed to practice as an architect. He wrote several books, of which *Contrasts between the Noble Edifices of the Middle Ages and Corresponding Buildings of the Present Day*, 1836, and *True Principles of Pointed or Christian Architecture*, 1841, are the most notable. In these he railed against classic architecture and praised Gothic in unrestrained language that became ridiculous. He had a large ecclesiastical practice, and was an able draughtsman, with intimate knowledge of Gothic detail, which made Sir Charles Barry entrust him with the detailing of the Houses of Parliament. Scarisbrick Hall (Figs. 297, 298) was designed by him in 1837 and added to by his son, Edward Welby Pugin, in 1867. The elaboration of the details and the care lavished upon them brought the cost up to more than £300,000, and made it the most interesting example of the Gothic Revival. A. W. N. Pugin lost his reason and was succeeded by Edward Welby Pugin (1834-75) at the age of seventeen, who enjoyed a large practice and designed numerous churches—of course, of Gothic character.

The elaborated detail of Scarisbrick Hall should be compared with the contemporary Scotney Castle (Figs. 299, 300), by Anthony Salvin (1799-1881),

[1] Vol. i, p. v.

a pupil of John Nash, whose work was more restrained and better suited to its purpose.

To such a pass had architectural taste come that the glass-and-iron Crystal Palace, designed to house the Great Exhibition of 1851, was hailed as a new architecture that would meet modern requirements and supersede all other styles. Critics of current works did not fail to point out how professional architects had failed in the public competition for the Exhibition building, alleging that this was due to lack of enterprise and because they were unable to tear themselves away from tradition. They proceeded to show

> " how mistaken we had been in endeavouring to copy from ancient examples ; that the architecture of the future should be the architecture of common sense; and that if the same principles which had inspired the designer of the Exhibition building had been applied to the Houses of Parliament, to the British Museum, and to the new churches then in course of erection, millions of money would have been saved and a better class of art secured."[1]

The adulation poured forth over Paxton's big greenhouse is remarkably like that bestowed upon the products of some revolutionary architects of the present day. Time will show whether these are better justified.

What we term the Classic Revival (which we may date, approximately, as beginning *c.* 1760) was essentially a copying and adaptation of Italian and (later) of Greek details.

Although these supplanted Palladian design as fashions, Palladian design continued contemporaneously and has never ceased to be the architecture of the grand manner; moreover, architects like the brothers Adam, who were apostles of the Revival, designed, also, Palladian buildings.

The fact is that the Revival was more decorative than architectural, its novelties being in trimmings rather than in form.

The fashion for rococo ornament, which Isaac Ware deplored, but to which he was compelled to bow, was succeeded by intensified devotion to the antique, which, beginning as a popular practice in collecting pictures, statuary, and *objets d'art* (for displaying which great houses having spacious apartments were built), developed into copying every form of antique ornament and decoration and applying them to these apartments. Economy with display—in other words, the desire to produce imposing effects as cheaply as possible—led to simplification of design and repetition of details by means of moulds, by which walls could be enriched at small cost with applied plaster ornament. In all this, however, proportion and rules of good architectural design were not ignored.

Important influences upon architecture of the latter half of the eighteenth century were the brothers Adam, of whom the most distinguished was Robert. Born in 1728, he was second son of William Adam, architect, engineer, and

[1] *A History of the Gothic Revival*, by Charles L. Eastlake, London, 1872, pp. 281-2.

master mason to the Board of Ordnance in Scotland. William Adam, an architect of ability, who worked in the Palladian manner, succeeded Sir William Bruce as the leading architect in Scotland, and published *Vitruvius Scoticus* in imitation of Colen Campbell's *Vitruvius Britannicus*. He was architect of many great houses built for Scottish peers, and of notable public buildings in Edinburgh, Glasgow, and Dundee.

Robert Adam was a good-looking young Scotsman, having suave manners and considerable charm in company. Between 1754 and 1758 he made a tour, mostly in Italy and to Spalatro in Dalmatia, where he made drawings of Diocletian's palace, which were engraved by Bartolozzi and published in 1764. On his return to England he embarked upon architectural practice and became the most fashionable architect of the day. He succeeded in ousting other architects, as James Paine from Kedleston which Adam carried out to Paine's plans, and at Harewood, Yorks, designed and built by John Carr of York, the completion and decoration of which was put into the hands of Adam. Although Adam completed, altered, and decorated many great houses, his name cannot be attached to any of the very large ones as entirely designed and built by him. Amongst houses where he was engaged may be mentioned:

Shardeloes, Bucks, 1759-61; Sion House, Middlesex, additions, 1761-62; Kedleston Hall, 1761-62 (Fig. 258); Osterley, 1761-73; Shelburne (now Lansdowne) House, 1765; Kenwood, Highgate, 1761-67; many London houses from 1768, including No. 20, St. James's Square (Figs. 267, 268). Stowe, Bucks, is his design, which was carried out, with slight modifications, by an Italian, Signor Borra, whilst certain buildings there are by Vanbrugh, Kent, Leoni, and other architects (Figs. 269, 270, 346). Adam seems to have been captivated by light forms of Italian and Etruscan decoration, of which he made drawings and which he copied or adapted for English houses. His brother James, who was associated with him in much of his work and may alone have been responsible for Portland Place, studied in Italy (1760-63). He was concerned with the Adelphi speculation, which almost involved the brothers in ruin. Another brother, William (1738-1822), was the financial and business partner, who, as William Adam & Co., traded in Liardet's stucco, which the architect brothers employed largely in their own works, the extent of which may be gathered from the record that 3,000 men were employed in 1772 upon these speculative building enterprises.

The changes in architectural design wrought by Robert and James Adam are best described in their own words. In the Preface to *The Works in Architecture of Robert and James Adam, Esquires*, London, 1778, they state:

> " We have not trod in the path of others, nor derived aid from their labours. . . . The skilful . . . will easily perceive within these few years a remarkable improvement in the form, convenience, arrangement, and reliefing of apartments; a greater movement and variety in the outside composition, and in the decoration of the inside an almost total change. The massive entablature,

the ponderous compartment ceiling, the tabernacle frame, almost the only species of ornament formerly known in this country, are now universally exploded, and in their places we have adopted a beautiful variety of light mouldings, gracefully formed, delicately enriched, and arranged with propriety and skill."

Footnotes develop this theme. Of " the massive entablature " they say:

" Nothing can be . . . more sterile and disgustful, than to see for ever the dull repetition of Doric, Ionick and Corinthian entablatures in their usual proportions, reigning round every apartment, where no order can come or ought to come, and yet it is astonishing to think that this has been the case in the apartment of every house in Europe, that has any pretensions to magnificence, from the days of Bramante down to our time. In smaller rooms the places of architrave and frieze have been ponderously supplied by a cornice of most ample proportions fit for the temple of Jupiter Tonans, from which it was . . . probably copied."

The following of their definitions are interesting:

" *Movement* is defined as " meant to express the rise and fall, the advance and recess, with other diversity of forms, in the different parts of a building, so as to add greatly to the picturesque of its composition. For the rising and falling, advancing and receding, with the convexity and concavity, and other forms of the great parts, have the same effect in architecture, that hill and dale, foreground and distance, swelling and sinking have in a landscape : that is, they serve to produce an agreeable and diversified contour, that groups and contrasts like a picture and creates a variety of light and shade, which gives great spirit, beauty and effect to the composition. It is not always that such variety can be introduced into the design of any building, but where it can be attained without encroaching upon its useful purposes, it adds much to its merit as an object of beauty and grandeur."

Tabernacle frame : " The whole dressing of a door, window, niche or chimney, when the dressing consists of columns or pilasters, with an entablature and pediment over them."

(Figs. 438, 798.)

Compartment cielings : " The heavy compartment cielings adopted in France were introduced into England by Inigo Jones with as much weight but less fancy and embellishment. Vanbrugh, Campbell and Gibbs followed too implicitly the authority of this great name."

(Figs. 380, 743, 745, 748.)

The authors of these views must have shocked the Palladians of their day: indeed, there seems to have been more than a little enmity between the Adam brothers and Sir William Chambers, who was the leading contemporary exponent of Palladianism.

The self-appreciation proceeds:

" We have introduced a great diversity of cielings, freezes and decorated pilasters, and have added grace and beauty to the whole, by a mixture of grotesque stucco and painted ornaments together with the flowing rainceau with its fanciful figures and winding foliage."

The definition of *Grotesque* is given in the footnote:

" By *grotesque* is meant that beautiful, light stile of ornament used by the ancient Romans, in the decoration of their palaces, baths and villas. . . . The Italians . . . give to ruins dug up and cleared the name of ' grotto ' . . . hence the modern word ' *grotesque*.' "

Of *Rainceau* they say:

" This French term is used by artists of this country to express the winding and twisting of the stalk or stem of the acanthus plant . . . often intermixed with human figures, animals, birds, imaginary or real, also with flowers and fruits. . . . Well composed, attains a wonderful power of pleasing."

A final thrust at fellow-architects runs:

" Among architects destitute of genius and incapable of venturing into the great line of their art, the attention paid to those rules and proportions " (of the Orders) " is frequently minute and frivolous. The great masters of antiquity were not so rigidly scrupulous, they varied the proportions as the general spirit of their composition required, clearly perceiving that however necessary these rules may be to form the tastes and to correct the licentiousness of the scholar, they often cramp the genius and encumber the ideas of the master."

In this passage, Adam (for Robert was the moving spirit amongst the brothers) shows himself to have been an independent thinker, not tied to Palladian or other conventions, but who searched for truth himself. He enters more fully into details in his disquisitions upon Orders, their entablatures, mouldings, and correct *versus* current wall decoration.

Here, in 1778, we have an instance of genius in rebellion against convention, and particularly against stereotyped use of the Orders. The parallel between his attitude and that of some modern architects is apparent, but Adam was no iconoclast, and his heresy was regulated by the discretion of well-balanced judgment arising from profound study. His activities extended to designing for arts and trades connected with architecture in general, and with the house in particular, including every description of furniture and textile, far surpassing the scope, in these directions, even of William Kent. So prolific was Adam, and so extensive were his incursions into these minor arts, that he has been regarded as being more a decorator and designer of fittings than an architect— a summary which scarcely does him justice, and which no one familiar with his completed works would endorse.

An obituary notice[1] stated that:

" Mr. Adam produced a total change in the architecture of this country : and his fertile genius in elegant ornament was not confined to the decoration of buildings, but has been diffused into almost every branch of manufacture."

The notice goes on to say:

" To the last period of his life, Mr. Adam displayed an increasing vigour of genius and refinement of taste : for in the space of one year preceding his death, he designed eight great public works, besides twenty-five private buildings, so various in their style, and so beautiful in their composition, that they have been allowed by the best judges, sufficient of themselves, to establish his fame unrivalled as an artist."

[1] *The Gentleman's Magazine*, 1792.

Amongst architects of the later eighteenth and early nineteenth century was George Dance the elder (1700-68), clerk of City works, who was architect of the Mansion House, since altered. His son, George Dance the younger (1741-1825), studied in Italy and was one of the original forty Royal Academicians. He was architect of several domestic buildings having little distinction—Ashburnham Place, Sussex, is one of them—but is best known as the architect of Newgate Prison, a fine building, now demolished.

Robert Morris, born early in the eighteenth century, was brought up by a relative (Roger Morris, carpenter) who had a considerable architectural connection, his most important building probably being Inveraray Castle, Argyllshire. Robert was author of several books on architecture, amongst which were a volume of *Lectures* (1736), *Rural Architecture* (1750), *Architecture Improved* (1755), and in conjunction with William and John Halfpenny, " architects and carpenters," and with T. Lightoler, " carver," he produced, in 1742 and 1757, *The Modern Builder's Assistant*, which included the inevitable directions for drawing the Orders, together with plans, elevations, and sections of small and large houses and outbuildings, with brief specifications and approximate estimates of costs; also designs for chimneypieces, windows, doors, stairs, and decorations, with sections of roof construction. Morris's share in this book is not defined, but apparently he was responsible for the text and the Orders. The designs for buildings were by the Halfpennys and by Lightoler, whose name is attached to a mansion, estimated to cost £10,676. Lightoler also provided the decorative illustrations, both for walls and ceilings, which sufficiently indicate the vogue in large and small houses. Morris, with S. Wright, designed the centre block of the White House, Richmond Park (Fig. 248), as well as other large country houses. He was the designer of the Palladian bridge at Wilton, which probably was the prototype of those at Bath and Stowe (Fig. 347), which closely resemble it.

William Halfpenny, who was one of those associated with Morris in *The Modern Builder's Assistant*, and who described himself as " architect and carpenter," is stated to have been a carpenter named Hoare, of Richmond, Surrey. He was author of a dozen works, including (1722) *Magnum in Parvo: or The Marrow of Architecture*; (1725) *The Art of Sound Building*, which was a practical work, showing how to set out, geometrically, brick arches, niches, columns, pilasters, and included a few draughts of buildings and staircases. This was essentially a tradesmen's textbook; indeed, in the preface, the author disclaims any intention to " teach our Architects," and gives as his reasons for publication:

" the daily errors that I saw Workmen commit in framing their Works for Buildings, on account of their Want of Knowledge of the Proportions contain'd in this Book, being the only Thing, that I know of, that is wanting to make the Art of Building compleat."

In 1749 he published *A New and Compleat System of Architecture Delineated in a Variety of Plans and Elevations of Designs for Convenient and Decorated Houses*. The distinction between " Convenient " and " Decorated " houses is naïve. This work included sundry details and estimates of costs of erecting the buildings illustrated. It was, actually, an advertisement of the writer as " architect," but in the preface he acknowledges indebtedness to " Robert Morrice, Architect." Other publications by Halfpenny were *Rural Architecture in the Gothic Taste* and *Rural Architecture in the Chinese Taste*, both, no doubt, designed to meet current fashions, for which he was prepared to cater.

The practical illustrations for setting out roof timbers, steeples, staircases, etc., are augmented in the second edition of *The British Carpenter* by a supplement containing the Orders according to Palladio, with " the ornaments of doors and windows."

With the exception of Batty Langley's, probably the works of William Pain, " architect and joiner," had the greatest sale of any during the latter half of the eighteenth century. He published in 1763 *The Builder's Pocket Treasure*; in 1774 *The Practical Builder's and Workman's General Assistant*, which contained Rules of Carpentry, Details of the Orders, and Plans and Elevations of Houses. In 1781 appeared *The Builder's Golden Rule*, which consisted mostly of copperplate illustrations covering the usual subjects; and in 1786 *The British Palladio*. In 1790 *The Practical House Carpenter* appeared and quickly ran into several editions, the seventh being dated 1805. Although covering the same ground as previous works, including his own, the selection of subjects and the practical nature of the working drawings were superior and, no doubt, so useful as to cause demand for copies. At the end of this book are lists of prices of materials and labours in considerable and orderly detail. The elevations for houses are consistently bad, as are the plans when the author departs from those for small and moderately sized houses, such as those upon which he was accustomed to work. The list of tradesmen-architects might be extended to include A. Swan, J. Crunden, and others who wrote useful books. Most of these men were carpenters. They wrote for other carpenters and tradesmen. They all emphasized the importance of knowledge of the Orders and of designing in strict accordance with them. The details which they circulated are still to be found, copied or varied to taste, all over the country. These were the textbooks of village tradesmen, who read, mastered, and applied them to their daily works, to which their names are not attached, but which are still convenient, dignified, and reasonably scholarly dwellings. Such tradition is lost even more irretrievably than the Gothic vernacular tradition, because that is still perpetuated by the workman copying examples and following customs; but the " village classic " is dead : how dead may be realized if we try to imagine a village builder of today applying himself to set up a Doric doorway according to Palladio. It is doubtful whether there is now one in all England capable of doing what was a commonplace act in his trade 150 years ago.

Amongst legitimate architects, Sir Robert Taylor (1714-88) was son of a stonemason and was apprenticed to Sir Henry Cheere, sculptor and mason. He studied in Italy and returned to England to practise as a sculptor, an example of his art being the sculpture in the pediment of the Mansion House. About this date (1753) he devoted himself to the practice of architecture, and during the next thirty-five years designed many buildings of importance in London and in the country. Of the latter, Heveningham Hall, Suffolk, may be mentioned, and Ely House, Dover Street, W. (Fig. 543), was built for the Bishop of Ely, 1772. Heveningham was altered later by James Wyatt; indeed, many of Taylor's buildings have been modified or destroyed. He held the appointment of Architect to the Bank of England from 1765 to 1788, when he was succeeded by Sir John Soane. He was a sound architect, well versed in Palladian design.

Until the advent of the brothers Adam, Sir Robert Taylor and James Paine (1716-89) shared most of the important architectural practice. In 1767 was published *Plans, Elevations and Sections of Noblemen and Gentlemen's Houses*, by James Paine, architect, " one of the Directors of the Society of Artists of Great Britain," in the preface to which he records that:

> " The Author . . . began the study of architecture in the early part of his life, under the tuition of a man of genius,[1] and at the age of nineteen was entrusted to conduct a building of consequence[2] in the West Riding of Yorkshire, in the execution of which he acquitted himself so much to the satisfaction of his employer . . ."

The *Dictionary of the Architectural Publication Society* gives a long list of his works, with notes of the alterations made to them by other hands. Beginning as a Palladian, Paine had to follow the fashion set by Adam, and in plate xci of his book he illustrates ceilings at Brockett Hall, which abound in representations of animals in the Etruscan manner and in thin ornament.

John Wood the younger, of Bath, succeeded his father and completed certain works begun by him. Of his own work, Royal Crescent, 1769, is illustrated (Fig. 257), and may be compared with his father's terrace houses in Queen Square (Fig. 232).

James Stuart (1713-88), whose long residence in Greece and publication of the first volume of *The Antiquities of Athens*, 1762, secured for him considerable reputation and the appellation of " Athenian Stuart," designed the St. James's Place front of Spencer House, the finer front to the park and the plan being by John Vardy the elder. Stuart was also the architect of No. 15, St. James's Square (Fig. 256); an early essay in Greek architecture in London.

James Gandon (1743-1823) was a pupil of Sir William Chambers, who, with John Wolfe (architect to the Board of Works), published vols. iv and v of *Vitruvius Britannicus*. His works were mostly public buildings in Dublin, of which the Custom House is the finest.

---

[1] Mr. Thomas Jorfy.   [2] Nostell Priory. Illustrated in *Vitruvius Britannicus*, iv.

Sir William Chambers (1726-96), whose father was a Scotsman, was born at Stockholm, and sent to Yorkshire to be educated. At the age of sixteen he went as a ship's supercargo to the East, and the impress of Indian and Chinese architecture is often a feature of his own works. In 1757 he published *Designs of Chinese Buildings, Furniture, Dresses, &c.*, from notes and measurements made whilst at Canton. One effect of this book is to be seen in furniture of the period, popularly known as " Chinese Chippendale." In 1759 Chambers published *A Treatise of Civil Architecture*, the third edition of which, published in 1791, he entitled *A Treatise on the Decorative Part of Civil Architecture*. Gwilt's edition of this work, published 1825, is the best known. This was, at the same time, the most scholarly and most complete book upon the subject which had been produced. Chambers studied both in France and in Italy, and, on returning from his first visit in 1755, was appointed instructor in architecture to the Prince of Wales, afterwards George III. Shortly after, he designed the gardens and buildings at Kew, some of which, like the Pagoda, are " in the Chinese taste "; others, as the Orangery, 1761 (Fig. 255), follow a more sober fashion. He was architect of many great buildings, the most distinguished being Somerset House, 1776, and the most beautiful, perhaps, the Casino at Marino, Clontarf, Ireland (Fig. 252). Melbourne House, Piccadilly, now Albany, 1767 (Fig. 263), shows his treatment of a purely domestic building. Chambers was the greatest rival of the Adam brothers. Of contemporary architects, he was least affected by the fashions they introduced, and succeeded in avoiding the eccentricities of the opposing schools. His style was Palladian, tempered by experience obtained during Continental journeys and by his own sound discrimination. He kept burning the candle of true classic tradition, which still threw its beams in a " naughty world " of Gothic and Classic Revivals.

Thomas Leverton (1743-1824), son of a builder at Woodford, Essex, was an architect of the Adam school, who built many houses in town and country. Parts of Bedford Square, W.C., are by him, and he lived for some years in No. 13. He employed J. Flaxman, the sculptor, upon his decorations.

Henry Holland (*c.* 1746-1806) is best known in his association with the rebuilding, 1788-90, of Carlton House (demolished 1827) for the Prince of Wales. He was a fashionable architect who enjoyed a large practice. He built Brooks's Club, St. James's Street, 1777; Southill Park, Bedfordshire, in the decoration of which he combined Greek and Roman Classic Revival with the French manner of Louis XVI. He showed independence in design, contrasting with the slavish imitation, by other architects, of the brothers Adam.

To every architect who has a sense of artistic composition there is temptation to demolish existing buildings, or to alter them to suit those of his own conception. Respect for ancient things and appreciation of their qualities are restraints which have preserved to us many of those buildings which we value greatly, but some designers have been drastic and remorseless. Of these, the

Wyatts (James, 1746-1813, and his nephew, Jeffry, 1766-1840, who changed his name to Wyattville and was knighted 1828) are notorious. A mere list of the alterations made to existing houses and cathedrals, and of the buildings demolished to make room for their own compositions, would be a lengthy one. Even their successes in producing picturesque results, as in the alterations at Windsor Castle, cannot excuse their cruel treatment of what should have been regarded as national monuments entitled to respect. James Wyatt well merited the name of " Wyatt the Destroyer " with which Pugin branded him, and his nephew was equally unscrupulous.

The two architects who most influenced architecture during the closing years of the eighteenth and the first quarter of the nineteenth centuries were Sir John Soane and John Nash, but upon very different lines.

Sir John Soan, or Soane (1753-1837) was son of a mason, pupil of George Dance the younger and of Henry Holland. Distinctions won whilst studying in the Royal Academy Schools induced Sir William Chambers to introduce him to George III, following which Soane set out upon the Grand Tour, which included Rome, Sicily, and Malta, but stopped short of Athens. On his return in 1780 he quickly built up a practice, and in 1788 won, in competition, the position of architect to the Bank of England, where his supervision of building operations extended from 1794 to 1823, by which date the whole structure had become one design. The essential difference between his decoration and that of Adam (which consisted of the adaptation of Etruscan and grotesque ornaments) was the substitution by Soane of a linear and surface treatment peculiarly his own,[1] an instance of which is seen in inlaid rectangular lines of wood in mahogany doors, panelling, etc. (Figs. 472, 477), and in similar incised lines, as in the porch at Mells Park (Fig. 468), and in the mantelpiece (Fig. 814). Notwithstanding these originalities and his differences with Sir William Chambers, and Sir Robert Taylor, whom he supplanted, Soane was a staunch classicist, who inclined towards the Greek, and whose catholicity is manifest in his Lectures[2] delivered to students of the Royal Academy, 1809-36, and in his completed works, as at Tyringham, Bucks (Fig. 283), Pitzhanger (Fig. 289), and his own house at No. 13, Lincoln's Inn Fields. The quality of Soane's composition is manifest in his design for the entrance gateway at Tyringham (Fig. 348), where he handles simple masses with consummate ability.

John Nash (1752-1835) was a pupil of Sir Robert Taylor, and the most fashionable architect of the early years of the nineteenth century. In 1793 he designed Regent's Park, in 1811 the houses near it, and in 1813-20 Regent Street, which completed the scheme. He also designed the eastern portion of Carlton House Terrace, following the demolition of Carlton House. Few architects have opportunity of designing such important and

[1] Introduction to A Description of the Residence of Sir John Soane, by Arthur T. Bolton, F.S.A., 11th edition, Oxford. [2] Edited by Arthur T. Bolton, Publication No. 14, Soane Museum.

extensive town areas as these cover, and Nash accomplished his task with credit.

Although other architects (including Soane, Decimus Burton, Smirke, and Abraham) furnished designs for various buildings, the general scheme and the Regent Street façades were left to Nash, as architect to the Commissioners. His handling of the street had scale and unity, which the new Regent Street lacks, the new quadrant alone possessing any of the qualities of the old one. Nash recognised that it was not sufficient to design street blocks as complete compositions, but that successful design must take cognizance of the street as a whole, and the relation of each block-unit to those adjoining and opposite. It may be recalled that, although, for many years preceding rebuilding, Regent Street was devoted entirely to trading purposes, Nash designed its buildings as shops with residences over them, which were described as suited for occupation by retired Indian Civil Servants and their families (Fig. 291). Although Nash showed ability in town planning and in the picturesque disposition of masses, his work had nothing of the great manner and cannot be regarded as other than debased classic, although the degradation had not proceeded as far as it was to do at the hands of his successors. His own house in Dover Street (Fig. 290) illustrates his abilities and his limitations. Nash perceived the possibilities of the use of stucco (which the Adam brothers had done much to popularize), recognizing the economy by which effects could be produced with it and its suitability to the climate of London, in the ease with which grimy buildings could be freshened up by repainting. His devotion to stucco was wittily recorded in the lines:

" Augustus at Rome was for building renown'd,
For of marble he left what of brick he had found ;
But is not our Nash, too, a very great master ?
He finds us all brick and he leaves us all plaster."

James Paine,[1] writing of an architect's " requisites," said:

" It is indispensably necessary that an architect should be perfectly acquainted with the quality and value of every material employed in the construction and decoration of a building, and also with the value of the labour of the several artificers. Without this knowledge it will never be in his power to do justice to his employer, for if he is ignorant in these particulars, he must necessarily call in the aid of workmen, and, in that case, unavoidably submit to the gratification of their avarice . . . and, thus, instead of being the principal. become subordinate."

Paine had no opinion of " the born architect," holding that

" an architect should be bred an architect."

Sir John Soane defined the duties of an architect almost exactly in accordance with modern standards:

[1] *Plans, Elevations and Sections of Noblemen and Gentlemen's Houses*, London, 1767.

" The business of the architect is to make the designs and estimates, to direct the works and to measure and value the different parts ; he is the intermediate agent between the employer, whose honour and interest he is to study, and the mechanic, whose rights he is to defend. His situation implies great trust ; he is responsible for the mistakes, negligences and ignorances of those whom he employs ; and above all he is to take care that the workmen's bills do not exceed his own estimates. If these are the duties of an architect, with what propriety can his situation and that of the builder or contractor be united ?" [1]

In his first Lecture, delivered to students of the Royal Academy, 1809, Soane also says:

" In this country we have long had too much reason to complain of mechanics of every description, from the bricklayer to the paperhanger, being identified with Architects ; and, what is equally fatal to the advancement of the Art, that Architects who ought always to be the intermediate persons between the employer and the employed, lose that high distinction and degrade themselves and the Profession by becoming Contractors, not only in the execution of their own designs but likewise those of others. Let our young Artists follow closely the precepts of Vitruvius . . . that our great Public and Private works will no longer be entrusted to ignorant mechanics, nor our streets and public places disgraced by the errors of mercenary men, nor by the mistaken and misapplied fancies of speculators." [2]

No doubt Soane had in mind the brothers Adam and also such practitioners as William Pain, architect and joiner (to whom allusion has been made), who, in the preface to his *Practical Builder*, published 1774, described his intentions:

" The Deficiencies and confined plans of those Books now used by Workmen, is another Inducement to collect together in one View, the most easy and certain Rules to carry on the Building Art. These are the Result of Experience, and by the Author long used in conducting Business, who now offers the Public a general practical Treatise, wherein his great Care has been plainly and faithfully to answer the Purpose of the manual Artificer : It is not meant to instruct the professed Artist, but to furnish the Ignorant, the Uninstructed, with such a comprehensive System of Practice, as may lay a Foundation for their Improvement, and thereby enable them to execute with Ease and Precision the various Branches of the Profession."

There is no doubt, however, that Pain and his kind increased in popularity and in practice, for the quality of their productions justified their pretensions.

No student is likely to allege that the decadence of architecture in the nineteenth century was due to these tradesmen-architects. It is clear that they followed the lead set by the great men of the profession, who must shoulder all the odium. It is to be observed that at the present day speculative tradesmen-builders are to be seen erecting houses, in the designs of which they embody features which architects once used, but discarded some twenty years ago—the wide bargeboard, painted white, is an instance. Every architect designing

---

[1] *Plans, Elevations and Sections of Buildings*, London, 1788.
[2] *Lectures on Architecture*, by Sir John Soane, edited by Arthur T. Bolton, F.S.A., London, 1929, p. 24.

domestic buildings towards the end of the nineteenth century employed it, and builders have only recently abandoned its use.

    Comparison of:—Tyringham, 1796 (Fig. 283),
      with   Cresswell Hall, 1820 (Fig. 294);
      or   Royal Crescent, Bath, 1767 (Fig. 257),
      with   The Paragon, Blackheath, c. 1790 (Fig. 276),
      —or—   29 Dover Street, W.C., 1810 (Fig. 290),
      with   86 East Hill, Colchester, 1819 (Fig. 295),

sufficiently illustrates the steady deterioration of classic design, without the inclusion of later and more flagrant examples.

The improvement in house accommodation, particularly of the working classes, marched with the improvement in wages, which in 1805 were 5s. per diem for a carpenter, 4s. to 4s. 6d. per diem for a bricklayer, and 3s. to 3s. 3d. per diem for his labourer—these for a working day of ten hours.

    " Wages in any part of England ; corrected, 1805."[1]

In later eighteenth-century plans we find some of the larger houses still designed with central blocks having two or four smaller blocks connected by corridors, as at Kedleston (Fig. 259) and Basildon Park (Fig. 265). The provision, in large houses, of halls and galleries for the display of works of art continued. Nash's own house in Lower Regent Street had extensive

    "galleries of painting and of architecture."

Considerations of sites upon which houses were to stand naturally influenced the designs of town houses more than those in the country. The brothers Adam refer to this:

> " The smallness of the sites upon which most houses in London are built, obliges the artists in this country to arrange the apartments of the Ladies and Gentlemen in two floors . . . we can only introduce both these upon the principal floor in our country houses, where our space is unconfined."[2]

The plans of No. 20, St. James's Square (Fig. 268), show that Adam arranged Sir Watkin Wynn's rooms on the ground floor, whilst Lady Wynn's were on the first or " principal floor." At Kedleston, Lady Scarsdale's rooms faced due north.

The most obvious change is in apartments having other than rectangular plans. Sometimes these were octagonal, as in Fig. 275, from Plaw's *Rural Residences*, and in Fig. 268 of the Adam house at No. 20, St. James's Square. In each of these plans we find, also, rooms with curved ends, sometimes semicircular, sometimes segmental; as employed, also, by Sir John Soane at Tyringham (Fig. 281). The circular salon affected by Palladian architects, as

---

[1] *The Practical House Carpenter*, by William Pain, 7th edition, 1805.
[2] *The Works of Architecture of Robert and James Adam*, 1777, Preface.

at Mereworth (Fig. 223), was used by their successors, who also planned rooms which were perfect ellipses. It happened sometimes that provincial designers were unsuccessful in imitation of these, or realized the difficulties of fitting furniture against curved walls and so broke the curve of the ellipse by making a short length of wall straight. The greater architects, like Adam, overcame the difficulty by designing furniture to fit the curve. A favourite practice was to form a semicircular end in a dining-room and to design the sideboard to fit this. Wood's semicircular end for a staircase well at Queen Square, Bath, 1729 (Fig. 234), became a favourite feature in the late eighteenth century, and Soane seems to have been particularly attached to this treatment, as used at Tyringham (Fig. 281) and at Buckingham House (Fig. 857).

The plan from Nicholson (Fig. 301), c. 1823, shows plan crystallization into the form which was adopted with little variation for middle-class houses and villas during the first fifty years of the Victorian period.

In the examples given, plans have been chosen of houses which are typical, each of its period, because these are less confused than plans of buildings to which additions and alterations have been made from time to time, as, naturally, has happened to many houses, in some of which the changes may be traced more easily than in others. Fig. 273 shows the development of a farmhouse in Lincolnshire.[1] First the typical " two-down and two-up " East Anglian cottage, probably roofed with reed and in its ground plan recalling the earlier hall-house. About 1780 agricultural prosperity warrants a trim Georgian addition and rearrangement, which result in a good farmhouse. After the Napoleonic wars a more grandiose addition is made, built as an independent building against the last house front. The last stage of all is the recent sub-division into cottages for occupation by smallholders, by closing up the communicating doors and the addition of a staircase in the kitchen. A house front having a plan similar to that of the third stage is shown in Fig. 274, but this is an eighteenth-century front.

Architects of the second half of the eighteenth century had every variety of classic design of the preceding 200 years upon which to draw for inspiration or imitation. Their elevations comprised each type—roofs with eaves, roofs hidden or partially hidden by parapets, division of fronts into three or five or more principal divisions, narrow fronts having a triangular pediment across the whole width, wider buildings with pediment over the centre division only, or pediments supported by pilasters or columns. Frequently fronts bore so much decoration as to be remarkable, as in the Adam work (Fig. 260, the caption of which quotes Horace Walpole's censure). Sir John Soane showed more structural ingenuity. He affected horizontal skylines, and his handling of masses, often devoid of decoration or trimmings of any description, anticipated our most recent modern

---

[1] The drawings and description by courtesy of Edwin Gunn, from *The Architect and Building News*, March 2, 1928, p. 331.

practice. A fine example is the entrance gateway at Tyringham (Fig. 348). After him the deterioration of design was rapid and complete. Roman and Greek classic features were used without stint, but proportion was ignored. Elevations were attenuated or clumsy, as also were doorway, window, and all other details. Design, like the people of the Victorian age, was utilitarian, uninstructed, and devoid of taste. The art patron gave way before the *nouveau riche*, who now called the tune.

One charming feature of later eighteenth-century and early nineteenth-century houses was the use of ironwork for balconies and verandas (Figs. 871, 872, 873), which served practical purposes and harmonized well with front designs. Most of the ironwork was wrought, but later examples were cast. Provision of iron railings round areas and to steps leading up to doorways continued, and, particularly for town houses, lamp-holders with or without link extinguishers were contrived as decorative adjuncts (Figs. 454, 455).

The adaptations of classic details introduced into England by the Adam brothers revolutionized interior decorations. The authors acknowledged one source of inspiration, in the preface to the second volume of their book, already cited:

> " Although the style of the ornament and the colouring of the Countess of Derby's dressing-room are both evidently imitated from the vases and urns of the Etruscans, yet we have not been able to discover, either in our researches into antiquity, or in the works of modern artists, any idea of applying this taste to the decoration of apartments."

Of another room in the same house they say:

> " The ornaments are all in stucco : and the grounds, both of the cieling and the side-walls, are all picked in with different tints of green, which has a simple and elegant effect."

Of the second withdrawing-room:

> " The ornaments of the pilasters, arches and the pannels of the doors, are beautifully painted by Zucchi."

Of the great withdrawing-room:

> " The ornaments of the cieling and entablature are chiefly of stucco, gilt, with a mixture of paintings. The grounds are coloured with various tints. The frames for glasses, the pedestals and vases in the niches and the girandoles on the piers, are of wood, gilt. This room is hung with satin, and is undoubtedly one of the most elegant in Europe, whether we consider the variety or the richness of its decoration."

The effects of the gradual industrialization of England have been described by an historian as influencing changes in habits of living:

> " In the industrial world, members of the new middle class ceased to live over the workshop, and built themselves separate villas and mansions in imitation of the life of the gentry. They no longer formed one household with their apprentices and journeymen. The landed gentry, for their part, were enlarging

the manorhouse for the heir and the parsonage for the younger son, and too often replacing a tumble of gabled roofs that had grown up piecemeal in the last three hundred years, by a gorgeous 'gentleman's seat' in the neo-Palladian style."[1]

This prosperity was reflected in the profuseness of internal decoration. Ceilings and walls were panelled, stuccoed, painted with floral, formal, landscape, and legendary subjects. Walls were hung with damasks, figured silks, wall-papers from China, flock papers in imitation of cut velvets, velvets strained or pleated; tooled, coloured and gilded leather from Spain and the Low Countries; and magnificent tapestries. The most ordinary villa had walls stuccoed with flowing designs interspersed with tablets in higher relief bearing groups of classic figures (Figs. 660, 661, 812), all usually in white, with a background of pale blue, green, or other tint, which produced light, graceful, but somewhat cold effects.

Care was taken correctly to proportion rooms and details. A dining-room, measuring 30 ft. by 20 ft. by 15 ft., was described as :

> " intended to be hung with damask or paper. The order is preserved in the several parts of the walls."[2]

The space to be hung with damask or to be papered was that between the dado (pedestal) and the frieze—viz., that space which, had the walls been decorated with an Order, instead of only being proportioned to one, would represent the height of the column or pilaster (see Fig. 640).

Another dining-room, all four sides of which are illustrated in one of the carpenter-architect's books,[3] measured 42 ft. by 30 ft. by 16 ft. It has a recess at one end, the full width of the room, from which it was divided by Corinthian columns, which, like the wall divisions, were carefully proportioned. Large profiles are given of the mouldings, those of the panels being similar to those at Chandos House (Fig. 656). In the same volume, and for the same house, illustrations are given for a library, entirely lined with bookshelves, and measuring 26$\frac{1}{2}$ ft. by 17$\frac{1}{2}$ ft. by 16 ft.

Sir William Chambers, writing in 1795, of the proportions of rooms, gives the height of an oblong room as equal to its width—additional height to be allowed for coved rooms. He recognizes the difficulty of varying heights of rooms on the same floor, which must generally be the same, and says:

> " The usual method in buildings where beauty and magnificence are pre-ferred to economy, is to raise the hall, salons and galleries, higher than the other rooms, by making them occupy two stories ; to make the drawing-rooms, or other largest rooms, with flat ceilings ; to cove the middle-sized ones a third, a quarter, or a fifth of their height, according as it is more or less excessive ; and in the smallest apartments, where even the highest coves are not sufficient to render the proportion tolerable, it is usual to contrive mezzanines over them, which

[1] History of England, by G. M. Trevelyan, 1926, " The Reign of George III," p. 612.
[2] The Builder's Magazine, 1774, [p. 1], Plate ii.
[3] The Practical House Carpenter, by William Pain, 7th edition, published 1805, but the plates (Nos. 117-24) are dated 1791.

afford servants' lodging rooms, baths, powdering rooms, wardrobes and the like ; so much the more convenient, as they are near the state apartments, and of private access. . . . Holkham is a masterpiece in this respect . . . and does great credit to the memory of Mr. Kent." [1]

In his Lectures, delivered to students of the Royal Academy, 1809-36, Sir John Soane said:

" If in fixing the proper Heights of Rooms Convenience were the only object to be attended to, ten or twelve feet in rooms of moderate dimensions would be sufficient for every useful purpose, but when Elegance and Magnificence are consulted, the Height of a square room with a flat ceiling is usually not less than four-fifths of its breadth, nor more than five-sixths. If the ceiling of such a room be coved the Height should be equal to one side of the square. In a room, the Length of which exceeds its Breadth, the Height should be equal to the latter dimension, and, if the room be one-third or one-half more than its width, the two dimensions should be added together, and half the total allowed for the Height. If the Room be coved, one-fourth or one-fifth more must be allowed." [2]

Wallpaper is a perishable form of decoration so easily removed and replaced that few examples of early ones have come down to us; so few, indeed, as to give an impression of less frequent use than may have been the case. In the fifteenth century they were in use in France, as contemporary records show, and about the same time (1482) statute 1 of Richard III, cap. 12[3] (which was to prevent unemployment in England caused by importation of manufactured articles from the Continent), ordained that certain articles should not be imported into England, among which were

" painted glass, painted papers, painted images, painted cloths."

Painted cloths are referred to in ancient inventories as cheap substitutes for tapestries, and association in this statute of painted cloths and painted papers is significant.[4] Add to this the facts that painted wallpapers were then in use in France, that contemporary examples have been found in England, and that not only was paper made in the fifteenth century in quantities but that paper of old documents was reused, there can be little doubt that painted wallpapers were employed as substitutes for painted cloths, just as the latter were substitutes for arras, and, further, that wallpapers were used for decoration of walls concurrently with paintings on plaster, like those illustrated in Figs. 695, 696, 699.

Designs for these early wallpapers were heraldic, or formal or floral similar to those employed for brocades, damasks, and other textiles. Others may have been inspired by tempera wall decorations. In some cases sheets were pasted together and rolled. An early English paper (c. 1509) was found at Christ's College, Cambridge. This was a formal pine-cone, strap and foliage design,

[1] *Civil Architecture*, Gwilt, ed. 1825, pp. 390-1.
[2] *Lectures on Architecture*, by Sir John Soane, edited by Arthur T. Bolton, London, 1929, pp. 122-3.
[3] Quoted by C. C. Oman in *A Catalogue of Wallpapers*, V. and A. Museum 1929, from which also other information has been derived.
[4] See page 71.

such as is associated with brocades, and was printed on the paper from a wood block. The design was printed on old documents which had writing on one side only. Another sixteenth-century paper is illustrated (Fig. 727), the design of which would have been applicable equally to textile fabrics. Seventeenth-century designs of architectural subjects exist, and in this century there was important development of flock papers, in which a ground colour is first applied and, when dry, the desired design printed or painted in an adhesive. Upon this flock is dusted—flock being fine wool waste, and this only sticks to the pattern painted in adhesive (Fig. 729).

In the eighteenth century, wallpapers, which hitherto had been substitutes for more costly decorations, became fashionable, and fashion favoured papers designed and produced in China. Chinese designs of the early seventeenth century were such as are associated with painted silks. The fashionable Chinese papers of the second half of the eighteenth century were of three types: (1) Birds and plants; (2) human figures engaged in various pursuits, as that illustrated from Ramsbury Manor (Fig. 728); and (3) a combination of the two. These papers were frequently mounted on canvas, strained and lightly fixed to walls from which they could be removed.

Although a patent was granted in 1753 to print from copper cylinders, the development and popularizing of wallpapers by this means was achieved by calico-printers of the nineteenth century, who turned out immense quantities at low prices and were the real progenitors of the modern paper-stainer, whose productions revolutionized wall decoration not only by superseding panelling, stucco reliefs, and textile hangings (Fig. 730 still shows the influence of classic wall-paintings), but by eliminating the horizontal division of walls in proportion of the order and covering the whole surface from skirting to ceiling with patterned papers.[1]

The use of fir and deal boards, often knotty, for flooring was one factor favouring the increasingly popular practice of covering floors with carpets. Another treatment, less familiar, is referred to in the lines, written early in the nineteenth century:

" These all wear out of me, like Forms with chalk
Painted on rich men's floors for one feast-night."[2]

Although the proportions for later eighteenth-century external doorways were laid down in the books as a double square, heights were generally more than twice the widths of openings and the minimum of these 6 ft. 6 in. by 3 ft. Designers also allowed themselves some latitude in proportions, which were

[1] *Catalogue of Wallpapers*, by C. C. Oman, London, V. and A. Museum, 1929. "English Wallpapers of the Sixteenth and Seventeenth Centuries," by H. Jenkinson, *Antiquaries' Journal*, 1925.
[2] *Personal Talk*, William Wordsworth's Poems, London, 1888. Poem beginning " I am not one who much or oft delight . . ."

subordinated to those of the fronts. During the third quarter of the century Roman Orders were still in favour, both for columns and pilasters. The Tuscan Order was seldom employed, the Doric (Fig. 450) most, and after it the Ionic (Figs. 448, 467), generally with triangular pediments, as Fig. 448, but also with horizontal entablatures. Later, as Fig. 467, Greek Orders came into favour, with horizontal entablatures, supported by consoles. All these doorways had fanlights over them to light entrance halls, which often were narrow and depended upon these and light from a window half-way up the stairs for illumination. These fanlights were filled with delicate and beautiful glazed tracery in wood, lead, or cast iron (Figs. 463, 464, 466, 469, 870). Doors (painted dark green or brown) were framed up in six or more panels, which, earlier, were raised and sunk later. Where doorways were of stone, the doors might be painted white as was stipulated for all houses in The Royal Crescent, Bath, by the architect, John Wood the younger. Often the lower panels were flush with the framing, from which they were separated only by a bead and quirk. Brass handles were small by comparison with nineteenth-century patterns, and there was considerable diversity in design of brass door-knockers (Fig. 874).

For internal doorcases the triangular pediment was being replaced by a horizontal entablature on consoles (Fig. 465). These, the frieze, and the architrave and pilasters (where they were included) were enriched with carved and applied ornament (Fig. 465). Where doors were of pine or fir they, like fir panelling, were painted (Fig. 462). In the best houses the doors were of mahogany, the six panels made from beautifully figured wood and framed with horizontal fluting, with paterae at the angles and enriched with carving (Figs. 465, 474). The brass furniture on these doors was delicately modelled and gilded (Fig. 476).

There was great variety in sash-window design, casements only being used for cottages and very small houses. The proportion of window openings was the double square, but judgment was exercised in varying this, and we find those of a principal floor, $2\frac{2}{5}$ or more to 1 (Figs. 258, 272), with those of the second floor a little more or a little less than a square (Figs. 258, 262). For important buildings the tabernacle frame might be used (Figs. 262, 343), in others windows were furnished with a moulded architrave and key-block as the middle window (Fig. 251), and immense numbers had flat gauged brick arches without architraves (Fig. 272). By Act of Parliament—

"After the 1st day of June 1709 no Door Frame or Window Frame of Wood, to be fix'd to any House or Building within the Cities of London and Westminster, or their Liberties, shall be set nearer to the outside Face of the Wall than four inches."[1]

This accounts for reveals (often plastered and painted white like the frames) to be seen in London houses (Fig. 272), whereas, in the provinces window frames were

[1] 7 Annæ, fol. 263.

flush, or almost flush, with the wall-face, as Fig. 261. Some later Venetian windows were embellished with fan treatment over the arch (Fig. 545). In smaller houses three-light sash windows were introduced, but the sashes of the side-lights might be fixed (Figs. 261, 546). Round-headed (semicircular) windows were used for dormers (Fig. 286) and in many other ways (Figs. 262, 542); about the middle of the century, bow, segmental, and other forms of bay windows became common (Figs. 279, 280, 544, 548). Some of these were designed with columns and with pilasters (Figs. 547, 548); indeed, much ingenuity was shown in devising novel forms. Other dormer windows were flat and segmental headed (Figs. 271, 287), as well as furnished with the triangular and segmental pediments of the earlier part of the century (Fig. 534).

A radical change took place in the sections of glazing bars; a width of 2 in. in the time of Wren was reduced by 1820 to $\frac{1}{2}$ in. These glazing bars were also made on the curve and " in the Gothic taste " (Figs 279, 280).

Stair balustrades in the earlier manner, as that at Stowe (Fig. 853), developed into lighter and more wiry design (Fig. 855), in its turn followed by graceful ironwork as that by Adam (Fig. 856). This became less decorative (Fig. 857), and ultimately the balusters were plain square bars of wood or of iron, having a section of 1 in. or $1\frac{1}{4}$ in., carrying a narrow mahogany handrail. Staircases were also curved in plan, as Fig. 858, or were in long straight flights. The Chinese taste of the middle of the eighteenth century produced balustrades after the style of that in Fig. 854. Ultimately the staircase tended to become merely a contrivance for traffic and lost character as one of the chief features of the house interior.

Mantelpieces differed more in the diversity of their details than in general design. They were not " continued " with superstructures as those earlier in the century (Figs. 794, 800), but walls above were decorated with stucco or other panels (Fig. 812), or provided with mirrors (Fig. 810). The mantelpiece itself consisted of a frieze with entablature, forming a wider shelf than hitherto, supported by pilasters, consoles, or columns. The material might be:

(a) White marble (Figs. 808, 811).
(b) White and coloured marbles (Figs. 807, 810).
(c) White marble, inlaid with coloured marbles (Fig. 812).
(d) Wood, carved, ornament applied and all painted (Fig. 813).

The friezes were often enriched by sculpture as in Figs. 808, 811. Such ornament on wood mantels was cast or modelled in composition or even in soft metal and then painted.

Two chimneypieces (which no longer exist), one in the great withdrawing-room, the other in the Countess of Derby's dressing-room, are described in the Adam book as follows:

" The former is finely executed in statuary marble, inlaid with various coloured scagliola and brass ornaments, gilt in *or moulu*. . . . The latter . . . in the Etruscan style, both in regard to the form of ornament and the peculiarity of the colouring."[1]

Openings (so spacious in medieval fireplaces, Figs. 771, 776) had long been contracted, and the fireback and andirons, which lingered during the reign of William and Mary in Dutch designs (Figs. 792, 793), were replaced by the fire-basket (Fig. 780), which, indeed, the increasing practice of burning coal had made necessary. The firebasket developed into a handsome combination of fireback, basket and standards, which raised it well above the hearth (Figs. 785, 799), more simple forms of which are shown in Figs. 807, 809. Then came the hob-grate (Fig. 800) and its development in the " duck's nest " (Figs. 784, 811). An early nineteenth-century form is seen in Fig. 774, a later hob-grate in Fig. 814, and the familiar mid-Victorian grate in Fig. 616.

Enough nineteenth-century examples have been illustrated to show the trend of taste—or lack of it—as still to be seen in the architecture of the suburbs of every large town. The sight is a melancholy one, and when the course of the degradation is realized pursuit of the theme can profit little. The dawn of better things is so recent as to belong to a chronicle of current events rather than to history. We cannot say yet what homes the new day may bring. It may produce chaos, but indications promise rational plans and seemly buildings.

[1] *The Works of Robert and James Adam*, vol. ii, description of plate vi.

M

EXTERIORS AND PLANS

For other Illustrations of EXTERIORS see—

EXTERNAL WALL TREATMENT, pages 274 to 281

ENTRANCES, pages 284 to 326

c. 1130.   *King :* Henry I.

FIG. 41.—THE KEEP, CASTLE HEDINGHAM, from the south-west.

FIG. 41.—The earliest Norman castle to be built in stone was the Tower of London, *c.* 1087. Then Rochester Castle and Castle Hedingham, both *c.* 1130. The keep of Rochester Castle is much the larger of these two, but Castle Hedingham keep is in remarkably good state, except that the superstructure of the forebuilding and the embattled parapet which once crowned the walls and towers have been destroyed, as also have two of the four turrets. A great hall stood south-west of the keep (a little behind the point from which the above photograph was taken). Here also the foundations of oriel, buttery, and chapel have been traced, all of uncertain date. The centre buttress on the south front encloses the flues from fireplaces in the two halls, but the openings on each side of the buttress, through which smoke escaped, are now closed up.

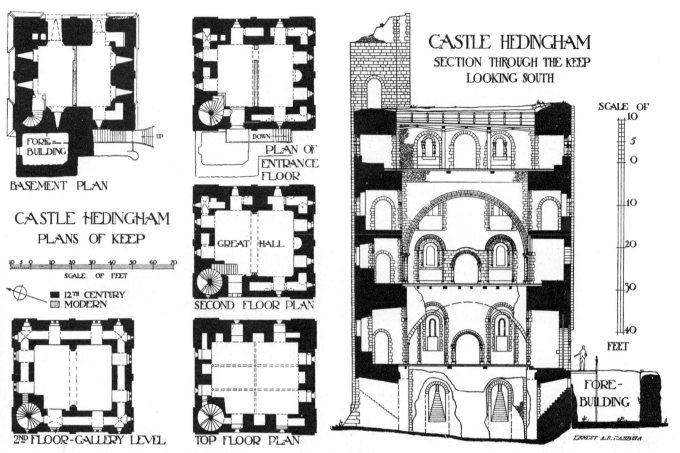

BASEMENT PLAN

FORE-BUILDING

CASTLE HEDINGHAM
PLANS OF KEEP

SCALE OF FEET

■ 12TH CENTURY
▨ MODERN

2ND FLOOR-GALLERY LEVEL

PLAN OF ENTRANCE FLOOR

DOWN

GREAT HALL

SECOND FLOOR PLAN

TOP FLOOR PLAN

CASTLE HEDINGHAM
SECTION THROUGH THE KEEP
LOOKING SOUTH

SCALE OF

FEET

FORE-BUILDING

ERNEST A.R. RAHBUL

F_IG_. 42.—Reproduced from Volume I, *Essex N.W., Royal Commission on Historical Monuments (England)*, by permission of the Controller of H.M. Stationery Office.

c. 1130. *King :* Henry I.

F_IG_. 43.—T_HE_ K_EEP_ _OF_ R_OCHESTER_ C_ASTLE_.

F_IG_. 43.—The general effect is spoilt by the mutilation of the window openings. Stairs, now external but once enclosed, lead to the doorway of the forebuilding. Two newel stairs in the towers give access to the upper floors.

c. 1140.   *King: Stephen.*

FIG. 44.—CASTLE RISING.

FIG. 44.—The upper portion is ruinous, but most of the structure of the forebuilding (destroyed at Castle Hedingham) remains. In this were the stairs leading to the doorway of the Guard chamber (the arch of which can be seen).

Photo: S. Smith, Lincoln.

c. 1150.   *King: Stephen.*

FIG. 45.—THE JEWS' HOUSE, LINCOLN.

FIG. 45.—There are few town houses of this period, and those remaining have been mutilated or altered. In this (one of two on Steep Hill, Lincoln) are some remaining features of interest. There was one room each on the ground and first floors, the latter having the fireplace, which is set over the archway of the door; but the chimney was destroyed during the nineteenth century. The circular-headed windows had two lights each, separated by shafts which formed the mullions or monials.

c. 1150.   *King:* Stephen.

FIG. 46.—A Norman house at CHRISTCHURCH, HANTS.

FIG. 46.—This house measures only 70 ft. by 24 ft., yet was the residence of an earl.
The ground floor was lighted by loopholes.   The first floor was the hall, which has two-
light windows at the sides and ends and possibly had one end partitioned off to form a
private chamber.   It contains the only fireplace, the circular chimney of which remains.
Although a ruin, the gable and side walls remaining enable a good idea to be formed of
its form and bulk.   A stream of the river Avon flows between the footpath and the
elevation illustrated.   Traces of other buildings remain, but we know from Alexander
Neckham (*c.* 1157–1217) that the accommodation of a house (that is, the residence
of a person of importance) consisted of hall, chamber, kitchen, larder, and sewery or
servery.   The last three were often "lean-to" or similarly flimsy structures.   Walls
were rendered with plaster, decorated with paintings of sacred or other subjects, but
wainscot does not seem to have been in vogue until the next century.

Photo : W. Lee, Grantham.

c. 1180.   *King:* Henry II.

FIG. 47.—THE MANOR HOUSE, BOOTHBY PAGNELL, near GRANTHAM.

FIG. 47.—This building marks the transition from Norman to Early English.   Like that at
Christchurch, it consists of two floors, the upper having the fireplace.   Access was by an
external stair, but that existing is not original.   The four-light window is a fifteenth-
century insertion, but the two-light windows are contemporary with the building.   Like
other twelfth-century buildings, it has been re-roofed.

FIG. 48.—A sixteenth-seventeenth-century cottage at ST. ANDREWS.

FIG. 48.—The stone castles which the Normans introduced into England had the living-rooms on upper floors, the ground floor being used for storage. But the Saxon hall had always been on ground level (the illustration in the Bayeaux tapestry of King Harold and his nobles drinking in a first-floor *aula* is drawn by a Frenchman), and we shall find that this Saxon practice (subject to occasional exceptions, as at Liddington, Fig. 614) gradually superseded the Norman hall on an upper floor, which all the preceding examples and several which follow illustrate. The French tradition (originally defensive) of having living-rooms on the upper floors survived in Scotland, however, where external stairs were constructed as recently as the eighteenth century, and in modern Scottish houses the drawing-room is still on the first floor. The photograph shows a typical Scottish cottage with the living-room on the first floor, approached by external stairs, the ground floor being used for storage : the ground-floor windows are later insertions.

Photo : Henwood and Son, Oakham.

c. 1180.   *King:* Henry II
FIG. 49.—OAKHAM CASTLE, RUTLAND.

FIG. 49.—Oakham Castle has a hall of the Saxon type with the floor at ground level and open to the roof within. This hall, an example of the transitional period between Norman and Early English, is the only building that remains of a residence of Henry II. The roof is modern but has the same pitch as the original. The doorway (like practically all entrances to medieval halls) was nearer the end—actually in the position of the two-light window on the extreme right of the illustration. The gable finials are original : the one on the left is a centaur, that on the right a woman seated on the back of a scaly animal.

Photograph by Aero Films Ltd.

c. 1180–1190.

FIG. 50.—DOVER CASTLE.

King : Richard I.

FIG. 50.—Few stone castles were built by the Normans until about seventy years after the Conquest. Dover Castle, *c* 1180-1190, is the product of many periods, and occupies the site of important and extensive predecessors. Even the Norman keep has suffered from alterations. As a general picture of a large fortress the air view gives a better impression than would any plan. It stands on a precipitous hill ; the present easy road up from the town is modern, and access to the entrance (in right-hand lower corner of the photograph) would be by a steep path. To reach the entrance gateway a deep ditch is crossed by a drawbridge. Entering through this gateway and across the Outer Bailey, another gatehouse in the inner ring of the fortifications has to be passed to reach the Inner Bailey, in the centre of which stands the keep. Although much altered, Dover Castle still conforms to the plan of a large Norman fortress. To study unmutilated details we must go to contemporary castles which (though semi-ruinous) are in their original unaltered state.

c. 1190.   *King:* Richard I.

FIG. 51.—BAMBURGH CASTLE, NORTHUMBERLAND.

FIG. 51.—By contrast with the scanty remains of the wood-building Saxons, England is filled with Norman castles, churches, and even a few remains of small houses, for the Normans built in stone and stone endures. Of these Bamburgh Castle was built about 1190, though on this site an extensive Saxon timber fortress (long since demolished) stood in the sixth century. Although the castle has undergone many alterations of detail (the Tudor windows are most noticeable in the view above) the castle as a whole retains its Norman character and presents an imposing appearance. In photographing Bamburgh Castle it happens that roofs of low buildings are shown nestling under it as if for protection (just as buildings undoubtedly did in the twelfth century), by which a remarkably realistic impression is conveyed.

c. 1240 and 1291.   *Kings:* Henry III and Edward I.

FIG. 52.—STOKESAY CASTLE, SHROPSHIRE.

FIG. 52.—A view from the south-west, with the church tower beyond. The south tower on the right and the north tower on the left suggest defence, and the other buildings domesticity.

c. 1240 and 1291. *Kings :* Henry III and Edward I.

FIG. 53.—STOKESAY CASTLE, SHROPSHIRE, from beyond the moat.

The buildings are of several dates: The lower part of the north end (on right). *c.* 1115; the upper part *c.* 1620; the hall and upper end (solar, etc.), *c.* 1240; the south tower on left, *c.* 1291; the timber and plaster gatehouse (FIG. 335), *c.* 1600.

FIG. 53.—The external stairs up to the solar and from the solar to the south tower had a pentice roof, the sloping weatherings over which can be seen on the wall in the illustration. So far as nature of accommodation went, the Norman house was little better than the Saxon, but there is a gradual increase in the number of rooms. The hall was still there, but instead of being the only apartment it became the principal one of several, though the total, even in the king's residences, was meagre. The change was so gradual that only by comparing several houses of one period with those of another can we realize the growth of accommodation. Stokesay Castle was really a fortified house (not a castle), for protection was necessary near the borders of Wales. The south tower was a special feature; but the parallelogram, which included the hall with lower end chambers near its entrance, and upper end chambers at

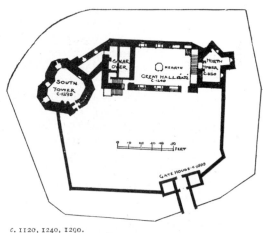

c. 1120, 1240, 1290.

FIG. 54.

its south end, was in accordance with the usual medieval house-plan. The courtyard, measuring about 120 ft. by 80 ft., was entered through a gatehouse, and the whole was surrounded by a deep moat. In addition there were buildings (such as the kitchen) which formerly stood in the court. This was an important place in the thirteenth century, the residence of the de Says, the Ludlows, and later of the Vernons, who maintained considerable forces requiring corresponding accommodation.

c. 1260-1280.   *Kings:* Henry III and Edward I.

FIG. 55.—The south-east angle of LITTLE WENHAM HALL, SUFFOLK.

FIGS. 55, 56 AND 57.—This is a remarkably well-preserved and carefully restored example of a knight's house of the latter part of the thirteenth century. Though domestic, it is fortified, and although it had no moat, it would be protected by some kind of enclosure, within which would be subsidiary buildings of a less substantial nature. The ground floor is vaulted, and consists of a large chamber under the hall and a small one under the chapel. The windows are narrow outside and deeply splayed within, but in the chapel these are not furnished with window seats as are those in the hall, nor is there any fireplace. There is an entrance doorway on the ground level at the north end, which opened into the large room from which a winding stair gave access to the first and second floors and the roof. A doorway opens into the hall at the first-floor level, access to which was gained by an external staircase, which may have occupied the position of the modern wooden stairs seen in Fig. 55. Another doorway on the same level on the west side is an Elizabethan insertion, *c.* 1585. The hall and chapel occupy the first floor. The entrance doorway, modern stairs, and two-light windows are at the south end of the hall. The tower contains the chapel (first floor) and one chamber over it. The turret encloses the newel staircase. The chamber under the hall is vaulted with brick, and has stone ribs. Slight alterations and repairs were made during Elizabeth's reign, and further necessary repairs were made at the end of the nineteenth century, but the general appearance of the house and the details of its windows, etc., are substantially what they were during the reigns of Henry III and Edward I. The church, which stands near, was built at the same time. This building is, perhaps, the most interesting of the few now existing of its period, and is the earliest brick dwelling-house remaining in England. (*Measured drawings and plans are given on the following two pages.*)

By courtesy of Miss Margaret Crisp.

LITTLE WENHAM HALL. SUFFOLK.

SCALE OF FEET

EAST ELEVATION

SKETCH IN LOWER ROOM

WEST ELEVATION

THE SOUTH DOORWAY WAS AC-
CESSIBLE BY AN EXTERNAL STAIR-
CASE WHICH SEEMS TO HAVE
CURVED ROUND THE S.W.-ANGLE
BUT HAS BEEN REMOVED AND
ACCESS IS NOW GAINED BY A
LADDER

SOUTH ELEVATION

Measured and Drawn by;
Geoffr. William Leighton
March 1889.

Kings : Henry III and Edward.

EXTERIOR

PLAN

SEAT

STONE

A WINDOW IN HALL

INTERIOR

SCALE FOR DETAILS

THE MATERIAL OF THE WALLS OF THIS HOUSE
IS CHIEFLY BRICK, MIXED IN PARTS WITH FLINT
THESE BRICKS ARE MOSTLY OF THE MODERN
FLEMISH SHAPE BUT THERE ARE SOME OF OTHER
FORMS AND SIZES. THE COLOUR OF THE GROUND
VARIES CONSIDERABLY.
ALL THE BUTTRESSES ABOVE THE LEVEL OF THE
PLINTH ARE BUILT ENTIRELY OF STONE SOME OF
A VERY HARD STONE
THE COPINGS ARE OF TERRA COTTA SOME OF
WHICH ARE ORIGINAL AND OTHERS OF A LATER
PERIOD

SECTION A B

FIG. 56.—Elevations and Sections of LITTLE WENHAM HALL, SUFFOLK.

c. 1260–1280.

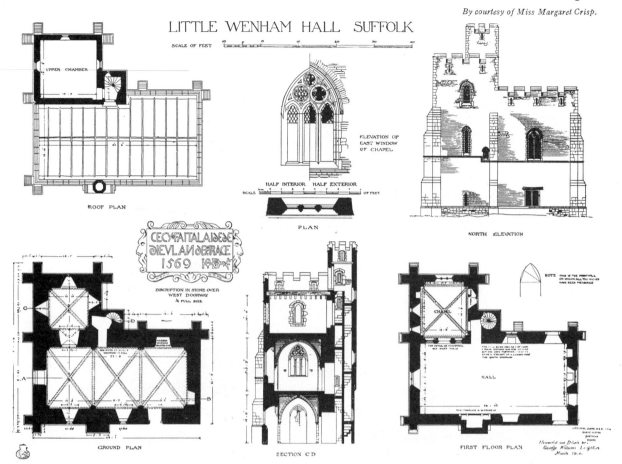

By courtesy of Miss Margaret Crisp.

LITTLE WENHAM HALL SUFFOLK

SCALE OF FEET

UPPER CHAMBER

ROOF PLAN

ELEVATION OF
EAST WINDOW
OF CHAPEL

HALF INTERIOR   HALF EXTERIOR

SCALE   OF FEET

PLAN

NORTH ELEVATION

CECY·FATTALAISESE
SIEVLAN·DEGRACE
1569

INSCRIPTION IN STONE OVER
WEST DOORWAY
¼ FULL SIZE

GROUND PLAN

SECTION CD

CHAPEL

HALL

FIRST FLOOR PLAN

FIG. 57.—Plans and Elevations of LITTLE WENHAM HALL, SUFFOLK.

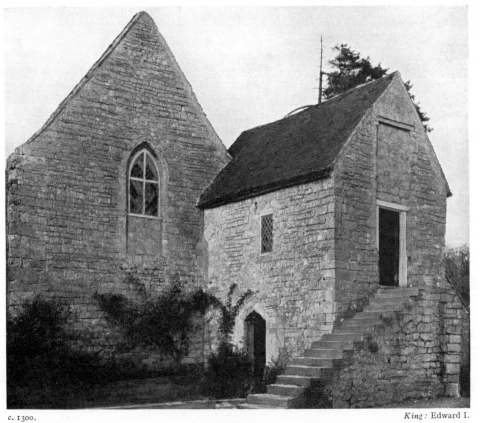

c. 1300.   *King:* Edward I.

FIG. 58.—The east end of the hall and chapel, OLD SOAR, PLAXTOL, KENT.

c. 1300.   Chapel.   Chamber.   Hall.   Turret staircase.

FIG. 59.—The north-west angle of OLD SOAR.

FIG. 58—The tracery has been removed from the hall windows and from the south and east windows of the chapel. The latter has been mutilated further by the insertion of a doorway, the steps up to which are modern, though built partially with old stones. Notwithstanding its condition, this is a valuable example of a late thirteenth-century house, because it is small, and the chances against small houses surviving 600 years are infinitely great.

FIG. 59.—The building on the left is the chapel, and that in the foreground is a chamber, lighted only by four cross-loops. The high building on the right (with a part of the window shown) is the hall. The low, semi-circular tower, with stone roof, on the right of the hall, contains the winding staircase. See also the east elevations and plan (Figs. 58 and 60).

FIG. 60.—Old Soar was at one time the seat of the Colepeppers, who afterwards became the largest land-owning family in Kent and Sussex by the simple expedient, it has been stated, of kidnapping heiresses, whom they forcibly married. As at Little Wenham Hall, the apartments are on the first floor. The ground-floor room under the hall has a stone vault, but the chapel and chamber floors are of timber.

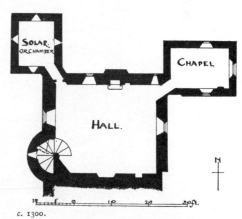

c. 1300.

FIG. 60.—The first-floor plan of OLD SOAR.

(From Turner's *Domestic Architecture.*)

Photo: Gibson, Hexham.

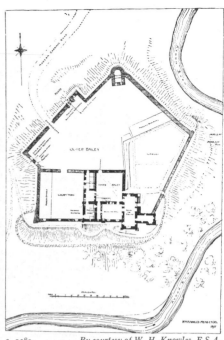

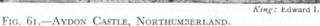

c. 1280.   *King: Edward I.*

FIG. 61.—AYDON CASTLE, NORTHUMBERLAND.

c 1280.   *By courtesy of W. H. Knowles, F.S.A.*

FIG. 62.—AYDON CASTLE.   General plan.

FIG. 61.—The Inner Court, showing steps to the Upper Hall doorway, two-light windows of hall and
north end of solar building with windows.   The doorway, with modern window inserted, was the original
entrance to the Lower Hall; that at foot of steps is later.   The channel in the wall over the steps shows
the line of the pentice roof which once protected them.

Photo: Gibson Hexham.

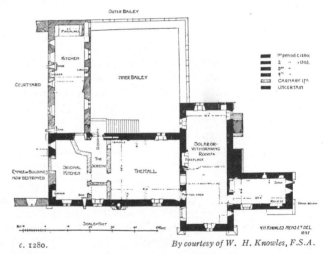

c. 1280.   *By courtesy of W. H. Knowles, F.S.A.*

FIG. 64.—AYDON CASTLE, NORTHUMBERLAND.
Plan of principal (first) floor.

FIG. 63.—This foreshortened view shows the
south-west buttress of the solar wing. Beyond
this is the wall chimney of the Lower Hall,
carried up only to the string course and having
side openings for escape of smoke. Further are
the windows of the Upper Hall, the lower lighting
the entry, the upper (with pointed lights) the
gallery over the screens, now destroyed. The
furthest windows lighted the original kitchen on
the Upper Hall level and west of the screens.

c. 1280.   *King : Edward I.*

FIG. 63.—AYDON CASTLE, NORTHUMBERLAND.   South
front from the east.

Photo by Aerofilms.

Mainly fourteenth and sixteenth centuries.

FIG. 65.—HADDON HALL, DERBYSHIRE.

FIG. 65.—This air photograph from the south-west angle gives a general idea of the group of buildings which are of several periods—many on earlier foundations. Between the two courts is the great hall (with pitched roof), *c.* 1330, entered from both courts, the parlour (with solar over) is at its south end, whilst the kitchen and buttery are at its north end. The early exterior walls of the east front (eleventh to twelfth century) retain their defensive character. The original entrance to the courtyard was from the north front under the Eagle Tower situated in the north-east angle. The long gallery (sixteenth century) with its three bay windows faces the lawn. The Chapel (fifteenth century) occupies the south-west angle.

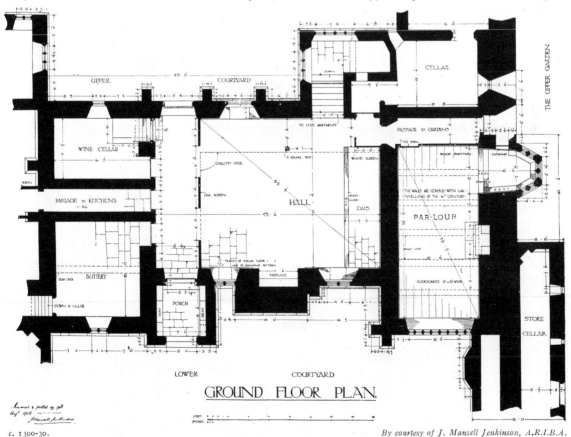

GROUND FLOOR PLAN.

c. 1300-30.   *By courtesy of J. Mansell Jenkinson, A.R.I.B.A.*

FIG. 66.—HADDON HALL, DERBYSHIRE. Ground floor plan.

FIG. 66.—There is no better known or more romantic domestic building of the medieval period than Haddon Hall. Although portions were built as early as the thirteenth century, it is about the central block of hall, upper-end and lower-end chambers, that interest centres. Yet the ground plan is the same as other houses of the period and differs little from that of Penshurst (FIG. 80), 150 miles away.

N

:ELEVATION TO LOWER COURTYARD:

c. 1300–30.   *By courtesy of J. Mansell Jenkinson, A.R.I.B.A.*
FIG. 67.—HADDON HALL, DERBYSHIRE.

FIG. 67.—The principal entrance to the great hall, like others, has another door opposite. The drawing brings out clearly the fine masses of masonry pierced by well-proportioned windows, the treatment of which may be compared with those at Penshurst (b. 1341), FIGS. 79, 81.

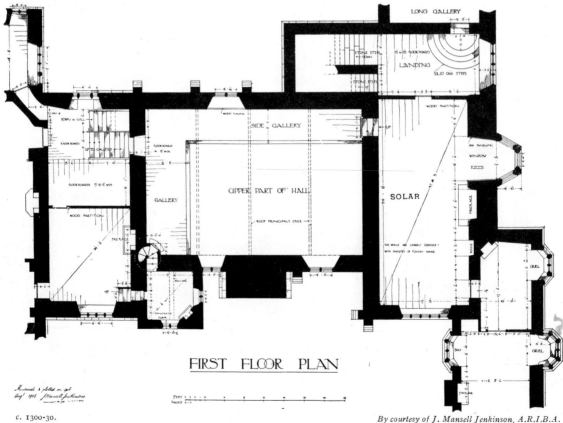

FIRST FLOOR PLAN

c. 1300-30.   *By courtesy of J. Mansell Jenkinson, A.R.I.B.A.*
FIG. 68.—HADDON HALL, DERBYSHIRE. First-floor plan.

FIG. 68.—Interest in the first-floor plan is in its completeness and (except the galleries in the hall) in its all being medieval.

Photo: Gibson, Hexham.

c. 1310.   *King: Edward II.*

FIG. 69.—The approach over the moat through the gatehouse at
MARKENFIELD HALL, near RIPON, YORKSHIRE.

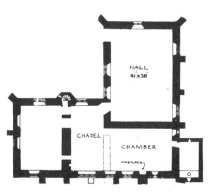

FIG. 70.—The first-floor plan of
MARKENFIELD HALL.

Photo: Gibson, Hexham

c. 1310.   *King: Edward II.*

FIG. 71.—The fourteenth-century building occupying the north-east angle of the courtyard
of MARKENFIELD HALL, near RIPON, YORKSHIRE.

Photo: Gibson, Hexham.

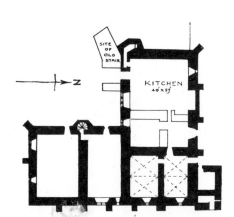

FIG. 72.—The ground-floor plan of
MARKENFIELD HALL.

c. 1310.   *King: Edward II.*

FIG. 73.—The east elevation of MARKENFIELD HALL, near RIPON, YORK-
SHIRE, showing the chapel window of three lights with geometrical tracery.

FIG. 69.—The fourteenth-century house occupies one angle of the courtyard, which is surrounded by
a moat. The gatehouse and other buildings are of the fifteenth-sixteenth centuries.

FIG. 71.—The hall is at the first-floor level, and was originally entered by a doorway from an external
stair, the line of the roof over which can be seen by the weathering on the wall above the ground-floor
doorway. The hall is lighted by four-light (transome) geometrical traceried windows, two on each side.
The square windows are contemporary. The low building on the right is not included in the plans.

FIG. 73.—The two chimneys shown are (left) of the fourteenth and (right) of the fifteenth century.

FIG. 74.—The fourteenth-century tower, once self-contained, gradually had added to it a hall, kitchen, and other buildings, and was surrounded by a courtyard, the sides of which remain. Yanwath Tower has three storeys and very thick walls; the ground-floor apartment has a barrel vault, and the windows are narrow without, but deeply splayed within to admit the maximum of light. An Elizabethan ceiling in the first-floor room is one of the later alterations. The original, and at one time the only, stair was of the newel type. The stone rainwater spouts which drain the tower roof are designed as projections of the moulded string courses. The top of a contemporary chimney, having a conical cap and side-loop vents, can be seen just over the battlements. Such towers show little development from the Norman keeps of a date 200 years earlier. This fact alone indicates the still disturbed state of the Border country, which stifled progress towards that comfort in house design which the more settled south was already beginning to enjoy; peace and security have ever been necessary to house development.

c. 1325.   *Kings:* Edward II and Henry V.
FIG. 74.—YANWATH TOWER, WESTMORLAND. Tower c. 1325. Hall with kitchen beyond, on the right, is fifteenth century.

FIG. 75.—A plan of an upper floor at YANWATH TOWER, WESTMORLAND.

FIG. 76.—This building is of several periods, but possesses a number of characteristic and interesting fourteenth-century details. The chapel window (one of two) is a fine example of reticulated tracery, a rarity in domestic work. The 18-light window of the great hall and the 8-light window are perpendicular. The "Dutch" gable is seventeenth century. The porch and entrance doorway are fourteenth century, but the square window over is of later date.

FIG. 77.—At a time when monasteries were places of entertainment for travellers, the hospitality of such establishments as Glastonbury was prodigious. The accommodation afforded varied with the rank and importance of the guests, but was equal to providing for the retinue of a great lord, and even for the King himself. The kitchen (the only remaining portion of the domestic buildings) is of a type current at this period. There is another at Durham, one at Stanton Harcourt, and one with a similar roof at Raby Castle, co. Durham. The chimneys which stood on the four angles of the square lower storey have long since disappeared, but the openings in the lantern provided for the escape of steam and foul air remain.

c. 1320.   *King:* Edward II.
FIG. 76.—CLEVEDON COURT, SOMERSET.

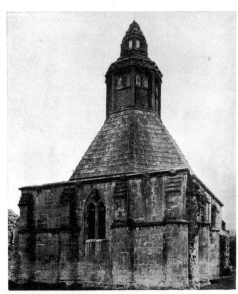

c. 1320.   *King:* Edward II.
FIG. 77.—THE ABBOT'S KITCHEN, GLASTONBURY.

c. 1330.   *King:* Edward III.

FIG. 78.—THE GREAT BARN, GLASTONBURY, SOMERSET.

FIG. 78.—Allusion has been made to the similarity of church, domestic and agricultural buildings built during the medieval period. Except that the walls are pierced by loops instead of windows, this building might well be the great hall of some lord or prelate. The upper part of each gable is pierced by a window having three trefoiled lights. Under the window is a panel carved with a winged bull, the emblem of St. Luke, and emblems of the other three Evangelists are found displayed elsewhere on the building. This barn, and the Manor House, Meare, are said to have been built by Abbot Adam de Sodbury.

FIG. 79.—The brick building on the right is a sixteenth-century addition. The windows (restored) show two forms of decorated tracery—geometric and flowing.

c. 1341.   *King:* Edward III.

FIG. 79.—The north entrance to the great hall, PENSHURST PLACE, KENT.

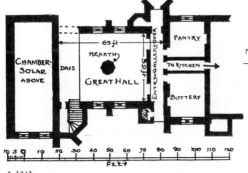

c. 1341.

FIG. 80.—PENSHURST PLACE, KENT.

FIG. 80.—The plan of Penshurst should be studied, for it is the plan of the typical medieval house. There were other types—tower-keeps; halls over vaulted ground-floor chambers; halls consisting of one room only; others having two apartments; and heterogeneous buildings added from time to time within the walls as found necessary for a large household. But the nucleus of these was the hall like that at Penshurst, having "upper-end" chambers consisting of the chamber or parlour or bower behind the dais, and above this room the solar, which was the bed-sitting-room of the lord and his lady. At the "lower end" were the screens and gallery with the passage (entry) between the two entrance doors. Beyond the entry were pantry, buttery, and kitchen, the latter often a relatively flimsy structure. Frequently

(Continued overleaf.)

c. 1341.   *King :* Edward III.

FIG. 81.—The south elevation of PENSHURST PLACE, KENT.

there was also a chapel. When the planning of large houses was quadrangular with a central court, the Penshurst type of plan formed the nucleus to which other lodgings were added, as shown at Bodiam Castle (Fig. 86) and (modified) at Eltham Palace (Fig. 94). The plan of the hall with upper-end and lower-end chambers was that both of great and small houses, and large numbers of the latter exist in Kent and other counties, where they have been converted into farmhouses and cottages. It will be seen that while at the south end of the dais a contemporary doorway to the stairs is shown, no indication is given as to what was originally at its north end. At the present time there are steps to a doorway (at the dotted lines) leading to the sixteenth-century portion of the house. Before this was built there was another window, but probably not a bay window, which was a fifteenth-century feature. Two terms are frequently misapplied to these halls, which have been called " baronial halls " or " banqueting halls." They are not baronial ; they were built long after the barons, and they were the chief apartments of every house, great or small. Nor is the term " banqueting " more correct. The hall was the room in which men and women and children ate, lived, and slept ; and the word " banqueting " (applied correctly to the hall of Whitehall Palace, *c.* 1622, which was built for that specific purpose) is misapplied to medieval halls : indeed, the term and the particular apartment came in with the Renaissance. and the banqueting hall was not introduced earlier than the sixteenth century.

FIG. 81.—The stair tower to the solar is on the left. The entrance to the hall is on the right of the transomed windows ; the pantry, buttery, and other lower-end chambers are to the extreme right. The increasing prosperity and freedom of burghers (whether merchants or otherwise engaged in trade) are manifest in this noble building, erected by a London merchant, Sir John de Poulteney, who was four times Lord Mayor of London, and " who played an important part in the commercial treaties and negotiations during the first half of the reign of Edward III, and was one of those rich traders from whom that King frequently borrowed money. He acquired lands and manors in various counties and in the City parish of St. Lawrence, for which he did so much that it is called after him to this day." That a merchant should be in a position to build and occupy so stately a place is a notable development in emancipation from the domination of nobles, prelates, and soldiers. It also indicates security of person and of property.

. 1350.   *King* : Edward III.

FIG. 82.—THE FISH HOUSE, MEARE, SOMERSET.

FIG. 82.—The small size of this building (32 by 16 ft.) and the simplicity of its details make it particularly interesting. All the windows of this elevation have square heads, but one at the end, shown in Fig. 597, has flowing tracery. The pointed doorways have simple chamfers. The ground floor was divided across the centre, one half forming the kitchen and the other half being divided into two rooms, entered by narrow stone doorways (Fig. 597). Access to the upper floor was by an external stair to the doorway, shown in the illustration ; between this and the doorway to the ground floor can be seen the remains of the chimney base, which served the fireplace in the kitchen and that of the hall above. The woodwork of the interior and the roof open to the first-floor room were burnt out a few years ago, but the roof was almost identical in character with that of Martock Manor House (Fig. 596).

FIG. 83.—The plan of this little house is normal, except that there are no chambers at the upper end of the hall, which was lighted by a large four-light transomed window (Fig. 596), and also by two four-light transomed windows on each side. The portion placed transversely to the hall may be of slightly earlier date ; certainly the two-light window of its upper storey is of earlier character than the windows below and those of the hall. One of the two doorways shown is a later insertion. The modern roof-covering replaces the original stone slates and spoils the general appearance of the building. The small building, part of which is shown on the extreme right, was the kitchen, and is of slightly later date.

c. 1350.   *King* : Edward III.

FIG. 83.—THE MANOR HOUSE, MARTOCK, SOMERSET.

Photo : Gibson and Son, Hexham.

Late fourteenth century.

FIG. 84.—WRESSELL CASTLE, YORKSHIRE.

FIG. 84.—Wressell Castle illustrates several forms of window treatment, including piercing which is akin to plate tracery, lights with ogival heads, and lights having cusping of a character which became general in the fifteenth century. Two of the original chimneys remain. The castle was " slighted " during the Parliamentary wars.

c. 1386.   King: Richard II.

FIG. 85.—BODIAM CASTLE, SUSSEX.

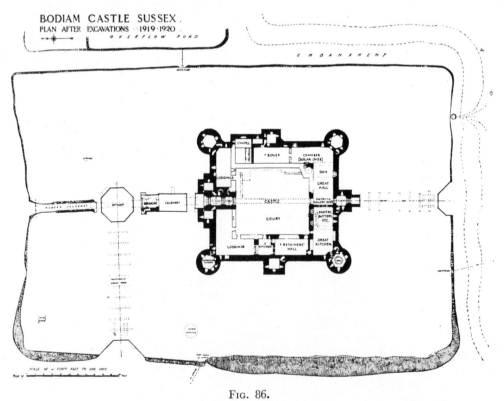

FIG. 86.

(Reproduced from Lord Curzon's book by the courtesy of the publishers, Messrs. Jonathan Cape.)

c. 1386.   *King:* Richard II.

FIG. 87.—Interior of BODIAM CASTLE, looking from the Gatehouse towards the entrance to the Great Hall.

FIG. 85.—A view from the south-east showing the postern, the four-light window of the great hall, the two-light chamber and solar windows, and the three-light window of the chapel. Although the licence to build was granted in 1386, the details are of fifteenth-century character. There are drum towers at each angle, connected by curtain walls, with square towers between them. The gatehouse and postern towers are machicolated. This is the most interesting of all remaining medieval castles, for it has never been altered, and the exterior presents almost the same appearance as it did over five hundred years ago. The south-west drum tower (on the left) contains the well; in its upper storey there is a columbarium to ensure a supply of fresh meat in winter. The only dungeon is in the north-east drum tower.

FIG. 87.—The south side of the court showing the entrance to the great hall, the postern doorway beyond, the four-light great hall window on the left, and those of the kitchen and other offices on the right. Reference to the plan, Fig. 86, will show that the entrance to the hall was in the centre of the court and directly opposite the principal entrance to the castle, as was the usual practice. Most of the roofs at Bodiam were pitched slightly in one direction, but apparently the roof of the great hall was an open roof, having coupled rafters of steep pitch like those of other halls illustrated.

Photo: Gibson, Hexham.

FIG. 88.—A plan of the ground floor of LANGLEY CASTLE, NORTHUMBERLAND.

(From Parker's *Domestic Architecture.*)

c. 1385.   *King:* Richard II.

FIG. 89.—The west elevation of LANGLEY CASTLE, near HEXHAM NORTHUMBERLAND.

FIGS. 88 AND 89.—The small two-light window in the centre has flowing tracery, others are square-headed or are mere loops. The large traceried windows, the entrance doorway and the windows on each side of it are modern. The chimney flues, in the thickness of the walls, terminate in the merlons of the battlements. There are four floors, each providing one large central room, with a smaller apartment in each tower. Four garderobes were provided for each of three floors. The tunnels from these discharged into a pit through which a stream of water was turned, as at Wells and elsewhere. The only original entrance was the narrow one in the north front at the foot of the newel stair.

Fourteenth and fifteenth centuries.
FIG. 90.—ST. CROSS HOSPITAL, HAMPSHIRE.

FIG. 90.—The entrance gateway and tower are of mid-fifteenth-century date. The hall, which is reached by the doorway with stairs, is late fourteenth century. The doorway to the left of it is that of the master's house, and the other buildings, which are of fifteenth-century date, are the lodgings of the brethren. The side from which the photograph was taken is open, except for the church which stands in the right-hand angle. The remaining side on the right has an ambulatory (Fig. 361) with an infirmary above. It will be seen that this institution for indigent persons conformed to the quadrangular plan and also had a gate-house and common hall. Beyond the gatehouse is an entrance court, in which is the hundred-men's hall where the poor were fed.

Late fourteenth or early fifteenth century.
FIG. 91.—GREVEL HOUSE, CHIPPING CAMPDEN.

FIG. 91.—An early fifteenth-century town house with its original doorway and bay window.

c. 1445–1456.   *King:* Henry VI.

FIG. 92.—HURSTMONCEAUX CASTLE, SUSSEX.

FIG. 92.—One of the great English castles of the fifteenth century, built of brick in the manner of French castles.

c. 1465.   *King:* Edward IV.

FIG. 93.—The south-east front of OCKWELLS MANOR, BRAY, BERKSHIRE.

FIG. 93.—A richly decorated half-timbered house of the fifteenth century. The lower-end chambers are on the left of the entrance, the hall and hall bay on the right of it, with the parlour and solar to the right of these   The hall windows and heraldic glass are original.

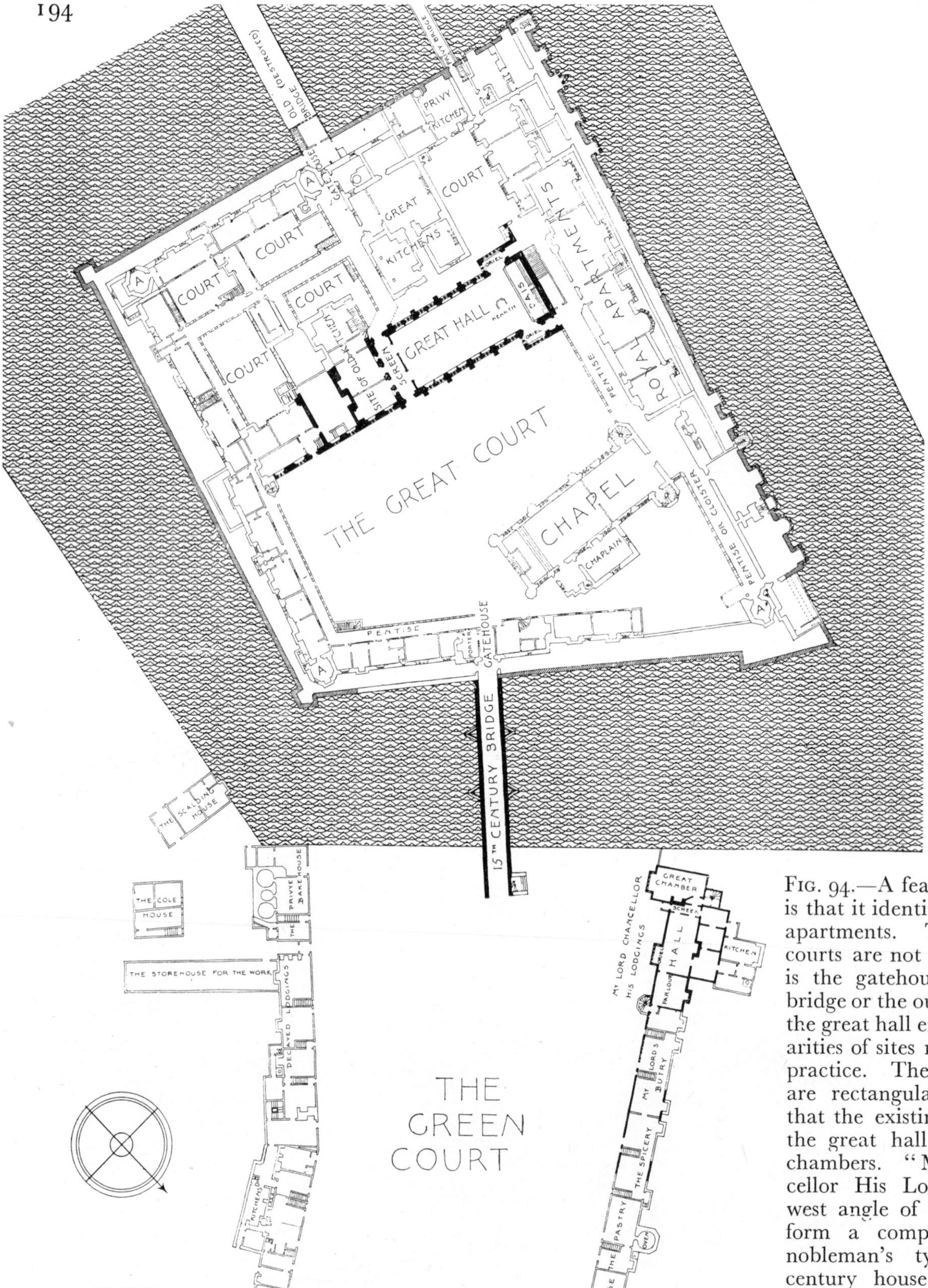

(FORMERLY) BRIDGE OLD

PRIVY KITCHEN

GREAT COURT

COURT

COURT

COURT

COURT

COURT

GREAT KITCHENS

SITE OF OLD HALL

SCREEN

GREAT HALL

HEARTH

ORIEL

ROYAL APARTMENTS

PENTISE

CHAPEL

CHAPLAIN

PENTISE OR CLOISTER

THE GREAT COURT

PENTISE

PORTICO

GATEHOUSE

A

15TH CENTURY BRIDGE

THE SCALDING HOUSE

THE COLE HOUSE

THE PRIVY BAKEHOUSE

THE STOREHOUSE FOR THE WORK

DECAYED LODGINGS

THE GREAT BAKEHOUSE

KITCHEN

DECAYED LODGINGS

GATE HOUSE

DECAYED LODGINGS

THE SLAUGHTER HOUSE

THE GREEN COURT

GREAT CHAMBER

SCREEN

MY LORD CHANCELLOR HIS LODGINGS

HALL

KITCHEN

PARLOUR

MY LORDS BUTTERY

THE SPICERY

THE PASTRY

THE COLE HOUSE

OVEN

OUTER COURTYARD

THE LAUNDRY

ELTHAM PALACE

PLAN DRAWN BY W.H. GODFREY FROM THE ORIGINAL PLANS OF JOHN THORPE.

EXISTING REMAINS BLACKED IN • OLD FOUNDATIONS SHADED • BISHOP BEC'S TOWERS MARKED 'A'

FIG. 94.—A feature of this plan is that it identifies many of the apartments. The two large courts are not rectangular, nor is the gatehouse axial to the bridge or the outer gatehouse to the great hall entry, but peculiarities of sites modified general practice. The smaller courts are rectangular. It happens that the existing buildings are the great hall and lower-end chambers. "My Lord Chancellor His Lodgings" at the west angle of the green court form a complete unit as a nobleman's typical fifteenth-century house, but the hall has the great chamber at the lower end, the kitchen and offices being placed at the back of the hall. The parlour is at the upper end, as usual, and beyond it are the buttery, spicery, pantry, coal-house, slaughterhouse and lodgings, the range of these offices forming one side and angle of the court. There is no connecting passage.

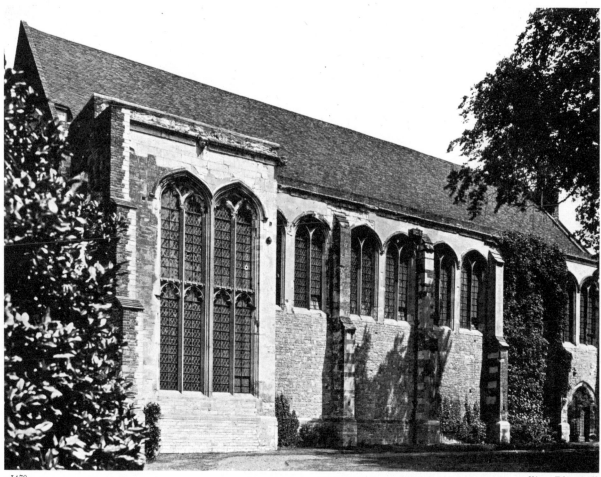

. 1479.   King: Edward IV.

FIG. 95.—THE GREAT HALL, ELTHAM PALACE, KENT.

FIG. 95.—One of the two bay windows and the clerestory windows.

Photo by courtesy of Lt.-Col. R. Cooper.

c. 1480.   King: Edward IV.

FIG. 96.—COTHAY MANOR, WELLINGTON, SOMERSET.

FIG. 96.—A general view of the gatehouse and manor-house; the upper part of the former has been restored.

Photo by courtesy of Lt.-Col. R. Cooper.

c. 1480   *King:* Edward IV.

FIG. 97.—COTHAY MANOR, WELLINGTON, SOMERSET.

FIGS. 97, 98.—The east front to the court, opposite which is the gatehouse shown on the plan. This house is particularly interesting because it retains so much of its medieval character. It stands isolated, and both in general effect and in unspoiled details is one of the most characteristic and perfect fifteenth-century manor-houses in the country.

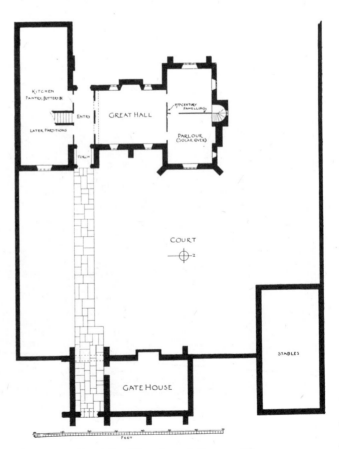

FIG. 98.—The plan of COTHAY MANOR.

Late fifteenth century.

FIG. 99.—SYNYARDS, OTHAM, KENT.

Late fifteenth century.

FIG. 100.—A hall house, recently standing at BENENDEN, KENT.

FIG. 99.—A fifteenth-century hall house into which floors were inserted in the late sixteenth century and a gabled dormer and large chimney added in the seventeenth century. The four-light window is modern. To the right of the entrance doorway are the offices, and in the centre (occupying the whole length of the recessed portion) is the hall, on the left of which is the parlour with a solar over. Many similarly altered hall houses may be found in Kent and other counties, which, like this example, retain their medieval character notwithstanding later alterations and additions. This illustration may be compared with the plan of a yeoman's house, Fig. 101, which is of kindred design.

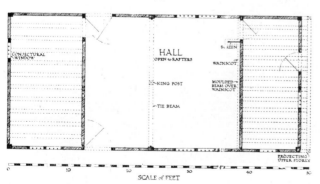

FIG. 101.—Plan of a yeoman's house of timber and plaster. until recently at BENENDEN, KENT.

FIGS. 100, 101.—This is the typical house of a Kentish small freeholder, or yeoman. The chimneys are modern. At the lower end of the hall are the usual external doorways, on opposite sides, but there are no screens nor gallery over as are found in more important halls. At the upper end is a spur, speer, or screen, which protected the master from the draught of the door when he sat at his high table at that end of the hall. The fire was of the central hearth type, there being no fireplace or chimney. The windows are furnished with oak bars of square section, set diagonally and closed by shutters. (See Fig. 506.)

Late fifteenth or early sixteenth century.   *King:* Henry VII.

FIG. 102.—MANOR HOUSE, LIDDINGTON, RUTLAND. (Once a residence of the Bishops of Lincoln.)

FIG. 102.—The hall is on the first floor. The bay window is that of which the interior is shown in Fig. 614. The windows, chimneys and other details are good types of this lime-stone district.

Early sixteenth century.   *King:* Henry VIII.

FIG. 103.—THE ABBOT'S LODGINGS, THAME PARK, OXON.

FIG. 103.—The interiors of these buildings have been reconstructed at various periods, but a tention may be drawn to the remarkable likeness which the elevation bears to those of hall houses, having upper-end and lower-end chambers. The first-floor room of the tower which was panelled by Abbot King, *c.* 1530, is illustrated in Fig. 613.

Early sixteenth century.   *King:* Henry VIII.

FIG. 104.—THE TRIBUNAL HOUSE, GLASTONBURY, SOMERSET.

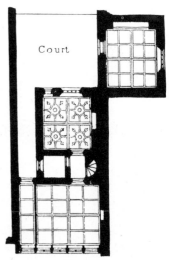

FIG. 105.

FIGS. 104, 105.—The scarcity of town houses, which were more liable to destruction for improvements than were country houses of the period, makes this building particularly interesting. In the street front can be seen the familiar Tudor details of mullioned windows with depressed four-centred heads, a doorway of similar character, and an oriel window to the principal room, situated on the first floor. In the ground-floor window the use of alternate thicker or master mullions confers an air of stability. Except for the entrance doorway (which occupies just the space two extra lights would have done) the front is symmetrical, but even the departure from strict symmetry does not destroy that balance which is characteristic of Tudor buildings.

Early sixteenth century.   *King:* Henry VIII.

FIG. 106.—COMPTON WYNYATES, WARWICKSHIRE.

FIG. 106.—Probably the most romantic house of this period of romantic architecture, Compton Wynyates is unexcelled—even by Haddon Hall. Its situation, the warmth of its colouring, its masses of roofs, its towers and the variety of its chimneys rising above picturesquely windowed walls, are unique, and its beauties, atmosphere, and romance appeal with certainty to the hearts of tens of thousands who have been privileged to visit it. In its present state it is essentially English—not a castle nor a mansion, but a peaceful English home ; yet in the sixteenth century a moat encircled it.

O

c. 1520.   King: Henry VIII.

FIG. 107.—LAYER MARNEY HALL, ESSEX.

FIG 107.—One of the two finest brick and terra-cotta buildings of
this period—Sutton Place being the other. The large windows
and parapet are of cream-coloured terra-cotta made by Italian
workmen, the walls of red brick of rough texture and many
shades of colour laid with thick mortar joints and diapered
with dark grey headers into patterns. The whole of the
terra-cotta is of Italian design, the whole of the brickwork of
English Gothic design.

c. 1525.   King: Henry VIII.

FIG. 108.—SUTTON PLACE, GUILDFORD, SURREY

FIG. 108.—The fourth side of the court, which included the gatehouse and towers, was
destroyed in 1782. The house is built of thin red bricks, mostly of deep colour, and the
dressings of windows, doorways, parapets, etc., are of terra-cotta, which also varies in colour,
but the prevailing tint of which is creamy. Although most of the ornament of the terra-cotta
is in the Italian manner, the forms of doors, windows, etc., are Tudor. The same subordination of foreign designers and workmen is found in contemporary houses. In one respect
only was departure made from English design. This was the entrance to the hall, which
was in its centre—not at one end as customary. This, with the symmetrical composition
of the elevation, was a concession to Italian taste.

c. 1525 and later.   King: Henry VIII.

FIG. 109.—COWDRAY HOUSE. MIDHURST, SUSSEX.

FIG. 109.—Although Cowdray was gutted by fire in 1793,
those portions of the buildings which remain give an excellent
idea of a house of its period. The entrance to the court is
by the gatehouse here illustrated ; opposite is the great hall,
with extensive upper-end and lower-end chambers. The
right and left sides of the court consisted of lodgings, with long
galleries over them at the first-floor level.

c. 1525 and later.   King: Henry VIII.

FIG. 110.—COWDRAY HOUSE. MIDHURST. SUSSEX.

FIG. 110.—The entrance porch is opposite the gatehouse. The
pointed windows and great bay window light the hall (c. 1520-
30 and 1535-39). The two bays on the left of these, which
were built by the second Viscount Montagu (c. 1592-1629)
light the upper-end chambers. The parlour is at the hall-
floor level, and the great chamber above the parlour.

FIGS. 111 AND 112.—An example of how the fortified castle developed into a great residence. The defensive character of the entrance gatehouse has gone, and in its place there is a portal over which is the richest and most ornate of oriel windows. No longer do large windows open only into the central court; those in external walls are planned upon an equally generous scale. Passing through the entrance archway the court is entered; opposite is the great bay window of the open-roofed hall. The building is still *Medieval* in plan, *Perpendicular* in its details, but entirely *Domestic* in its character and appointments. It was built for a rich city merchant, Sir Thomas Kytson, and detailed accounts of the materials used, the costs of these and of the labour, together with the names of the principal craftsmen, are still in existence. The chimneys (many of which are built of brick) have shafts enriched with diaper ornament, twisted screw threads, etc., like those illustrated in Fig. 562.

c. 1525–1538.   *King:* Henry VIII.

FIG. 111.—HENGRAVE HALL, BURY ST. EDMUNDS, SUFFOLK.

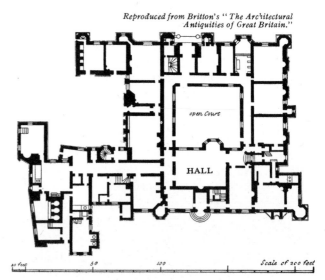

Reproduced from Britton's " The Architectural Antiquities of Great Britain."

open Court

HALL

10 feet   50   100   Scale of 200 feet

FIG. 112.—HENGRAVE HALL, BURY ST. EDMUNDS, SUFFOLK.

c. 1530   *King:* Henry VIII

FIG. 113.—DENVER HALL, NR. DOWNHAM MARKET, NORFOLK.

FIG. 113.—The products of Italian workers in terra-cotta at Layer Marney (Fig. 107) and Sutton Place (Fig. 108) had some influence upon English clay workers. The illustration shows tablets, heraldic devices, and chimney details moulded from the same clay as that from which the walling bricks were made. Similar and more elaborate work exists at East Barsham and elsewhere in Norfolk.

FIG. 114.—This most famous of all half-timbered houses—of which Lancashire and Cheshire still possess many rich examples—is surrounded by a moat—its only protection. The entrance over the bridge (Fig. 334) leads through the building into the courtyard. The long gallery (Fig. 621) is on the top floor.

FIG. 115.—Passing over the moat and through the gatehouse, a court is entered, on the opposite side of which is the door-way leading into the hall, the hall bay, and the parlour bay. Above the upper windows, carved in relief, are the words " God is al in al thing. This window whire made by William Moreton in the yeare of our Lorde MDLIX." Over the parlour window are carved the words : " Richarde Dale carpeder made this window by the grace of God." The sills are all laid on stone bases which raise them sufficiently above ground level to preserve the wood. The

c. 1559   *Queen :* Elizabeth.

FIG. 114.—The entrance front, MORETON OLD HALL.

centre of the west side of the court (left) is open for about 30 ft., so that the court is not so confined and damp as, otherwise, a small court would be. The original cusped and pierced barge boards, the richness of which can be inferred from inspection of the aprons over the upper windows, have disappeared.

c. 1559.   *Queen :* Elizabeth.

FIG. 115.—MORETON OLD HALL, CONGLETON, CHESHIRE.

c. 1550 or later.

FIG. 116.—EASTBURY MANOR HOUSE, BARKING, ESSEX.

Reproduced by courtesy of H. C. V. Curtis, Esq.

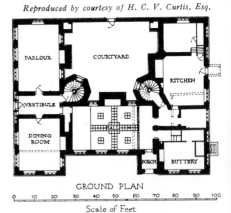

GROUND PLAN

Scale of Feet

FIG. 117.—EASTBURY MANOR HOUSE.
The ground plan.

FIG. 116.—The date of this house is difficult to determine. The plan (Fig. 117) shows developments associated with the later half of the sixteenth century. The hall (see plan) is not open to the roof, as was customary in this part of England until the beginning of the seventeenth century, but is ceiled, and has a room over it. On the other hand much of the detail is early in character. The entrance doorway (not illustrated) is in the manner of 1525, as also are such details as the gable finial mouldings and the newel staircases.

FIG. 117.—An **H**-type plan in which the exposed side of the courtyard is enclosed by a wall.

Mid-sixteenth century.   *Queen: Mary.*

FIG. 118.—LITTLE WOLFORD MANOR, WARWICKSHIRE.

FIG. 118.—The porch (d. 1671), Fig. 376, is in front of the original doorway which gives into the entry. The hall windows may be seen between the porch and the turret enclosing the stairway to the solar. The solar windows are on the right, and the parlour has the unusual feature of an external doorway. Beyond the porch the building is returned at a right angle towards the front.

This house is extremely interesting as being a typical fifteenth-century house built after the middle of the sixteenth century. In remote country districts, men built as their fathers and grandfathers had done, introducing little variations or scraps of ornament of newer manner which they had picked up.

FIG. 119.—The back has undergone little alteration. The solar and parlour wing is on the left. A gabled bay is built to take the fireplace of the hall. The doorway is opposite the front entrance; the windows on the right of it belong to the offices and kitchen. This elevation is in even more perfect state than that of the front.

Mid-sixteenth century. *Queen:* Mary.

FIG. 119.—LITTLE WOLFORD MANOR, WARWICKSHIRE.

Mid-sixteenth century.

FIG. 120.—A cottage at BIGNOR, SUSSEX.

FIG. 120.—This is one of the most beautiful and intimately homely houses which have come down to us from our ancestors. The interior of the roof is not accessible for examination, but the form of the exterior indicates that here is a small hall house having upper-end and lower-end chambers. The original doorway, which is the left-hand one of the two shown in the illustration, led into the hall. The large plaster panels suggest the first half of the sixteenth century as the period of its construction. The original filling of the panels was wattle and daub (Fig. 303), a portion of which is exposed in a panel of the end wall near the bracket. The panels of the first floor on the left of the recess are filled with flints embedded in mortar (Fig. 308). The brick nogging (Fig. 304), both horizontal and herringbone, is of later date. The latter fills the four lights of the original window of the hall, which is now divided horizontally by a floor into two storeys. The chimney is of seventeenth-century date. From the explanation given of its altered features, it will be seen how little this small building differs from the Kentish hall houses illustrated in Figs. 16, 99, and 100.

Reproduced by courtesy of the Soane Museum.

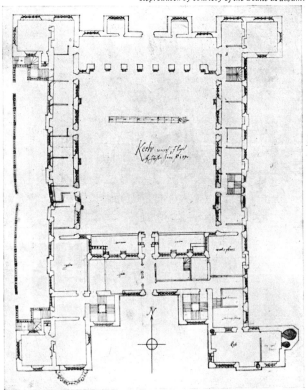

c. 1572.   *Queen :* Elizabeth.

FIG. 121.—The ground plan, dated 1570, of KIRBY HALL.   FIG. 122.—KIRBY HALL, NORTHANTS.

FIG. 121.—Kirby Hall is an example of a large country house in which the great hall, upper-end and lower-end chambers are placed at the (south) end of the large central court. Around the court are *lodgings*, to which access was obtained only from the open court.

FIG. 122.—The wealth of detail concentrated upon the porch and gables, and the beautifully designed chimneys, are worthy of especial attention. The illustration is of the porch entrance from the court to the great hall, and shows, also, hall windows and hall bay. The date of the later pedimented window over the entrance is *c.* 1638.

Photo : Bedford Lemere & Co.

c. 1580.   *Queen :* Elizabeth.

FIG. 123.—The ground plan of WOLLATON   FIG. 124.—North front of WOLLATON HALL, NOTTS.
HALL, NOTTS.

FIGS. 123 AND 124.—One of many extravagant architectural compositions of the Elizabethan period. Robert Smithson's name is contemporarily associated with it as the surveyor or architect. The great central tower is the upper part of a central hall, lighted only by the tower windows. This hall, now entered from the centre of one of its sides, was once reached through the screens. The elevations consist of a hotchpotch of units, ill-chosen and ill-disposed. The treatment of the chimneys is fantastic, and the whole is a travesty of the best Elizabethan architecture.

Photo : G. Hepworth.

c. 1595.   *Queen :* Elizabeth
FIG. 125.—BORWICK HALL, CARNFORTH, LANCASHIRE.

FIG. 125.—The entrance front of Borwick Hall. The hall is situated to the left of the porch Chimneys, gables, windows, etc., are like those on the north front of the more important Montacute in Somerset (Fig. 128).

c. 1595.   *Queen :* Elizabeth.
FIG. 126.—HUNTS FARM, CRUNDALE, WYE, KENT.

FIG. 126.—At this period the close timber studding and narrow panels of the fifteenth century had usually been superseded by large plaster panels, but occasional persistence in using narrow panels often accounts for the assignment of too early dates to buildings. The plaster panels of the gable are impressed with a pattern. The barge boards are carved with an S pattern, but are not pierced. The brick chimney is of characteristic Kentish design ; the moulded rib starts from a cut brick corbel. The porch may be of a little later date.

FIG. 127.—Flint panel and flint chequer-work are found in counties where flints abound. The rich work at the gatehouse of St. Osyth's Priory, Essex, is shown in Fig. 330, and in this illustration is seen that chequer-work which was a feature of ordinary building practice in Wiltshire. Symmetry is the dominating factor of the elevations, and some skill is shown in handling the groups of chimney shafts where their placing departs from strict symmetry.

Late sixteenth century.   *Queen :* Elizabeth.
FIG. 127.—LAKE HOUSE, AMESBURY, WILTSHIRE.

FIG. 128.—The north front of MONTACUTE HOUSE, SOMERSET.

FIG. 129.—A garden house at MONTACUTE HOUSE, SOMERSET.

FIG. 128.—The doorway, bay, and screen (*c.* 1525) were brought from Clifton Maubank when that house was demolished in the late eighteenth century. Attention may be drawn to the chimneys, square sectioned and set diagonally on the north front, but fashioned as columns and furnished with hoods on the other fronts. The sobriety of the elevation, at a period when great house design ran to extraordinary excesses, is notable. Comparison with preceding illustrations of exteriors will emphasize the similarity of such details as gables, windows, and chimneys of stone buildings in widely separated counties.

FIG. 129.—One of two garden houses at the extreme angles of the garden south of the house.

c. 1580–1600.   *Queen:* Elizabeth.

FIG. 130.—MONTACUTE HOUSE, SOMERSET.

c. 1580–1600.   *Queen:* Elizabeth.

FIG. 131.—The south and east fronts of MONTACUTE HOUSE, SOMERSET.

FIG. 130.—Detail of the south front and terrace.   In the north and south porches are the words:

"Through this wide opening gate
   None come too early, none return too late,"   "And yours, my friends."

FIG. 131.—Montacute was built by a Phelips and is still owned by a Phelips. The proportion of window to wall area is good; the interior is well lighted, and the building is stately without being pompous. The garden lay-out, beyond the balustrade shown in the photograph, is contemporary.

Late sixteenth or early seventeenth century.   *Queen:* Elizabeth.

FIG. 132.—HUSH HEATH, GOUDHURST, KENT.

FIG. 132.—This is not a hall house, and although its external appearance suggests a fifteenth-century or early sixteenth-century date, the plan and details are of late sixteenth-century character, notwithstanding the close studding and narrow panels. The detail of the barge boards (no longer cusped), the ovolo mouldings of the windows, the carving of the bressumer beam and brackets, show the course of ornamental development.

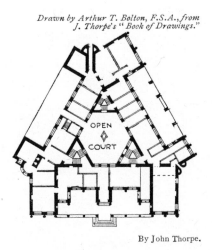

Drawn by Arthur T. Bolton, F.S.A., from J. Thorpe's "Book of Drawings."

OPEN COURT

By John Thorpe.

FIG. 133.

By courtesy of Arthur T. Bolton, F.S.A.

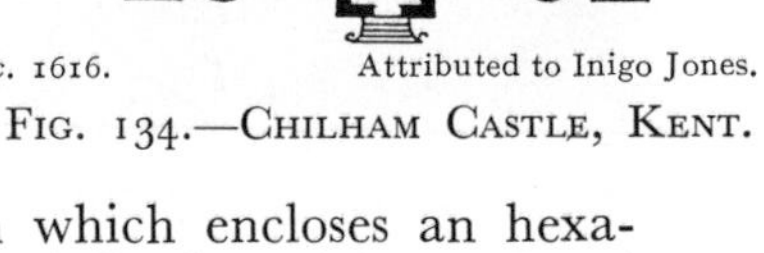

c. 1616.   Attributed to Inigo Jones.

FIG. 134.—CHILHAM CASTLE, KENT.

FIG. 133.—A design for a triangular plan which encloses an hexagonal court. The plan of the front is substantially that of the medieval hall house. Longford Castle, Wiltshire, is similarly triangular in plan, and has a round tower at each of the three angles.

FIG. 134.—Another *freak* plan in which the wings converge. The medieval plan is still the basis of the design. The authors of these plans were influenced by such Italian buildings as the Farnese Palace of Caprarola, by Vignola.

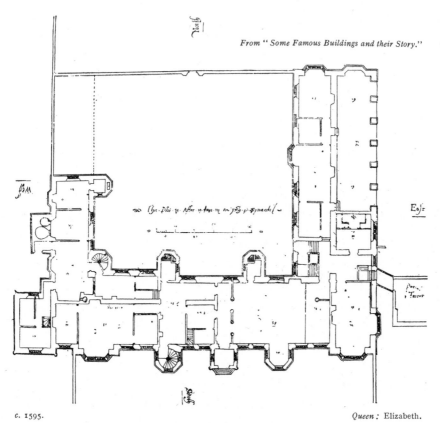

From " Some Famous Buildings and their Story."

c. 1595.   *Queen:* Elizabeth.

FIG. 135.—The ground plan of BEAUFORT HOUSE, CHELSEA, LONDON.
(Sir Thomas More's house.)
Drawn by J. Symonds.

FIG. 135.—A rambling extension of the medieval house plan.

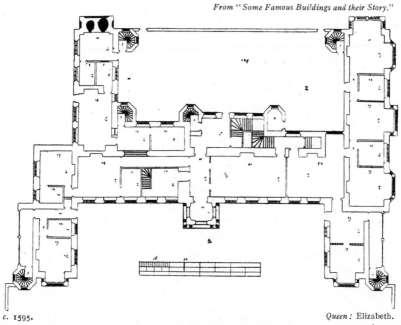

From " Some Famous Buildings and their Story."

c. 1595.   *Queen:* Elizabeth.

FIG. 136.—The ground plan for the suggested rebuilding of BEAUFORT HOUSE,
CHELSEA.
Drawn by Spicer.

FIG. 136.—A scheme prepared in connection with the proposed
rebuilding of the house (Fig. 135), which shows a more orderly
arrangement of the rooms and the adoption, approximately, of the
H-type of plan.

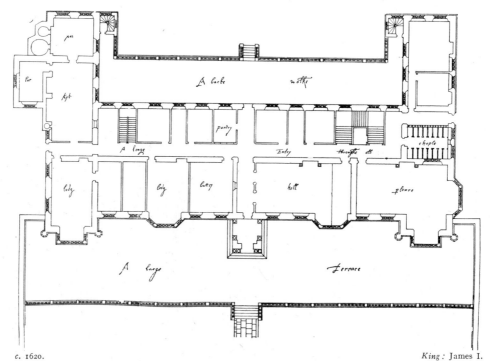

c. 1620.   *King:* James I.

FIG. 137.—The ground plan of BEAUFORT HOUSE, CHELSEA, as it was rebuilt.
Drawn by J. Thorpe.

FIG. 137.—In Thorpe's plan of the house, as actually rebuilt, the position of
the hall is changed ; indeed, nothing of the original plan (Fig. 135) is retained,
yet the medieval hall, with its upper-end and lower-end chambers, still forms
the nucleus of the house. By contrast, the provision of a central corridor anticipates a feature which did not become general practice for nearly another
hundred years. Thorpe's plan is well considered and orderly, and is much
in advance of that shown in Fig. 136.

Reproduced by courtesy of the Soane Museum.

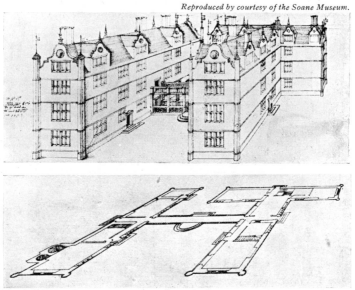

FIGS. 138, 139.—A " freak " design and plan for an Elizabethan house
by John Thorpe.

FIGS. 138 AND 139.—Although the plan of the Elizabethan house generally
took the form of the letter **H**, or had the wings extended at the back to form
a court, as at Kirby Hall (Fig. 121), there were a few *freak* plans, of which that
designed by John Thorpe for himself (but not carried out) is an instance.
The perspective shows the design of the towers has been contracted to mere
angle turrets and the introduction of double curved pediments, in the Dutch
manner, for gables.

c. 1606.   *King:* James I.

FIG. 140.—BRAMSHILL, EVERSLEY, HAMPSHIRE.

FIG. 140.—The house, of which a view from the south-west is shown here, is of the pierced parapet type and has a curved pediment. Its plan is of ⊥ form with a long connecting arm in which a narrow court divides the rooms of the north-west and south-east elevations, just as the " long entry " does in the plan of Beaufort House, Chelsea (Fig. 137). Like most Elizabethan and Jacobean mansions, Bramshill has an imposing entrance, the design of which is more than usually original in its conception.

FIG. 141.—The view is of the south-east and north fronts, and shows the pierced parapet and a gable-pediment in the centre of the north-east front. The projecting wings of the south-east front have arcaded loggias between which is a narrow, raised terrace. This elevation has that air of dignity and repose, undisturbed by pretentious " centre-pieces," which is the characteristic of many large Elizabethan and Jacobean houses of native design. The type is admirably adapted to domestic buildings : the window treatment provides ample lighting for the rooms, and although strictly symmetrical at Bramshill, it is capable of considerable variation from symmetry without spoiling the design, a variation which would be impossible with a classic front.

c. 1606.   *King:* James I.

FIG. 141.—BRAMSHILL, EVERSLEY, HAMPSHIRE.

c. 1607–11

Kin.: James I.

c. 1607–11

King: James I.

FIG. 142.—HATFIELD HOUSE, HERTFORDSHIRE.
Robert Lyminge, *Architect.*

Reproduced from Kerr's " The English Gentleman's House."

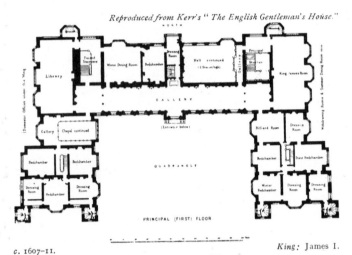

c. 1607–11.

King: James I.

FIG. 143.—HATFIELD HOUSE, HERTFORDSHIRE.

FIG. 142.—The south elevation, with its pierced parapet and curved pediments, represents the ultimate development of Jacobean architecture. There are no gables, and the roofs are hidden by the pierced parapets. The pediments, which take the place of gables, have curved outlines —recalling the aphorism, " Early curly, later straighter." A feature of the wings is their width, which is no longer one room thick (as is the main block) but widens to include as many as three rooms in the spaces between the turrets. The flatness of the skyline is broken by the turrets, by the central clock tower, and by the admirable grouping of the brick chimney shafts.

FIG. 143.—A plan of the first (principal) floor of Hatfield House.

c. 1607–11.

King: James I.

FIG. 144.—HATFIELD HOUSE, HERTFORDSHIRE. Centre of south front and east wing.
Robert Lyminge, *Architect.*

FIG. 144.—The filling in and glazing of the arcading is modern; originally it was a covered walk or ambulatory.

c. 1635.   *King:* Charles I.

FIG. 145.—BROOME PARK, DENTON, KENT.

FIG. 145.—One of the finest brick houses of its period. The porch is modern, and its marble doorway was imported from Italy. The curved and triangular pediments are particularly interesting for the variety of their details, which are carried out in cut and moulded brick. The painted wood window frames and the glazing, though renewed, are characteristic of the period, and so is the varied design of the chimneys.

d. 1631.   *King:* Charles I.

FIG. 146.—KEW PALACE, LONDON, S.W.

FIG. 146.—Built by a Dutch merchant, Samuel Fortrey, it was long known as " the Dutch house," just as in Eastern and South-Eastern counties similar gables are still called " Dutch gables." The sashes replace the original mullion and transom windows. Kew Palace is one of the earliest examples in England of a building in Flemish bond. It is also the earliest built in gauged brickwork. Further, many of the moulded bricks are axed by hand, and the Ionic and Corinthian capitals are built up with ordinary brick and carved. The Doric order of the doorway has been removed. Like Broome Park, Fig. 145, and Cromwell House, Highgate, Kew Palace is a remarkable piece of brickwork, unlike anything hitherto built in England, but such pedimented gables soon gave place to pediments of lower pitch, in the full Italian manner.

P

c. 1620. *King:* James I.
FIG. 147.—A house at OUNDLE, NORTHAMPTONSHIRE.

c. 1620–38. *Kings:* James I and Charles I.
FIG. 148.—RAYNHAM HALL, NORFOLK.

FIG. 147.—The court is enclosed by buildings on three sides, and may be compared with Figs. 116, 117. On the fourth side there is a wall with a doorway. The gables have battlemented finials, and the bay windows are mullioned, one of them still retaining its battlemented parapet. The wall doorway has a Tudor arch, but the pediment is semicircular in shape, with three of those obelisk finials which are typical of Jacobean work.

FIG. 148.—The north-west angle of the house, showing its curved and triangular pediments. The projection of the wings of the **H** form of plan have shrunk to 7 ft. only in this west elevation and to a few inches in the east elevation. The scrolls of the gables are treated with much greater freedom than are those at Broome Park (Fig. 145). The central doorway (Fig. 410) is Italian in character, and the composition of the whole elevation is good. Originally, the window openings were furnished with mullioned and transomed frames as at Broome Park (Fig. 145).

Photo: Gibson, Hexham.

c. 1620. *King:* James I.
FIG. 149.—CHIPPING CAMPDEN, GLOUCESTER.

Early seventeenth century. *King:* James I.
FIG. 150.—PLANKLEY MILL HOUSE, VALLEY OF ALLEN, SOUTH TYNEDALE, NORTHUMBERLAND.

FIG. 149.—A small house of the gabled type in which Gothic details can be seen. The winding stairs partly housed in the semicircular turret are not far removed in form from those at Old Soar, Plaxtol, Kent (see Fig. 59).

FIG. 150.—A cottage having the characteristic North Country features of thick stone walls, small windows, stone slated roof, and sturdy chimneys. The decoration is restricted to the dripstones over the doorway and windows. The attached later building has the old type of external stairs to the upper floor.

Photo: Frith, Reigate.

d. 1633.   *King: Charles I.*

FIG. 151.—COLBY HALL, ASKRIGG, YORKSHIRE.

FIG. 151.—A typical substantial Yorkshire stone house. The walls are of rubble, harled (rough-cast) to protect from driving rains. The stone slated roofs are of low pitch, and both verges and eaves have slight projection. For description of doorway see Fig. 412.

c. 1634.   *King: Charles I.*

FIG. 152.—BATEMAN'S, BURWASH, SUSSEX.

FIG. 152.—Another example of the gabled type of house where the gables have copings or tabling. The porch archway shows the influence of the Renaissance in its semicircu'ar head. The brick chimneys are square in section and are set lozenge fashion, whilst the treatment of the caps may be compared with the design of those of stone illustrated in Fig. 128.

c. 1640.   *King :* Charles I.

FIG. 153.—GREAT WIGSELL, BODIAM, SUSSEX.

FIG. 153.—The new architecture had little influence as yet even in districts within 50 miles of London. In this house are all the sixteenth-century characteristics of high pitched roofs, gables, mullioned windows with ovolo mouldings, chimney shafts in pairs or larger groups. The only concession to fashion is the entablature over the doorway, but the latter has the Tudor four-centred head which springs from curious imposts.

FIG. 154.—Although the composition of the elevation is unusual, it embodies many typical details of windows, gables, and chimney, such as are found in other small houses of the same period in the vicinity. The introduction of scroll ornament is feeble.

c. 1636.   *King :* Charles I.

FIG. 154.—HOUSE AT GREAT WELDON, NORTHAMPTONSHIRE.

By courtesy of Eric W. Chapman, A.R.I.B.A.

b. 1653. Commonwealth.
FIG. 155.—UNSTONE HALL, NEAR DRONFIELD, N.E. DERBYSHIRE.

By courtesy of J. Mansell Jenkinson, A.R.I.B.A.

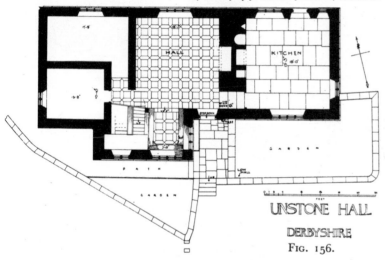

UNSTONE HALL
DERBYSHIRE
FIG. 156.

FIG. 155.—Like Yorkshire houses built of hard millstone grit, the design is simple, mouldings are few and plain. The roofs, which are covered with heavy grey slates, are of low pitch. The hall is not open to the roof, but is ceiled and has apartments over.

FIG. 156.—A typical Derbyshire and Yorkshire house. The L plan is found in houses of many periods, probably originating in the practice of placing the parlour (with solar over) transverse to the hall. Here the toe of the L contains the hall bay and the staircase. This is substantially the medieval plan with slight local variations. The hall was never open to the roof, but had bedrooms over. The pavings of the hall and kitchen are of stone, but for the former they are shaped geometrically. The entrance doorway gives directly into the hall, or houseplace as it is often styled in the North. The bay on the south side of the hall has two windows and a fixed seat round three sides. The bay here is far from the fireplace and seems an example of such an oriel as mentioned in the quotation from Dorset, page 45. The fireplace (now contracted) was a wide one with stone arch or lintel.

Photo : Gibson, Hexham.

FIG. 157.—A house said to have been built by the community as a place of refuge against attack by Scottish raiders ; a very late example of a fortified building, and of earlier character than the house at Plankley (Fig. 150).

c. 1642. *King : Charles I.*
FIG. 157.—BASTLE HOUSE, MILLBRIDGE, NORTHUMBERLAND.

Late seventeenth century.

FIG. 158.—Cottage at LITTLE BARRINGTON, GLOUCESTERSHIRE.

Photo: B. C. Clayton.

FIG. 158.—The character of the building is seventeenth century, but traditional building in the district is so strong that it may have been built in the eighteenth century. Local characteristics are : (1) The bell-cast of the roof, caused by the wall-plate being placed on the inside of the thick walls. (2) The diminishing sizes of stone slates—large at eaves, the small under ridge. (3) The swept valley at intersection of roofs, the slates being cut to the curve. (4) The placing of a **V**-shaped ridge coping, *inverted* at point of intersection of gable ridge with main roof —this to throw off wet from a vulnerable point. The setting of this house, with its garden wall of the same stone, produces the impression of its having grown out of the soil. This effect can only be achieved when local materials are employed : imported materials look alien.

FIG. 159.—The street front is 70 ft. long. The framework of the house is Elizabethan—1567—but the front, including carved oak, windows, and pargeting, is of the third quarter of the seventeenth century. The pargeting was restored 1850. The general appearance is Elizabethan, notwithstanding the details and decorative work having been carried out a hundred years later.

Late seventeenth century.   *King:* Charles II.

FIG. 159.—SPARROWE'S HOUSE, IPSWICH.

Photo : Gibson, Hexham.

c. 1698.   William and Mary.

FIG. 160.—House at CORBRIDGE, NORTHUMBERLAND.

FIG. 160.—This type of dormer window is found also in contemporary Scotch houses. Its design and workmanship are clumsy by comparison with dormers in Northamptonshire (Fig. 520). The debased Tudor door arch is surmounted by a triangular classic pediment.

d. 1702.   *Queen :* Anne

FIG. 161.—LOWER STANDARD FARM, NINFIELD, SUSSEX.

FIG. 161.—A small house which combines gables, chimneys, mullion and transom windows in the old manner, but quoins, cornice, and doorway with bolection-mould architrave and entablature in the new. Thus the country builder gradually developed.

1619-22.   *King:* Charles I.
FIG. 162.—THE BANQUETING HOUSE, WHITEHALL, LONDON.
Inigo Jones, *Architect.*

FIG. 162.—This is the first *building* to be erected in England in the purely Italian style, and probably the façade illustrated has never been surpassed. A drawing (in the Duke of Devonshire's collection at Chatsworth) made by Inigo Jones shows the centre surmounted by a triangular pediment, and the whole roof hipped, the balustrade being omitted. This would have been an early instance, in this country, of a hipped roof design. The variation of the pediments to the ground-floor windows and the use of flat entablatures at the first floor was, no doubt, an innovation. The windows were furnished originally with mullioned wood frames, filled with lead lights.

1618-35.   *King:* Charles I.
FIG. 163.—The south elevation of the QUEEN'S HOUSE, GREENWICH.
Inigo Jones, *Architect.*

FIG. 163.—The first *dwelling-house* in England designed in the full Italian manner was built astride the Dover-London road. The position of this architectural novelty over the road may account for the contemporary description of the house as a " curious devise." The road passed under the house where the colonnades now stop. Tradition has it that the queen objected to crossing the road in order to reach either the park or the river. The house is like an Italian palace, but the loggia faces south, instead of north as it would have done in Italy.

FIG. 164.—The two courts served to light the Dover road which passed through the house at the ground-floor level. The north and principal entrance opened into a square salon or hall which was the height of two stories, with a gallery encircling it at the first-floor level. Except the gallery, there were no passages or corridors, and rooms opened off one another. The principal and original staircase is the *round* one illustrated in Fig. 832.

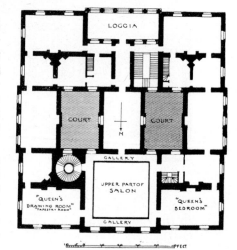

FIG. 164.—Plan of the first floor, the
QUEEN'S HOUSE, GREENWICH.

1618-35. The colonnades were built *c.* 1807.   *King:* Charles I.

FIG. 165.—The north elevation of the QUEEN'S HOUSE, GREENWICH.

FIG. 165.—Fully to realize the difference between this new style and that which it superseded, the illustration should be compared with those of other houses which were built during the first third of the seventeenth century. (See Figs. 140, 142, 145, 152.)

From "Vitruvius Britannicus."

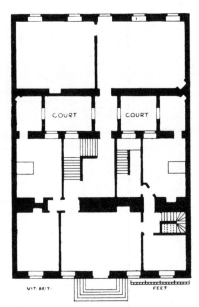

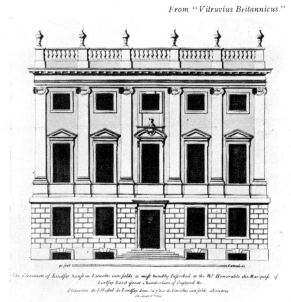

1641.

FIG. 166.—The ground-floor plan, LINDSEY HOUSE, LINCOLN'S INN FIELDS, LONDON.

King: Charles I.

FIG. 167.—The elevation, LINDSEY HOUSE, LINCOLN'S INN FIELDS, LONDON.

From a drawing by Colen Campbell.

FIG. 166.—Notwithstanding the exigencies of the site and the symmetrical Italianated elevation, the entrance doorway of Lindsey House gives into a large room having a fireplace and a chamber at each end—an arrangement reminiscent of the medieval plan, though the hall was no longer a common living-room but had become an entrance hall—the introduction of the staircase into the hall was to come a little later.

FIG. 167.—Comparison is interesting between this early town house of the school of Inigo Jones, the early sixteenth-century house at Glastonbury (Fig. 104), and the early seventeenth-century house at Oundle (Fig. 147). The contrast with timber and plaster-fronted houses (as that at Ipswich, Fig. 159), of which many town examples survive, is still more striking. Lindsey House still exists, but has been altered by lowering the window sills and doubling the doorway; consequently, the drawing by Colen Campbell gives a better idea than a photograph would of the front and its proportions.

c. 1656.   Commonwealth.
FIG. 168.—THORPE HALL, PETERBOROUGH, NORTHAMPTONSHIRE.

FIG. 168.—The south-west angle and screen wall to kitchen court (see Fig. 340). The large windows in the west elevation are of doubtful date. The house is attributed to John Webb, but not with certainty.

c. 1656.   Commonwealth.
FIG. 169.—The north front of THORPE HALL, near PETERBOROUGH.

FIG. 169.—This square building with its hipped roof, cornice and pedimented windows is far removed, in its Italian manner, from gabled and pedimented buildings of the **H** plan, like Broome Park (Fig. 145). Probably the porches are the first of their type to be built in England. The original wooden window frames with mullions and transoms, like most others of this period, have been destroyed. Novel features are the windows of the ground and third floors which have simply moulded architraves, and those of the first floor which have alternately triangular pediments and flat entablatures—except the centre window, which has a segmental pediment and (outside the architrave) pilasters springing from ramped volutes such as are found elsewhere in the house.

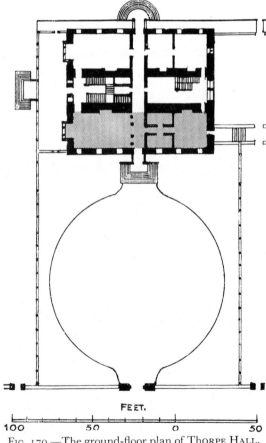

FEET.

100   50   0   50

FIG. 170.—The ground-floor plan of THORPE HALL.
From Hakewell's drawing.

FIG. 170.—Notwithstanding the otherwise completely Italianated plan and elevations, the medieval plan lingers in the shaded portion, which consists of an entry giving into the hall on the left and with passages to the offices on the right. The plan consists of two passages crossing each other and dividing the chambers (and the house) into four equal divisions. The portion of the layout illustrated shows the entrance court, which is approached through gate piers and enclosed by a balustrade. Outbuildings stand in the court on the west of the house.

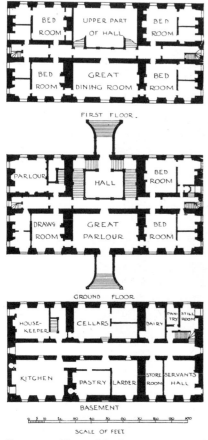

FIG. 171.—Plans of the basement, ground floor and first floor at COLESHILL.

c. 1662.   *King:* Charles II.

FIG. 172.—COLESHILL, BERKSHIRE.
Sir Roger Pratt, *Architect.*

FIG. 171.—The placing of a large staircase hall and a great parlour beyond it—the two occupying the whole depth of the centre of the house—is a practice which is found in plans after this date. These plans should be compared with those of Eltham Lodge (Fig. 175), where the staircases are placed in a central passage or staircase hall. Both methods are found in other houses. The contemporary nomenclature of the rooms completes the impression of the great breach between these plans and those of the Jacobean house (see Figs. 137 and 143) ; indeed, the plans of Coleshill include no trace of the medieval plan but approximate closely to modern design, in which they differ from the plan of the Queen's House, Greenwich (Fig. 164), which, however, resembles neither medieval nor modern English practice.

FIG. 172.—Coleshill (long attributed to Inigo Jones, but actually designed and carried out by his friend, Sir Roger Pratt) is one of the finest houses in the country. Its qualities are due to its admirable proportions : to the disposition of the windows in three groups, the spacing of those in the centre group being wider than those on each side ; to the substantial and well-proportioned chimneys well placed, and to the crowning of the whole by a handsome cupola through which access to the balustraded roof is gained. The windows have simple architraves and entablatures. The contrast between this building in the Italian manner and such a Gothic house as Ockwells Manor (Fig. 93) is striking. At Ockwells, though the building has a wide front, the predominating lines are vertical ; at Coleshill the lines are horizontal. At Coleshill pediments have taken the places of gables ; at Ockwells the windows are divided by mullions into many lights, whereas, originally, at Coleshill each window had one mullion and a transom. Ockwells has many breaks in its front, such as the projections of the porch and bays, but Coleshill has flat surfaces. At Ockwells the windows are disposed without regard to symmetry (though the elevation is well balanced) ; at Coleshill everything is absolutely symmetrical. The plan of Ockwells, like that of all Gothic houses, is rambling ; at Coleshill it is as symmetrical as its elevations.

FIG. 173.—This front was built or faced for Sir Christopher Hatton, afterwards Lord Hatton. Although attributed to Inigo Jones, there is no evidence that he was the architect, but, certainly, it may be said to be of his school and is in the Italian manner.

1638-40.   *King:* Charles I.

FIG. 173.—The north front of KIRBY HALL, NORTHAMPTONSHIRE.

c. 1664.   *King:* Charles II.

FIG. 174.—ELTHAM LODGE, KENT.
Hugh May, *Architect.*

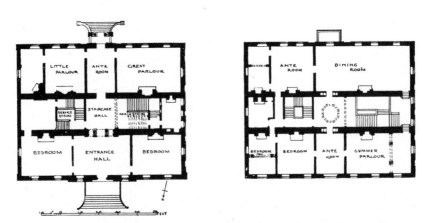

FIG. 175.—Plans of the ground floor and first floor of ELTHAM LODGE, KENT.
Reproduced by courtesy of H.M. Office of Works and H.M. Stationery Office.

FIG. 174.—Like Coleshill (Fig. 172), this house has a hipped roof, a fashion
which became firmly established after the Restoration. The proper mullion
and transom windows have been replaced by late sashes having attenuated
glazing bars. These windows were designed without architraves or pediments
of any description. Originally the roof " platform " may have had a
balustrade, like that at Coleshill.

FIG. 175.—Here is complete emancipation from medieval planning. The
ground floor has passages north and south, east and west, which cross. The
stairs and their hall occupy the centre third of the house. The thick inner
walls contain fireplaces with their flues, securing warmth. The names attached
to the apartments are based upon those of other houses of the same period.
The great parlour and dining-room were transposed later.

c. 1680.   *King: Charles II.*

FIG. 176.—The entrance front of RAMSBURY MANOR, WILTSHIRE.

c. 1680.   *King: Charles II.*

FIG. 177.—The north front of RAMSBURY MANOR.

Reproduced by courtesy of Sir Francis Burdett, Bart.

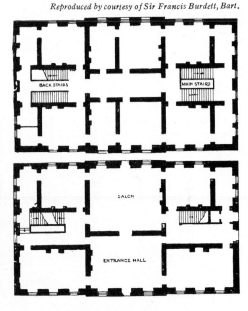

FIG. 178.—Ground-floor and first-floor plans.

FIG. 176.—The use of brick revived with the Restoration, being well suited to that intimate and homely house design which was current during the second half of the seventeenth and the first quarter of the eighteenth centuries. This elevation may be compared with that of Eltham Lodge, Fig. 174, of which it is a logical and scholarly development. There are no pilasters, but the slight breakforward under the pediment is accentuated by stone quoins, which are also used at the angles of the building. All windows have architraves; those of the ground floor have entablatures, but those of the first floor are carried up into the frieze of the main cornice. The doorway and window above form one composition. The panelled chimneystacks are of the form associated with Wren's work, but here have stone margins and caps with panels of brick. The architect is unknown (possibly it was Captain Wynne, the architect of Hampstead Marshall), but the whole design and workmanship are of the highest quality.

FIG. 177.—The hipped roof has a lead flat. The elevations, in the centres of which the handsome cornice taken up as triangular pediments (an early instance of which, at Eltham, was illustrated in Fig. 174), became a fashionable type of house after the Restoration. Windows of the principal floor (sometimes of two floors) were designed with a height of twice (or more) their width and furnished with architraves and perhaps simple horizontal entablatures.

FIG. 178.—The plan of the ground floor combines features of Coleshill, Fig. 171, and of Eltham Lodge, Fig. 175. Unlike these houses, all the reception rooms at Ramsbury are on the ground floor.

d. 1685.   *King:* Charles II.

FIG. 179.—HONINGTON HALL, WARWICKSHIRE.

FIG. 179.—A further example of a house with a hipped roof and cornice, in which is seen another type of elevation of this period, where the hipped roof is brought forward over slightly projecting wings. This should be compared with Ramsbury Manor, Fig. 176, which has a central pediment. In each the doorway gives into a square entrance hall. The busts in niches are uncommon embellishments which are also to be found at Ashdown House, Berkshire, and at Ham House, Surrey.

c. 1690.   William and Mary.

FIG. 180.—The centre of the east front of HAMPTON COURT PALACE.

FIG. 180.—An outstanding instance of that graceful richness which Wren imparted to his work. The width of the whole front is 300 ft., and of the Corinthian order or " Porticu " which forms the centrepiece, 95 ft. Wren's method of using an order in such a position (a practice which became common in the eighteenth century) may be compared with Hugh May's at Eltham, Fig. 174, and with elevations by other architects who succeeded him. The carvings in the tympanum of the pediment were the work of Gabriel Cibber.

c. 1690.   William and Mary.

FIG. 181.—The east and part of the south front of HAMPTON COURT PALACE.
Sir Christopher Wren, *Architect.*

Reproduced from Volume IV. of the Wren Society.

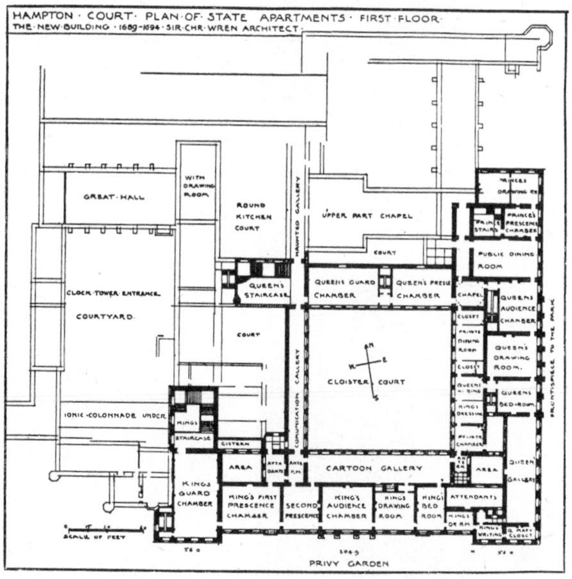

FIG. 182.—First-floor plan of HAMPTON COURT PALACE.

FIG 181.—The gaiety and grace of these elevations exceed those of the Louvre and Versailles, by which no doubt they were inspired. This is largely owing to the association of red brick with the white of Portland stone, but skilful composition and admirable proportions also play their parts. The windows of the *piano nobile*, punctuated by the circular ones, and emphasized by the square windows of the attic story, are well supported by the arched heads of the lower openings of the ground floor. It will be seen that the gables, which produced diversified and broken skylines, and the predominating vertical lines of Elizabethan and Jacobean buildings, are replaced by strong horizontal lines, symmetrical fronts, the uniform repetition of windows and other details, all characterized by great breadth of effect.

FIG. 182.—This plan of the principal (first) floor of the Wren buildings at Hampton Court Palace shows, also, their relation to the Wolsey and Henry VIII buildings, and may be compared with Fig. 181, which illustrates the south-east external angle. Although the state-rooms open one off another, each has separate access, but many of the private apartments can only be reached by passing through other rooms. Such imperfect planning (though characteristic of medieval buildings) shows limited progress at the end of the seventeenth century and indicates the difficulty which even Wren experienced in departing from convention.

Late seventeenth and early eighteenth centuries.   FIG. 183.—GREENWICH (PALACE) HOSPITAL, from the River THAMES.

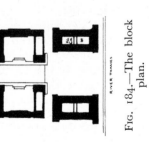

FIG. 184.—The block plan.

FIG. 183.—The building beyond the statue is the Queen's House, designed by Inigo Jones; that on the distant skyline is the Observatory. The other buildings are by various architects to the plans and elevations of Sir Christopher Wren, in association with Sir John Vanbrugh. The building on the extreme right (part only of which is shown) is that portion of King Charles's palace which, together with the Queen's House, Wren had to incorporate into his scheme. The position of the two domes (over the chapel and the hall respectively) on the angles is an essential feature of the composition.

FIG. 184.—Nothing marks the change in architectural styles and methods more strongly than the magnificent and orderly planning of the sites and settings of buildings. This is apparent in the association of gardens and parks with houses, but perhaps is brought out in its highest form in Wren's layout plan for Greenwich Hospital. First projected and begun as a palace, the block plan shows the relation of the buildings and the skill of their disposition, which is far beyond anything hitherto produced in England and ranks with the compositions of eminent French and Italian architects. The relatively simple elevation of the Queen's House was a difficulty, but the great gap dividing it from the colonnaded blocks separated it from them, even when viewed from a distance; yet it effectually closed the vista.

Late seventeenth century.

FIG. 185.—House at HIGH WYCOMBE, BUCKS.

c. 1700.   William and Mary.

FIG. 186.—DRAYTON HOUSE,
NORTHAMPTONSHIRE.

FIG. 185.—The incorporation of Gothic detail in a Renaissance building was often disastrous, as the steep gable termination of the centre of this front. In other respects the elevation is a good one, though sashes have been substituted for the original mullioned and transomed windows of the type remaining in Fig. 187.

FIG. 186.—Drayton House is a building of many periods. This elevation to the court is in the full Wren manner, and may be compared with Hampton Court, though there is no reason to connect it with Wren himself. The composition shows considerable originality: the slight relief of the scroll pediments of the windows on each side of the doorway connects them with it as subsidiary parts of the central composition; the triangular and segmental pedimented windows, having greater relief, form a separate division of the front. Other details worthy of scrutiny are the graceful doorway with its cornice surmounted by a carving of trophies, the square panels containing brackets bearing sculptured busts, and the fluted and rusticated treatment of the angle pilaster. The iron balustrade to the steps belongs to this period.

d. 1699.   William and Mary.

FIG. 187.—RAMPYNDENE, BURWASH, SUSSEX.

FIG. 187.—This house, with its high hipped roof, no balustrade around the lead flat, and a cornice in place of eaves, which had gone out of fashion, possesses many of the features of its period and district. The doorway has the typical shell-shaped hood enriched by modelled plasterwork on which is the date. The mullioned and transomed windows are of the latest phase; those of the ground floor have been replaced by sashes—a common practice (Fig. 525); the wood cornice breaks out round the slightly projecting centre of the front; the wall-tiling on timber framing is in the manner current in Kent and Sussex. The fine roof is pierced by flat-headed dormers, and is surmounted by two panelled brick chimneys into which all the flues in the house are gathered.

c. 1700   *Queen : Anne.*

FIG. 188.—EAGLE HOUSE, MITCHAM, SURREY.

FIG. 188.—A house with a hipped roof, lead flat surrounded by a balustrade, and a bold cornice carried up over the pediment. The resemblance to Coleshill, Fig. 172, and the even more remarkable resemblance to Clarendon House and Horseheath (which have similar pediments), all by Sir Roger Pratt (not illustrated), are notable.

FIG. 189.—The cornice is one of the richest remaining examples of a period when handsome cornices were prevalent. Although locally attributed to Wren, there is no reason to suppose that he was the architect. Illustrations of narrow fronts, deeply recessed between projecting wings, are frequently found in the eighteenth-century books on architecture. The finely gauged red brickwork of the angle pilasters, window arches and aprons contrasts admirably with the duller and rougher walling. The dormers are disproportionately large and, probably, are later.

c. 1715.   *King : George I.*

FIG. 189.—House at SOUTH CROYDON, SURREY.

c. 1701.   *William and Mary.*

FIG. 190.—MOMPESSON HOUSE, SALISBURY.

Late seventeenth or early eighteenth century.   *Queen : Anne.*

FIG. 191.—THE MANOR HOUSE, CROOM'S HILL.
GREENWICH.

FIG. 190.—The lead rainwater heads above the entrance are dated 1701. The whole front, including the doorway and cornice, is of stone. The slight projection of the centre window, round which the cornice breaks, is an illustration of one of those details introduced to vary fronts, and may be compared with the pediment at Ramsbury, Fig. 176, and the slightly projecting wings at Honington, Fig. 179. The provision of a forecourt to houses in country towns had become popular, and gave scope for handsome iron gates and a clairvoyée.

FIG. 191.—A house with gabled walls, and a roof finishing in front over a bold cornice with a concealed gutter. These small houses were extremely simple, yet their fronts were well proportioned. External embellishments were confined to the entrance doorway and to the main cornice.

c. 1701.   William and Mary.

FIG. 192.—CHICHELEY HALL, BUCKINGHAMSHIRE (attributed to Thomas Archer, *Architect*)

c. 1701.   William and Mary.

FIG. 193.—CHICHELEY HALL.

FIG. 192.—A house of unusual design in the Dutch manner. Many Dutch architects were established in England during the second half of the seventeenth century. The roofs are entirely hidden by the attic storey.

FIG. 193.—Shows the projections of the front elevation and the treatment of the angle where Corinthian and Doric orders meet. The detail of the lead rainwater head is exceptionally rich.

c. 1705.   *Queen:* Anne.

FIG. 194.—No. 30, QUEEN ANNE'S GATE, formerly
11, QUEEN SQUARE, LONDON.

c. 1720   *King:* George I.

FIG. 195.—No. 14, TOOK'S
COURT, LONDON.

By courtesy of the L.C.C.

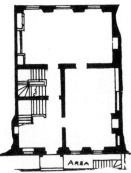

FIG. 196.—Ground-floor
plan of No. 30, QUEEN
ANNE'S GATE.

FIG. 194.—The window-heads have straight, not curved,
arches; these are gauged and furnished with keystones carved
with masks. The woodwork of the windows is set back only
an inch from the wall surface, as, no doubt, were the original
frames. The door-head is similar to those of adjoining
houses, but is of a design only found in this street.

FIG. 196.—The plan of the ground floor as originally built
(note that later alterations have confused the plan which here
is reconstructed from the unaltered first floor). Both the
ground and first floors are divided into only two rooms each.
The entrance hall is also the staircase hall; an arrangement
which became almost universal in town houses, and also
general in country houses.

FIG. 195.—A street front of rough brick with finely gauged segmental window
arches and having gauged pilasters the whole height of the building. The
Ionic capitals are of similar brick to the pilasters; they were built up and then
carved. The cornice is of moulded and gauged bricks. The windows are set
back from the wall surface, showing four-inch reveals in conformity with the Act
of Parliament of Queen Anne (1709), which also required the heads of windows to
be arched. The Act applied to buildings in London and Westminster and their
Liberties. The plastered reveals were coloured white like the painted
woodwork.

Late seventeenth or early eighteenth century.   William and Mary.

FIG. 197.—THE MANOR HOUSE, TINTINHULL, SOMERSET.

FIG. 197.—A stone house with a hipped roof, pediment and cornice. Although this house combines a classic façade and doorway together with the hipped roof which only came in with Inigo Jones, it has one remaining Gothic touch in its mullion and transom windows. Near the angles, pilasters take the place of rusticated quoins.

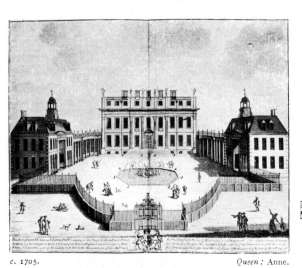

c. 1705.   *Queen: Anne.*

FIG. 198.—BUCKINGHAM HOUSE. LONDON.
Captain Wynne, *Architect.*

Reproduced from " Vitruvius Britannicus."

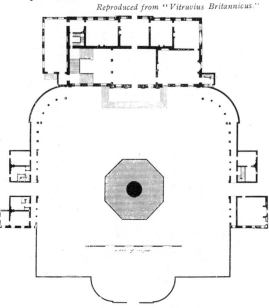

FIG. 199.—Plan of BUCKINGHAM HOUSE, LONDON.

FIG. 198.—This engraving conveys an impression which a photograph cannot do, for it is complete with details and even includes persons in contemporary costumes. It shows an early example of curved colonnades connecting the centre block with wings flanking it; but this plan was anticipated by Inigo Jones at Stoke Park, Northamptonshire, *c.* 1604. One wing of the buildings contains the kitchen and offices, and the other the servants' lodgings.

FIG. 199.—An original plan in which the grand staircase, of easy flights, is separated from the great entrance hall by a colonnade. On the right is the dining parlour, and behind is a suite of rooms; the whole effect is simple, dignified, and stately.

1702–11.   *Queen: Anne.*

FIG. 200.—The west front of EASTON NESTON.
Nicholas Hawksmoor, *Architect.*

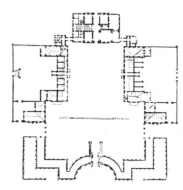

FIG. 201.—Ground plan of
EASTON NESTON.

FIG. 200.—Easton Neston was designed by Hawksmoor some time after he had become assistant to Sir John Vanbrugh. The west front shown here is more ponderous than that facing east (Fig. 202).

FIG. 201.—Hawksmoor's plan, including the subsidiary buildings and court (which were not carried out, though recently a stately setting has been designed and built), shows the influence of Vanbrugh in the planning, as well as in the centre feature of the west front. The medieval plan of the hall, upper-end and lower-end chambers, is obvious in the main block.

1702–11.   *Queen: Anne.*

FIG. 202.—The east front of EASTON NESTON, TOWCESTER, NORTHANTS.

FIG. 202.—It is interesting to see how Hawksmoor abandoned the two-floor big-scale and introduced small windows in the north front to meet internal requirements. Frequently a high ground floor was divided into two lower floors where small rooms were wanted. Where this was not done the height of small rooms gave them the proportions of a well. In the composition of this nine-window front one sees how the architect varied his grouping of windows, the effect of wider or narrower wall spacings between them, and of the forward breaks of the fronts. Comparison may be made also with the nine-window front of Coleshill (Fig. 172), where the same factors are differently handled.

Photo: Geo. Hepworth, Brighouse.

1702-14.   *Queen: Anne.*

FIG. 203.—CASTLE HOWARD, YORKSHIRE.
Sir John Vanbrugh, *Architect.*

FIG. 203.—This was the architect's first building, before the erection of which his chief claim to fame
was as a poet.   It is altogether in a lighter and gayer manner than Blenheim, begun some four years
later (1706), the plan of which (Fig. 206) has much that is akin to that of Castle Howard.

Reproduced from "Vitruvius Britannicus."

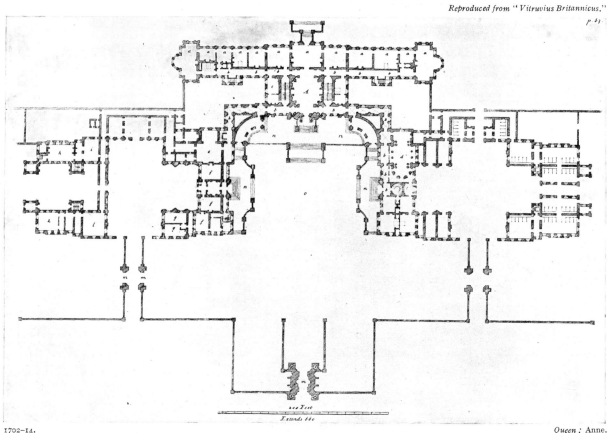

1702-14.   *Queen: Anne.*

FIG. 204.—The General Plan of CASTLE HOWARD.
Sir John Vanbrugh, *Architect.*

KEY TO PLAN.

A, The Great Hall; *a*, the principal apartments, making a line of 300 feet; *b*, the corridors; *c*, the private eating
parlour; *d*, the chapel; *e*, the kitchen; *f*, the hunting apartments; *g*, the dairy; *h*, the laundry; *i*, the washhouse; *k*, the
brewhouse; *l*, the bakehouse; *m*, the gates; *n*, the terraces; *o*, the Great Court.

FIG. 204.—Sir John Vanbrugh's plan.   The total width of the elevations is 660 feet.   The architect
(like others of the period) so planned the rooms that when communicating doors were opened extensive vistas might be obtained.

1706-24.   Anne and George I.

FIG. 205.—BLENHEIM PALACE, OXFORDSHIRE.
Sir John Vanbrugh, *Architect*.

FIG. 205.—The west entrance portico and the buildings on the north side of the Great Court, which are shown in. this illustration, have similar buildings facing them on the south side of the court. This is one of the most satisfactory views of the house, for the grouping of masses, primary, secondary, and tertiary, is good, the whole effect produced being noble and magnificent.

FIG. 206.—The plan of Blenheim Palace is many years in advance of its time. The principal floor of "the body of the house" consists of a central hall and a salon, in each side of which is one suite of apartments, each having its own drawing-room, ante-rooms, and bedrooms. The whole of the south front is given up to the great gallery. Every apartment can be entered from a corridor as well as from adjoining rooms. The kitchen and offices are in separate buildings connected by a colonnade. The total length of the front is 850 ft.; there are three acres of lead roofs. Although the finishing of Blenheim was not done under Vanbrugh's supervision, the workmanship was so accurate that "it is possible to look through the key-holes of ten doors and see the daylight at the end over 300 feet off."—*Quoted by Francis Lenygon from "Blenheim and its Memories," by the Duke of Marlborough.*

A, The body of the house; B, Great Court; C, chapel; D, stable court; E, coach houses; F, a greenhouse; G, the gates; H, kitchen court; I, kitchen; K, the common hall; L, bakehouse; M, laundry; N, back courts; O, greenhouse; P, the gates; Q, terraces; R, the Great Gate; S, the terraces; T, the colonnade on the Great Terrace; V, water cistern; W, little porticoes; X, passages; Y, principal approach and way by the Great Bridge.

Reproduced from "Vitruvius Britannicus."

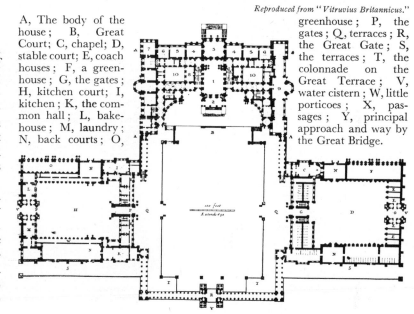

FIG. 206.—Ground plan of BLENHEIM PALACE.

KEY TO ROOMS IN THE MAIN BLOCK.

1, The Great Hall; 2, portico; 3, salon; 4, antechambers; 5, drawing-rooms; 6, great bedchambers; 7, great cabinet; 8, little dining-room; 9, the Great Gallery; 10, Little Courts.

1706-24.   Anne and George I.

FIG. 207.—The east and north fronts of BLENHEIM PALACE.

FIG. 207.—This view is heavier and less pleasing. The finials of the angle blocks or towers are unfortunate and give the whole building the effect of being upside down—it has been compared with an elephant on its back. In justice to Vanbrugh it should be recorded that although completed by the Duchess of Marlborough to his designs, for several years Vanbrugh had no part in supervising the works. He spoke of her as "spoiling Blenheim in her own way." The view shows the east and north fronts. The subsidiary building on the north (right of.illustration) is the kitchen.

c. 1710.   *Queen : Anne.*

FIG. 208.—COMPTON BEAUCHAMP, BERKSHIRE.

FIG. 208.—A new front has been built to an older house, and the application of such a style to a small house is interesting. There are few embellishments ; the elevation depends for its effects upon the basic qualities of good proportion and the able grouping of masses, with results which are distinguished and admirable. The severity of the building is softened by the curves of the wall flanking the entrance and by the circular pool.

FIG. 209.—A severely Palladian house having a heavy attic story. The whole forms a fine mass and impresses the eye by its reticence and dignity. The tall doorway has the only ornamental details, but the gate piers, iron gates, and screen give touches of gaiety. This house is not of a popular type, but it shows the architect to have been a man of real ability who eschewed mere prettiness and studied essentials.

c. 1710   *Queen : Anne.*

FIG. 209.—No. 68, THE CLOSE, SALISBURY.

c. 1710.   *Queen : Anne.*

FIG. 210.—A house at BURFORD, OXFORDSHIRE.

FIG. 210.—One of the best small houses in the Palladian style. The two floors are of equal importance. The divisions of the front by Corinthian pilasters are subtly contrived so that the repetition of windows and pilasters is not monotonous. The doorway is tall and narrow, and confers an air of dignity upon the front, the beauty of which is enhanced by the wrought-iron clairvoyée through which it is seen. There were stone vases on the angle dies of the parapet until they were removed about 1850 when the building was gutted and transformed into a Methodist chapel.

d. 1706.   *Queen: Anne.*

FIG. 211.—A cottage at STAPLECROSS, SUSSEX.

FIG. 211.—A small house or cottage of homely, comfortable type, substantially built of brick and tile.

FIG. 212.—A street house front of brick; the doorway and cornice are of wood, which is painted as also are the bands at floor levels and the quoins. The second-floor balconies are of the early nineteenth century, when also the windows opening on to them may have been lowered. During the later seventeenth and the whole of the eighteenth century great numbers of squares and streets in London were rebuilt with houses having these simple brick fronts. All are simple and unpretentious, yet each has distinctive details (in this example in its quoins, bands, and entrance doorway)—but they depended chiefly for their effects on such fundamental qualities as scale, proportion, and the relation of solids to voids. From most, the thick glazing bars, which furnished the windows, have been replaced by thin ones, some even by sheets of plate glass, which rob them of an important detail for lack of which they suffer. The red and plum-coloured bricks of the late seventeenth and early eighteenth centuries were superseded by grey stocks, which Ware and other architects said consorted better with stone dressings (and painted imitations) than red bricks did.

c. 1702.   *Queen: Anne.*

FIG. 212.—No. 44, LINCOLN'S INN FIELDS.

FIG. 213.—THE RED HOUSE, SAWBRIDGEWORTH, HERTFORDSHIRE.

FIG. 213.—Another example of a type of small house found in country towns. Built of red brick, the window dressings are gauged, and those of the middle window are rusticated to give it additional importance, in order that, with the doorway, it may form an effective focal point. The cornice is of moulded brick, with a painted wood addition over it. The handsome doorway has Ionic columns and a segmental pediment.

c. 1718.   *King:* George I.
FIG. 214.—Houses (now destroyed) in the south-west corner of HANOVER SQUARE, LONDON.

c. 1714.   *Queen:* Anne.
FIG. 215.—A house in KING STREET, KING'S LYNN, NORFOLK. Henry Bell, *Architect*.

FIG. 214.—The three houses show a variety of treatment of the window arches and dressings—all in brick—which is characteristic of work at this period.

FIG. 215.—Almost every country town possesses houses of the eighteenth century designed by local architects, but often credited to Inigo Jones, Christopher Wren, or other prominent men. This house by Bell of Lynn is an example of a small Palladian house which has all the virtues, but none of the eccentricities, of the style. The slightly increased height of the first-floor windows with their entablatures gives them proper importance. The increased emphasis given to the centre windows accentuates the doorway as a focal point.

FIG. 216.—The brick house, with or without stone dressings, but always scholarly, was perhaps the most popular type during the first three-quarters of the eighteenth century. Here the doorway is of stone; later, wood (already well established) became the favourite material for doorways.

c. 1720.   *King:* George I.

FIG. 216.—No. 69, THE CLOSE, SALISBURY.

Photo: Gibson, Hexham.

c. 1721.   *King:* George I.

FIG. 217.—The south front of SEATON DELAVAL, NORTHUMBERLAND.
Sir John Vanbrugh, *Architect.*

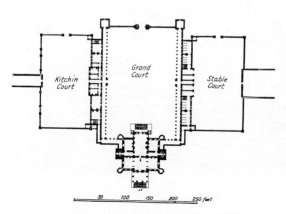

FIG. 218.—The ground plan of SEATON DELAVAL.

FIG. 217.—Only the shell of the main block of the buildings remains. Its design, the grouping of masses, and the lighter treatment of detail, show the development of the architect's powers and greater restraint in exercising them.

FIG. 218.—Although a small establishment by comparison with Blenheim Palace, the same method has been pursued in arranging the stables and offices in wings on each side of a court, at one end of which is the main building, while that opposite is left open.

Photo by courtesy of Moor Park, Ltd.

c. 1720.   *King:* George I.

FIG. 219.—MOOR PARK, HERTFORDSHIRE.
Giacomo Leoni, *Architect.*

Reproduced from "Vitruvius Britannicus."

FIG. 219.—Only the centre block remains of this house, which was originally furnished with flanking colonnades which screened the offices. It is an example of the unnecessary imposition of an immense portico upon a building. Compare with Easton Neston, Figs. 200, 202.

FIG. 220.—The plan of "Sir Lawrence Dundas's house," showing the main block illustrated in Fig. 219, the colonnades, wings, and the original layout.

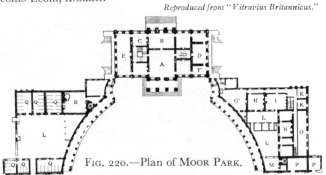

FIG. 220.—Plan of MOOR PARK.

A, Hall; B, salon; C, library; D, dining-room; E, gallery; F, bath; G, servants' hall; H, steward's room; I, kitchen; KK, pantries; LLL, courts; M, laundry; N, housekeeper's room; O, greenhouse; PP, coach-houses; QQQ, stables; R, brewhouse.

1723-5   *King:* George I.

FIG. 221.—The south and east elevations of MEREWORTH CASTLE, KENT.
Colen Campbell, *Architect.*

Reproduced from "Vitruvius Britannicus."

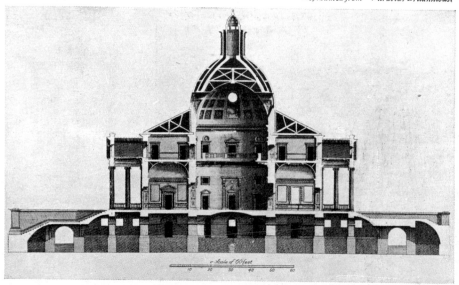

1723-5. *King:* George I.

FIG. 222.—Section of MEREWORTH CASTLE, KENT.

Reproduced from "Vitruvius Britannicus."   *Reproduced from "Vitruvius Britannicus."*

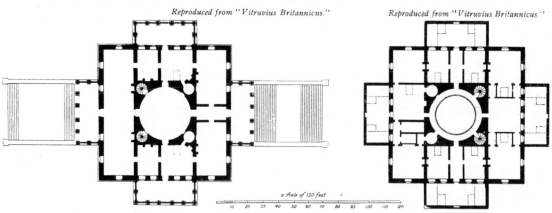

FIG. 223.—Plan of the principal floor.   FIG. 224.—Plan of the attic floor.

FIG. 221.—A copy of the Villa Almerico at Vicenza by Palladio, the principal variation from which is the carrying up of chimney flues in the thickness of the dome to discharge under the copper callot. Whereas the Villa Almerico stood on a hill, commanding views from the porticoes, there is but one distant prospect at Mereworth. This building (notwithstanding its unsuitability to the English climate and requirements) appears to have attracted the Palladians, for three other copies were built : one at Chiswick by the Earl of Burlington ; one called Nuthall Temple, in Nottinghamshire, by Wright ; and another at Foots Cray, in Kent. None, however, so closely followed Palladio's design as Mereworth, of which Campbell was inordinately proud. The entrance front is flanked by two buildings, of which one, which supplements the scanty bedroom accommodation, is shown ; the other belongs to the stables.

FIG. 222.—The section shows the construction of the dome. Campbell writes : " The Dome consists of thin shells. The first is carpentry with Stucco, which forms the ceiling of the Salon (Fig. 646). The outward is also carpentry, covered with Lead. . . . Between these two Shells, there is a strong Brick Arch, that brings 24 Funnels to the Lanthorn, which is finish'd with a Copper Callot, without any injury to the Smoke, which was not the least difficult Part of the Design."

FIG. 223.—The plan of the principal story shows a square house having a large hexastyle portico with triangular pediment to each elevation. The apartments surround a circular hall, which is 35 ft. in diameter and 60 ft. in height. The south front is given up to the gallery. The north front has a narrow entrance hall with a room on each side. The east and west fronts have each a state bedroom and an ante-room ; other bedrooms are in the attic. The kitchen and offices are in the basement.

FIG. 224.—Access to the first or attic floor is by two circular staircases up to the gallery in the central hall. Each bedroom in a pediment is lighted only by one small circular window.

Photo by courtesy of H. W. Fincham, F.S.A.

1723. *King: George I.*

FIG. 225.—ARGYLL HOUSE, KING'S ROAD, CHELSEA, LONDON.

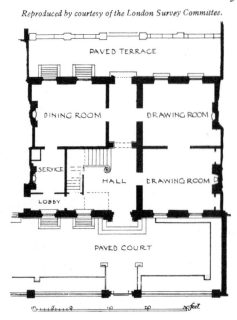

Reproduced by courtesy of the London Survey Committee.

FIG. 226.—Ground-floor plan of ARGYLL HOUSE. Giacomo Leoni, *Architect.*

FIG. 225.—This house should be compared with Moor Park, Fig. 219, to see how differently the architect designed—Moor Park in the full Palladian manner; Argyll House in the more homely style of the new vernacular, but with individual touches in the details of doorway and windows, which show development upon classic lines from such houses as No. 69, The Close, Salisbury, Fig. 216, and the Red House, Sawbridgeworth, Fig. 213.

FIG. 226.—A simple, practical plan devoid of pretentious state-rooms and contrasting with that of Moor Park, Fig. 220.

1721. *King: George I.*
FIG. 227.—A house at WITNEY, OXON.

c. 1725. *King: George I.*
FIG. 228.—FINCHCOCKS, GOUDHURST, KENT.

FIG. 227.—A street front, severely plain but possessing distinction.

FIG. 228.—The country squire followed the prevailing fashion and the historian records that " Edward Bathurst rebuilt this seat in stately manner." The front is reached through trees from the right, and the approach, being close to the building, produces an exaggerated impression of size. It is, however, a country designer's production, and the clumsiness of its proportions mars its good qualities. Once there were four central chimneys—symmetrically disposed; one of them, made of wood and painted to simulate brick, collapsed about fifty years ago. The building is an interesting provincial reflection of fashionable architects' work as seen by the eyes of a Kentish squire and his builder.

Photo: Bullock Bros., Macclesfield.

c. 1726.   *King:* George I.   1728.   *King:* George II.

FIG. 229.—SUDBROOKE PARK, RICHMOND, SURREY.   FIG. 230.—PEAR TREE HOUSE, JORDANGATE, MACCLESFIELD,
James Gibbs. *Architect.*   CHESHIRE.

Reproduced from Gibbs' "Book of Architecture."

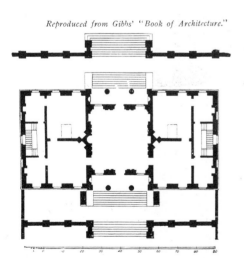

FIG. 231.—Ground-floor plan of SUDBROOKE
PARK.

FIG. 229.—The architect says of this house: "Here is a cube room of 30 ft., handsomely adorned and lighted by two porticoes. It has two apartments off it and over them Lodging Rooms. There are vaults and other offices underground." Although the house has undergone minor alterations (the vases have disappeared from the dies of the parapet and the steps have been modified), the illustration shows the house much as it was built by Gibbs.

FIG. 230.—A provincial builder's essay in domestic Palladian architecture. The parapet is missing, and the roof appears to be a later alteration. The window architraves are heavy and the doorway poorly proportioned. The treatment of the shutters is ingenious, but the piers which stop the iron railings are meagre. This house will not bear comparison with another provincial house at King's Lynn, Fig. 215.

FIG. 231.—The plan shows that everything was sacrificed to the Cube Room; indeed, two staircases were necessary to reach the first-floor apartments separated by the upper part of this room.

Reproduced rom "Vitruvius Britannicus."

c. 1729.   *King:* George II.

FIG. 232.—The north side of QUEEN SQUARE, BATH.
John Wood the elder, *Architect.*

*Reproduced from " The Eighteenth Century Architecture of Bath," by courtesy of Mowbray
A. Green, Esq., F.R.I.B.A.*

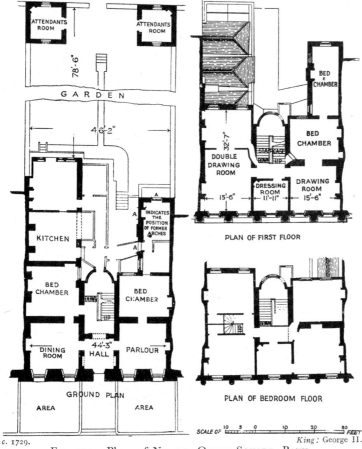

1724.   *King:* George I.

FIG. 233.—General Wade's house, GREAT
BURLINGTON STREET, LONDON.

c. 1729.   *King:* George II.

FIG. 234.—Plans of No. 24, QUEEN SQUARE, BATH.
John Wood the elder, *Architect.*

FIG. 233.—Of this house Colen Campbell wrote: " This beautiful Design is the Invention of the Right Honourable the Earl of Burlington, who is not only a great Patron of the Arts, but the first Architect." General Wade complained that the house was inconvenient and uncomfortable, whereupon Lord Chesterfield advised him to occupy a house on the other side of the street, where he might enjoy the prospect of his own house with the comfort which he desired.

FIG. 232.—An early instance in England of the grouping of dwelling-houses to form a terrace of one composition. Wood was also a pioneer of systematic town planning. This early essay by him is one in which the elevations are scarcely surpassed in subsequent terrace architecture.

FIG. 234.—As an eighteenth-century terrace house special interest attaches to these plans. The centrally placed entrance gives into a small square lobby, beyond which an arch leads to the staircase hall. The parlour and dining-room are only $15\frac{1}{2}$ ft. square, and behind each of these rooms there is a badly lighted bed-chamber. The staircase has a centrally placed window in its apsidal half-landing. Above the dining-room, and extending over the bed-chamber behind it, is a double drawing-room occupying the whole depth of the house on this floor, which consequently is lighted back and front. A smaller drawing-room (having only two windows) is over the parlour. The second floor has five rooms, and stairs up to the garrets. The garden in the rear of the house extends to Queen's Parade Place, and in each back angle has an outbuilding called an " attendants' room." In the light of greater knowledge, we can see how this plan betrays the inexperienced designer of terrace houses.

King: George II.

FIG. 235.—LAMB HOUSE, RYE, SUSSEX.

c. 1745. King: George II.

FIG. 236.—THAME PARK, OXFORDSHIRE.

FIG. 236.—The west front of Thame Park, designed by " Smith, of Coventry," stands at right angles to the early sixteenth-century south front illustrated in Fig. 103 ; indeed, other sixteenth-century buildings were pulled down to make way for that shown here. The wide front of eleven windows, divided into three groups in the usual way, is exceptionally flat, for the pedimented centre breaks forward only a few inches. It furnishes an instance of uninspired design, only distinguished by its academical precision.

FIG. 235.—This illustration of a country town house has details of good workmanship. The date of the bay window on the left is c. 1755 ; what appears to be brickwork between its plinth and the window-sill is actually brick tiling (see Fig. 326). The walling is in Flemish bond with grey headers. The entablatures over the gauged window arches are of moulded brick. The window-frames are almost flush with the wall face, those of the first floor being set slightly farther back than those of the ground floor ; the frames with thin glazing bars are of later date. The doorway has a flat hood and carved brackets ; there are ten raised panels in the door, and the dormer windows are half hidden behind the parapet.

FIG. 237.—The south front was described by its architect as " The best tetrastyle frontispiece in square pillars that hath yet been executed in or about Bath. The windows of the principal storey are dressed so as to become complete tabernacles, while those of the half-storey are adorned with single architraves ; and the mouldings in the whole front, proper to be carved, are all enriched in the best manner the workmen were then masters of."— *Quoted by Mowbray A. Green in " The Eighteenth Century Architecture of Bath," Bath, 1904, p. 74.*

c. 1734. King: George II.

FIG. 237.—BELCOMBE BROOK VILLA (now BELCOMBE COURT), BRADFORD-ON-AVON.

John Wood the elder, *Architect.*

King: George II.

FIG. 238.—HOLKHAM HALL, NORFOLK. South front.
William Kent, *Architect.*

1734–61.

King: George II

FIG. 239.—HOLKHAM HALL, NORFOLK. North front.
William Kent, *Architect.*

1734–61.

Reproduced from "Vitruvius Britannicus."

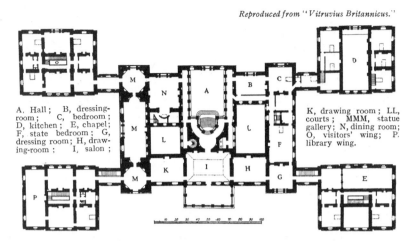

A, Hall ; B, dressing-room ; C, bedroom ; D, kitchen ; E, chapel ; F, state bedroom ; G, dressing room ; H, drawing-room ; I, salon ;

K, drawing room ; LL, courts ; MMM, statue gallery ; N, dining room ; O, visitors' wing ; P. library wing.

FIG. 240.—Plan of the principal floor of HOLKHAM HALL.

FIG. 238.—Built at a time when great landowners vied with one another in the erection of immense palaces, in the designing of which they personally took part. Lord Leicester at the same time reclaimed extensive areas of marsh, formed his park out of waste, and created one of the finest domains in the country out of clay and wilderness.

FIG. 239.—Built of cream-coloured brick ; the base, the columns and some of the dressings of stone.

FIG. 240.—The plan of a central block having subsidiary blocks connected with it by short corridors, as here, or by curved colonnades, as Fig. 220, was frequently adopted for great country houses during the eighteenth century. The centre of the kitchen, D, is 200 feet from the centre of the dining-room, N.

c. 1734-61.   *King :* George II

FIG. 241.—*Perseus and Andromeda.* Fountains on the terrace of the south front, HOLKHAM HALL, NORFOLK.

c. 1740.   *King:* George II.   c. 1750.   *King:* George II.

FIG. 242.—ST. SWITHIN'S, LEWES, SUSSEX.   FIG. 243.—UNDERDOWN FARM, EDDINGTON, KENT.

FIG. 242.—This house in the High Street is singularly bare, but is not without character. The door-way (which originally occupied the position of the nearest window) and cornice are good, and the keystones of the flat arches over the windows (which are without architraves) are effective.

FIG. 243.—The brick house with a five-windowed front and a handsome painted wood doorway, with a cut or purpose-moulded brick cornice and a hipped roof wholly or only half concealed by the parapet, is to be found in many counties. The brickwork was built in Flemish bond, and the window frames were almost flush with the wall face, except in houses within a radius of fifteen miles from London, where 4-in. reveals were established by law. The flat window arches were carefully gauged, and a band of moulded brick two, three, or four courses deep projected over the ground-floor window arches. The painted wood doorways were always the principal features of these fronts. That illus-trated is not well proportioned to the elevation, but many others were altogether admirable.

c. 1742.   *King:* George II.

FIG. 244.—"RANGER'S HOUSE," GREENWICH.

FIG. 244.—Lord Chesterfield's " villa at Blackheath." His town house is illustrated in Fig. 247. In the central features of this house the hand of the Palladian architect can be traced, just as in Argyll House, Chelsea (Fig. 225).

Reproduced from Ware's "Complete Body of Architecture."

Fig. 246.—The ground-floor plan of Chesterfield House, Mayfair, London.
Isaac Ware, *Architect.*

1753.   *King:* George II.

Fig. 245.—House on School Hill, Lewes.

Fig. 245.—Such square houses, well planned and comfortable, are to be found in many country towns. A lantern light over the staircase was the usual way by which the larger "cube houses" were lighted. The iron railing is not contemporary.

Fig. 246.—Chesterfield House was described by its architect as "a town house of the greatest elegance." The wings and colonnade have been rebuilt, reducing the width of the court by one half. The architect says: "The house being intended for elegance and magnificence must have the parts great . . . not to be thrown into a number of small rooms, for this would disgrace the external form. . . . A dressing-room in the house of a person of fashion is a room of consequence. . . . The morning is a time many chuse for dispatching business; and as persons of this rank are not to be supposed to wait for people of that kind, they naturally give them orders to come about a certain hour, and admit them while they are dressing. This use of the dressing-room shows also the necessity of a waiting-room." The following is a key to the plan: (A) Hall and staircase; (B) back stairs; (C) dining-parlour; (D) ante-room; (E) waiting-room; (F) dressing-room; (G) library; (H) drawing-room; (I) lobby; (K) water-closet; (L) colonnades; (M) porters' lodges.

1749.   *King:* George II

Fig. 247.—Chesterfield House.
Isaac Ware, *Architect.*

Fig. 247.—The centre block of Chesterfield House is the only unaltered feature. Ware wrote: "This rich and elegant order (the Corinthian) may be employed equally to the decoration of the great door of a house or to the door of an inner room of state. . . ." (See Fig. 438 at Mereworth Castle.)

c. 1750   *King:* George II.

FIG. 248.—THE WHITE LODGE, RICHMOND PARK, SURREY.
Centre portion by Robert Morris and Stephen Wright, *Architects*.

FIG. 248.—The wings, now hidden by trees, were built later and are connected with the
block illustrated by curved ground-floor links. A typical Palladian design, dull and having
no particular character, yet possessing that dignity which even the most conventional classic
composition does not entirely lack.

1753.   *King:* George II.
FIG. 249.—BROAD FARM, HORSHAM ROAD, SUSSEX.

FIG. 249.—The desire for "correctness" in design extended even
into remote country parishes, being interpreted by the local
builder according to his abilities, and was often combined with
the hipped roof and other features of the second half of the seventeenth century. Lack of knowledge is apparent here in the differing pitches of the triangular pediments of front and dormers, as
well as in the general clumsiness of the design.

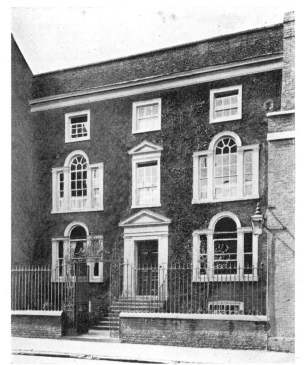

c. 1750.   *King:* George II.
FIG. 250.—House in TRUMPINGTON STREET, CAMBRIDGE.
James Essex, *Architect.*

1760.   *King:* George III.
FIG. 251.—House at WITHAM, ESSEX.

FIG. 250.—Houses by provincial architects have special interest, for usually their names are not connected with their buildings. The drawing for this elevation is in the British Museum (Essex Coll. Add. MSS. 6776–89), and states the house was built for Dr. John Randall, organist to King's College Chapel. The substitution of large sheets of glass for small ones in two windows is a serious disfigurement. The Venetian window was usually employed as a focal point (as at Boreham Street, Fig. 535, at Holkham, Fig. 239, and in the Adelphi, Fig. 545), and Essex's design confirms such use as its proper application. As the semicircular heads are above ceiling levels, they are intersected by the floors, and the back of their glass is painted black.

FIG. 251.—A sober square house having an unusually distinguished central feature.

c. 1760.   *King:* George III.
FIG. 252.—THE MARINO CASINO, CLONTARF, DUBLIN.

FIG. 252.—Although from Ireland, this illustration is given as an example of Sir William Chambers' scholarly designing. Recently it has fallen into a ruinous state. Figs. 255 and 263 show other buildings designed by him.

c 1760.   *King :* George III.

FIG. 253.—HOUSE AT DEAL, KENT.

c. 1750.   *King :* George III.

FIG. 254.—HOUSE, EAST STREET, COLCHESTER.

FIG. 253.—A brick front where certain features are of painted wood, whereas in earlier work the cornice might have been of moulded brick, and the bands and window dressings of rubbed brick. The scale of the bay window cornices increases as·they rise upwards, that of the second storey being the same as the main cornice, so that those furthest from the eye are the largest.

FIG. 254.—The bay windows are built of brick and may be compared with the bays of wood at Deal (Fig. 253).

1761.   *King : George III.*

FIG. 255—THE ORANGERY, KEW GARDENS, LONDON.
Sir William Chambers, *Architect.*

1763-5.   *King: George III.*

FIG. 256.—NO. 15, ST. JAMES'S SQUARE,
LONDON.

James Stuart, *Architect.*

FIG. 255.—Chambers was the architect of several pagodas and fantastic buildings at Kew, reflecting that Oriental taste which he acquired on his voyages to China and the East Indies ; this orangery, however, is sober and architectural in its design.

FIG. 256.—This elevation of a town house, by " Athenian Stuart," may be compared with a front of similar width at No. 20, St. James's Square (Fig. 267), by Robert Adam, who had not studied in Greece.

c. 1767.   *King : George III.*

FIG. 257.—THE ROYAL CRESCENT, BATH.
John Wood the younger, *Architect.*

FIG. 257.—The " Crescent " is more nearly a semi-ellipse. Its fine effect is produced by the Ionic columns, two floors in height, and the bold curve of the horizontal lines above and below. The designer relied entirely upon the curve and upon the Order for his effects : there is no attempt to embellish with added detail. Whereas the masonry both of base and entablature keeps the curve of the semi-ellipse, that between the columns is flat and not curved on face. Thus economy was achieved with little detriment to the effect. In front is a great lawn enclosed by iron railings.

By courtesy of " Country Life."

c. 1767.   *King:* George III.

FIG. 258.—The south front of the centre block of KEDLESTON, DERBYSHIRE.
Robert Adam, *Architect.*

Reproduced from "Vitruvius Britannicus."

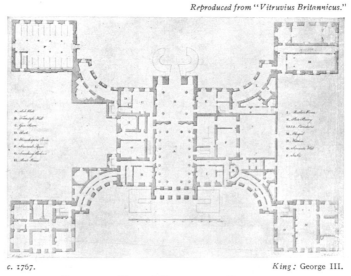

c. 1767.   *King:* George III.

FIG. 259.—Plan of KEDLESTON, DERBYSHIRE.

FIG. 258.—The wings of this elevation, shown in the plan (Fig. 259), were never built, and the centre suffers for lack of their support.

FIG. 259.—The scheme of a centre block with four subsidiary blocks connected by quadrants was conceived by Matthew Brettingham (who had assisted Kent at Holkham) and developed by James Paine for Sir John Curzon, who wished to build himself a house which would surpass Houghton and Holkham. Adam accepted the plan and elevations, but himself designed and built the south front (see Fig. 258). The angle with which each curved corridor terminates at its outer end enabled a window to be provided, which greatly assisted the lighting ; this treatment followed the practice of Palladio. The floors of these quadrants are laid with oak boards, cut to the same curve. Dr. Johnson wrote of the house in his diary under the date of July 19, 1777, that it is " very costly but ill-contrived . . . the grandeur is all below. The bedchambers are small, low, dark and fitter for a prison than a house of splendour. The kitchen has an opening into the gallery by which its heat and fumes are dispersed all over the house." The plan shows the distance from the kitchen to the dining-room to be 80 feet.

b. 1763-74. *King: George III.*
FIG. 260.—House in ADAM STREET, ADELPHI, LONDON.
The brothers Adam, *Architects*.

c. 1760. *King: George III.*
FIG. 261.—THE MILL HOUSE, WYE, KENT.

b. 1768-9. *King: George III.*
FIG. 262.—No. 3, THE TERRACE, RICHMOND HILL, SURREY.

FIG. 260.—In an obituary notice this design was attributed to James Adam. The brothers Adam introduced the use of stucco freely into their elevations as well as for the decoration of interiors. Referring to these elevations in a letter (July, 1773), Horace Walpole wrote: "What are the Adelphi Buildings?—warehouses laced down the seams, like a soldier's trull in a regimental old coat."

FIG. 261.—Notwithstanding the popularity of grey stock bricks in the London district, the use of red brick continued elsewhere, and many admirable little houses were built of it. Often the only decorative feature of these houses was the wooden entrance doorway, the variety of designs for which, in vogue during the eighteenth century, defies illustration. This house has also a neat cut-brick cornice of slight projection and three-light windows, the good proportions of which add to the whole effect.

FIG. 262.—Architects practising at this time vacillated between comparatively robust forms of Palladian design, as this front, and the more attenuated compositions, having slight applied ornament, which were popularized by the brothers Adam, who designed also in the more virile manner.

Photo by Bedford Lemere & Co.

c. 1767. *King: George III.*
FIG. 263.—ALBANY, PICCADILLY, LONDON.

c. 1770. *King: George III.*
FIG. 264.—A house at LEWES, SUSSEX.

FIG. 263.—Illustrating a domestic elevation by Sir W. Chambers. The buildings on the right and left of the court were designed as stables and offices.

FIG. 264.—A well-proportioned elevation with segmental bay windows and a segmental head to the doorway. The cornice is slight and compares unfavourably with earlier ones: the parapet has been destroyed.

Reproduced by courtesy of Messrs. Robersons Ltd.

c. 1776.

FIG. 265.—BASILDON PARK, PANGBOURNE, BERKSHIRE.
John Carr, Architect.

King : George III.

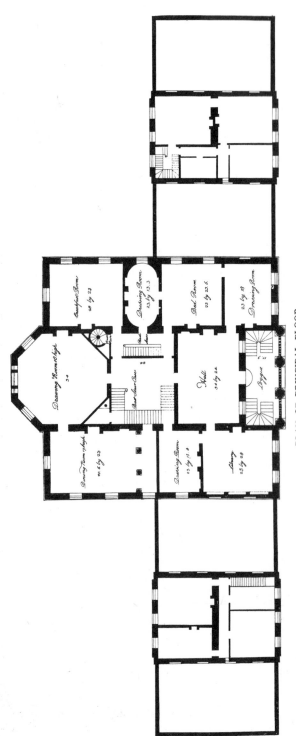

PLAN OF PRINCIPAL FLOOR.

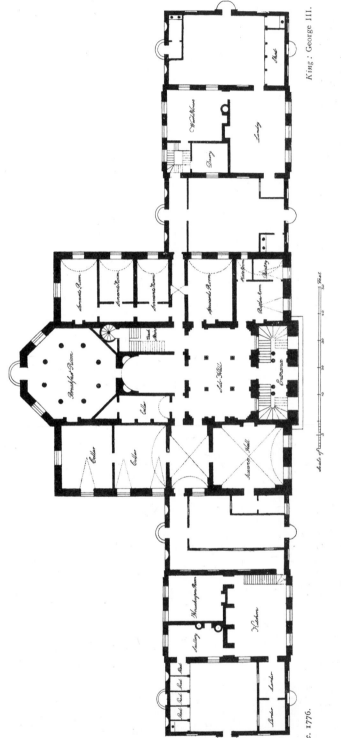

PLAN OF GROUND FLOOR.

FIGS. 266A AND B.—BASILDON PARK, PANGBOURNE, BERKSHIRE.

FIG. 265.—A large house of the late eighteenth century of imposing appearance, but extended plan, the frontage being 275 feet wide. As a composition of primary and secondary masses with connecting links extended to form a wide base, the design is excellent; but reference to the plans confirms the impression of domestic deficiencies which the elevation conveys.

FIGS. 266A AND B.—A distance of 170 feet had to be traversed between the centres of the kitchen and the breakfast room. Another breakfast room and the dining room are on the floor above. Unlike the smaller Georgian house, which suits modern purposes with little alteration, Basildon Park has been found so inadaptable to modern requirements as recently to have been demolished.

Reproduced from " The Works of Robert and James Adam."

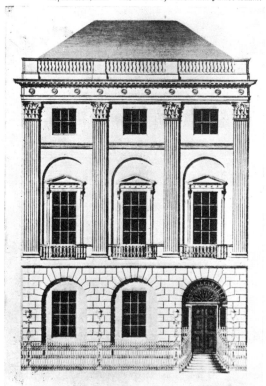

1772. *King:* George III.

FIG. 267.—No. 20, St. James's Square, London.
Robert Adam, *Architect.*

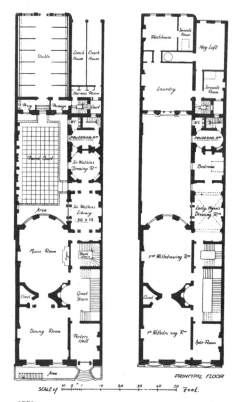

1772.

FIG. 268.—Plans of No. 20, St. James's
Square.

FIG. 267.—The house is described by the architect in the following words : " Where variety and grandeur in composition cannot be obtained (the front is only 46 feet wide) we must be satisfied with a justness of proportion and an elegance of style."—*The Works of Architecture of Robert and James Adam, Esquires,* vol. ii, London, 1779.

FIG. 268.—As plans of a narrow-fronted town house, these show development since the earlier work by John Wood the elder, at Queen Square, Bath, in 1729 (Fig. 234). Both premises extended to streets at the back, but whereas the house at Bath has a garden, that in London has the space occupied by stables and offices, an open area near the middle of the plot being designed as a court. The London staircase is less happy than it appears in the plans. The semicircular spaces are only niches, so that they do not actually increase the width of the staircase hall, the lankness of which is accentuated by its height and by the long flight of stairs in its length (Fig. 856). On both ground and first floors there are reception rooms of good design and proportions, the smaller rooms on each floor being designed as the private apartments of Sir Watkyn and Lady Wynn respectively ; both suites look out into the paved court. These plans show vigour and ability which are lacking in the cruder plans of John Wood.

c. 1777 *King:* George III.

FIG. 269.—Stowe, Buckinghamshire.
Robert Adam, *Architect.*

FIG. 269.—The south front of Stowe was designed by Robert Adam, but was slightly modified by the Italian, Signor Borra, who carried out the work and who was responsible for the internal decorations. The elevation has a width of 900 feet. The horizontal skylines of the three main blocks are broken only by the lower height of their connecting links.

c. 1777.

FIG. 270.—A detail of the south front of STOWE,
BUCKINGHAMSHIRE.

c. 1780. King : George III.

FIG. 271.—A house in HIGH STREET,
LEWES, SUSSEX.

FIG. 270.—This detail of a wing of the garden (south) front is a good example of the architect's work in the grand manner of the Italian Renaissance, and shows that Adam was capable of greater architecture than the mere shallow prettinesses for which, alone, he is often given credit.

FIG. 271.—A house, the timber-framed front of which is covered with " mathematical tiles," arranged to imitate brick heading bond ; the quoins are of wood, painted. Such construction is found throughout the south-coast countiès (see Fig. 326).

Photo : Bedford-Lemere & Co.

c. 1780. King : George III.

FIG. 272.

No. 13, DEVONSHIRE PLACE,
LONDON.

Reproduced by courtesy of Edwin Gunn, Esq.

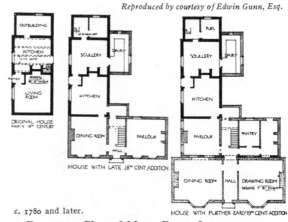

c. 1780 and later.

FIG. 273.—Plan of MAZE FARM, LINCOLNSHIRE.

FIG. 273.—Shows the development of a seventeenth-century cottage, based on the medieval hall house plan, by additions about 1780, and again forty years later, the latest front being like that in Fig. 274. A detailed description is given, page 160.

FIG. 272.—Where brick was used for the upper floors, the treatment was usually simple, emphasis being placed upon brick details, such as gauged window arches, rather than upon the introduction of dressings of stone. In this house the ground storey is rusticated, stuccoed, and painted; often, however, this storey was also of red brick. Here the handsome doorway and ironwork unite to confer additional charm.

S

c. 1780.   *King:* George III.
FIG. 274.—A house near ROLVENDEN, KENT.

c. 1785.   *King:* George III.
FIG. 275.—A plan of a small
country house.

FIG. 274.—A frame house covered with painted weatherboarding. The inside of the
framing is lathed and plastered, and the air space, thus enclosed, ensures a house warm in
winter and cool in summer. The roof is covered with red sand-faced tiles; the doorway, cornice, and joinery show the little crudenesses of a local tradesman's work. Such
houses continued to be built for many years.

FIG. 275.—This plan, from *Rural Architecture*, by John Plaw, London, 1794, plate liv, shows
the accommodation provided for a " villa " at the end of the eighteenth century, and the
naming of the rooms gives them special interest. The fashion for semicircular ends to
rooms is varied in the eating-room by making the exterior of the bay window a semi-
hexagon. The semicircular staircase landing was also a favourite treatment of Sir John
Soane's. The taste for "shaped" rooms is varied in the library, which is an oblong
hexagon, with recesses on four sides.

c. 1790.   *King:* George III.
FIG. 276.—THE PARAGON, BLACKHEATH, LONDON, S.E.

FIG. 276.—A grouping of houses connected by Doric colonnades to form one composition,
which is in many respects more interesting than ordinary terrace treatment, and produces
a sense of unity that detached buildings would not have possessed. Notwithstanding the
linking up, each house preserves its individuality.

c. 1790.   *King:* George III.

FIG. 277.—No. 24, WEST STREET, FARNHAM, SURREY.

c. 1790.   *King:* George III.

FIG. 278.—MILTON ABBAS, DORSET.

c. 1790.   *King:* George III.

FIG. 279.—A house and shop in HIGH STREET, HASTINGS.

FIG. 277.—The introduction of pateræ and flutes into the frieze is a happy instance of carpenters' detail. The doorways are of a favourite design, found in many towns, and no doubt taken from a handbook.

FIG. 278 —The whole village of thirty or forty standardized pairs of cottages was built at the same time. The walls are cream coloured and the roofs are of thatch. There is a joint doorway to each pair of cottages. The street winds up the slight incline of a narrow valley; half-way up is the church, and opposite it a row of almshouses. At the top of the street is the inn. Between each pair of cottages horse-chestnuts (planted when the buildings were erected) have grown into fine trees and soften the repetitive arrangement of the cottages. Except that the common entrances would not now find favour, this eighteenth-century housing scheme is not inferior to a modern one, whilst the rough grass, broken by paths trodden where wanted, compare favourably with untidy scraps of gardens enclosed by cheap fencing.

FIG. 279.—This building is timber-framed, lathed and plastered. The detail, which may be compared with that in Figs. 277, 280, is all of excellent design and workmanship and shows carpenters' work at its best.

Reproduced by courtesy of the Curator of the Soane Museum.

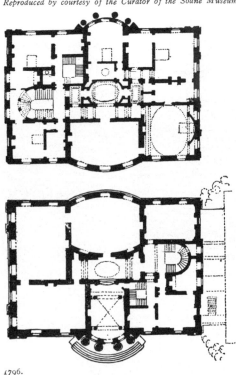

c. 1790.

FIG. 280.—A house and shop at WITHAM, ESSEX.

1796.

FIG. 281.—Plans of TYRINGHAM.

Reproduced from *The Works of Sir John Soane, R.A.,*
by Arthur T. Bolton.

FIG. 280.—The glazing bars of the doors belong to the Gothic revival, those of the lights over being in the "Chinese manner." At this date the window entablatures have become very thin.

FIG. 281.—The offices are in the basement and in a low building adjoining. Much space is wasted on the first floor in passages and in lighting the ground floor (see Figs. 283, 284).

c. 1798 and later.

King: George III.

FIG. 282.—HOLLYDALE KESTON, KENT.

FIG. 282.—A distinguished centre to which wings and other additions have been made. The aurora in the tympanum of the pediment is an instance of well-placed detail, which, though small, confers distinction upon the elevation.

c. 1796.   King: George III.

FIG. 283.—TYRINGHAM, BUCKINGHAMSHIRE.
Sir John Soane, *Architect*.

FIG. 283.—Soane's predilection for horizontal skylines did not always produce satisfactory effects. This engraving, dated 1820, shows the house in its original form, where the columns and their entablature serve no useful purpose, the whole design being vague and incomplete. For lack of an adequate base the building appears to have been thrust upwards out of the ground, as a modern gasometer rises out of its pit. (See Fig. 281.)

Photo: Bedford Lemere and Co.

c. 1796 and twentieth century.

FIG. 284.—TYRINGHAM, BUCKINGHAMSHIRE.
Sir John Soane, *Architect*.

FIG. 284.—The same building made reasonable by the modern addition of a dome and by an adequate base in the form of balustraded garden walls.

c. 1795.   *King: George III.*
FIG. 285.—A pair of cottages at MARDEN, KENT.

Late eighteenth century.   *King: George III.*
FIG. 286.—THE WHITE HOUSE, CHIPPING ONGAR, ESSEX.

Photo by courtesy of Mrs. J. D. Griffiths.

FIG. 285.—These were built as cottages and not converted from a better-class house. They illustrate a local method of building in brick up to first floor and continuing in timber framing covered with weather tiling. The only marked classic features are the entablatures on the consoles over the doorways.

FIG. 286.—A late eighteenth-century front. The practice of furnishing the windows with slight architraves and bringing the glass line out almost as far as the wall face, confers a certain quality upon the façade which would be lacking were the frames set back within $4\frac{1}{2}$-inch reveals.

c. 1800.   *King: George III.*
FIG. 287.—BARLBOROUGH RECTORY, CHESTERFIELD.

FIG. 287.—The main block is symmetrical, and the offices in the lower building are, as usual at this date, screened from the front by a plantation of trees or shrubs. Towards the close of the century the growing tendency to starve details produced mean cornices, whilst window architraves and dressings were reduced to mere flat bands, and often not even these. Stucco was supreme.

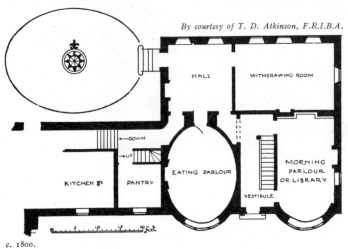

By courtesy of T. D. Atkinson, F.R.I.B.A.
c. 1800.
FIG. 288.—Ground plan of BARLBOROUGH RECTORY.

FIG. 288.—An ingenious plan for symmetrical effects. The north front of the main building is regular and unrelieved except for a slight pediment over the central window. The south front (Fig. 287) is symmetrical. The doorway from the hall to the eating parlour is square-headed, but those on each side have round heads. In the eating parlour the true curve of the ellipse has been preserved in the door and in the glazing of the windows, but there is a straight length of about 5 ft. on each of the longer sides which mars the effect; this has been corrected in the drawing, because such rooms were usually set out correctly. The principal staircase rises to a central landing, around which four bedrooms are grouped.

Reproduced by courtesy of the Curator of the Soane Museum.

c. 1802.   *King:* George III.

c. 1810.   *King:* George III.

FIG. 289.—PITZHANGER MANOR, EALING, LONDON.
Sir John Soane, *Architect.*

FIG. 290.—No. 29, DOVER STREET,
LONDON.

John Nash, *Architect.*

FIG. 289.—Comparison with the Adam centre block at Kedleston (Fig. 258) will show how much Soane was influenced by that design. Whereas at Kedleston the columns support the main cornice, those at Pitzhanger do not ; indeed, with their statues they produce the impression of being unnecessary " trimmings," having no structural functions or relation to a design which would be complete without them. In other respects Pitzhanger has the Soane characteristics of reticence, able grouping of masses, and the introduction of sculpture. The mouldings are simple and project little. There is such a remarkable similarity between Soane's design and a painting of classic ruins, not identified, by G. P. Pannin, that it cannot be regarded as an original composition.

FIG. 290.—This is perhaps one of the best of Nash's fronts, but it is a poor composition and suggests an assemblage of stock units rather than a considered design.

1813–20.   *King:* George III.

1818–21.   *King: George* III.

FIG. 291.—The west side of old REGENT STREET, LONDON.
John Nash, *Architect.*

FIG. 292.—CASTLE PLACE, No. 166,
HIGH STREET, LEWES, SUSSEX.

FIG. 291.—The chief merit of Nash's Regent Street was its unity. Each block was a complete composition and designed also in relation to adjoining blocks and to the whole street. The illustration shows how the ground floor of a block was designed for shops, and the upper floors as fashionable residences. The angle of the block beyond shows variety in design, whilst, however, maintaining general unity.

FIG. 292.—A façade built by Dr. Gideon Mantell, the famous geologist. The capitals of the pilasters have volutes in imitation of ammonites—hence the term "ammonite order," a shell variation of the Ionic volute, which, Mr. Arthur T. Bolton has pointed out, was also used by George Dance, R.A., in 1789 at a gallery in Pall Mall for Boydell.

FIG. 293.—The segmental bays, the doorway entablatures on consoles, and the parapet with a deep frieze, are all stuccoed and painted after the fashion of the period. The window awnings are of later date.

Early nineteenth century.   *King:* George III.
FIG. 293.—Houses on STRAND, DAWLISH, DEVON.

Photo by Thompson, Newcastle.

1820–4.   *King:* George IV.
FIG. 294.—CRESSWELL HALL, NORTHUMBERLAND.
John Shaw, *Architect.*

FIG. 294.—The influence of so eminent an architect as Soane extended far into the provinces and blossomed forth in interpretations which varied with the abilities of their architects. Here the result is a coarse imitation of Tyringham (Fig. 283).

c. 1819.   *King:* George III.
FIG. 295.—No. 86, EAST HILL, COLCHESTER, ESSEX.

c. 1846.   *Queen:* Victoria.
FIG. 296.—WHITE ROCK, HASTINGS.

FIG. 295.—A house in the heavy and clumsy manner into which the " Greek Revival " degenerated. The walls are stuccoed, lined, and painted in imitation of ashlar.

FIG. 296.—A decadent and uninspired composition in the Corinthian Order where proportions are bad—these are most obvious in the windows, entablature, and attic.

Photo: T. J. Gidden, Southport.

1837: Augustus W. N. Pugin.   1867: Edward W. Pugin.   Queen: Victoria.

FIG. 297.—SCARISBRICK HALL, ORMSKIRK, LANCASHIRE.

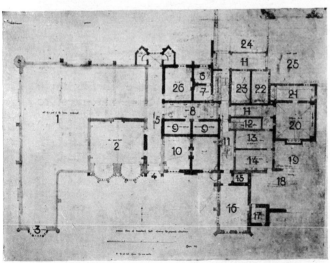

1837: Augustus W. N. Pugin, Architect.   1867: Edward Pugin, Architect.

FIG. 298.—SCARISBRICK HALL, ORMSKIRK, LANCASHIRE.
Augustus W. N. Pugin's plan of the ground floor.

FIG. 297.—Probably the finest and most elaborate example of Gothic revival applied to domestic building which, however, although rich, dignified, and picturesque, is unsuitable for a dwelling-house. This will be realized by reference to the plan (Fig. 298), in which rooms are badly arranged and ill-proportioned.

FIG. 298.—The square hall (Fig. 670), which has a high open roof, is provided with two bay windows, one fireplace, and a gallery. Lighting of the central corridor (8 in plan) is inadequate, being by overhead lights on each side of the corridor of the first floor; indeed, the whole plan is ill-conceived and inconvenient, showing its subordination to the picturesqueness of the elevations.

KEY TO PLAN.

1, All this part of the house unchanged; 2, the great hall; 3, new library window; 4, entrance; 5, principal corridor; 6, 7, butler's room; 8, upper passage; 9, store room lit from passage; 10, usual visitor's room; 11, passage; 12, way down to cellar; 13, housekeeper's room or still room; 14, housekeeper's room; 15, strong room, fireproof; 16, business room; 17, clock tower; 18, laundry; 19, court; 20, kitchen; 21, scullery; 22, dry larder; 23, wet larder; 24, hall; 25, courtyard; 26, butler's pantry.

b. 1837.

FIG. 299.—SCOTNEY CASTLE, LAMBERHURST, KENT. East elevation.
Anthony Salvin (1799–1881), *Architect.*

b. 1837.

FIG. 300.—SCOTNEY CASTLE, LAMBERHURST, KENT.

FIG. 299.—Salvin was a pupil of John Nash of stucco-classic fame, but these elevations will
bear critical scrutiny.   They show Gothic revival at its sanest and best.

FIG. 300.—Built·at the same time as Scarisbrick Hall (Fig. 297), this is a more sober example
of Revival work.   It is a sane and practical adaptation of Elizabethan-Jacobean architecture
to modern requirements.

*Reproduced from Nicholson's " Practical
Builder."*

c. 1823.   *King :* George IV.

FIG. 301.—A villa plan of the
early nineteenth century.

FIG. 301.—A villa plan of the early
nineteenth century which continued
the prevailing type for more than
fifty years.

FIG. 302.—A variation of Nicholson's villa plan.   The kitchen and
offices are relegated to the basement, which is lighted by an area.
The exterior is a cube of yellow
brick with a low-pitched slate roof
and deep eaves.

*Villa plan from Nicholson's " Practical
Builder."*

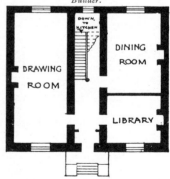

c. 1860.   *Queen :* Victoria.

FIG. 302.—A variation of Nicholson's villa plan.

EXTERNAL WALL TREATMENT

For other examples of WALL TREATMENT see—

EXTERIORS, pages 170 to 272

Sixteenth century.

Fig. 303.

FIG. 303.—Wattle and daub panel from the house illustrated in Fig. 120. The wattles are interlaced with the oak studs (one of which is visible) which are fixed at regular intervals between the oak rails. The daub, which is composed of loam and reeds, was applied simultaneously by a man on each side of the wall. Such panels are found in houses throughout the medieval period, of which this is a late example. Another example of similar treatment is illustrated in Fig. 558.

FIG. 304.   *c. 1530.*   FIG. 305.—HALES PLACE, TENTERDEN, KENT.

FIG. 304.—Brick nogging of two types—herringbone and horizontal. These are of different periods. The four upper panels fill an older window, the three lower replace wattle and daub panels (see Fig. 120).

FIG. 305.—Brickwork rendered with a thin coat of plaster (lime and sand) to imitate stone. This treatment was applied to the cut and moulded brickwork—the wall surfaces being left as brick.

c. 1546.   *King:* Henry VIII.   Sixteenth century.
FIGS. 306 AND 307.—BECKINGHAM HALL, TOLLESHUNT   FIG. 308.
MAJOR, ESSEX.

FIG. 306.—The practice of decorating external walls with colours was still in favour, but few examples have withstood exposure to weather. The brickwork of the gatehouse at Beckingham Hall was rendered with plaster and covered with a pattern now almost black.

FIG. 307.—A detail of the decorative pattern in black.

FIG. 308.—Panels of flints in mortar in a timber-framed building (Fig. 120), an alternative treatment to wattle and daub.

Photo: B. C. Clayton.

Late seventeenth century.   *King:* Charles II.
FIG. 309.—SPARROWE'S HOUSE, IPSWICH.

FIG. 309.—The long street front of 70 feet is a seventeenth-century facing of a medieval house, the oak and pargeting being contemporary. The pargeting was restored about the middle of the nineteenth century. Details of other plaster panels on this house are illustrated in Figs. 529 and 530.

d. 1692.   William and Mary.

FIG. 310.—CROWN HOUSE, NEWPORT, ESSEX.

FIG. 310.—The plaster panels are defined by moulded borders, in which is floral ornament not dissimilar to that at Earl's Colne (Fig. 311). The crown over the door hood is in higher relief.

d. 1685.   *King:* Charles II.

FIG. 311.—COLNFORD HOUSE, EARL'S COLNE, ESSEX.

FIG. 311.—Pargeting decorated with fruit and foliage in relief. In the centre of one panel is a cartouche bearing the date 1685. The doorway and windows are eighteenth century.

Photo: B. C. Clayton.

Plaster, late seventeenth century.   *King:* Charles II.

FIG. 312.—House at CLARE, SUFFOLK.

FIG. 312.—A fifteenth-century house, the walls of which were pargeted towards the end of the seventeenth century. The design is a vague floral pattern. The fifteenth-century barge boards, oriel windows, and blocked-up doorway are in good preservation.

Eighteenth century.

FIG. 313.—Pargeting at NEWPORT, ESSEX.

FIG. 313.—Applied to a timber-framed wall. The damaged corner shows the first coat scored to form key for the second and final coat, which is roughly panelled. This scale pattern combing is a favourite with plasterers and is found in many counties.

Seventeenth century.
FIG. 314.—DUKE'S PLACE, near MEREWORTH, KENT.

FIG. 315.—FORD PLACE, TROTTERS-
CLIFFE, KENT.

Eighteenth century.
FIG. 316.—Pargeting at THAXTED, ESSEX.

FIG. 314.—Plasterer's decoration was not confined to repetitive detail or to divisions of wall space into panels, but extended to formal geometrical designs which called for skill in setting out the wood templates. These were fixed in position upon the first coat of plaster and removed when the final coat had been applied. Similar treatment was used to represent tablets bearing initials or dates, also armorial and other devices.

FIG. 315.—Pargeting of older brickwork to represent stone. The channels are coloured with lime to a lighter tint than the blocks, which enhances the stone-wall effect. This illustration and that in Fig. 317 are highly developed instances of the ancient practice of rendering walls with plaster and lining them to imitate masonry.

FIG. 316.—The wall surface is divided into panels, which are decorated with impressed chevron ornament. The framing is moulded with bead and quirks.

FIG. 317.—House at COLCHESTER, ESSEX.

FIG. 317.—The pargeting of these earlier (sixteenth-century) houses is channelled to simulate masonry.

Eighteenth century.

FIG. 318.—House at SAWBRIDGEWORTH, HERTFORDSHIRE.

FIG. 318.—House having pargeted front divided into panels, the framing worked with bead and quirk moulding, the surfaces of the panels left rougher than those of the framing. The panel over the doorway has a sunk geometrical pattern. The window architraves project from the wall surface that the plaster may be stopped by them. The whole is coloured cream.

T

Photo: B. C. Clayton.

Late sixteenth or early seventeenth century.

FIG. 319.—House front at HIGHAM FERRERS, NORTHAMPTONSHIRE.

Seventeenth century. *King:* Charles II.

FIG. 320.—House at SMARDEN, KENT.

Sixteenth century

FIG. 321.—House at SMARDEN, KENT.

FIG. 319.—Panel of arabesques in white plaster on a black ground, which is studded with small pebbles.

FIG. 320.—The owner's name, date 1671, and two sheep indicate some branch of the wool trade.

FIG. 321.—The bressumer of the gable is carved with animals in relief, and coloured white on a black ground.

Photo: B. C. Clayton.

Early seventeenth century.

FIG. 322.—House front at EXETER, DEVON.

FIG. 322.—Wall slating where slates have been cut to fancy shapes. The panels between the windows bear armorials in wreaths which are executed in plaster.

Eighteenth and nineteenth centuries.

FIG. 323.

Eighteenth and nineteenth centuries.

FIG. 324.—Weather boarding.

FIG. 325.

FIG. 323.—Wall tiling with plain tiles was another method of covering old walls through which rain penetrated. Tiles were used also on new buildings, wholly or partially built of timber framing. Other wall tiles (as those of Fig. 325) were of ornamental shapes. In Western Counties wall-slating is found (Fig. 322).

FIG. 324.—The walls of small houses of the second half of the eighteenth and of the nineteenth century often were covered with feather-edged boarding—$7'' \times \frac{3}{4}'' \times \frac{1}{4}''$ boards, lapped and nailed to timber framing. Usually this weatherboarding was painted white, as in Fig. 274. Such buildings with red-tiled roofs are picturesque features of the Eastern, South-Eastern and Home Counties.

Eighteenth century.

FIG. 326.—"Mathematical" or brick
tiles.
Header and stretcher.

FIG. 326.—These tiles (bedded in mortar) were nailed to wood studding or boarding. At the angles of the building were quoins of wood, chamfered to represent blocks of stone (see Fig. 271). Such tiling is almost indistinguishable from brickwork and evaded the Brick Tax (1784–1850), but was in use earlier in the eighteenth century. It was employed also to encase timber and plaster walls of ancient buildings for which, also, ordinary plain tiles (Fig. 285), slates, and weatherboarding (Fig. 274) were used.

ENTRANCES

c. 1340.   *King:* Edward III.

FIG. 327.—The north elevation of the gatehouse, BATTLE ABBEY,
SUSSEX.

FIG. 327.—Alan, Abbot of Battle (1324-51),
obtained Royal licence in 1339 to fortify and
embattle his monastery, the gateway of which
belongs to this period.　It stands on one side
of a triangular open space, up to which the
narrow High Street leads, and as an example
of ecclesiastical arrogance and domination it
would be difficult to surpass.　The detail on
the south side is similar, but that shown is
in a better state of preservation.　The geometrical traceries of the two-light window
and arcading are excellent: other openings
have cinquefoil, trefoil, and ogee heads.

FIG. 328.—The entrance to the gatehouse, showing one of three portcullises by which it was
protected.　The massiveness of the whole, the
deeply machicolated parapet, the narrow loops
and windows, and the relatively small and well-
protected entrance are real military features
which became entirely conventionalized in gate-
houses in the course of the succeeding hundred
years.

c. 1386.   *King:* Richard II.

FIG. 328.—BODIAM CASTLE, SUSSEX.

FIG. 329.—The grooves were for the drawbridge chains. The door is modern but made in the style of the fifteenth century. Built some sixty years after the gatehouse at Bodiam, it is less massive but still a piece of pure fortification. The drawbridge was raised by chains; at Bodiam it was simply drawn away from over the space above the moat which it spanned.

FIG. 330.—This gatehouse, built about fifty years before the house (the entrance doorway and oriel window of which can be seen through the archway), is a beautiful example of flint panelwork, specimens of which are to be found also in East Anglian churches. In the parapet the work is varied by diamond chequering.

c. 1445–6. *King:* Henry VI.

FIG. 329.—HURSTMONCEAUX CASTLE, SUSSEX.

c. 1475. *King:* Edward IV.

FIG. 330.—The gatehouse to ST. OSYTH'S PRIORY (or ABBEY).

c 1482.   *King:* Edward IV.
FIG. 331.—OXBURGH CASTLE, NORFOLK.

FIG. 331.—A house built round a quadrangular court and surrounded by a moat. Through the gatehouse on the opposite side of the courtyard can be seen the hall doorway. The towers of the gatehouse show the development from short squat towers, as at Bodiam (Fig. 85) and Hurstmonceaux (Fig. 329), to slight towers with more stories, a development which was continued in the early sixteenth century. Towers were designed now more for appearance than for defence, and machicolations were merely ornamental.

FIG. 332.—The gateway has lost much of the fortified character of those at Bodiam, Hurstmonceaux, and Oxburgh (Figs. 328, 329, and 331). The doorway seen through the arch is the entrance to the hall.

Early sixteenth century.   *King:* Henry VIII.
FIG. 332.—The gateway to the court at COMPTON WYNYATES, WARWICKSHIRE.

FIG. 333.—The entrance doorway, oriel, and towers are no longer defensive in character. They are typical of the best work of the period and are significant of the change in style—as yet confined to details—which was in progress. The archway is *Perpendicular* in design, as also are the corbelling out of the oriel, the windows, the tracery, the crockets of the cupolas, the crenellations over the oriel and at the bases of the cupola and of the parapet. On the other hand, the figures supporting the armorial shields under the window show the new influence, as also do the enrichments of the corbel mouldings.

FIG. 334.—The entrance through the gatehouse is reached by a bridge over the moat. The gabled projection on the left contains garderobes serving two stories. Four cusped braces in each square panel form quatrefoils, and two of simpler shape form each of the arches of the blind arcading. The smaller quatrefoils in the coving are painted on the plaster.

FIG. 335.—A late example of the detached gatehouse which is on the opposite side of the court to the hall entrance. The gatehouse is reached by a light footbridge over the moat which encircles the castle and courtyard. See plan, Fig. 54.

c. 1525–38.   *King:* Henry VIII.

FIG. 333.—HENGRAVE HALL, BURY ST. EDMUNDS, SUFFOLK.

Mid-sixteenth century.   *Queen:* Elizabeth.

FIG. 334.—MORETON OLD HALL, CONGLETON, CHESHIRE.

Late sixteenth or early seventeenth century.

FIG. 335.—The Gatehouse at STOKESAY CASTLE, SHROPSHIRE.

Early seventeenth century.   *King:* James I.   *c.* 1626.   *King:* Charles I.

FIG. 336.—COKE'S HOUSE, WEST BURTON,   FIG. 337.—STANWAY HOUSE,
SUSSEX.   GLOUCESTERSHIRE.

FIG. 336.—A simple and homely work in the new manner, but having a Tudor arch.   See also Fig. 147.

FIG. 337.—This gatehouse shows a variety of "Dutch" gable which has somewhat exaggerated curves. Although the archway is mainly classic in its design, the arch itself is the four-centred Tudor type.   The building well illustrates the design of finials, chimneys, and parapets current at the time.

c. 1640.   *King:* Charles I.

FIG. 338.—The gateway in the screen wall at KIRBY HALL,
NORTHAMPTONSHIRE.

FIG. 338.—The gateway was built at the same time and was probably designed by the author of the elevation illustrated in Fig. 173. All the elements, triangular pediment, escutcheon and swags, rusticated jambs, niches and balustrading, are in the Italian manner: all are firm gand robust in design and well proportioned, which indicated thoroughly preconceived design instead of design largely developed during construction.

c. 1656.   Commonwealth.

FIG. 339.—THORPE HALL, near PETERBOROUGH, NORTHANTS.

FIG. 339.—The walls enclosing the extensive gardens are pierced at several points by approaches which are flanked by piers similar to those illustrated here; they are features which we find attached to great houses during the remainder of the seventeenth century. The piers are always substantial—the slight ones not coming into fashion until the eighteenth century.

FIG. 340.—The croisettes (breaks in the architraves) and the ramped volutes or scrolls were favourite and effective motifs found in Italian buildings, by which, no doubt, they were inspired. See Fig. 168 for setting.

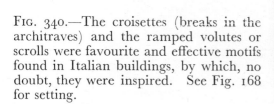

c. 1656.   Commonwealth.

FIG. 340.—THORPE HALL, near PETERBOROUGH.

c. 1662.   *King:* Charles II.

FIG. 341.—COLESHILL, BERKSHIRE. (Sir Roger Pratt, *Architect.*)

FIG. 341.—These piers are remarkable amongst many fine ones of the seventeenth century, and impress the eye by the simplicity and severity of their design. Yet every detail has been carefully considered, as, for example, the shapes of the studs of the panel borders, those at the top being treated as voussoirs.

d. 1666.   *King:* Charles II.

FIG. 342.—BROMLEY COLLEGE, KENT.

FIG. 342.—The finials of the piers are the mitre of John Warner, Bishop of Rochester, the founder.

c. 1680.   *King :* Charles II.

FIG. 343.—RAMSBURY MANOR, WILTSHIRE.

FIG. 343.—Gate piers of stone or brick, measuring 4 ft. square or more in plan, usually had heraldic finials and formed imposing entrances to parks. The lodges here on either side are of eighteenth-century date.

c. 1701.   William and Mary.

FIG. 344.—DRAYTON HOUSE, THRAPSTON, NORTHAMPTONSHIRE.

FIG. 344.—Ironwork for gates and screens was extensively used during the last quarter of the seventeenth century. Every great house had at least one magnificent entrance of this character, the spaces between the gate piers of which were filled with ironwork.

1706–24.

FIG. 345.—BLENHEIM PALACE, WOODSTOCK, OXFORDSHIRE.
Sir John Vanbrugh, *Architect*.

FIG. 345.—The gateway and interior of the kitchen court at Blenheim possess a severity which conveys a singular air of reserve and dignity.

c. 1730.   *King:* George II.

FIG. 346.—STOWE, BUCKINGHAMSHIRE.
Giacomo Leoni, *Architect*.

FIG. 346.—A gateway in a screen in baroque manner.

Mid-eighteenth century.   *King:* George II.

FIG. 347.—The Palladian Bridge, STOWE, BUCKINGHAMSHIRE.

FIG. 347.—Bridges almost identical in design were built by Robert Morris at Wilton, Wiltshire, in 1736, and (possibly by Wood) at Prior Park, Bath, in 1756. The bridge at Stowe spans a shallow pond and can only have been designed for pictorial effect.

1795.

King: George III.

FIG. 348.—TYRINGHAM, BUCKS.
Sir John Soane, *Architect.*

FIG. 348.—Such a composition shows Soane at his best, in skilful handling of masses having the minimum of decorative adjuncts, yet losing nothing by stark severity. It might be regarded as the prototype of modern essays in construction in concrete.

d. 1824.

King: George IV.

FIG. 349.—The gateway and lodges to the park at EASTON NESTON, TOWCESTER, NORTHAMPTONSHIRE.

FIG. 349.—An excellent design in the eighteenth-century manner, recalling that by Adam for Syon House, of which he said : " The colonnade and iron rail beneath not only give an air of magnificence to this building, but were also intended by His Grace to gratify the curiosity of the public, by giving travellers an opportunity of viewing from the road the park, lawn, bridge, river; and the house itself, at a little distance, closing the beautiful scene."

Photo by courtesy of Sir Ambrose Elton, Bart.

c. 1320.   *King:* Edward II.
FIG. 350.—CLEVEDON COURT, SOMERSET.

c. 1341.   *King:* Edward III.
FIG. 351.—PENSHURST PLACE, KENT.

c. 1386.   *King:* Richard II.
FIG. 352.—BODIAM CASTLE, SUSSEX.

FIG. 350.—The three interior doorways led respectively to the pantry, kitchen, and buttery. Opposite these (on the left) would be openings through the screen to the hall. The entry from the porch is illustrated in Fig. 363.

FIG. 352.—The entrance doorway to the great hall. The doorway to the postern is opposite, and the doorways to the pantry, buttery, and kitchen are on the right; the hall is on the left. See plan, Fig. 86.

FIG 351.—The interior of the porch to the north entrance, showing the entry and openings in the screens. The south door is at the opposite end to the entry, as is usual in medieval halls. It would be difficult to find a better groined roof of this period. The door is probably of the same later date as the screens, but the whole conveys an excellent impression of the principal entrance to an important fourteenth-century house.

Fifteenth century.
FIG. 353.—LINK FARM, EGERTON, KENT.

Late fifteenth century.
FIG. 354.—A house at TENTERDEN, KENT.

FIG. 353.—The two halves of the pointed door-head are each formed with its post in one piece by cutting these out of a tree at a point where there was a large bough. Within the door may be seen the doorways to the pantry and buttery; the hall is on the left of the doorway. See Fig. 16 for an illustration of the house.

FIG. 354.—Within, on the right, are the doorways to the offices; the hall is on the left. The crenellated moulding and the sunk tracery in the spandrels of the door-head are characteristic decorations of the period.

Photo by courtesy of the Rev. C. E. Carnegie.

c. 1350.   *King:* Edward III.   c. 1465.   *King:* Edward VI.

FIG. 355.—NORTHBOROUGH MANOR   FIG. 356.—OCKWELLS MANOR, BRAY,
HOUSE, NORTHAMPTONSHIRE.   BERKSHIRE.

FIG. 355.—The doorways from the entry to the offices show the development of ornament in characteristic decorated ogee arches, enriched with crockets and ball-flower ornament. The hall is on the right of the illustration.

FIG. 356.—The panelled framework of the screens is characteristic of early panels, being narrow and tall in heavy framing, but the muntins are not mason-mitred. The cinquefoil tracery in the lower panels is more unusual. The carvings in the spandrel of the porch arch, and the arch itself, are typical of the Tudor period.

Late fifteenth century.   *King:* Henry VII.

FIG. 357.—TURK FARM, SMARDEN, KENT.

FIG. 357.—The first door on the left leads to steep stairs, the treads of which are solid blocks of oak. The second and third doors lead to the lower-end chambers. The moulded beam over the doorways is contemporary, the moulded ceiling joists are of sixteenth-century date. To the right is the hall, originally open to the roof.

U

Early sixteenth century.   *King:* Henry VIII.   Mid-sixteenth century.   *Queen:* Mary.

FIG. 358.—COMPTON WYNYATES,   FIG. 359.—LITTLE WOLFORD MANOR
WARWICKSHIRE.   WARWICKSHIRE.

FIG. 358.—The entry, which is under the gallery, looks towards the doorway leading to the court. The panelled door leads to the lower-end offices. The linen panels of the partition are very tall, and the framing is mitred with masons' mitres. The development of these panels from the plain, earlier ones to be seen at Ockwells Manor (Fig. 356) is obvious, but there were intermediate stages of development.

FIG. 359.—The entry (under gallery). The entrance to hall is on the right. The woodwork may be compared with the earlier work at Ockwells (Fig. 356) and Compton Wynyates (Fig. 358).

Late fifteenth or early sixteenth century.   Late fifteenth or early sixteenth century.

FIG. 360.—LONG ALLEY ALMSHOUSES, ABINGDON,   FIG. 361.—ST. CROSS HOSPITAL, WINCHESTER, HAMPSHIRE.
BERKSHIRE.

FIG. 360.—An example of arcading in oak: a treatment also found in porches. Here it forms both an ambulatory and a covered way, giving access to the apartments. The brickwork is modern.

FIG. 361.—Late fifteenth-century or early sixteenth-century ambulatory, which serves the same purpose as that at Abingdon in Fig. 360. The wall has been rebuilt. (See also Fig. 375.)

c. 1130.   King: Henry I.
FIG. 362.—Stairway to the GUEST HALL, CANTERBURY.

c. 1320.   King: Edward II.
363.—Porch, CLEVEDON COURT.

c. 1250.   King: Henry III.
FIG. 364.—THE DEANERY, WINCHESTER.

c. 1250.   King: Henry III.
FIG. 365.—THE PRIORY (now the DEANERY), WINCHESTER.

FIG. 362.—The covered ways over the stairs to Rochester and Hedingham Keeps have been destroyed, but that at Castle Rising (Fig. 44) remains. This one at Canterbury is of about the same date. The original roof has long gone. It has been renewed several times, but each new one seems worse and less in keeping with the arcading than that which preceded it. It will be seen how like to those at Rochester and Castle Hedingham are the capitals and mouldings.

FIG. 363.—A semi-fortified entrance. Although the portcullis is modern, it is in the original portcullis grooves.

FIG. 364.—This beautiful and unique porch includes several types of arches in the Early English style. The three arches of the entrance are very acute, and, unlike the rear arches, have no shafts. The spandrels have niches for statues.

In FIG. 365 the details of shafts, caps, arcading, etc., of the interior of the porch should be studied, as similar ones will be found in doorways and windows of the same period, and in this porch several types are assembled. Attention may be drawn to the shouldered lintels (also called flattened trefoil arches) between the outer and inner piers. This form of opening is found also in contemporary doorways and windows. See Figs. 389, 493.

Late fifteenth century.   *King:* Henry VII.

FIG. 366.—SEYMOUR COURT, BECKINGTON, SOMERSET.

FIG. 366.—Porch with room over. The transverse ridge and gables enable a fireplace and chimney to be provided, which usually were lacking in porch rooms.

FIG. 367.—The porch and screen were brought from Clifton Maubank. Over the inner door are the words "And yours my friends." The detail is of earlier character than that of Montacute, and while generally in the manner of the Renaissance, some of the mouldings, as those of the strings, the cusping of the pierced parapet, and the crenellations of the bases on which the terminal heraldic beasts stand, are distinctly Gothic in character, as also is the entrance archway. Comparison may be made with the entrance to Hengrave Hall (Fig. 333).

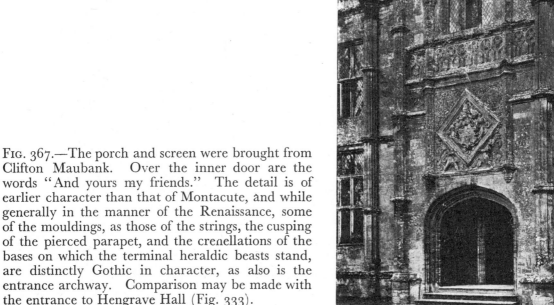

c. 1525.   *Queen:* Elizabeth.

FIG. 367.—MONTACUTE HOUSE, SOMERSET.

FIG. 368.—Porches, having rooms over, rising the height of the building to which they were attached, were usual in Elizabethan and Jacobean houses (see Figs. 122, 125, 128, 131). This porch is entirely classic in character, and is of a type of which many seventeenth-century examples exist. There is no Gothic detail, from the influence of which the designer seems to have been emancipated.

d. 1594.   *Queen:* Elizabeth.

FIG. 368.—COBHAM HALL, KENT.

d. 1594.   *Queen:* Elizabeth.

FIG. 369.—COBHAM HALL, KENT.

FIG. 369.—Interior of the porch illustrated in Fig. 368. A crude interpretation of the classic as transmitted to us through the Low Countries, but nevertheless having much Italian character and anticipating Inigo Jones's purer design.

c. 1606.   *King:* James I.
FIG. 370.—BRAMSHILL, EVERSLEY, HAMPSHIRE.

c. 1606.   *King:* James I.   *c.* 1611.   *King:* James I.
FIG. 371.—BRAMSHILL, EVERSLEY. HAMPSHIRE.   FIG. 372.—HATFIELD HOUSE.

FIG. 370.—In the detail of the entrance to the south-west front (see Fig. 140), the arcading, like that in Fig. 371, has some Italian feeling.   The Orders and other details show marked evidence of the influence of the Low Countries upon a building in which there is also something of Gothic flavour, notably in the corbelled oriel window.

FIG. 371.—In this and the corresponding loggia at the opposite end of the raised terrace (Fig. 141) restraint has been exercised by the designer which was lacking in the centre feature of the entrance front (Fig. 370). This arcading bears resemblance to that of Holland House, Kensington, which was designed by John Thorpe.

FIG. 372.—The south entrance is one of those stupendous and magnificent entrances without which no palace built at this period would have been considered complete.   The ability of the designer to use the Orders is overshadowed by excessive application of elaborate detail.

c. 1656.   Commonwealth.
FIG. 373.—THORPE HALL, near PETERBOROUGH.

c. 1630.   *King:* Charles I.   *d.* 1637.   *King:* Charles II.
FIG. 374.—UPPER SWELL MANOR,   FIG. 375.—MORETONHAMPSTEAD, DEVON.
GLOUCESTERSHIRE.

FIG. 373.—Recent examination of the porches at Thorpe Hall (one of which is illustrated) proves that they are contemporary with the house, as also are the ironwork of the balustrade over, and the plaster-work of the ceiling. Amongst the Inigo Jones drawings illustrating scenes for masques, etc., are examples of several porches of this kind (with Tuscan and Doric Orders) but having over-porches. The ironwork should be compared with that of the staircase at Greenwich, Fig. 832.

FIG. 374.—The entrance is of later date than the house. An earlier doorway can be seen within the porch. The segmental pediment, the scrolls round the cartouche and the strapwork of the frieze are characteristics of the period. This progress may be compared with the persistence of old design shown at Little Wolford (Fig. 376), built forty years later.

FIG. 375.—Four dwellings having an arcaded ambulatory in common. Compare with Almshouses at Abingdon (Fig. 360), where the arcading is of oak. Here the whole structure is of the local granite. The columns and mouldings are simple as befits so hard a stone.

d 1671.   *King:* Charles II.   1729.   *King:* George II.   *c.* 1740.   *King:* George II.

FIG. 376.—LITTLE WOLFORD MANOR, WARWICKSHIRE.   FIG. 377.—RAINHAM HALL, ESSEX.   FIG. 378.—No. 9, THE CLOSE, SALISBURY.

FIG. 376.—The porch was added to the Elizabethan building illustrated in Fig. 118. Its details (as the outer doorway mouldings) show little change in style since the house itself was built more than one hundred years earlier. The inner door is of the sixteenth century.

FIG. 377.—The fine quality of design, richness of detail, and excellent workmanship lavished upon internal doorcases is reflected in entrance doorways, of which this is probably the best remaining example. The door is modern, but conforms to eighteenth-century details. The window frames are not original, though in the eighteenth-century manner. Segmental, gauged, brick window arches are characteristic of this period.

FIG. 378.—An entrance porch with columns carrying a segmented hood. The shallow, recessed panels have small ogee mouldings.

1706-24.   Anne and George I.   1723-5.   *King* George I.

FIG. 379.—The east front entrance of BLENHEIM PALACE. Sir John Vanbrugh, *Architect*.   FIG. 380.—MEREWORTH CASTLE, KENT. Colen Campbell, *Architect*.

FIG. 379.—The portico and centre of the east front has scale too large for a domestic building. The square openings in the frieze are windows lighting the rooms behind the entablature. The great heights of the floors, which are suited to rooms having large floor areas, make the proportions of smaller rooms unpleasing and uncomfortable to occupy.

FIG. 380.—A detail of the south portico at Mereworth Castle showing the pediment mouldings and the design of the plaster ceiling.

Second half eighteenth century.   *King:* George III.   1769   *King:* George III.   *c.* 1775.   *King:* George III.

FIG. 381.—No. 32, SCHOOL HILL, LEWES, SUSSEX.

FIG. 382.—CHANDOS HOUSE, CHANDOS STREET, W.

Robert Adam, *Architect.*

FIG. 383.—PORCH IN ST. JAMES'S STREET, LONDON, S.W.

J. Crunden, *Architect.*

FIG. 381.—Doric porch added to earlier house.

FIG. 382.—A porch which became a stock feature of nineteenth-century houses, particularly in towns. Here it is well-proportioned and complete with its iron railings, lamp-holders, and torch extinguishers. In Fig. 295 is a travesty of this type of porch.

FIG. 383.—The area railings are of earlier character than those over the porch.

Early nineteenth   *King:* George III.   Early nineteenth century.   *King:* George III.   Late eighteenth century and nineteenth century.
century.   *King:* George III.

FIG. 384.—COLCHESTER, ESSEX.

FIG. 385.—PETERSHAM HOUSE, SURREY.

FIG. 386.—THE WHITE HOUSE, CHIPPING ONGAR, ESSEX.

FIG. 384.—Ionic porch of decadent design. The proportions are bad, the columns attenuated, the frieze too deep, the ornament meagre. Compare with Figs. 381, 382, the designs of which are virile and the proportions good.

FIG. 385.—Porch and iron gateway (added to an earlier house) in the manner of Sir John Soane.

FIG. 386.—The projecting porch is of later date than the columns of the doorway.

c. 1130.   *King:* Henry I.

FIG. 387.—The entrance doorway of CASTLE HEDINGHAM, ESSEX.

FIG. 387.—The stonework is well preserved, and the characteristic Norman
details are similar to others inside.

Photo : W. Lee, Grantham.

c. 1150.   *King :* Stephen.   *c.* 1180.   *King :* Henry II.

FIG. 388.—THE JEWS' HOUSE, LINCOLN.   FIG. 389.—BOOTHBY PAGNELL MANOR HOUSE.

FIG. 388.—An unusual feature is the arch above the doorway, which carries the chimney of the first-floor fireplace. The open-heart moulding of the doorway arch is in good state. In the jambs only the voluted capitals remain, the nook shafts having been destroyed.

FIG. 389.—The entrance doorway to the vaulted room has a square-headed trefoil or "shouldered arch" (Early English).

c. 1232–40.   *King :* Henry III. *c.* 1260–80.   *Kings :* Henry III and Edward I.

FIGS. 390 AND 391.—The Great Hall at WINCHESTER CASTLE.   FIG. 392.—LITTLE WENHAM HALL, SUFFOLK.

FIG. 390.—The south doorway. The inner pointed arch is very flat; the hood-mould has characteristic Early English ornament. FIG. 391.—The west doorway. The arch is more pointed than that of the south doorway, and the vertical lines of the mouldings at the springing are more marked. In both doorways the shaft capitals and bases are early examples of their type—restored.

FIG. 392.—Internal doorway having Early English hood-mould, mouldings and stops. Students of church details will appreciate the simplification of these when applied to a domestic building.

c. 1290–1300.   *King:* Edward I.   *c.* 1300.   *King:* Edward I.   *c.* 1340.   *King:* Edward III.

FIG. 393.—THE MANOR HOUSE, GODMERSHAM.   FIG. 394.—OLD SOAR, PLAXTOL, KENT.   FIG. 395.—The Entrance to Gatehouse at BATTLE ABBEY.

c. 1341.   *King:* Edward III.   *c.* 1440.   *King:* Henry VI.

FIG. 396.—PENSHURST PLACE, KENT.   FIG. 397.—The School at EWELME, OXON.

FIG. 393.—Probably the effigy over the mutilated doorway at the Manor House, Godmersham, is that of the builder, Prior Henry. This doorway may be compared with those at Winchester (Figs. 390, 391), where the same details have been used. Attention may be drawn to the trefoil arch and the cusping and piercing of the plate.

FIG. 394 shows a simple doorway at Old Soar, leading to the ground-floor room under the chapel.

FIG. 395.—The shafts of the pier from which the groined vault springs can be seen through the open gate. The general appearance and the detail of the caps are early in character for this date, but the licence was granted in 1339.

FIG. 396.—In the north entrance doorway and porch the sandstone used is stained by iron; the intensity of the orange-red stain varying. The builder has used this stratum to produce a beautiful radiating effect. The tablet above the doorway is a modern addition.

FIG. 397.—The doors are of an early type of woodwork carved to represent tracery and are imitative of mason's work. The brickwork is modern.

Photo : B. C. Clayton.

c. 1470.   *King:* Edward IV. Late fifteenth century.   Late fifteenth century.   *King:* Henry VII.

FIG. 398.—ELTHAM PALACE, FIG. 399.—YANWATH HALL, WESTMOR- FIG. 400.—TURK FARM, SMARDEN, KENT.
KENT.   LAND.

Photo : Gibson and Son, Hexham.

Late fifteenth or early sixteenth century.   Early sixteenth century.

FIG. 401.—SKIPTON CASTLE, YORK- FIG. 402.—PAYCOCKES, GREAT COGGESHALL,
SHIRE.   ESSEX.

FIG. 398.—The doorway in the bay of the great hall. The door is modern.

FIG. 399.—The stopping of the ribs of the hall door illustrates an intermediate stage in the development towards complete linenfold panelling.

FIG. 400.—Doorway to a lower-end chamber having four-centred head and sinkings in the spandrels. A characteristic of the fifteenth-century timber work is the massive framing of which these doorposts are an example. The contemporary door is made of overlapping boards (clapboard) nailed to ledges with iron studs.

FIG. 401.—The entrance doorway and bay window in the court. The Clifford arms can be seen over the doorway.

FIG. 402.—These folding doors have definite, but not fully developed, linenfold panels. Comparison with the doors at Ewelme (Fig. 397), and with the intermediate type at Yanwath Hall (Fig. 399), will show the change in design and treatment which had taken place in the course of fifty years.

c. 1525.   King: Henry VIII.   c. 1572-5.   Queen: Elizabeth.   Sixteenth century.

FIG. 403.—SUTTON PLACE, GUILDFORD,   FIG. 404.—KIRBY HALL,   FIG. 405.—TURK FARM,
              SURREY.   NORTHAMPTONSHIRE.   SMARDEN, KENT.

FIG. 403.—The development of the Renaissance influence during the first half of the sixteenth century was of a partial nature. At Sutton Place, for instance, the doorway is of Tudor character in its design and mouldings, but it was built of terra-cotta designed and made by Italian workmen. The tablets over the lower dripstone are also of Italian design and workmanship. So, too, are the intermediate balusters and other framing, which are of the same red colour as the bricks of the walling.

FIG. 404.—This doorway is more nearly in the Italian manner than others of this date.

FIG. 405.—The head and jambs moulded with shallow mouldings stopped by four-leafed pattern with carved stop below (see Fig. 882). The crenellated beam over is of the fifteenth century. The door is of boards, nailed to ledges, the boards tongued, grooved and moulded with bead and quirk.

Late sixteenth or early seventeenth century.   Late sixteenth or early seventeenth century.
FIG. 406.—FORD PLACE, TROTTERS-   FIG. 407.—A House in WINECHEAP,
              CLIFFE, KENT.   CANTERBURY.

FIG. 406.—The doorway and door probably have been moved from their original position. The very heavily moulded door frame and stops, carved with arabesques, are characteristic of some late Elizabethan work. The moulded and studded plank door is contemporary.

FIG. 407.—The stops on the jambs are characteristic work of the Elizabethan period (see Fig. 882 for detail of similar stop). The light above the door is of later date. The knocker is Georgian.

Reproduced by courtesy of the Director of the Victoria and Albert Museum.

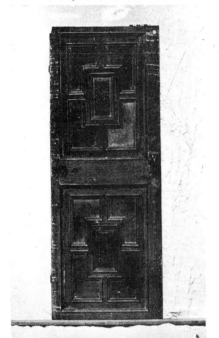

Early seventeenth century.   *King:* James I.

FIG. 408.

c. 1620.   *King:* James I.

FIG. 409.—CAMPDEN HOUSE, CHIPPING CAMPDEN.

c. 1636.   *King:* Charles I.

FIG. 410.—RAYNHAM HALL, NORFOLK.

FIG. 408.—An oak door with a raised panel, set in the centre of L-shaped panels, all of which are formed with applied mouldings.

FIG. 409.—The door is a typical one of its period, having channelled and moulded stiles, rail, and muntins. The semicircular head is a copy of the original but retains its general character.

FIG. 410.—The arms of Sir Roger Townshend, who died in 1637 and who built the house, indicate the date of a design of a character many years in advance of English practice. Although charming and graceful, the elongation of the columns and pedestals produces an attenuated effect and suggests lack of experience in drawing the Orders, such as one would expect of William Edge, mason, who accompanied his master to London and the Continent and whose services in making drawings appear in the accounts.

House, *c.* 1580-1601.   *Queen:* Elizabeth.

FIG. 411.—MONTACUTE HOUSE, SOMERSET.

FIG. 411.—In this door-case and door of a bedroom at Montacute, there are a number of elements current in woodwork of the early seventeenth century. The pilasters of the Order are inlaid with various woods, and the spaces between the inlaid areas are furnished with applied panels, in the centre of each of which is the faceted ornament which developed later into the rounded cabochon. Both arcaded and rectangular panels are introduced into the door. The postillion's boots are of mid-seventeenth-century date.

Photo: Frith, Reigate.

d. 1633.
FIG. 412.—COLBY HALL,
YORKSHIRE.

1618–35.   King: Charles I.
FIG. 413.—THE QUEEN'S
HOUSE, GREENWICH.

c. 1656.   Commonwealth.
FIG. 414.—THORPE HALL, near
PETERBOROUGH.

FIG. 412.—Doorways having semicircular heads, springing from moulded imposts and sometimes having moulded jambs, are found in stone counties. For a Sussex example see Fig. 152, and for one in Gloucestershire, Fig. 374. These heavy, moulded imposts are found also with the sixteenth-century four-centred arches (Fig. 337). The association of such imposts with semicircular arches has produced traditions that such doorways are Norman work removed from ruined abbeys, whereas they are of the period of the houses to which they are the entrances. There is considerable variety of Yorkshire doorheads, some of which are fanciful. Louis Ambler in *The Old Halls and Manor Houses of Yorkshire*, page 13, gives a comparative series of twenty kinds.

FIG. 413.—The door-case on the first floor to the S.W. rooms. For this door-case, as for all others in the house, the material used is stone (not wood) which has been painted. The small ramped and flattened volute is characteristic of the Inigo Jones school, and is a detail which the Palladians copied a hundred years later.

FIG. 414.—The panel construction of this door differs little from that in Fig. 415, but here it is enriched with carving. The architrave is a stiff version of acanthus leaf ornament, which was shortly to be used in a more naturalistic manner.

FIG. 415.—All the mouldings are small and project slightly. The panels are sunk within the framings and mouldings. The panels of the doors are raised, but the margins round the raised portions are not bevelled and their faces are not brought forward as far as the face of the framing. The centres of the panels are raised with ovolo and fillet moulding, but an ogee was often used for this purpose. This kind of raising was called " revailing " by contemporary joiners; see Fig. 478c.

c. 1656.   Commonwealth.
FIG. 415.—THORPE HALL, near
PETERBOROUGH.

c. 1660.
FIG. 416.—DRAYTON HOUSE,
THRAPSTON, NORTHAMPTONSHIRE.

FIG. 416.—Door-case and picture panel over in the manner of John Webb, who designed the overmantel in the same room (Fig. 633). The room is hung with tapestries, but a fragment of earlier small panelling is exposed on the right of the picture panel.

From " A History of English Brickwork."

c. 1654.   Commonwealth.   *d.* 1692.   William and Mary.

Fig. 417.—Tyttenhanger Park, St. Albans, Herts.   Fig. 418.—House at Newport, Essex.

Fig. 417.—An early example of a wooden door-hood on brackets. The windows have architraves and, alternately, segmental and triangular pediments. The design of the cut brickwork of the centre window may be compared with the doorway at Thorpe Hall (Fig. 340).

Fig. 418.—The shell hood and pargeted panels are contemporary.

c. 1685.   *King:* Charles II.   *c.* 1662.   *King:* Charles II

Fig. 419.—Honington Hall,   Fig. 420.—Coleshill, Berkshire.
Warwickshire.   Sir Roger Pratt, *Architect.*

Fig. 419.—The coved door-hood (semi-elliptic or semicircular) was introduced towards the close of the seventeenth century. Late examples were carved in the form of shells instead of being filled with fruit, flowers, acanthus leaf, birds, and amorini; but other examples combine both treatments.

Fig. 420.—At Whitehall the entrance doorway to the Banqueting Hall is insignificant, and at the Queen's House, Greenwich (Figs. 163, 165), Inigo Jones does not accent the entrance doorway of either front. At Coleshill, his friend Pratt goes further in this direction by designing a fine entrance, but the reserve he shows contrasts markedly with the Jacobean profuseness (Figs. 370, 372), which the Italian school was ousting.

W

c. 1690.   William and Mary.
FIG. 421.—THE COMMUNICATION GALLERY, HAMPTON COURT PALACE.

c. 1690.   William and Mary.
FIG. 422.—HAMPTON COURT PALACE. Sir Christopher Wren, *Architect.*

c. 1690.   William and Mary
FIG. 423.—DENHAM PLACE, BUCKINGHAMSHIRE.

FIG. 421.—Typical Wren door architrave and panel mould.

FIG. 422 shows the door-case and window shutters in the King's Drawing-Room, the authorship of which makes them particularly interesting. The bold bolection moulding of the door frame is enriched with carving. The door and shutter panels are raised and fielded.

FIG. 423.—The library is panelled in oak, with recessed bookshelves. All the mouldings are enriched with carving. Although there are neither columns nor pilasters the proportions of the Order have been observed ; the dado rail represents the pedestal-cap, and above this two panels occupy the approximate height of a column ; then come the frieze and cornice. Compare with the haphazard proportions in Fig. 690.

c. 1690.   William and Mary
FIG. 424.—DENHAM PLACE, BUCKINGHAMSHIRE.

c. 1701.   William and Mary.
FIG. 425.—MOMPESSON HOUSE, SALISBURY.

FIG. 424.—Oak door panelling with bolection mouldings enriched by carving.
FIG. 425.— Eight-panel door and door-case enriched with carving.

Late seventeenth or early eighteenth century.

FIG. 426.—MANOR HOUSE, CROOM'S HILL.

Early eighteenth century. *Queen : Anne.*

FIG. 427.—No. 45, SHEEN ROAD, RICHMOND, SURREY.

Early eighteenth century. *Queen : Anne.*

FIG. 428.—No. 11, THE GREEN, RICHMOND.

FIG. 426.—Handsome carved brackets supported flat, triangular, and semicircular or semi-elliptic hoods, which were frequently enriched with carving in the form of a shell, animals, fruit, foliage, etc.

FIG. 427.—Many late seventeenth-century and early eighteenth-century doorways still exist which are constructed of wood, richly carved. They are usually approached by a flight of Portland stone steps, flanked by wrought-iron balustrading. The door panels vary in number from six to ten.

FIG. 428.—Another typical doorway with wrought-iron balustrade and steps.

c. 1700. William and Mary.

FIG. 429.—The east entrance to DRAYTON HOUSE, NORTHAMPTONSHIRE.

FIG. 429.—The iron balustrade is in the manner which succeeded that of Jean Tijou. It is formed in upright panels, and at the landings a shallow "lying" panel is added. The easy appearance of the ascent is an effect produced by the wide landing half-way up.

c. 1701.   William and Mary.   *c.* 1702.   *Queen :* Anne.   *c.* 1702.   *Queen :* Anne.

FIG. 430.—MOMPESSON HOUSE, SALISBURY,   FIG. 431.—LOWER STANDARD FARM,   FIG. 432.—THE GRANGE, FARNHAM,
WILTSHIRE.   NINFIELD, SUSSEX.   SURREY.

FIG. 430.—Stone doorway in the Wren manner, with a contemporary eight-panel door.

FIG. 431.—The large bolection moulding used round fireplace openings is here applied to a doorway.

FIG. 432.—The substitution of painted wood for stone entrance doorways produced a remarkable diversity of designs based (more or less) upon the Orders; usually these were beautiful and well proportioned.

c. 1709.   *Queen :* Anne.   *c.* 1714.   *King :* George I.   *c.* 1715.   *King :* George I.

FIG. 433.—THE BLUECOAT SCHOOL,   FIG. 434.—BRADBOURNE PARK,   FIG. 435.—No. 179, CLAPTON ROAD,
WESTMINSTER, LONDON.   LARKFIELD, KENT.   LONDON.

FIG. 433.—Doric doorway, which is a vigorous and masculine rendering of the Order.

FIG. 434.—Flat door hoods were often supported by elaborately carved brackets. Whereas the fanlight usually filled a semicircular opening, as in Figs. 448, 453, here the leaded glasswork fills the whole space of the rectangle. The eight or ten panelled door is here replaced by folding doors, the glazing of which is of later date, but is carried low down. Similar correct treatment of door glazing is shown in Fig. 377.

FIG. 435.—A fine doorway in the Corinthian Order. The pilasters are set on pedestals—a practice less often seen later in the eighteenth century. The ramped Portland stone steps and their iron railings complete an excellent composition.

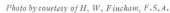
Photo by courtesy of H. W. Fincham, F.S.A.

1723.   *King:* George I.

FIG. 436.—ARGYLL HOUSE, KING'S ROAD, CHELSEA.

Giacomo Leoni, *Architect*.

FIG. 436.—A doorway incorporating details current at the time, but having distinct originality. The balustrade and vases are exceptional, but the whole effect is satisfactory, for the doorway and centre window have been treated as one composition.

d. 1727.

FIG. 437.—FITZWILLIAM HALL,
CAMBRIDGE.

c. 1723-25.   *King:* George I.

FIG. 438.—MEREWORTH CASTLE,
KENT.

FIG. 437.—A doorway of the period of the date on the brickwork.

FIG. 438.—The gallery doorway leading into the salon reaches, perhaps, the summit of Palladian design and workmanship.   See also Fig. 247.

FIG. 439.—The salon has a domed ceiling of eight diminishing sides enriched with octagonal sunk panels.   The walls have large panels with enriched mouldings, and the windows are in the three external sides of the octagon.   Amorini reclining on the pediment are Italian details.

c. 1744.   *King :* George II.

FIG. 439.—HONINGTON HALL, WARWICK-
SHIRE.

1723.   *King :* George I.

FIG. 440.—MEREWORTH CASTLE, KENT.
Colen Campbell, *Architect.*

c. 1745.   *King :* George II.

FIG. 441.—THAME PARK, OXFORD-
SHIRE.

FIG. 440.—The doorway in the south portico has a horizontal entablature supported by consoles.   The narrow pilasters are panelled, and the pulvinated frieze is carved with laurel leaves and crossed ribbons; the architrave mouldings are also enriched with carving. Comparison with the window (Fig. 536) shows how little the treatment of openings varied, the same *motifs* being used for them all.

FIG. 441.—In the door-case, dado, and panel moulds, all the mouldings are enriched with carving.   Both wall and door panels are sunk.

c. 1740.   *King :* George II.   *c.* 1740.   *King :* George II.
FIG. 443.—House in HIGH STREET,   FIG. 444.—MANOR HOUSE, PETERSHAM,
COLCHESTER, ESSEX.   SURREY.

c. 1744.   *King :* George II.
FIG. 442.—HONINGTON HALL,
WARWICKSHIRE.

FIG. 442.—The horizontal entablature for door-cases, which thirty years later was almost entirely to supersede pediments, is seen here. Stucco tablets had ousted pictures in over-door panels.

FIG. 443.—Recessed Doric doorway with columns, the steps carried forward over the pavement. Compare with step treatment in Fig. 457.

FIG. 444.—The door is narrow, but the substantial nature of its setting the outward sweep of the iron railings and the deep reveals prevent any impression of lankness.

d. 1731.   *King :* George II.   *c.* 1750.   *King :* George II.
FIG. 445.—CHURCH HOUSE, BECKLEY,   FIG. 446.—BRANCASTER STAITHE, NORFOLK.
SUSSEX.

FIG. 445.—A Doric doorway with pilasters and cornice, the whole being severely rectangular in design. Glass has been substituted wrongly for two of the wooden panels. Figs. 377 and 434 show the right treatment.

FIG. 446.—The pulvinated frieze of this Ionic doorway is carved with acanthus in a manner verging upon the rococo. The staircase is a good example of the type, found in country houses, rising from a square hall, which is no longer the principal apartment, but has become a mere entry.

1747.　　　　　　*King:* George II.
FIG. 447.—Doorway of a house,
NORTHIAM, SUSSEX.

Mid-eighteenth century.
FIG. 448.—THE BARONS, REIGATE,
SURREY.

c. 1745.　　　　　*King:* George II.
FIG. 449.—MONTROSE HOUSE,
PETERSHAM, SURREY.

FIG. 447.—Another variety of consoles supporting a horizontal hood. Often, instead of consoles, the brackets are of earlier character as the section imposed on the illustration.

FIG. 448.—A well proportioned Ionic doorway. Such columns were not solid but built up of thin boards on a backing, thereby avoiding distortion through warping of the wood.

FIG. 449.—Semi-elliptical arches to door-cases are more uncommon than at entries to passages and under stairs of houses built during the first fifty years of the eighteenth century. Probably the four-panel door (though it matches the panelling) is later work.

Mid-eighteenth century.
FIG. 450.—CASTLE STREET,
FARNHAM, SURREY.

c. 1750.　　　　　　　　　　　　　　*King:* George II.
FIG. 451.—No. 44, GREAT ORMOND STREET, LONDON.

FIG. 450.—Similar Doric doorways, with pilasters or columns and triangular pediments, dating from 1750 to 1780, are to be seen in many old towns.

FIG. 451.—The panels of the railings are filled with straight and scroll work—one merging into the other—and are surmounted by scrolled crestings. The elaborate leaf treatment of Tijou was discarded by the Georgian smiths, their effects being produced by curving and scrolling the bars.

c. 1760.   *King:* George III.
FIG. 452.—MILL HOUSE, WYE, KENT.

c. 1765.   *King:* George III.
FIG. 453.—ELMER HOUSE,
FARNHAM, SURREY.

c. 1768.   *King:* George III.
FIG. 454.—ALFRED HOUSE, BATH.
John Wood the younger, *Architect.*

FIG. 452.—Ionic doorway of house in Fig. 261. The applied decoration of the frieze and the " Gothic taste " of the light are distinctive features. The Portland stone steps have moulded nosings.

FIG. 453.—A doorway of unusual design and fine quality. The scrolled ends to the lower step are frequently seen also in earlier work.

FIG. 454.—A fine example of a doorway in the classic manner. The form of the pediment on which the bust of Alfred the Great stands anticipates the manner of Sir John Soane. The window arches are peculiar, inasmuch as each extends over two windows, the keystone being over the intervening pier. All the window reveals are splayed—an unfortunate modern alteration. The ironwork of the lampholder and the torch extinguishers on each side are excellent examples of this date. The railings are simple, having neither panels nor scrolls.

c. 1768-74.   *King:* George III.
FIG. 455.—No. 13, JOHN STREET,
ADELPHI, LONDON.

Second half eighteenth century.
FIG. 456.—DEAL, KENT.

Second half eighteenth century.
FIG. 457.—DEAL, KENT.

FIG. 455.—An example of applied decoration to a doorway by the brothers Adam. The ironwork is complete with lampholders and link extinguishers.

FIG. 456.—Doorway with pilasters and triangular pediment, all of very simple character and economical to make. The town abounds in such examples of the joiner's craft applied to small houses.

FIG. 457.—Doorway including five steps up to ground floor which forms a shelter. For another step treatment at Colchester see Fig. 443.

Reproduced by courtesy of Messrs. Robersons Ltd.

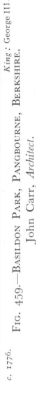

c. 1776.   FIG. 459.—BASILDON PARK, PANGBOURNE, BERKSHIRE.   *King :* George III.
John Carr, *Architect.*   Compare with Figs. 461 and 474.

Reproduced by courtesy of Messrs. Robersons Ltd.

c. 1776.   FIG. 458.—BASILDON PARK, PANGBOURNE, BERKSHIRE.   *King :* George III
John Carr, *Architect.*

FIG. 458.—Carved and painted door-case. The mahogany door panels are carved with key pattern border. Compare with Figs. 461 and 474.

c. 1769.   *King : George III.*   1772.   *King : George III.*

FIG. 460.—NO. 3, THE TERRACE, RICHMOND HILL, SURREY.   FIG. 461.—20, ST. JAMES'S SQUARE, S.W. 1.

Robert Adam, *Architect.*

FIG. 460.—Doorways in rusticated ground stories have been illustrated in Figs. 165, 262, 538. Here the key block is given special prominence, as also in the window arches. The iron railings are round the area in front of the house (Fig. 262). The wrought iron scrollwork, with which the panels are filled, stands between double-baluster iron standards of circular section having vase finials. The vertical bars of the railings are square in section with spear points. On the ramp the necking of these points is cut on the rake.

FIG. 461.—Painted door-case with folding doors of mahogany. For detail of panel and brass furniture see Fig. 476 ; of mouldings, Figs. 724, 725, 726.

FIG. 462.—A door-case and folding doors painted and gilded. The decoration is by Valdré (see Fig. 723 : detail of panels, Fig. 719).

FIG. 463.—Unusually ornate doorway of this period, belonging to the house illustrated in Fig. 260. The panelled doors are of nineteenth-century date.

c. 1777.   *King : George III.*   c. 1768-74.   *King : George III.*

FIG. 462.—STOWE PARK, BUCKS.   FIG. 463.—ADAM STREET, ADELPHI.

Signor Borra, *Architect.*   The brothers Adam, *Architects.*

c. 1780.   *King:* George III. *c. 1780.*   *King:* George III. *c. 1785.*   *King:* George III.

FIG. 464.—No. 38, THE CLOSE,   FIG. 465.—No. 13, DEVONSHIRE   FIG. 466.—WEST STREET,
          SALISBURY.   PLACE, LONDON.   FARNHAM, SURREY.

FIG. 464.—Greek influence is to be seen in the detail of this doorway. The fanlight semi-circle is stilted.

FIG. 465.—A door-case with a mahogany door of the best design and workmanship. " The door of great elegance and expence, wrought of mahogany . . . and decorated with sculpture . . . those who have been familiar with such, will not approve a painted door in an elegant apartment " (*The Builders' Magazine*, London, 1779). The walls are covered with green damask with an applied border. For detail of panel see Fig. 474.

FIG. 466.—Tall, narrow doorways, tending more towards Greek than Roman classic, were fashionable and accorded well with the light, elegant decoration current. The tracery of the fanlight is a departure from conventional patterns. The door has four raised panels, and two flush panels which are only outlined by bead and quirk.

Photo by courtesy Victoria and Albert Museum.   *By courtesy of the Curator, Soane Museum.*

c. 1795.   *King:* George III. Late 18th or early   *King:* George III. *c. 1800.*   *King:* George III.
                                        19th century.

FIG. 467.—No. 36, GREAT GEORGE   FIG. 468.—MELLS PARK, SOMERSET,   FIG. 469.—No. 111, HIGH STREET,
  STREET, WESTMINSTER, LONDON.   Sir John Soane, *Architect*.   RYE, SUSSEX.

FIG. 467.—The doorway and doors, as usual, are of pine.

FIG. 468.—The outlining of panels in this porch by incised channels is characteristic. Similar effects were produced by Soane in internal woodwork by inlaying mahogany with bands of ebony or other contrasting material. (See Fig. 477.)

FIG. 469.—Although this doorway has considerable charm, the detail of the pilaster panels and the panels over them is characteristic of the decline in design. The door panels are sunk with croisetted mouldings. The scraper is recessed in the wall.

Early nineteenth century.   *King :* George III.
FIG. 470.—DEAL, KENT.

FIG. 470.—Door and window of shop front.   Such
reeding of column and caps is a late feature.   See also
Figs. 469, 471.

Early nineteenth century.   *King :* George III.
FIG. 471.—DEAL, KENT.

c. 1812.   *King :* George III.
FIG. 472.—No. 13, LINCOLN'S INN FIELDS,
LONDON.

FIG. 471.—Doorway and bow window, probably intended for use as a shop front.   Reeded
pilasters and architraves having square pateræ (enriched with lion masks or other ornaments)
are found also in internal doorcases and windows.   Other forms of reeding are shown in
Figs. 469, 470.

FIG. 472.—Door recess, door and wall treatment showing how Sir John Soane used the figure
and grain of wood, inlaid bands of ebony and shallow mouldings.   The wall is painted and
grained closely to match the figuring of the mahogany of the door.   For detail of door panel,
etc., see Fig. 477; of mouldings, see Figs. 724, 725, 726.

From " A History of English Brickwork."

c. 1820.   *King:* George III.
FIG. 473.—POLE HOUSE, KING'S LANGLEY,
HERTS.

c. 1780.   *King:* George III.
FIG. 474.—No. 13, DEVON-
SHIRE PLACE, LONDON.

1794.   *King:* George III.
FIG. 475.—BUCKINGHAM HOUSE,
PALL MALL, LONDON.

FIG. 473.—Doorway in Regency manner. The window canopies and cast-iron railings are contemporary. The house is built of yellow stock bricks.

FIG. 474.—Detail of a panel in a mahogany door (see Fig. 465). The paterae in the angles and
the transverse bands of fluting are fine examples of Adam design, though the work in this house
cannot be attached to him with certainty. It may be compared with Fig. 476 by Adam.

FIG. 475.—Detail of door-case on stairs (Fig. 857), showing the simplification of architrave and
entablature which is characteristic of early nineteenth-century work. Later, the entablature was
omitted, and the case composed of architrave and linings only.

1772.   *King:* George III.
FIG. 476.—No. 20, ST. JAMES'S SQUARE, LONDON.
ROBERT ADAM, *Architect.*

1812.   *King:* George III.
FIG. 477.—No. 13, LINCOLN'S INN FIELDS,
LONDON.
Sir John Soane, *Architect.*

FIG. 476.—Detail of enriched door panel in mahogany and of the metal fittings. See doors, Fig. 461.

FIG. 477.—Detail of door panels and painted wall treatment. For doorway see Fig. 472, for drawing
of section see Figs. 724, 725, 726.

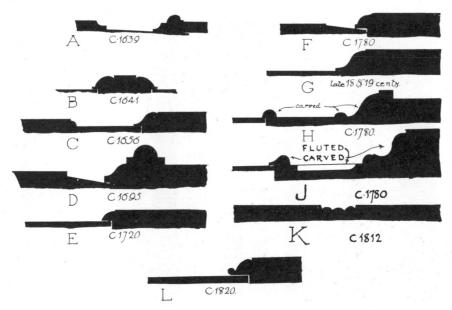

FIG. 478.—Comparative sketches of door panel moulds.

A.—Cromwell House, Highgate. Transition from sixteenth-century type (see Fig. 39), but having a raised panel.

B.—Great Wigsell, Bodiam, Sussex. A door, having six panels, the rails and muntins of which are moulded (see Fig. 827). Similar mouldings are also found on doors of more pronounced Renaissance character.

C.—Thorpe Hall, Peterborough, Northants. Large panels framed in small mouldings, the centres of the panels slightly raised (see Figs. 414, 415).

D.—Hampton Court Palace. Bolection moulding (*i.e.*, a moulding raised above the framing) with raised and fielded panels (see Fig. 422).

E.—Early eighteenth-century type, contemporary with and succeeding the heavy bolection moulding. The ovolo mould has only one fillet.

F.—Later eighteenth-century type. The ovolo has two fillets, but type E is also found in use concurrently. Some panels were raised as here, and some not.

G.—Eighteenth-century and early nineteenth-century panels often had this ogee moulding.

H.—Stowe Park, Bucks. A sunk panel enclosed by mouldings which are enriched by carving (see Fig. 719).

J.—No. 20, St. James's Square, London. Sunk panel surrounded by enriched mouldings and by a band of transverse fluting by Robert Adam (see Fig. 461).

K.—Sir John Soane's House, No. 13, Lincoln's Inn Fields, London.

L.—From Nicholson's *Builder*. Decadent mouldings in great variety, of which this is one.

Generally.—The sixteenth-century mouldings consisted of many small members, and panels were small. The mid-seventeenth-century mouldings were small and simple, enclosing large panels. The late seventeenth-century mouldings were very large, enclosing large panels. The early eighteenth-century mouldings reverted to the mid-seventeenth-century type—small mouldings round either raised or sunk panels; but the Palladians also used mouldings with large members, particularly when these were enriched with carving, as Figs. 539, 717. The later half of the eighteenth century brought mouldings, often of stucco, having larger members and forming wider borders to panels, which sometimes were raised but more often were sunk (Figs. 656, 661).

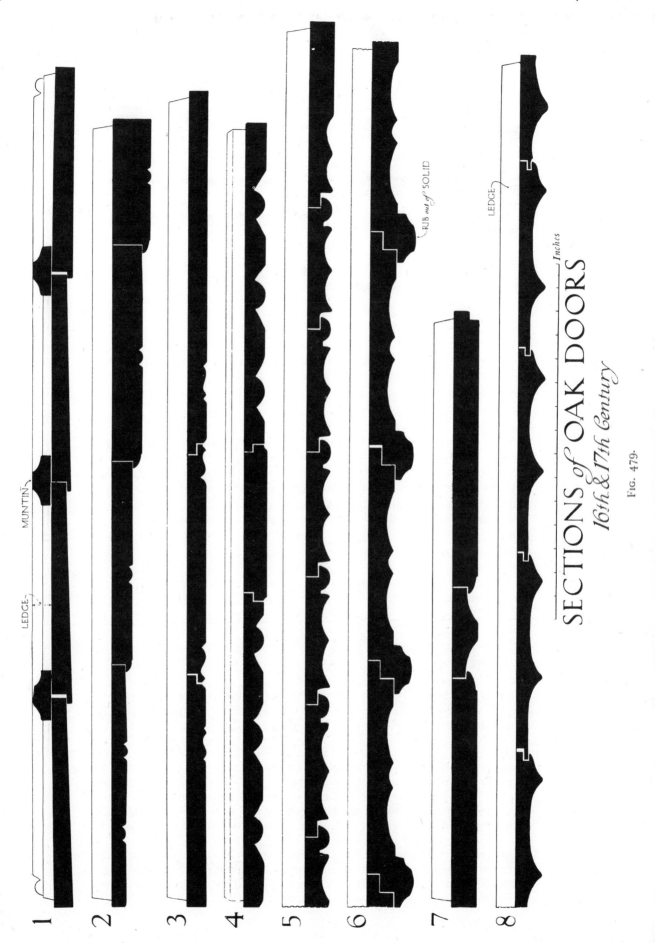

SECTIONS of OAK DOORS
16th & 17th Century

FIG. 479.

WINDOWS

For other examples of Exterior Windows see—
Exteriors, pages 170 to 272

For other examples of Interior Windows see—
Interiors, pages 352 to 392

c. 1130.   *King:* Henry I.

FIG. 480.—ROCHESTER CASTLE.

c. 1130.   *King:* Henry I.

FIG. 481.—CASTLE HEDINGHAM.

Photo: S. Smith, Lincoln

c. 1150.   *King:* Stephen.

FIG. 482.—THE JEWS' HOUSE, LINCOLN.

c. 1150.   *King:* Stephen.

FIG. 483.—A Norman House at CHRISTCHURCH, HANTS.

Transition c. 1160 or later.   *King:* Henry II.

FIG. 484.—MOYSES HALL, BURY ST. EDMUNDS.

Photo: W. Lee, Grantham.   *Photo: Heawood and Son, Oakham.*

Transition *c.* 1180

Transition *c.* 1180.   *King:* Henry II.

FIG. 485.—BOOTHBY PAGNELL MANOR HOUSE.

FIG. 486.—OAKHAM CASTLE.

FIGS. 480 TO 486.—Owing to the defensive character of the buildings, Norman and Early English windows were very small, but, being splayed within, gave more light than might be supposed. The most certain way of determining the dates of buildings is by their mouldings, carvings, and other details ; but windows and doorways of houses seldom had that degree of elaboration which the same details reached in ecclesiastical buildings. The development from the massive windows at Rochester Castle and at Castle Hedingham to lighter and more spacious forms at Lincoln and Bury St. Edmunds marks transition from the fortress to the dwelling-house. The rectangular openings within the Norman arches at Bury are early, for rectangular windows are not necessarily products of later periods, as commonly believed. The windows at Boothby Pagnell and Oakham Castle are transitional ; at Oakham the transition takes the form of pointed window heads, though the same windows, within, have one semicircular rear-arch (see Fig. 581). The Boothby Pagnell window shows the " plate " over the round-headed lights, which later was pierced by a circular opening—the earliest form of " plate tracery," as in Figs. 488 and 489.

c. 1232-40.   *King:* Henry III.

c. 1260-80.   *Kings:* Henry III. and Edward I.

c. 1240   *King:* Henry III.

FIG. 487.—The King's Great Hall at WINCHESTER CASTLE.

FIG. 488.—LITTLE WENHAM HALL, SUFFOLK.

FIG. 489.—Three types of windows at STOKESAY CASTLE, SHROPSHIRE.

FIG. 490.—LITTLE WENHAM
HALL, SUFFOLK.

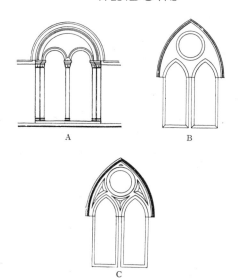

A   B

C

FIG. 491.

c.1260–80.   *Kings:* Henry III. and Edward I.
FIG. 492.—LITTLE WENHAM HALL,
SUFFOLK.

FIGS. 487 TO 493.—There is great variety of thirteenth-century (Early English) windows. In domestic work some have rectangular openings, but many more have pointed or other shaped heads. Where windows consist of two or more lights within a semicircular or a pointed outer arch or a dripstone, there is an area of wall above and between the arches of the lights and the containing arch. This tympanum the Normans frequently filled with carving or other decoration. Later it was pierced by a circular, trefoil or other opening, and in this simple form is termed "plate tracery." Next, the triangular areas round the openings (spandrels) were emphasized by sinkings, the effect of which was further to define the outlines of the openings to what is termed " bar tracery." Fig. 491 (*a, b, c*) shows unpierced plate tracery and bar tracery. In its latest development the latter was a three-quarter-round moulding. At

c. 1300.   *King:* Edward I.
FIG. 493.—OLD SOAR, PLAXTOL, KENT.

Old Soar the chamber opening off the hall is lighted only by cross-loops, one of which is shown in Fig. 493 —a survival of an opening designed for fortresses. In the same figure is a flat-headed trefoil window with splayed jambs and sill. This illustration also shows the corbelling of the walls and the treatment of the angle in forming the narrow passage from the hall to the chamber shown in the plan (Fig. 60). The windows at Winchester Castle (Fig. 487) (restored) illustrate plate tracery and are early examples of transomed windows. The upper lights were glazed, the lower ones had wooden shutters. Fig. 489 shows three types of windows at Stokesay Castle : (1) A single-light lancet with soffit cusping. Such narrow windows were often splayed inside so widely as adequately to light the interior. (2) The other single-light window has an ogee head. (3) Two-light transomed windows. The upper lights have soffit cuspings, and the head is pierced by a plain circle. Like the windows at Winchester Castle, the upper portions were glazed and those below the transom had shutters. The resemblance of domestic to church windows is remarkable ; in some cases details are identical. Inside, however, domestic windows were frequently built with seats in the thickness of the walls, as at Little Wenham (Fig. 490), and Winchester Castle (Fig. 584). Another type of window is shown in Fig. 586, between the hall and the chapel. In studying windows of a period, comparison should be made with doorways and arcadings, because the same details were used in all three.

FIG. 488.—Two-light window, with wooden shutters, between hall and chapel. The mullion is still a shaft with base and cap. The quatrefoil sunk in the tympanum is an early step towards plate tracery, as at Winchester (Fig. 487), where the piercing is completed.

FIG. 490.—Interior of two-light window, the exterior of which is similar to that illustrated in Fig. 492.

FIG. 492.—Two-light window having mullion in form of Early English shaft (which is a restoration) with base and cap. The plate is pierced by quatrefoil.

c. 1330.   *King:* Edward III.

FIG. 495.—THE MANOR HOUSE,
MEARE, SOMERSET.

c. 1341.   *King:* Edward III.

FIG. 496.—PENSHURST PLACE, KENT.

c. 1330.   *King:* Edward III.

FIG. 494.—THE MANOR HOUSE, MEARE,
SOMERSET.

FIG. 494.—The window which is at the north end of the first-floor hall has flowing tracery, while that of the room below has characteristic trefoil heads. The lead lights are not ancient, but the treatment of the cames in the cinquefoil heads of the lights is suitable.

FIG. 495.—One of the side windows of the hall, showing a cinquefoil foliated rear arch. Originally the lower portions of the lights were not glazed; the hooks of the shutter hinges remain, and there is a loop for the shutter bolt in the stone mullion.

FIG. 496.—One of the transomed windows of the great hall, restored, but furnishing a good illustration of decorated tracery. The walls pierced by these windows are thin, and the weight and thrust of the roof are taken by the segmental arches between the buttresses. (See illustrations of elevations, Figs. 79 and 81.)

FIG. 497.—Three types of windows are illustrated here: 1. Reticulated tracery, which is uncommon in ecclesiastical work, and very rare in domestic buildings. 2. Also fourteenth century, a two-light window in which the lights have trefoil heads. 3. An eight-light window of the late fifteenth century.

c. 1320.   *King:* Edward II.

FIG. 497.—CLEVEDON COURT, SOMERSET.

c. 1350.   *King:* Edward III.
FIG. 498.—THE MANOR HOUSE, MARTOCK, SOMERSET.

c. 1330.   *King:* Edward III.
FIG. 499.—THE MANOR HOUSE, MARTOCK, SOMERSET.

c. 1350.   *King:* Edward III.
FIG. 500.—THE MANOR HOUSE, MARTOCK, SOMERSET.

c. 1350.   *King:* Edward III.
FIG. 501.—THE FISH HOUSE, MEARE, SOMERSET.

Late fourteenth century.   *King:* Edward III.
FIG. 502.—THE MANOR HOUSE, MARTOCK, SOMERSET.

FIG. 498.—A window on the east side of the hall with a foliated inner arch and transom.

FIG. 499.—Exterior of window—interior shown in Fig. 498.

FIGS. 500 AND 502.—The upper window (of the solar) (Fig. 500) is of earlier character than that below (Fig. 502), and indeed than those of the hall; it has been suggested that the solar was originally a first-floor hall, like that at the Manor House, Meare, that the hall was added, and that the windows under the solar windows are later insertions. The evidence for this theory is the early two-light window with plate tracery, and the fact that the masonry of the hall wall is not toothed into that of the solar block, nevertheless, in a remote district an early type of window is not uncommonly found, while straight joints in masonry of this period are frequently seen.

FIG. 501.—Decorated window at end of hall; an interesting example of transition from plate tracery to flowing tracery. In this building there are also square-headed windows. For interior see Fig. 597.

Late fourteenth or early fifteenth century.   *King*: Henry IV.

FIG. 503.—GREVEL HOUSE, CHIPPING CAMPDEN.

c. 1405.   *King*: Edward IV.

FIG. 504.—OCKWELLS MANOR, BRAY, BERKSHIRE.

FIG. 503.—The valley between the gable and main roofs has the tiles swept in the old Cotswold way. At the junction of the ridge with the main roof an **L**-shaped stone is used to protect this vital point from penetration by rain. This beautiful window is a rare survival of an early bay window.

FIG. 504.—The glazing of the upper lights is heraldic, and is probably the best remaining example of domestic stained glass of the period. The brick nogging is later work. The design of the cusped and carved barge boards is particularly fine, and the panel work of the gable is uncommon and good.

c. 1440.   *King*: Henry VI.

FIG. 505.—A window of the school at EWELME, OXON.

FIG. 505.—Mention has been made of the fact that (contrary to popular ideas) square-headed windows are found in buildings throughout the medieval period, and to this it may be added that pointed windows were not always curvilinear. The heads of this two-light window are an example of such variation from common practice. The dripstone or label, so characteristic of medieval wall openings, here has enormous terminals.

FIG. 506.—Window of hall. Unglazed windows furnished with oak bars, set diagonally, are found in the smaller fourteenth-, fifteenth-, and sixteenth-century houses. As protection against wind and rain, they had shutters inside, those of the lower lights sliding in grooves on a sill, as in Fig. 513. The upper ones hinged on hooks, as in Fig. 508.

Late fifteenth century.   *King*: Henry VII.

FIG. 506.—House lately at BENENDEN, KENT.

Photo : Gibson and Son, Hexham.

Fifteenth century   *King:* Henry VII.

Fig. 507.—St. Cross Hospital, Winchester.

Early fifteenth century.   *King:* Henry VII.

Fig. 508.—The Old Manor House, East Meon, Hampshire.

Late fifteenth century.   *King:* Henry VII.

Fig. 509.—West Tanfield Castle Gatehouse, near Ripon.

Fig. 507.—A two-light window of Hundred Men's Hall, closed by wooden shutters, on hook and strap hinges.

Fig. 508.—Interior of the upper lights of a fifteenth-century hall window, showing the original shutter belonging to one of the lights.

Fig. 509.—Compare the tracery of this oriel window with that of the oak window at Dukes Place, Mereworth (Fig. 511).

c. 1465.   *King:* Edward IV.

Fig. 510.—Ockwells Manor, Bray, Berkshire.

Late fifteenth century.

Fig. 511.—Dukes Place, Mereworth.

c. 1480.   *King:* Edward IV

Fig. 512.—Eltham Palace, Kent.

Fig. 510.—Stained glass (of armorial design) was frequently introduced into fifteenth-century windows, but few could boast of such wealth of heraldic splendour.

Fig. 511.—The heads of the lights in this four-light window of the hall of a timber and plaster house are arched in a manner introduced late in the fifteenth century, but which became general in the sixteenth century. The slightly pointed form of earlier windows (as at Great Dixter, Fig. 513) has disappeared, and the arch itself is flattened.

Fig. 512.—The interior of one of the two bay windows of the hall, and part of one of the clerestory windows, showing the mouldings of the mullions. For exterior see Fig. 95.

Late fifteenth century.   *King:* Henry VII.
FIG. 513.—GREAT DIXTER, NORTHIAM, SUSSEX.

Fifteenth or early sixteenth century.   *King:* Henry VII.
FIG. 514.—THE HALL, VICARS' CLOSE, WELLS, SOMERSET.

FIG. 513.—The shutter of this two-light window is a copy of an old one, sliding on the sill and in the original head-groove of the wall-plate. This shutter is a typical fitting also of those barred windows (Fig. 506) which were unglazed.

FIG. 514.—The oriel window of the hall, and an earlier window with ogival heads to the lights.

c. 1525-28.   *King:* Henry VIII.
FIG. 515.—HENGRAVE HALL, SUFFOLK.

c. 1525.   *King:* Henry VIII.
FIG. 516.—SUTTON PLACE, near GUILDFORD.

c. 1525.   *King:* Henry VIII.
FIG. 517.—COWDRAY HOUSE, SUSSEX.

FIG. 515.—The bay window, like those adjoining, is Gothic in its design and details.

FIG. 516.—Like the doorway (Fig. 403), this terra-cotta window is entirely Gothic in design, but the hollows of the mouldings are enriched with arabesques in the Italian manner—the only concession made to the foreign terra-cotta worker.

FIG. 517.—The bay window and one of the clerestory windows of the great hall. Such bays are found in large halls of the early sixteenth century, another example being at Hampton Court Palace.

Middle sixteenth century.   *c.* Mary.

FIG. 518.—LITTLE WOLFORD MANOR.

Detail of small bay window, built late but of the early
type, as illustrated in Figs. 104, 401.

c. 1580–1600.   *Queen:* Elizabeth.

FIG. 519.—FORD PLACE, TROTTERSCLIFFF,
KENT.

FIG. 518.—Here the Tudor character is retained, with the four-centred heads to lights, but instead of the variety of mullion mouldings as at Skipton Castle (Fig. 401) and Glastonbury (Fig. 104), these consist of a bold hollow chamfer. Later the hollow is superseded by a convex (ovolo) moulding as at Broadway (Fig. 521).

FIG. 519.—An Elizabethan window with ovolo section mullions. The upper range of lights is less in height than the lower by the thickness of the transom—a proportion often to be observed. The window is built of purpose-moulded bricks and rendered with plaster (restored) to simulate stone.

Early 17th century.   *King:* James I.   *c.* 1604.   *King:* James I.

FIG. 520.—DUDDINGTON,
NORTHANTS.

FIG. 521.—AT BROADWAY, WORCESTERSHIRE.

FIG. 520.—Bay window, having a dormer roof of the type common in the district. The valley slates at the intersection of the roofs are swept.

FIG. 521.—The ovolo mullioned window was still current and persisted in the Cotswolds long after this date. The elements by which the Cotswold mason produced his results were few and simple. Here a wide window, having a larger (master) mullion in the centre, a drip stone which protects the openings from rainwater running down the wall face and casts a pleasant shadow on sunny days. Above all, a sunk tablet bearing the owner's name and the date of erection.

First quarter of seventeenth century.　　　　　　*King:* James 1.
FIG. 522.—KIRBY HALL, WELDON, NORTHANTS.

FIG. 522.—When departure from usual forms in the design of the windows occurs, it does not extend beyond the rearrangement of details. The semicircular bays have the same mullions and transoms, the same mouldings, pediments, and pyramidal finials as are found in contemporary buildings. A reference to the Thorpe plan (Fig. 121) will show that only one bay was at first contemplated. The design of the pediments may be compared with Fig. 337.

Early seventeenth century.　　*King:* James I.
FIG. 523.—THE DEANERY, WINCHESTER, HAMPSHIRE.

c. 1611.　　　　　　*King:* James I.
FIG. 524.—KNOLE, SEVENOAKS, KENT.

d. 1699.　　　　　William and Mary.
FIG. 525.

FIG. 523.—The four-light mullioned and transomed window of the seventeenth century was superseded by the sash window towards the close of that century. First constructed of stone or brick, it was latterly made of wood. The illustration is of a window with hollow chamfers ; other examples had the ovolo moulding (Fig. 521), and some the splayed chamfer (as Fig. 499), whilst others again had mullions of square section, slightly rounded at the angles.

FIG. 524.—The interior of a window in the gallery. The mullions have hollow chamfers.

FIG. 525.—The upper window frames are of wood, the design of which was the last phase of mullioned and transomed frames. These began to be superseded by sashed frames *c.* 1685. The lower windows have had the casements removed and sashes substituted. The mullioned windows have their upper lights slightly taller than a square, the latter being a proportion usually avoided.

*From "A History of English
Brickwork."*

c. 1690.   William and Mary.   *c.* 1700.   William and Mary.   *c.* 1730.   *King:* George II.

FIG. 526.—HAMPTON COURT PALACE.   FIG. 527.—DRAYTON HOUSE, THRAP-   FIG. 528.
                                         STON, NORTHAMPTONSHIRE.

FIG. 526.—A detail of the ground-floor windows of the elevations illustrated in Figs. 180, 181. The sturdiness of these windows, with their heavy architraves and segmental arched heads, lends stability to fronts pierced with many openings.

FIG. 527.—Designers of this period realized the dignity to be produced by very tall windows (the openings of these are nearly three times as high as the width), and "punctuated" them in various ways— Wren, at Hampton Court (Figs. 180, 181), by circular windows; the architect of Drayton by oblong panels, in front of each of which was a sculptured bust in a bracket, all so narrow as to increase the impression of height.

FIG. 528.—The upper window frame is of the date of the house. It has a segmental head of the same curve as the gauged brick arch and has thick glazing bars. The lower window is a later replacement where, for economy, the head is made straight and, in accordance with current practice, the glazing bars are very slight. The mouldings also may be compared.

Photo: B. C. Clayton.   *Photo: B. C. Clayton.*

Late seventeenth century.   *King:* Charles II.   Late seventeenth century.   *King:* Charles II.

FIG. 529.—SPARROWE'S HOUSE, IPSWICH.   FIG. 530.—SPARROWE'S HOUSE, IPSWICH.

FIG. 529.—Carved oak oriel window, the base decorated with pargeting.

FIG. 530.—Another window also with arched head to the centre lights, but all the glazing bars of wood. The pargeting is contemporary.

c. 1714.   *Queen : Anne.*   *c. 1715.*   *Queen : Anne.*

FIG. 531.—BRADBOURNE, LARKFIELD, KENT.   FIG. 532.

c. 1715.

FIG. 533.

FIG. 531.—Elliptic and bullseye windows were used with great effect (Figs. 228, 237). Usually these had wood glazing bars, others had lead lights, but always the curves and radiating bars were correctly set out. Gauged brickwork lent itself particularly well to the construction of these windows.

FIG. 532.—Detail of centre window, etc., over doorway illustrated in Fig. 435. The window is formed of finely gauged and rubbed red bricks set in thin putty joints. The pilaster caps are carried up with the main cornice, which breaks out to form them. The straight arch has a serpentine soffit on face only. The sash frame is almost flush with the brickwork, contrary to London law. More simple gauged windows are shown in Fig. 528.

FIG. 533.—Detail of the windows on each side of the doorway illustrated in Fig. 435. Wren used finely gauged brick dressings to windows, etc., to contrast with the rougher and thicker-jointed brick of the wallings, and such work continued in fashion in London up to about 1730, when grey stock bricks superseded red ones, and in the country until later in the eighteenth century when stucco became universal. Considerable variety is found in these window "arches." In the upper window the arch key is continued into the main cornice, the lower members of which break round it. This window has an apron-piece down to the entablature of the lower window, which has a simple key block—all of finely rubbed and gauged red brick.

c. 1720.   *King : George I.*

FIG. 534.—THE RED HOUSE, SAWBRIDGEWORTH, HERTS.

FIG. 534.—Dormer windows usually had segmental or triangular pediments (Fig. 213), but sometimes flat, slightly curved or semicircular heads (Figs. 228, 276, 277). Often they were placed behind the parapet.

1731.   *King:* George II.

FIG. 535.—MONTAGU HOUSE, BOREHAM STREET, SUSSEX.

1723.   *King:* George I.

FIG. 536.—MEREWORTH CASTLE, KENT.
Colen Campbell, *Architect.*

FIG. 535.—The Venetian window (used by Scamozzi in Venice) was freely employed by Palladian designers. The example at Montagu House is of stone and retains the original sashes, which have the usual divisions by wide glazing bars. Instead of being glazed with large squares, however, they are filled with separate lead lights, each containing four rectangular quarries.

FIG. 536.—The detail of this window, which resembles that of the doorway (Fig. 440), is in the best manner and workmanship of the period.

c. 1730.   *King:* George II.

FIG. 537.—LULLINGSTONE CASTLE,
KENT.

1734–61.   *King:* George II.

FIG. 538.—HOLKHAM HALL, NORFOLK.
William Kent, *Architect.*

FIG. 537.—A sash window having the substantial glazing bars of early type. The frame is moulded with ogee and bead. The gauged brickwork has a flat arch and a bead mould on the jambs.

FIG. 538.—In these large houses the entrance doorways were relatively unimportant. Ware describes Venetian windows as " very pompous in their nature and, when executed with judgment, of extreme elegance " (*A Complete Body of Architecture*, pp. 466-7, London, 1756). This Venetian window violates the rule laid down by Ware that the side lights should not be narrower than the centre light.

1744. *King: George II.*

FIG. 539.—HONINGTON HALL, WARWICKSHIRE.

FIG. 539.—Glazing bars, though not so thick as Wren's, were still substantial. Those of the windows in the octagon room are richly carved within, in harmony with the panel moulds of the shutters.

FIG. 540.—The blind window recalls the window tax imposed in 1695, increased six times between 1746 and 1808, and not repealed until 1851. The rusticated brickwork is well designed and gauged.

c. 1750. *King: George II.*

FIG. 540.—MONTROSE HOUSE, PETERSHAM, SURREY.

Mid-eighteenth century. *King: George II.*

FIG. 541.—Dormer at BIDDENDEN, KENT.

1768–69. *King: George III.*

FIG. 542.—NO. 3, THE TERRACE, RICHMOND HILL, SURREY.

FIG. 541.—Hipped dormer window, tiled, with moulded cornice and plastered cheeks.

FIG. 542.—The window reveals are furnished with boxed shutters; the panels are formed with applied mouldings. The architrave is broken and enriched with carved ornaments. A general view of the room can be seen in Fig. 663. The exterior of the window is shown in Fig. 262, 460.

FIG. 543.—Ground-floor and first-floor windows still in the Palladian manner.

FIG. 544. — Bay windows, curved or semi - hexagonal, became popular about the middle of the eighteenth century.

c. 1772.   *King:* George III.
FIG. 543.—ELY HOUSE, DOVER STREET, LONDON.

Sir Robert Taylor, *Architect.*

Second half of the eighteenth century.
FIG. 544.—CUPOLA HOUSE, FOLKESTONE, KENT.

1772–75.   *King:* George III.
FIG. 545.—A Venetian window in the ADELPHI, LONDON.

The brothers Adam, *Architects.*

Late eighteenth century.   *King:* George III
FIG. 546.—CASTLE STREET, FARNHAM, SURREY.

FIG. 545.—The fan filling of the arch over the centre window was a favourite device ; there is another example over the principal window of Boodle's Club, St. James's Street, London, which was designed by John Crunden (compare with the Venetian windows illustrated in Figs. 535, 538).

FIG. 546.—A three-light window in which the cases are treated as panelled pilasters (see Fig. 261 also).

Early nineteenth century.   *King:* George III.

FIG. 547.—IN HIGH STREET,
COLCHESTER, ESSEX.

Photo by courtesy of Hampton and Sons.

FIG. 547. — Three types of windows in the upper part of a house, showing variations in the use of components of the Orders.

FIG. 548.—Semicircular treatment of an oriel window lighting first and second floors. The remarkable variety of window forms about this time is witness to the ingenuity of carpenters.

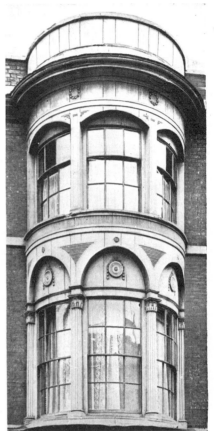

Early nineteenth century.   *King:* George III.

FIG. 548.—HIGH STREET, COLCHESTER,
ESSEX.

1772.   *King:* George III.

FIG. 549.—NO. 20, ST. JAMES'S SQUARE, LONDON.
Robert Adam, *Architect.*

c. 1819.   *King:* George III.

FIG. 550.—NO. 86, EAST HILL, COLCHESTER.

FIG. 549.—The interior of a Venetian window. For the exterior of a similar window see Fig. 545. Writing in 1756, Ware describes Venetian windows as " calculated for show, and very pompous in their nature, and, when executed with judgment, of extreme elegance."

FIG. 550.—Detail of windows (Fig. 295) where the entablatures are heavy and clumsy. Other windows had unmoulded (often heavy) architraves (Fig. 287), but more were simply openings in the walls whether these were of brick (Fig. 277) or stuccoed (Fig. 292)

Y

CHIMNEYS

For other examples of CHIMNEYS see—

EXTERIORS, pages 170 to 272

Photo: Gibson, Hexham.

*c.*1150.   *King: Stephen.*

FIG. 551.—A Norman house at CHRIST-
CHURCH, HANTS.

Late thirteenth century.

FIG. 552.—ABINGDON ABBEY, BERKSHIRE.

c. 1280.   *King: Edward I.*

FIG. 553.—AYDON CASTLE,
NORTHUMBERLAND.

FIG. 551.—The Norman builders frequently constructed chimneys circular
in plan, as at Christchurch (Fig. 46). One exists at Boothby Pagnell, the
cap on which appears in Fig. 47.

FIG. 552.—One outlet (low down on the left of the illustration) is merely a
baffle in front of the flue, the smoke from which escapes through the openings
in each side of the baffle stones. The other flue (from the fireplace in the
abbot's parlour) has a shaft, in the gabled terminals of which are lancet-
shaped openings for the escape of smoke.

FIG. 553.—A wall chimney with smoke outlets at sides.

Photo: B. C. Clayton.

c. 1290.   *King: Edward I.*   *c.* 1386.   *King: Richard II.*

FIG. 554.—THE MANOR HOUSE, OLD WOOD-   FIG. 555.—BODIAM CASTLE, SUSSEX.
STOCK, OXFORDSHIRE.

FIG. 554.—In the fourteenth century chimneys often were octagonal. The
example at Woodstock is weather-worn, but the gablets over the middle row
of openings are still distinguishable. The fireplace from which the flue to
this chimney rises is in a cross wall of the house (not in an external wall) on the
first floor, and has the shouldered lintel opening (Fig. 389) already illustrated
in windows and doorways.

FIG. 555.—Every room of this castle had a fireplace with a chimney, a degree
of comfort not attained in earlier fortresses.

FIG. 556.—This decorated chimney-shaft has its vents at the sides.

Fourteenth century.

FIG. 556.—GROSMONT CASTLE,
MONMOUTHSHIRE.

Fifteenth century.

FIG. 557.—Chimney at CROSCOMBE, SOMERSET.

Photo by permission of Arthur H. Bertwhistle.

Medieval.

FIG. 558.—A flue of timber, raddle and daub lately at DARWEN, LANCASHIRE.

FIG. 557.—An octagonal chimney with a crenellated cap.

FIG. 558.—The photograph shows the flue to have been constructed of substantial oak posts, having short rails at intervals; the spaces between were filled with stakes and branches intertwined like hurdles, and coated with clay plaster—local "raddle and daub" work (see also Fig. 559).

Medieval.

FIG. 559.—MARLEY FARM, SMARDEN, KENT.

FIG. 560.

FIG. 561.

FIG. 559.—Flue constructed, in the middle of a house, of oak timbers and clay "pug" over an open fireplace. So good is the composition of the "pug" filling that no stain of smoke or soot has penetrated it at any point. Though of medieval construction, this flue probably is of sixteenth-century or seventeenth-century date, is still in daily use and is swept regularly like any flue of stone or brick.

FIGS. 560 AND 561.—Wicker and thatched chimneys are still to be seen in Carmarthenshire, if not also on the English side of the border. Such a chimney indicates a higher degree of comfort than the "headless barrel" of Bishop Hall's satire, page 93. Fig. 560 shows the framework and Fig. 561 a completed chimney after thatching.

Early sixteenth century.　*King:* Henry VIII.
FIG. 562.—A chimney at NEWPORT, ESSEX.

Early sixteenth century.　*King:* Henry VIII.
FIG. 563.—ST. OSYTH'S PRIORY, ESSEX.

Late sixteenth century.　*Queen:* Elizabeth.
FIG. 564.—A chimney at WINCHCOMBE FARM, CRUNDALE, KENT.

FIG. 562.—An unspoiled example of cut and moulded brickwork which has its parallels in many counties. At some unknown date the cap was rebuilt with bricks moulded for the purpose, but apparently the curves of the old bricks have been correctly copied and the original proportions of the cap preserved.

FIG. 563.—During the first half of the sixteenth century chimney shafts of beautiful design were produced in stone and (more frequently) in brick. In the course of the second half of the century, the cut diaper patterns, spirals, etc., with which shafts had been decorated, went out of fashion, though the same bases, shafts, and caps continued to be used.

FIG. 564.—In the Elizabethan chimney many features of those of the reign of Henry VIII were preserved, but the shafts were no longer decorated.

c. 1572 1600.　*Queen:* Elizabeth.
FIG. 565.—KIRBY HALL, NORTHAMPTONSHIRE.

c. 1580–1600.　*Queen:* Elizabeth.
FIG. 566.—A chimney at MONTACUTE HOUSE, SOMERSET.

FIG. 565.—The tall chimneys are of exceptionally graceful design. The coupled chimney shafts are of a type adopted by designers who strove after classic effects by making their chimneys in the guise of columns.

FIG. 566.—The twisted chimney shaft was superseded by hollow columns complete with capitals; the hoods, to prevent a down draught, were later additions. Several patterns of chimneys are often found on the same house, as at Montacute (Figs. 128, 130, 131).

Early seventeenth century. *King:* James I.
FIG. 567.—Near TENTERDEN, KENT.

c. 1642.   *King:* Charles I
FIG. 568.—GREAT WIGSELL, BODIAM, SUSSEX.

FIG. 567.—Gradually, the early and mid-sixteenth century chimneys which had separate shafts for each flue were superseded by masses of stone or brick which enclosed all the flues. Brick chimneys of the type shown in this illustration are common in all the Southern Counties. Their designers diversified them by varying the vertical breaks and the projecting courses of their caps; other treatments are illustrated in Figs. 116, 126, 145.

FIG. 568.—Chimneys (square and diamond in plan) were designed singly, in pairs and in groups. When built of brick, the caps consisted simply of three or four oversailing courses; when of stone, of a simple moulding, as at Unstone (Fig. 155).

c. 1620.   *King:* James I.
FIG. 569.—CAMPDEN HOUSE,
GLOUCESTERSHIRE.

c. 1636.   *King:* Charles I.
FIG. 570.—House at GREAT WELDON,
NORTHANTS.

c. 1656.   Commonwealth.
FIG. 571.—THORPE HALL, near
PETERBOROUGH.

FIG. 569.—A chimney formed as a column. The finials and strapwork ornament also show the influence of the Low Countries, so characteristic of work at this date. There is one of these columns at each of the four angles of the building, but only one serves as a chimney; the others are merely decorative finials.

FIG. 570.—All the flues in this little house are gathered into one chimney, which is an excellent specimen of Northamptonshire design and craftsmanship. For more simple chimneys of the same type see Fig. 158.

FIG. 571.—A comparison of this chimney and of that at Coleshill (Fig. 572) with the Jacobean chimneys illustrated in Figs. 567, 569, 570, brings out the contrast between Renaissance designing in the Italian manner and in that derived from the Low Countries.

c. 1662. *King:* Charles II.
FIG. 572.—COLESHILL, BERKSHIRE.

Fig. 572.—The chimneys of Thorpe Hall and Coleshill are essential features of the general designs. Although so massive, the architects' construction was not always sound. On a copper plate (dated 1748) preserved at Coleshill are directions addressed to future owners, amongst which is the following respecting the chimneys : " Ye 4 middle stacks which are 6′ 4″ × 5′ 4″ project on decay'd oak 8 inches to ye N.W. and 8 inches to ye S.W. If ever they fail, rebuild without timber or diminucon, supporting each projection with an arch like that on ye Angula Stacks which (being originally 6′ 4″ × 6′ 4″ & projecting only inwardly on oak) inclined 15 inches & were thus rebuilt by

c. 1714. *King:* George I.
FIG. 573.—BRADBOURNE, LARKFIELD, KENT.

Sir Mark Pleydell, Bart. in 1744 by ye direct⁵ of ye Earls of Burlington & Leicester " (see Fig. 172). FIG. 573.—Chimney of brick, panelled and having moulded stone cap. Chimney design was becoming simplified ; the caps were shallow, and whether of cut brick or of stone, consisted of cymatium only. Fantastic chimneys imitating columns, etc., had gone out of fashion.

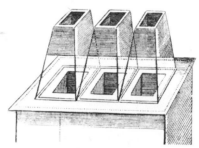

FIG. 575.
From " Fires Improved," by Monsieur Gauger, 1713. Made English and improved by J. T. Desaguliers, M.A., F.R.S., London, 1715.

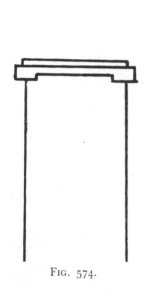

FIG. 574.

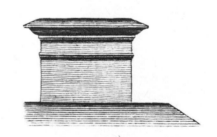

FIG. 576.
From " Essay on Chimneys," by Robert Clavering, London, 1779.

FIG. 577.
From " Essay on Chimneys," by Robert Clavering, London, 1779.

FIG. 574.—With the eighteenth century came decadence of chimney design hastened by the invention of chimney pots of various forms. Whereas before the era of pots, chimneys were built in the proportions of a column or of a pedestal (Fig. 576), the cap of which was the crowning feature, the pot required only a sufficiently sound base upon which it could be fixed—" well flaunched up and weathered in cement." The result was that in most buildings, the chimney cap was replaced by a shallow projecting band, as in Figs. 283, 291, 293, and 296, and Figs. 574 and 577. The earliest pots (*c.* 1715) were of pyramidal form (Fig. 575), but later in the century (1780) they had attained ugliness (Fig. 577) scarcely surpassed by modern inventions.
FIG. 575.—Truncated pyramids.
FIG. 576.—" The upper shaft of a chimney, terminating the building and finishing in the form of a pedestal regularly according to order."
FIG. 577.—" A chimney shaft, with pots fixed on it, which is now become the fashion in most of the new buildings."

INTERIORS

For other examples of INTERIORS see—

INTERIOR WALL TREATMENT, pages 394 to 419

CEILINGS, pages 422 to 432

STAIRCASES, pages 450 to 462

FIREPLACES, pages 434 to 447

c. 1130.　　　　　　　　　　　　　　　　　　King: Henry I.

FIG. 578.—ROCHESTER CASTLE KEEP.
The hall or great chamber.

FIG. 578.—The wooden floors have long since disappeared, but the positions of the floor joists of this chamber and of the floor above can be seen by the holes in the walls. The keep, though square in section, is divided by a thick wall for its whole height, but on the second floor this is pierced by four large arched openings that two rooms may be combined to form the great chamber. A shaft passes through the centre pier, with openings to every floor to enable water to be drawn up from the well. There is a fireplace in the outer wall of each half of the chamber, one shaft capital and a portion of the chevron-moulded work of which may be seen on the extreme left of the illustration (see also Fig. 761). About halfway up the chamber is a passage formed in the thickness of the walls passing all round the chamber. Attention may be drawn to the bold chevron (or zigzag) mouldings of the arches to the large scalloped capitals, and to the small, uncarved cushion capitals.

FIG. 579.—This is a second-floor chamber and, like that at Rochester Castle (Fig. 578), is the principal apartment. It must be remembered, however, that these keeps were fortresses and that in times of peace a less substantial structure (the great hall), which stood in the court, outside the keep, was that in daily occupation. Like that of the first floor in Fig. 580, it is divided by a stone arch. The gallery is 12 ft. above the floor, and (like that at Rochester) enables one to walk all round the chamber. The fireplace is similar in character to those at Rochester, but here is a double chevron moulding. The flue is cone-shaped and discharges through two rectangular openings (now closed) in the wall on each side of the centre buttress of the south elevation (Fig. 41). It will be seen that the scalloped capitals of the shafts are similar to those at Rochester. The garderobe is in the north-east angle; there are only two garderobes in this keep (Fig. 42). The arched window recesses have angle shafts with cushion capitals, and the semicircular arches are chevron-moulded. The portcullis was operated from the gallery over the entrance doorway below.

c. 1130.　　　　　　　　　　　　　　　　　　King: Henry I.

FIG. 579.—CASTLE HEDINGHAM KEEP.
The great hall is 39 × 31 × 26 ft. high.

c. 1130.   *King:* Henry I.

FIG. 580.—The inferior hall, CASTLE HEDINGHAM KEEP.

37 ft. × 29½ ft. × 18 ft.

FIG. 580.—The inferior hall is on the first, which is also the entrance floor, and is spanned by a stone arch (now imperfect), which reduced the lengths of the beams required for the floor above. The small arch within the larger one is the entrance to an L-shaped chamber contrived in the thickness of the N.E. angle of the walls. There are five chambers in the walls. The fireplace has shafts with scalloped capitals, and abaci with billet moulding. The hearth is segmental in plan, the flue cone-shaped, discharging smoke through the wall a few feet up. The arch is moulded with chevron ornament. In the N.E. angle is the garderobe. See plan, Fig. 42.

c. 1180.   *King :* Henry II.

FIG. 581.—Interior of the hall at OAKHAM CASTLE.

FIG. 581.—The windows, which are two-light transitional outside, are round-headed and splayed within. The entrance doorway should be in the position of the farthest window. There were also two doorways (now concealed by panelling) at the end illustrated, and another at the end from which the photograph was taken—these being in the usual positions for a medieval hall of this type, on ground level. The windows were furnished with iron bars and wooden shutters. It is doubtful whether glass was used for domestic windows in the twelfth century. The horseshoes which disfigure the walls were each given by a peer on the first occasion of his entering the town, a custom still prevailing.

c. 1180.   *King :* Henry II.

FIG. 582.—The ground floor of the MANOR HOUSE, BOOTHBY PAGNELL.

FIG. 582.—This vaulting is in a good state. Over it was the hall, the living-room of the house. Vaulting under halls is common in houses where the hall is on the upper (first) floor.

c. 1240.   *King:* Henry III.

FIG. 583.—The lower end of the great hall at STOKESAY CASTLE, SHROPSHIRE.

FIG. 583.—The entrance doorway opens directly into the hall, and, where the screens would usually be, there is a staircase in the hall itself. This variation from the usual medieval arrangement (see plan, Fig. 53) probably occurred because the lower-end chambers at Stokesay are situated in the older building, or north tower, to which the hall was added. The staircase, though reconstructed, seems to be in its original position. Portions of it, such as some of the solid oak treads and a part of the handrail, are of great antiquity, and may well be from the thirteenth-century stair, but it should be regarded as an exceptional and not a typical example. The doorway on the first landing has the contemporary lintel, and that at the top of the stairs, though of less early character, may be of the same date. The ledged and boarded and studded entrance door itself is an interesting one, though probably not of earlier than seventeenth-century date. This illustration of the lower end of the hall, with that of the upper end (Fig. 585), shows the roof detail, the reinforced and repaired timbers of which may be distinguished by their colour and texture. The dais is gone from the upper end, but the doorway leading to the upper-end chamber remains, and is just visible on the left of Fig. 585. The two " squints " in Fig. 585 enabled the lord in the solar to observe and communicate with his people in the hall below. The roof, though repaired, is contemporary. It has upper and lower collar beams, and has principals with curved braces springing from stone corbels.

c. 1232-40.   King: Henry III.

FIG. 584.—The great hall, WINCHESTER CASTLE, HANTS.

FIG. 584.—In its present state this view of the interior, looking west, shows the hall much as it was when built by Henry III in place of the eleventh-century Norman hall. The exterior has been drastically altered, particularly by the insertion of a pretentious nineteenth-century entrance where no medieval doorway would have been placed. The hall is practically all that remains of the ancient castle. The curved braces under the tie-beams of the roof were added c. 1470, the rose with the rays of Edward IV being carved at their junction.

c. 1240   King: Henry III.

FIG. 585.—The upper end of the great hall at STOKESAY CASTLE, SHROPSHIRE.

This photograph is taken looking towards the upper end of the hall, where the dais stood. Above the dais is a " tube " by which the king could communicate between the hall and the chamber beyond. In the " Liberate Rolls," 32nd Henry III, the king instructed the Sheriff of Southampton " to renew and repair the paintings above our dais." We know the walls were plastered, so the painting would be on the plaster. Unfortunately, the original plaster on many ancient buildings was removed in the nineteenth century, under the mistaken idea that our forefathers favoured bare, rough, stone walls in their rooms. Attention may here be drawn to the windows of an early form of plate tracery for which glazed frames were made. This hall was not only that of the king's house (last used as such by James I), but was put to public uses, and its historical associations are scarcely less important than those of Westminster Hall ; indeed, for centuries Parliament sat in the Winchester Hall, although it was actually and primarily the hall of the king's principal residence.

c. 1260–80.   *Kings* : Henry III and Edward I.

FIG. 586.—LITTLE WENHAM HALL, SUFFOLK.

c. 1260–80.

FIG. 587.—The chapel at LITTLE WENHAM
HALL.

FIG. 586.—Between the hall and chapel is a doorway with two-light windows on each side of it. The mullioned windows have wooden shutters and strap hinges (see Fig. 488). The illustration shows, through the doorway, the piscina in the chapel, with its detached shaft and pointed trefoil arcading.

FIG. 587.—This Early English vaulted roof is in excellent preservation. On the north side of the altar (modern) is an aumbry or locker, the arch of which has a hood mould. On the south are a piscina and sedalia (Fig. 586) having trefoil arches. The corbels on each side of the window were for images. The details vary slightly in each window.

c. 1260–80.   *Kings* : Henry III and Edward I.

FIG. 588.—The hall at LITTLE WENHAM HALL, SUFFOLK.

FIG. 588.—The roof is of sixteenth-century date. There are indications in the brickwork that the original fireplace may have had a hood like that at Boothby Pagnell (Fig. 762), which would have been in accordance with contemporary practice. Probably the original roof also was almost flat.

c. 1300. *King :* Edward I.

FIG. 589.—The hammer-beam roof in the PILGRIMS' HALL, WINCHESTER.

FIG. 590.

FIGS. 589 AND 590.—The timbers of this roof are very substantial: a characteristic of early work. The ends of the hammer beams are carved alternately with a king's or a bishop's head. Such heads are often seen on stone corbels, but this carving out of the end grain of a beam (Fig. 590) is probably unique. A modern floor has been inserted into the hall which divides it into two storeys.

FIG. 591.—During the eighteenth century a floor was inserted in the hall at plate level, and the upper portion was used for the storage of corn ; the photograph shows the detail of the roof construction. The two tie-beams are enclosed in the thickness of the seventeenth-century floor ; a portion of one is visible in the illustration. The tie-beams are rectangular in section, the only mouldings being a bowtel worked on each of the lower arrises. Roofs of this early date are rare. The plastering which hides the upper portion of the roof is modern.

TIE BEAM SECTION

c. 1300.   *King:* Edward I.

FIG. 591.—The roof of the hall at OLD SOAR, PLAXTOL, KENT.

Photo by courtesy of J. R. Wigfull, F.R.I.B.A.

Fourteenth century.   *King:* Edward III.

FIG. 592.—Interior of the Great Barn, GLASTONBURY, SOMERSET.

Hall, 1300–30.   Screens, mid-fifteenth century.

FIG. 593.—HADDON HALL.

FIG. 592.—A magnificent arch-braced collar-beam roof with wind braces. The upper collars are also arched, which is an unusual feature. Barn timbers are seldom if ever moulded, as are those of church and hall roofs, but constructionally they are identical.

FIG. 593.—The tall panels of the screens are framed up with masons' mitres, and many panels still retain their perpendicular tracery. Through the opening in the screens is the (open) W. entrance from porch to entry, and (closed) the door to the buttery.

c. 1341. *King:* Edward III.

FIG. 594.—The great hall, PENSHURST PLACE, KENT.

c. 1341. *King:* Edward III.

FIG. 595.—The roof of the great hall, PENSHURST PLACE, KENT.

FIG. 594.—Perhaps this is the most realistic of existing medieval halls. The screens are not contemporary, but were put in during the latter part of the sixteenth century, and include some modern work. The design and position of hearth and andirons are in keeping with medieval forms. As has been indicated already, some medieval halls were furnished with wall fireplaces (usually these halls were on the first-floor level); others had open hearths in the middle of the floor, as at Penshurst, where the smoke rose into the open roof and passed out through a louvre, which was often a highly decorative feature, though in mean houses it might be nothing more than a barrel open at both ends. These halls are easily identified by the smoke-stained rafters, and there are still great numbers remaining as cottages and farmhouses where, in the seventeenth century, the halls were divided by floors and partitions. In Kent and Sussex the smoke-stained rafters have caused them to be called "smoke houses," under the mistaken idea that at one period bacon was cured in them. The long tables (27 ft.) and their benches down each side of Penshurst hall are of fifteenth-century date, while that on the dais (not illustrated) is of the seventeenth century. The long tables (for accommodation of inferior persons), which were set on each side of the hall (as in this illustration), were usually composed only of boards on trestles, which were removed and placed against the walls between meals to clear the floor for occupations, and at night for bedding. There was no *salt* below which inferiors sat, and it will be clear that there was no place for it. The foolish and widely used expression " seated below the salt " is a romantic phrase which presupposes a long table running from the dais down the middle of the hall, at the upper end of which the " quality " sat, and below a certain point, where the saltcellar stood, the common people were placed. The medieval practice was for the lord, his family, and guests of the same social standing to sit at the table on the dais; other persons sat at the tables or trestles and boards down each side of the hall; moreover, there was not one *salt*, but several in use at each table.

FIG. 595.—The great hall roof has principals of the arch-braced collar-beam type. On the lower collars are king-posts supporting a collar purlin under the upper collars. A peculiarity of this roof is the use of short pieces of timber placed horizontally between the great purlin and each common rafter, so that the backs of these may come in the same plane as those of the principal rafters. The lower window at the end of the hall is an example of geometrical tracery.

King: Edward III.
FIG. 596.—The hall of the MANOR HOUSE,
MARTOCK, SOMERSET.

King: Edward III.
FIG. 597.—Interior of THE FISH HOUSE, MEARE,
SOMERSET.

FIG. 596.—This is a "ground-floor" hall, with a collar-braced roof. The boarding in place of common rafters is modern. That there were no chambers at the upper end of this hall is proved by the great transomed window, long blocked up, the sill of which came down as low as the transomes of the side windows.

Fourteenth and fifteenth centuries.
FIG. 598.—THE BRETHREN'S HALL, ST. CROSS HOSPITAL.

FIG. 597.—The photograph is taken from that half of the ground floor which was the kitchen. The fire which gutted the building was not able to ruin the great beam of the first floor—heart oak is highly fire-resisting. The two narrow doorways leading into small apartments are interesting. The hall was a first-floor apartment. The roof is modern.

FIG. 598 shows the upper end of the Brethren's Hall with the seats of the master and officials, one of the fourteenth-century windows, and the arch-braced collar-beam roof. The handrail and newel post (having Bishop Fox's pelican as a finial) of the stairs up to the solar are ancient. The brethren sit on forms at two long tables, one on each side of the hall. This disposition conforms in every respect to medieval domestic practice.

Photo: H.M. Office of Works, by courtesy of the Controller of H.M. Stationery Office.

c. 1393–99.   King: Richard II.

FIG. 599.—The arch-braced hammer-beam roof of WESTMINSTER HALL, LONDON.

FIG. 599.—This magnificent roof has no parallel at any period or in any country. It replaced on the same walls (raised 2 ft.) an earlier roof, which was completed in 1099, but the William II roof had oak posts like the barn illustrated in Fig. 18, which divided the hall into a central nave with aisles. To design a roof which should give a clear floor nearly 70 ft. wide was a remarkable achievement. This roof differs from other hammer-beam arch-braced roofs in the carrying of the great arch-brace through the hammer-beams and hammer-posts instead of under the point of junction of the hammer-beam and hammer-post, thereby balancing the vertical and oblique thrusts so perfectly as to permit the great span. The length of the hall is 236 ft., the width 69 ft., and the height 95 ft. For diagram of a section, see Fig. 33, page 37.

c. 1450.   King: Henry VI.

FIG. 600.—Upper end of great hall, GREAT DIXTER, NORTHIAM, SUSSEX.

FIG. 600.—The hammer-beam roof is combined with a tie-beam, king post and braces, the spandrels between the latter being filled with cusping. The faces of the hammer-beams are carved with shields of arms. The bay window is a restoration. The roof timbers are stained by soot from the fires on the central hearth. The unusual construction of the roof was necessitated by the timber walls, which required a tie.

Photo by courtesy of Lt.-Col. Reginald Cooper.

FIG. 601.—In counties where timber was the usual building material, fifteenth-century framing would be filled with vertical oak studs, which would form narrow panels of the same width as the oak, and not until the mid-sixteenth century would one expect to find large square panels such as those at the end of this hall. The wood panelling is seventeenth-century work. The roof is of the arch-braced, collar-beam type, of which only the principals can be seen, the common rafters being ceiled off. The door shown in the illustration is that of the parlour.

c. 1480.   *King:* Edward IV.

FIG. 601.—The upper end of the hall at COTHAY MANOR, WELLINGTON, SOMERSET.

Photo by courtesy of Lt.-Col. Reginald Cooper.

FIG. 602.—The openings in the screens to the entry at the lower end of the hall, and also those beyond to the lower end chambers, etc., can be seen. The gallery is enclosed except for a small opening in the centre. The pins for pikes are early features. The fireplace has a flat lintel and appears to be of sixteenth-century date, whilst the mouldings to the openings in the screens are of similar character. Probably there was a central hearth originally.

c. 1480.   *King:* Edward IV.

FIG. 602.—The lower end of the hall at COTHAY MANOR.

c. 1465.   King: Edward IV.

FIG. 604.—OCKWELLS MANOR, BRAY, BERKSHIRE.

FIG. 604.—The screens and the gallery over at the lower end of the hall. For the reverse side of the screens, showing their construction, see Fig. 356. The open door leads to the porch. The panelling under the window is seventeenth-century.

c. 1465.   King: Edward IV.

FIG. 603.—OCKWELLS MANOR, BRAY, BERKSHIRE.

FIG. 603.—In this view of the upper end of the hall can be seen the interior of the bay window, its fifteenth-century heraldic glass, and seventeenth-century panelling. The roof is of the arch-braced collar-beam type. There is now no dais.

_c. 1479._ _King : Edward IV._

FIG. 606.—ELTHAM PALACE, KENT.

FIG. 606.—This hall is singular in having two bay windows (one at each end of the dais), one of which is shown here. The doorways opening to the upper end apartments (now destroyed) are in these bays. The doors are modern. The illustration also shows a false hammer-beam roof of late type (see Fig. 31, page 37).

_c. 1480._ _King : Edward IV._

FIG. 605.—COTHAY MANOR, WELLINGTON, SOMERSET.

FIG. 605.—The solar, as usually the case, occupies the full depth of the building and is transverse to the hall. Under it are the parlour and the adjoining room shown in the plan, Fig. 98. The arch-braced collar-beam roof is open, as customary, and is double framed, with substantial principals. The common rafters are ceiled off. The circular window has interesting tracery.

c. 1490. *King:* Henry VII

FIG. 607.—The solar, GREAT DIXTER, NORTHIAM, SUSSEX.

FIG. 607.—The roof is single framed with common rafters only, but has two tie-beams and king posts, one respond to which is seen in the gable wall.   See Fig. 25, page 36.

Late fifteenth century. *King:* Henry VII.

FIG. 608.—Hall of a house lately at BENENDEN, KENT.

FIG. 608.—The exterior and plan of this house are shown in Figs. 100 and 101.   The oak-barred, four-light window and the wainscot at the head of the hall are typical Kentish details.

Late fifteenth or early sixteenth century.   *Kings:* Henry VII, VIII.

FIG. 609.—Lower end of RUFFORD HALL, LANCASHIRE.

Late fifteenth or early sixteenth century.   *Kings:* Henry VII, VIII

FIG. 610.—Upper end of RUFFORD HALL, LANCASHIRE.

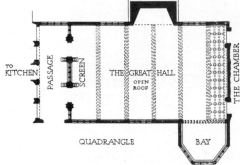

FIG. 611.—Plan of RUFFORD HALL.

FIG. 609.—The lower end of the hall has not the entry separated from the hall by screens but only partially by an arched opening flanked by speers. There is also a movable screen, the three finials of which are later additions. Originally there was a central hearth; the fireplace is of the late sixteenth century.

FIG. 610.—The upper end, showing coved ceiling over the high table and bench on wall behind. On the right is the opening to the bay window.

c. 1525.   *King:* Henry VIII.

FIG. 612.—HAMPTON COURT PALACE.   Cardinal Wolsey's Closet.

FIG. 612.—The fireplace and doorway are in their original positions.   The panelling is contemporary, but assembled here from other parts of the palace.   The panel framing has only a bead moulding.

c. 1530.   *King:* Henry VIII.

FIG. 613.—THE ABBOT'S LODGINGS, THAME PARK, OXFORDSHIRE.

FIG. 613.—This early sixteenth-century apartment is a valuable survival of its period. The fireplace has the late type of " four-centred " arch.   The linen-fold panelling is fully developed, but lacks the incised and punched representation of a stitched border, as that in Fig. 683.   The panelling was put in by Abbot Robert King (*c.* 1530), whose name and mitre appear on the upper panel on the right of the porch ; the arms are missing, however, having been cut away when the panels were mutilated.   The ceiling is shown in Fig. 736.

Late fifteenth or early sixteenth century.   *King:* Henry VII.

FIG. 614.—MANOR HOUSE, LIDDINGTON, RUTLAND.

FIG. 614.—The hall is on the first floor. (Exterior shown in Fig. 102.) The illustration shows the bay window and upper end of hall. Although the fan tracery, carved in wood, of the coving is exceptional, the boarded ceiling divided by moulded ribs of wood applied is a type of ceiling treatment of this period found elsewhere. A variation at Compton Wynyates is shown in Fig. 733.

c. 1559.   *Queen:* Elizabeth.

FIG. 615.—The parlour at MORETON OLD HALL, CONGLETON, CHESHIRE.

FIG. 615.—The beams and joists of the floor over the parlour are very massive; in this respect and in the sections of their mouldings the character is like late fifteenth-century work. The panelling also has exceptionally heavy framing. (See Fig. 39.)

Photo : George Hepworth, Brighouse.

c. 1575.   Queen: Elizabeth.

FIG. 616.—The great chamber, GILLING CASTLE, YORKSHIRE.

FIG. 616.—This plaster ceiling is of the fan and pendant type, a familiar example of which, from Sizergh Castle, is in the Victoria and Albert Museum. The centre panel of the overmantel contains the Fairfax arms, and those of Queen Elizabeth are to be seen on the panel above. The frieze is painted with scenes and bears many shields of arms. The panelling is in fairly large squares, divided by wide framing ; the lozenges are formed with slight, applied mouldings, and the field of these and their spandrels is inlaid. The frieze of the panelling is divided into panels (filled with gilt strapwork) by split balusters, an early instance of this favourite Jacobean ornament. The glass (c. 1585) also is heraldic, and is the work of a German artist named Dininckhoff.

Photo : George Hepworth, Brighouse.

FIG. 617.—The plan of this house is medieval in character, but the upper-end and lower-end rooms have been reversed at some later date. The illustration is of the upper end of the hall, which has a flat ceiling, and shows the fireplace, panelling, a gallery which gives access to the first-floor chambers, and a staircase with "dog gates" at its foot. Although the hall conforms to the medieval type, the extension of the gallery is an early and tentative step in the direction of a passage room into which the hall ultimately developed. Beyond the panelling at this end of the hall are rooms which are now used as a drawing-room, kitchen, pantry, etc. The lower end of the hall, which is entered from the porch, has screens with two arched openings, separated and flanked by coupled

c. 1583 and seventeenth century.   Queen: Elizabeth.

FIG. 617.—The upper end of the hall, OAKWELL HALL, near BRADFORD, YORKS.

Tuscan columns in oak ; these give access from the hall to the entry. What were originally lower-end apartments are now used as family rooms. Almost the whole of the wall opposite the hall fireplace is filled with a 30-light window.

Photo by courtesy of J. R. Wigfull, F.R.I.B.A.

Early sixteenth century.   *King:* Henry VIII.   Panelling *c.* 1545.   *King:* Henry VIII.

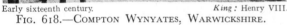

FIG. 618.—COMPTON WYNYATES, WARWICKSHIRE.   FIG. 619.—HADDON HALL. The Parlour.

FIG. 618.—The upper end of the great hall showing the bay window.

FIG. 619.—The parlour is entered from the upper end of the Great Hall. The panelling (*c.* 1545) has a simple framing with only a bead moulding, the panels tall, as earlier work. Those of the frieze and certain others are carved with heads, arms and geometrical devices. Compare with the seventeenth-century bay at Unstone Hall not many miles away (Fig. 156).

Late sixteenth century.   FIG. 620.—TURK FARM, SMARDEN, KENT.   *Queen:* Elizabeth.

FIG. 620.—Interior of a fifteenth-century hall (once open to the roof and having a hearth in the middle of the floor) after insertion of floors and chimney with fireplace, all *c.* 1600, yet all in the manner of the early part of the sixteenth century. The door is seventeenth century.

Late sixteenth century.   *Queen:* Elizabeth.

FIG. 621.—The Long Gallery, MORETON OLD HALL, CONGLETON, CHESHIRE.

FIG. 621.—The Long Gallery, which extends the whole width of the entrance front (Fig. 114), is approximately 70 ft. long and 12 ft. wide. The roof is stiffened by cusped wind braces, the spaces between which are plastered so that the common rafters are ceiled off. At each end of the room are examples of plaster-work in relief (see Fig. 691). The collar beams, mortised for ceiling joists, are of later date.

Photo by courtesy of J. R. Wigfull, F.R.I.B.A.

c. 1590.   *Queen:* Elizabeth.

FIG. 622.—HADDON HALL.

FIG. 622.—Portion of the Long Gallery on the first floor, built above the earlier walling. Such galleries were well lighted, and this important example may be compared with the more humble Moreton Old Hall, twenty-five miles away (Fig. 621). The plaster ceiling is coved. For detail of panelling see Fig. 687.

Photo : C. E. Keene, Derby.

c. 1597.   *Queen :* Elizabeth.

FIG. 623.—HARDWICKE HALL, DERBYSHIRE.

FIG. 623.—The presence chamber retains many features of its period. Two tendencies may be noted in the Elizabethan great house: (1) The increasing importance of the chamber, and (2) the placing of the chamber on the first floor.

The illustration shows : (1) The plaster frieze of scenes of Diana hunting ; the figures in relief and coloured in tempera. In the window recess Ver (Spring) is beating Cupid with a bunch of flowers ; (2) panelling of unusual shapes, painted and with stiles in the form of pilasters elaborately but ill designed ; (3) the marble fireplace and mantelpiece ; (4) the tapestries, which consist of eight panels and illustrate the story of Ulysses ; and (5) the farthingale chairs (on the right), which are of early seventeenth-century date. For detail of frieze see Fig. 694.

c. 1580–1601.   *Queen :* Elizabeth.

FIG. 624.—The hall screens at MONTACUTE HOUSE, SOMERSET.

FIG. 624.—These screens (which are of seventeenth-century character) bear evidence of changes in style. They are built of local stone, well designed and worked, except for the two figures which support the centre cresting, which are almost as ill-fashioned as any on a country joiner's mantelpiece. The screens may be compared with the medieval ones at Cothay Manor (Fig. 602), at Ockwells Manor (Fig. 604), and the Jacobean screens at Magdalen College, Oxford (Fig. 627).

c. 1605.   *King:* James I.
FIG. 625.—The great hall at KNOLE, SEVENOAKS, KENT.

c. 1610.   *King:* James I.
FIG. 626.—COKE'S HOUSE, WEST BURTON, SUSSEX.

c. 1605.   *King:* James I.
FIG. 627.—MAGDALEN COLLEGE HALL, OXFORD.

FIG. 625.—Open roofs for halls and solars were now no longer in fashion; in their place came flat plaster ceilings geometrically patterned and frequently furnished with pendants. The screens were very elaborate and richly decorated with pilasters—atlantes or caryatides, highly carved in relief, being introduced as terminals. Crestings and galleries were pierced—all in the Flemish fashion. The usual small, nearly square panel is used round the rest of the hall at Knole. The fireplace arch is in the Tudor manner, with an added classic mantel supported by columns.

FIG. 626.—A typical room of the period, in which the plaster frieze is worked with fruit, flowers, and foliage in relief.

FIG. 627.—The Jacobean screens are more correctly classic than those at Knole (Fig. 625) in the detail of their columns and arcading. Some of the arches are filled with cartouches bearing armorial charges. The tall pyramidal finials standing on four balls and terminating with one ball are typical Jacobean details. The frieze of the main Order is carved with scrolls terminating in grotesque animal heads, like those in the earlier frieze of the linenfold panelling (Fig. 682) on the other three sides of the hall. The doors are nineteenth-century insertions. The tables and benches, portions of which can be seen on either side in the illustration, are characteristic of domestic woodwork of the middle of the seventeenth century.

c. 1605.   *King:* James I.

FIG. 628.—KNOLE, SEVENOAKS, KENT.

FIG. 628.—The solar (now called the ballroom) at Knole is one of few remaining early seventeenth-century rooms, which, notwithstanding its later furniture, presents some resemblance to its original appearance. The fireplace is the design and work of some able marble mason like the Fleming, Ghiles de Witt, who worked those at Cobham Hall a few years earlier. The panelling, in which the squares are becoming larger, bears little relation to the pilasters dividing it. The rich frieze has many figures and devices modelled in high relief, no doubt by a Low Country craftsman, and the ceiling is a good example of strapwork in moderately high relief and without pendants.

c. 1607. *King:* James I.
FIG. 629.—CHARLTON HOUSE, KENT.

c. 1631. *King:* Charles I.
FIG. 630.—The King's breakfast room, KEW PALACE.

FIG. 629.—The long gallery. The plaster ceiling is ornamented with scrolled strapwork, in which are cabochon and pyramidal ornaments in relief and, at intervals, large diamond-shaped panels enclosing devices. (See also Fig. 742.) The fireplace with its Corinthian columns bearing entablatures is well proportioned.

FIG. 630.—Although pilasters were still foreign to the panel divisions, here they seem to have been designed together, for spaces have been left for them between the panels, and the mouldings of the pedestal capping are continued round the room as a dado capping.

c. 1634. *King:* Charles I.
FIG. 631.—BATEMAN'S, BURWASH, SUSSEX.

FIG. 631.—A parlour nearly square in plan, having mullioned and transomed stone windows with ovolo mouldings, small panels, and ceiling beams with oak joists between, all features of a small house of the period. Rooms of this type have a singularly intimate and domestic character. They are sometimes called " very English," a term, however, which we find popularly applied also to such dissimilar interiors as those of Elizabethan and Georgian houses (Figs. 615, 647).

c. 1656.   Commonwealth.

FIG. 632.—THORPE HALL, near PETERBOROUGH.

FIG. 632.—The panels are large and the horizontal divisions are approximately the divisions of the Order. Panel moulds are slight. The use of volutes (circular and compressed) is noticeable, as everywhere in this house.

FIG. 633.—A bedroom at DRAYTON HOUSE, THRAPSTON, NORTHANTS.

c. 1662.   *King:* Charles II.

FIG. 634.—The salon on the first floor at COLESHILL. Sir Roger Pratt, *Architect.*

FIG. 633.—The upper portion of the mantelpiece was designed by John Webb in 1653. The moulding round the fireplace is of the later seventeenth century, and the grate is of late eighteenth-century date.

FIG. 634.—The fruit and foliage ornament of the plaster ceiling is of the very compact nature, characteristic of this school, and should be compared later with the more free, open, and naturalistic treatment of the Wren period (Fig. 751).

c. 1680.   *King:* Charles II.

FIG. 635.—RAMSBURY MANOR, WILTSHIRE.

FIG. 635.—The woodwork and carving in the salon, *c.* 1680. The marble mantel-piece and the plaster ceiling, *c.* 1770.

c. 1690.   William and Mary.   Late seventeenth century.   William and Mary.

FIG. 636.—DENHAM PLACE, BUCKINGHAMSHIRE.   FIG. 637.—DRAYTON HOUSE, THRAPSTON, NORTHANTS.

FIG. 636.—The panelling is of fir, painted; the panels around the fireplace are carved. The firegrate is late eighteenth century.

FIG. 637.—Large panels framed in heavy bolection mouldings (Figs. 707, 708) were the fashion. Often these were filled with paintings, particularly the square and "lying" panels over doorcases (as at Denham, Fig. 423), for which landscapes, architectural and still life subjects were specially painted. Below the large panels, "lying panels" occupied the place of a dado (as at Cullompton, Fig. 640).

c. 1701.   William and Mary.   Early eighteenth century.   William and Mary.

FIG. 638.—CHICHELEY HALL, BUCKINGHAMSHIRE.   FIG. 639.—MOMPESSON HOUSE, SALISBURY.

FIG. 638.—The screen under the gallery (which connects the first-floor rooms at each end of the house) divides the entrance hall from the back, or staircase, hall.

FIG. 639.—The doorcase is of slightly later character than that in the hall (Fig. 425), as also is the stucco plasterwork of the ceiling and walls, most of which is more formal and less naturalistic than that in Figs. 749 and 751, and anticipates developments shortly to take place.

c. 1700.   William and Mary.

FIG. 640.—A house in HIGH STREET, CULLOMPTON, DEVONSHIRE.

FIG. 640 shows the entrance hall of an earlier house into which new stairs, fireplace, panelling, and plaster ceiling were introduced, *c.* 1700. The narrow shelf over the fireplace forms a base for the panel above : the wide shelf came in later. The square newels, twisted balusters standing on a string, and all the panel proportions and moulds, are good types. The beam is a survival from the older construction.

c. 1714.   *King:* George I.

FIG. 641.—BRADBOURNE, LARKFIELD, KENT.

1702–13.   *Queen:* Anne.

FIG. 642.—EASTON NESTON.

FIG. 641.—The salon contains the original furniture and pictures, mostly of the early eighteenth century. The exceptional height of this room is accentuated by the tall panels. In the panelling we still have raised panels, the framing of which is enriched with carved egg and tongue moulding, for the bolection mouldings and carvings of fruit, flowers, game, musical instruments, and trophies were already out of fashion. Oak panelling, also, had given place to pine, which was painted and enriched with gilding.

FIG. 642 shows the first-floor gallery which traverses the house. The semicircular-headed windows—one front and one back—are well proportioned to their positions. The great height of this floor has been well treated by lining the walls with panelling of large size, having tall pilasters and deep entablature. The division of the tall panels into two may be compared with those at Bradbourne (Fig. 641). In both interiors, but by different means, the effect of height to which the designers aspired was achieved.

Photo by courtesy of F. R. Yerbury, Hon. A.R.I.B.A.   *Photo by courtesy of F. R. Yerbury, Hon. A.R.I.B.A.*

c. 1716.

FIG. 643.—BLENHEIM PALACE, WOODSTOCK, OXFORD.

c. 1716. *c.* 1750.

FIG. 644.—BLENHEIM PALACE, WOODSTOCK.

FIG. 643.—The Great Gallery is over 180 ft. long : see plan (Fig. 206). The gallery was warmed by two fireplaces. How far Vanbrugh was responsible for the decoration of this interior is difficult to determine, for he did not finish Blenheim, having quarrelled with the Duchess of Marlborough, who in 1716 employed a glassmaker, named Moor, and others to complete the work.

FIG. 644.—The Great Gallery, showing the detail of the marble doorway, probably by Vanbrugh, and of the bookcases which were made to house the Sunderland Library (*c.* 1749) and are in the manner of that period.

Reproduced from " The English Interior," by Arthur Stratton (Batsford).

1702-14.

FIG. 645.—CASTLE HOWARD, YORKSHIRE.
Sir John Vanbrugh, *Architect*.

1723-5.   King: George I.

FIG. 646.—MEREWORTH CASTLE, KENT.
Colen Campbell, *Architect*.

FIG. 645.—The Great Hall illustrates English baroque and masons' workmanship at their best, and being in the centre of the house it is lighted by windows in the drum under the dome. The paintings (c. 1712) are by Antonio Pillegrini. The architect's views upon the comfort and convenience of this house are given on p. 125.

FIG. 646.—The circular central salon is lighted by circular windows in the dome and has a gallery or "Poggio" from which to reach the first-floor bedrooms. Campbell states that "the ornaments are executed by Signor Bagutti, a most ingenious artist."

Photo by courtesy of H. W. Fincham, F.S.A.

1723.   King: George I.

FIG. 647.—ARGYLL HOUSE, KING'S ROAD, CHELSEA, LONDON.
Giacomo Leoni, *Architect*.

FIG. 647.—In this front room on the ground floor, the panelling, mantelpiece, and the panel over with a picture in it, are characteristic of small house details; this room contrasts strongly with contemporary interiors of great houses, as those shown in Figs. 645, 646, and 649.

Photo by courtesy of the Director of the Victoria and Albert Museum.

c. 1730.   *King: George II.*

FIG. 648.—A panelled room at No. 26, HATTON GARDEN, LONDON.

FIG. 648.—This panelled room at No. 26, Hatton Garden, London, photographed before its removal to the Victoria and Albert Museum, should be compared with Fig. 632 (Thorpe Hall, Peterborough) in order to realize the influence of the Inigo Jones school on the Palladian architecture of 1730. A new feature was the niche (semicircular or semi-elliptic in plan, with or without doors) which was frequently introduced as a decorative feature of panelled rooms; its shelves served to display china. Such pinewood panelling was painted. Olive-green was most used, but other shades of green, light-blue, cream, buff, brown, and white are also found.

Reproduced from " The English Interior," by Arthur Stratton (Batsford).

c. 1722–35.   *Kings: George I, II.*

FIG. 649.—HOUGHTON HALL, NORFOLK.

c. 1730.   *King: George II.*

FIG. 650.—EASTON NESTON, NORTHANTS.

FIG. 649.—Just as the house was designed by Colen Campbell but erected and modified by Thomas Ripley, so the stone hall was designed by Campbell and decorated by others. Campbell describes it as " a cube of 40 feet . . . all in stone; the most beautiful in England." The ceiling and frieze are in stucco by Artari. The figures on the door pediments are by Rysbrach. The designing of the details is probably by William Kent.

FIG. 650.—The stucco wall decoration of the south-east room (now the dining-room) was probably the work of Artari or Bagutti, the Italian stuccoists. See also Honington Hall (Figs. 654, 851).

c. 1631 and c. 1740.

FIG. 651.—KEW PALACE, LONDON.

FIG. 651.—The dining-room is of two periods. The windows, doors, and panelling c. 1740. The pediment over the door, the ceiling rose, and the overmantel (except the centre panel) c. 1631. The stone fireplace probably is c. 1631, but William Kent, who was employed to make the eighteenth-century alterations, imitated works of the Inigo Jones period, and it may be Kent's work. The strapwork on the overmantel order indicates it as sixteenth-century work. The firegrate is an early type of hob grate. The heat given by such a grate would be inadequate to warm a large room having three windows on one side and two on another, yet the king (George III), queen, and princesses lived here for years towards the end of the eighteenth century. Subsequent progress in standards of comfort is remarkable.

Photo by courtesy of the Director of the Victoria and Albert Museum.

c. 1740.   *King:* George II.

FIG. 652.—Room from WOTTON-UNDER-EDGE, GLOUCESTERSHIRE.

FIG. 652.—Pine-panelled and painted room hung with Chinoiserie wallpaper (birds and plants), the original trellis-work border to which was replaced (c. 1800) by that illustrated. The wallpaper is used, not only to furnish the panels between dado (pedestal of the order) and cornice, but is carried round the doorcase so as to impair the architectural treatment of the walls. Ultimately the application of wallpapers extended from skirting to ceiling, and made the destruction complete.

Photo : Bedford Lemere & Co.

1749.   *King :* George II

FIG. 653.—CHESTERFIELD HOUSE, MAYFAIR, LONDON.
Isaac Ware, *Architect.*

FIG. 653.—The decoration is in the extreme French rococo style, of scrolls and C's and curves, which came into fashion in England *c.* 1740. The architect's own views upon such work are quoted on page 139.

FIG. 654.—For a small house, probably the decorations of the interior of Honington are unequalled. No record exists of the artists employed, but Artari did work at the Radcliffe Library, Oxford, and also, with Vessali and Serena, at Ditchley near Oxford, during this period; the demand for stucco ornaments, which extended from Northumberland to the English Channel, brought many craftsmen to England.

c. 1744.   *King :* George II.

FIG. 654.—HONINGTON HALL.

By courtesy of "Country Life."

c. 1767   *King: George III.*

FIG. 655.—KEDLESTON HALL.

FIG. 655.—The marble hall at Kedleston Hall, Derbyshire. An illustration of Robert Adam's work in the grand manner combined with that "light and graceful" decoration which he affected. The ceiling of this "Grecian Hall" was designed by George Richardson (author of several architectural books and designs), and carried out by Joseph Rose. The colouring was pink and green.

Photo: Bedford Lemere & Co.

FIG. 656.—The paintings in the ceiling of the first drawing-room are by Angelica Kauffman. The fillings of the wall panels have now disappeared, but they may, originally, have contained paintings similar to those at Osterley Park by Zucchi, or they may have been furnished with stucco ornament, like the panels in the eating-room at Osterley, which also contains smaller panels filled with paintings. Although the panel moulds in the first drawing-room ceiling at Chandos House are large, the detail is not coarse. The mantelpiece is contemporary.

1769   *King: George III.*

FIG. 656.—CHANDOS HOUSE, LONDON.
Robert Adam, *Architect.*

Photo by courtesy of Hampton and Sons.

1772.   King : George III.

FIG. 657.—No. 20, St. James's Square.
Robert Adam, *Architect*.

FIG. 657.—The entrance hall, showing the niche opposite the staircase. See also plan, Fig. 268. No doubt the architect introduced the niche in order to give an effect of greater width to the passage between this wall and the staircase opposite : an attempt which was only partially successful.

Photo by courtesy of Hampton and Sons.

FIG. 658.—In the large drawing-room the taste for curves is extended to a segmental or barrel ceiling, in addition to the segmental end of the room. Circles and ellipses are also conspicuous in the design of the ceiling ornament.

1772.   King : George III.

FIG. 658.—No. 20, St. James's Square, London.
Robert Adam, *Architect*.

Photo by courtesy of Hampton and Sons.

FIG. 659.—In the library, hexagonal panels predominate over circles, and although the recess at the end of the room is curved in plan, straight lines govern the design. The mouldings of the ceiling panels are in slight relief and may be compared with those at Moor Park (Fig. 758).

1772.   *King:* George III.

FIG. 659.—NO. 20, ST. JAMES'S SQUARE, LONDON.
Robert Adam, *Architect.*

FIG. 660.—The dining-room ceiling and walls show the slight and graceful decoration of the period, but it differs from the Adam designs in its free treatment and naturalistic motifs, which may be compared with Figs. 656, 658, 661. The colouring of the ceiling ornament is original. The framing of the sunk wall panels has a reeded moulding, with crossed ribbon ornament at intervals. Some panels contain pictures, whilst others have delicate stucco ornament in character with that of the ceiling. The panel over the fireplace contains a figure emblematic of Music. The mantelpiece is constructed of statuary, onyx and coloured marbles; the grate, doorcase, and sideboard are contemporary; indeed, except for the Venetian chandelier, the original decoration of the room is unusually complete.

c. 1770.   *King:* George III.

FIG. 660.—DRAYTON HOUSE, NORTHAMPTONSHIRE.

Photo by courtesy of Hampton and Sons. 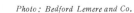 *Photo: Bedford Lemere and Co.*

1772. *King:* George III. *c.* 1770. *King:* George III.

FIG. 661.—No. 20, ST. JAMES'S SQUARE, LONDON.
Robert Adam, *Architect.*

FIG. 662.—HAREWOOD HOUSE, near LEEDS.
Robert Adam, *Architect.*

FIG. 661.—The music room is a complete example of Adam ceiling and wall decoration in his lightest manner. The mantel and grate are contemporary. For the plan of the room see Fig. 268.

FIG. 662.—The ceiling design of the gallery includes painted pictorial panels by Rebecca or Rebecchi, and the stucco work is by Rose. In this ceiling Adam's treatment is superior to that at Moor Park, which is heavy in appearance. The furniture was designed for the house and supplied by Chippendale.

1769. *King:* George III. *c.* 1773. *King:* George III.

FIG. 663.—No. 3, THE TERRACE,
RICHMOND HILL, SURREY.

FIG. 664.—No. 26, GROSVENOR SQUARE, LONDON
(since destroyed).

FIG. 663.—The practice of coving the angles of the wall and ceiling was sometimes extended to the rounding of other angles. In this room it has also been carried out in the door architrave and windows, Fig. 542.

FIG. 664.—This perspective drawing from *The Works of Architecture of Robert and James Adam, Esquires,* published 1777, shows the third drawing-room of Lord Derby's house. The heavy character of the illustration differs from the light and dainty nature of the Adam decoration, but is valuable because the room is represented complete with its decorative accessories.

By courtesy of Messrs. Robersons Ltd.

c. 1776.   *King:* George III.

FIG. 665.—BASILDON PARK, PANGBOURNE, BERKSHIRE.
John Carr, *Architect.*

FIG. 665.—Reception room, the decoration in the Adam style, but having the qualities of virility and good proportion. The tablet over the fireplace lacks support which *garniture de cheminée* standing upon the shelf would afford.

Photo: Bedford Lemere and Co.

c. 1777.   *King:* George III.   1780.   *King:* George III.

FIG. 666.—STOWE, BUCKINGHAMSHIRE.   FIG. 667.—NO. 13, DEVONSHIRE PLACE, LONDON.
Signor Borra, *Architect.*

FIG. 666.—The sculpture round the central hall represents a Roman triumphal procession.

FIG. 667.—The walls of the back drawing-room are hung with damask silk: that now fixed being modern. The ceiling, doorcase, doors (see Figs. 465, 474), and fireplace are all of the period.

FIG. 668.—The library at STOWE, BUCKINGHAMSHIRE.
Sir John Soane, *Architect.*

FIG. 668.—The detail of the flat ceiling is in the manner of the Henry VII chapel at Westminster. The mantelpiece, and the gates to the bookcases, are of bronze. The room was designed to house a collection of Saxon MSS. belonging to the Duke of Buckingham. On the whole, the pre-Ruskin Gothic detail (taken direct from English examples) is better than later work. The mantelpiece (arch, jambs, and shelf) somewhat resembles one illustrated (Plate 66) in *The Modern Builder's Assistant,* the joint production of William and John Halfpenny, architects and carpenters, Robert Morris, surveyor, and T. Lightoler, carver, published in 1757.

Reproduced by courtesy of the Curator, the Soane Museum.

FIG. 669.—No. 13, LINCOLN'S INN FIELDS, LONDON.
Sir John Soane, *Architect.*

FIG. 669.—The dining-room ceiling is divided into compartments in which are paintings by Henry Howard, R.A. The furniture, except the earlier chair at the far end of the table, is contemporary.

Photo by courtesy of Everard Scarisbrick, Esq.

1837.

Queen : Victoria.

FIG. 670.—SCARISBRICK HALL, ORMSKIRK, LANCASHIRE.
A. W. Pugin, *Architect.*

Reproduced by courtesy of the Curator, the Soane Museum.

1812.

King : George III.

FIG. 671.—NO. 13, LINCOLN'S INN FIELDS, LONDON.
Sir John Soane, *Architect.*

FIG. 670.—The Great Hall, like the exterior (Fig. 297), is an extremely interesting example of full-blooded Gothic Revival. Fig. 298 shows how far the hall plan (2) departs from medieval practice. Extraordinary pains were taken by the designer over all details for which he furnished full-size drawings. The attempt to adapt Gothic details by reducing them to the scale of a nineteenth-century chimneypiece is disastrous, notwithstanding the skill expended upon its execution : the tiny decorated ogee arch is particularly ridiculous. The wall is decorated by stencils of the architect's cypher, a P. Shields on the string bear an S. for Scarisbrick.

FIG. 671.—A view of the library and the dining-room beyond. The furniture is as it was in 1812. The fireplace and grate are designed in the severe rectilineal manner of Soane. (See Fig. 814.)

2B

Photo: Newtonian Illustrated Press Service.

Middle nineteenth century.   *Queen:* Victoria.

Fig. 672.—The Prince Consort's Writing-Room, BUCKINGHAM PALACE, LONDON.

FIG. 672.—A room similar to thousands of others in English homes at the same period, which illustrates the current fashion and public taste. A more restless combination would be difficult to imagine. The walls are covered with a strongly patterned paper divided into panels by equally aggressive borders and partly obscured by pictures—large and small. The mouldings of the woodwork are coloured, the frieze of the doorcase entablature is enriched by further scroll ornament in colours. The carpet is patterned all over, and the furniture covers—even the cushions—are crawling with decoration. The gasolier and its shades complete this picture of opulent ugliness.

INTERNAL WALL TREATMENT

For other examples of INTERNAL WALL TREATMENT see—

INTERIORS, pages 352 to 392

STAIRCASES, pages 450 to 462

Late fifteenth century.   *King:* Henry VII.

FIG. 673.—A house in CHURCH SQUARE,
RYE, SUSSEX.

Early sixteenth century.   *King:* Henry VIII.

FIG. 674.—COMPTON WYNYATES, WARWICKSHIRE.

FIG. 673.—An early type of wainscoting of oak clapboards, tongued and grooved, overlapping on the front and flush at the back, and nailed to a rail in the wall with square-headed studs. For section see Fig. 37, page 73

FIG. 674.—Clapboarding reversed, to present the smooth face towards the room. The boards are in two lengths and the horizontal joint is covered by a carved and pierced ribbon of oak.

Sixteenth century, but of an earlier type. *Queen:* Elizabeth.

FIG. 675.—STRAWBERRY HOLE FARM,
NORTHIAM, SUSSEX.

Fifteenth century.

FIG. 676.—WILSLEY HOUSE, CRANBROOK, KENT.

FIG. 675.—Clapboarding ribbed " lignum undulatum."

FIG. 676.—Single ribbed panels between structural studding.

Sixteenth century.

FIG. 677.—Panelled oak chest.

Late fifteenth or early sixteenth century. *King:* Henry VIII.
FIG. 678.—PAYCOCKE'S HOUSE, GREAT
COGGESHALL, ESSEX.

FIG. 677.—Chest with ribbed framing and panels. The panel ribs have stops of an elementary or primitve kind.

FIG. 678.—The framed oak panelling has ribs stopped in three ways, but none of them is similar to the true linenfold panel. The carved lintel over the fireplace is of oak.

Fifteenth or sixteenth century.
FIG. 679.—THE GUILDHALL, LAVENHAM, SUFFOLK.

Early sixteenth century. *King:* Henry VIII.
FIG. 680.—COMPTON WYNYATES,
WARWICKSHIRE.

FIG. 679.—Boards moulded in ribs. The ribs are stopped more elaborately than the panels in Fig. 677.

FIG. 680.—The panel ribs are stopped as folds, but the linenfolds are not yet fully developed.

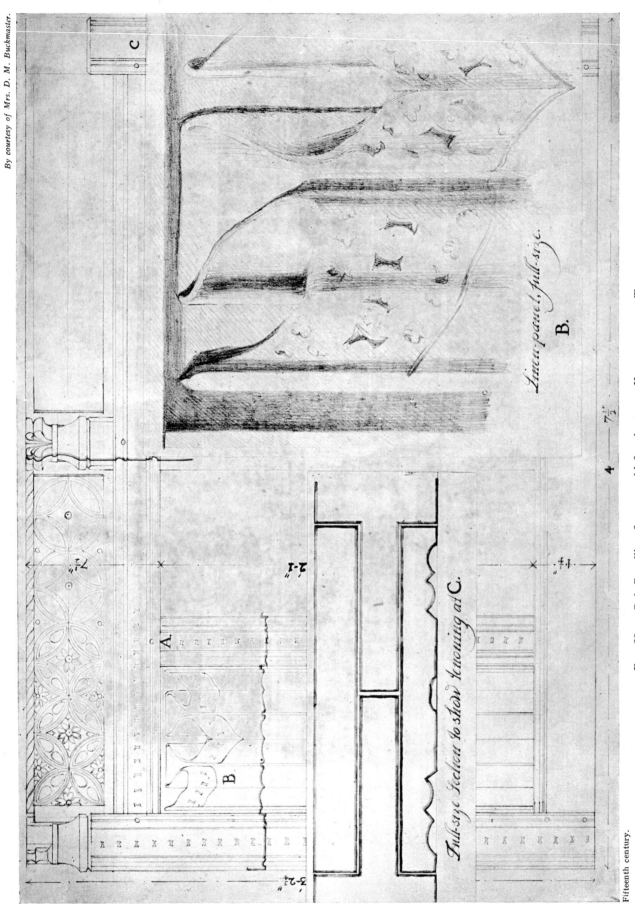

By courtesy of Mrs. D. M. Buckmaster.

Fifteenth century.

FIG. 681.—Oak Panelling from an old farmhouse at KINGSTON, near TAUNTON.

FIG. 681.—The ribbed panels are stopped in imitation of the margin of a folded cloth, and the edges punched to simulate stitchery. See Fig. 683.

By courtesy of the Director of the Victoria and Albert Museum.

c 1541.   *King:* Henry VIII.
FIG. 682.—MAGDALEN COLLEGE, OXFORD.

Fifteenth century.
FIG. 683.—Farmhouse at KINGSTON, SOMERSET.

FIG. 682.—True linen panelling.

FIG. 683.—Fullest development of the linen panel with punched border to represent stitchery.

By courtesy of the Director of the Victoria and Albert Museum.

Early sixteenth century.   *King:* Henry VIII.

FIG. 684.

FIG. 684.—Parchemin panels. The simple central rib with ogival splays (see Fig. 38, page 75) has become elaborated and enriched with vine ornament, etc.

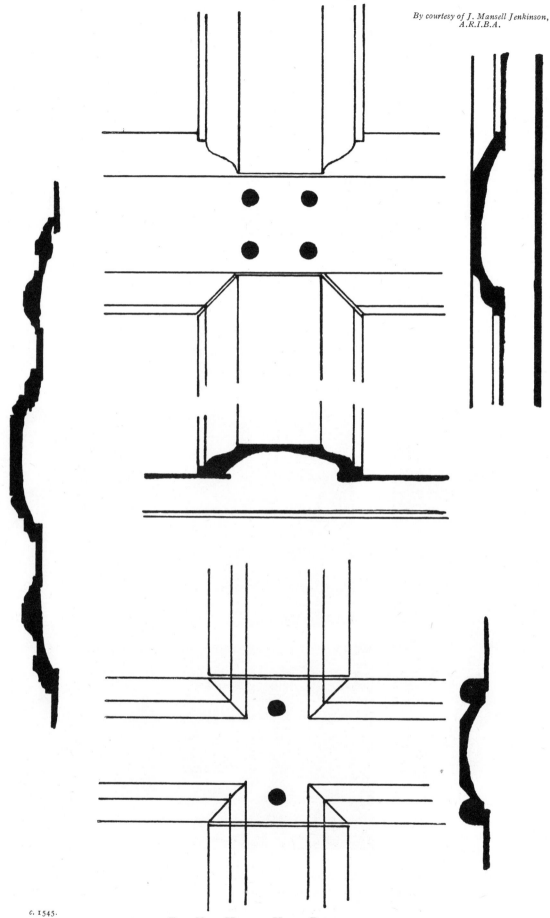

By courtesy of J. Mansell Jenkinson, A.R.I.B.A.

c. 1545.

FIG. 685.—HADDON HALL, DERBYSHIRE.

FIG. 685.—(*Left*) Full-size section of panelling in solar, and (*right*) full-size drawing of two treatments of the panelling in the parlour (see Fig. 619). For other sixteenth-century and seventeenth-century panel moulds see Figs. 697, 698.

By courtesy of the Director of the Victoria and Albert Museum.
By courtesy of J. R. Wigfull, F.R.I.B.A.

Early sixteenth century. *King:* Henry VIII.
FIG. 686.—WALTHAM ABBEY, ESSEX.

c. 1570–90. *Queen:* Elizabeth.
FIG. 687.—HADDON HALL, DERBYSHIRE.

FIG. 686.—Oak panel of Renaissance design; the heads, etc., in roundels with dolphin and other Renaissance ornament.

FIG. 687.—The design of the panelling is exceptionally architectural, and its horizontal lines follow the divisions of the pilasters. It is rare to find such harmony (though ill-proportioned) at so early a date. For interior of gallery see Fig. 622.

c. 1580. *Queen:* Elizabeth.
FIG. 688.—THE OLD HOUSE, SANDWICH, KENT.

FIG. 688.—Detail of the overmantel. The panels show (1) Samson carrying the gates of Gaza and (2) wielding an ass's jaw-bone. The fields of the large panels and of the lower frieze are inlaid, the former with ornament and the latter with spirited silhouettes of hounds. The shafts of the columns are formed of translucent size in which spirals of shavings and wood turnings are embedded before being turned into columns in the lathe. Such work is rarer in England than in the Low Countries, whence it originated.

Linen panels early sixteenth century. Carving and pilasters *d.* 1573.

Queen: Elizabeth.

FIG. 689.—THE PARSONAGE HOUSE, BRENCHLEY, KENT.

FIG. 689.—The ceiling beams and the stone fireplace are late fifteenth or early sixteenth century. The carved mantel and the Ionic pilasters are of the date 1573, which is carved over the doorway. The small square linen panels (with which the room is lined) were refixed at this time. As usual in early examples, where classic pilasters are used to divide the panelling into groups of panels, the horizontal divisions of the pilasters do not correspond with those of the panelling. In this example the pilasters must have been added when the linen panelling was refixed. The detail shows the centre panels, one bearing the arms of the Hendlys and of Elizabeth Fane, by whom the panelling was reconditioned, initialled and dated.

Photo by courtesy of the Victoria and Albert Museum.

c. 1575.   Queen : Elizabeth.   Late sixteenth century.   Queen : Elizabeth.
FIG. 690.—SIZERGH CASTLE.   FIG. 691.—THE LONG GALLERY, MORETON OLD HALL,
                                                        CONGLETON, CHESHIRE.

FIG. 690.—The lower portion of the wind porch is divided into geometrical panels, and the upper portion into arcaded panels between classic columns. The walls, which are of earlier date than the wind porch, are panelled at different heights from the latter, with geometrical panels below and arcaded panels with pilasters above. Most of the large pilasters are divided to correspond with the horizontal divisions of the panelling. The designer has been influenced by Flemish work. The inlay is profuse and is in light and dark poplar and bog oak.

FIG. 691.—The coloured plasterwork of the gable is one of many varieties of the current naturalistic treatment of foliage, and the sententious motto is characteristic of others, as at Earlshall, Fife, and Pinkie House, near Edinburgh. One at Earlshall runs :

> " A nice wife and a back doore
> Oft maketh a riche man poore."

The common rafters are ceiled off at Moreton Old Hall, but show the ornamental cusping of the wind braces.

Early seventeenth century.   King : James I.
FIG. 692.—A plaster panel in the great hall at MONTACUTE HOUSE, SOMERSET.

FIG. 692.—The panel, which contains two scenes in one, depicts the fate of a hen-pecked husband, who was forced to " ride the skimmington." In this case the cause of dissension was that the husband, who had been left in charge of the baby, was caught by his wife surreptitiously drawing beer. She hit him over the head with a shoe, making him drop the spigot, so that the beer continued to run. He is seen vainly trying to stop the leak with his finger. A tell-tale villager standing by informed the neighbours, who seized the unfortunate husband and carried him round the village sitting astride a pole, forcing him to play a pipe to their derisive chanting.

Photo: George Hepworth, Brighouse.

c. 1601–10.   Elizabeth and James I.
FIG. 693.—BURTON AGNES HALL, near BRIDLINGTON, YORKSHIRE.

FIG. 693.—The panelling and doorway are amongst the richest examples of the woodwork of their period, and contrast with the simpler square panels which were constructed during the same period, like those from Exeter (Fig. 701).

Photo: C. E. Keene, Derby.

c. 1597.   *Queen :* Elizabeth.
FIG. 694.—HARDWICK HALL, DERBYSHIRE.

FIG. 694.—Detail of plaster frieze in presence chamber—Diana and her court. Modelled in high relief and coloured in tempera. For interior see Fig. 623.

Copyright photo by permission of Mr. E. W. Attwood.

Sixteenth century.   *Queen :* Elizabeth.

FIG. 695.—3, CORNMARKET STREET, OXFORD, formerly the "CROWN TAVERN."

Photo by courtesy of J. Sanderson Furniss.

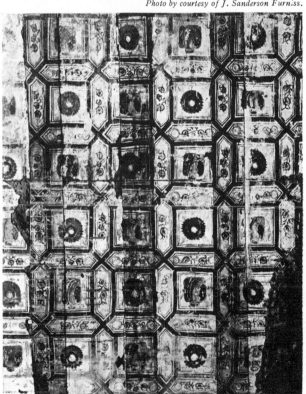

FIG. 695.—Mural painting in colours on orange-red ground. The painting is over the plaster and structural oak timbers, but for many years was hidden by canvas upon which were several layers of wall-papers. Of the usual pious inscriptions there remain " and last of thi rest be thou gods servant for that hold i best. In the mornynge Serve god Devoutlye. Feare god above allthynge and . . . the Kynge." The beautiful fresh condition of the painting and its extent, which enable a complete idea of the room to be formed, make it specially important and interesting.

FIG. 696.—Wall painting applied to a timber and plaster (clay daub) wall, covering both oak studs and panels. White ground. Interlaced octagons in black. The squares contain alternately a flower and seed fruit (pomegranate) in light and dark reds. Foliage in angles green (faded). The hexagons contain foliage in black. The design is a rude variation from that of the ceiling in Cardinal Wolsey's closet, Hampton Court, *c.* 1525 (Fig. 734), but probably of later date.

Sixteenth century   *Queen :* Elizabeth.

FIG. 696.—BARHAM'S MANOR HOUSE, HIGHAM, SUFFOLK.

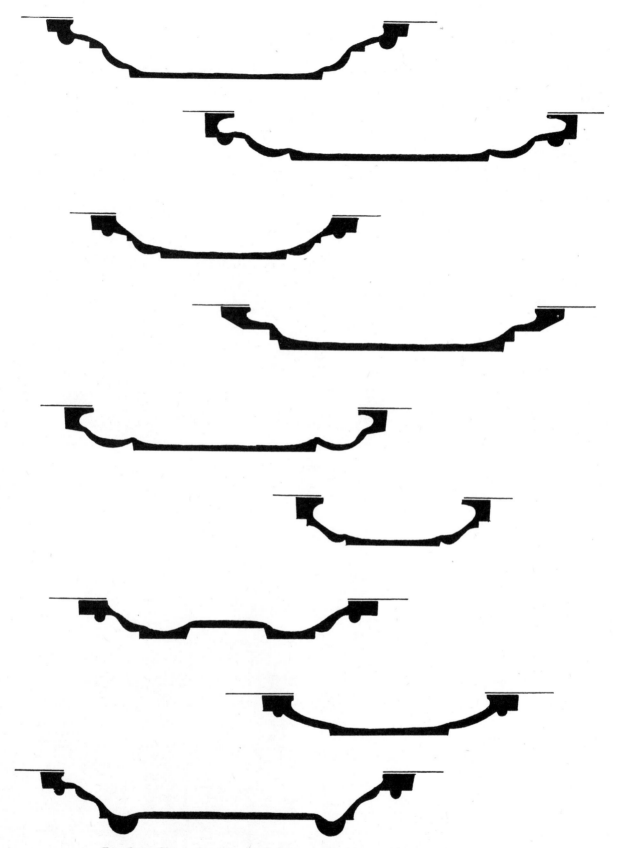

FIG. 697.—Sixteenth-century and seventeenth-century panel moulds (full size).

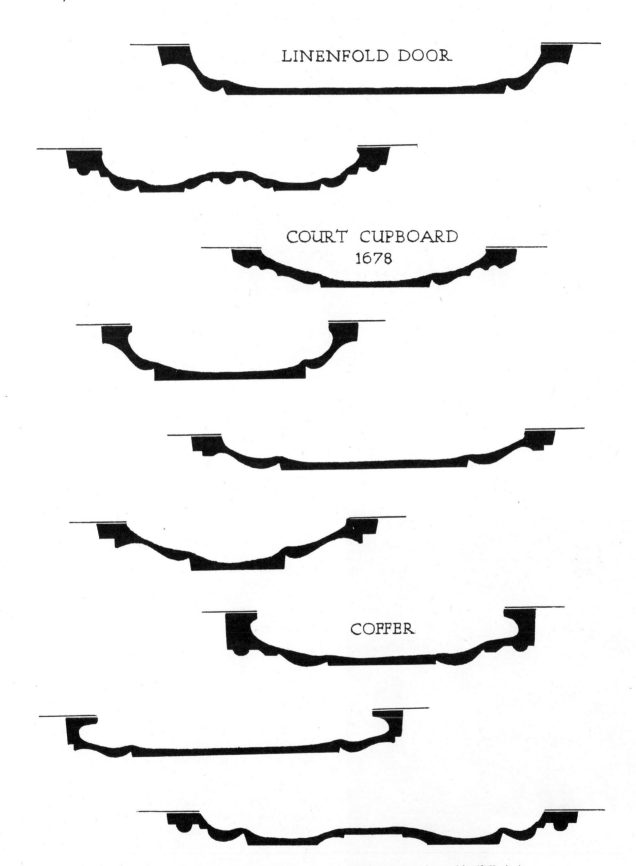

FIG. 698.—Sixteenth-century and seventeenth-century panel moulds (full size).

Early seventeenth century.   *King :* James I.

FIG. 699.—WEST STOW HALL, near BURY ST. EDMUNDS, SUFFOLK.

1618–35.   *King :* Charles I.

FIG. 700.—THE QUEEN'S HOUSE, GREENWICH.

Inigo Jones, *Architect.*

Reproduced by courtesy of the Director of the Victoria and Albert Museum, London

Early seventeenth century.   *King :* James I.

FIG. 701.—Oak panelling from EXETER.

FIG. 699.—Wall painting continued to be a common form of decoration, often floral in treatment, like the Italian-looking frieze illustrated. The subjects of the panel (which is over a fireplace) are : A boy with a hawk on his wrist—" Thus do I all the day." A man and woman courting—" Thus do I while I may." A middle-aged man looking at the couple—" Thus did I when I might." An aged man regarding the others—" Good Lord, will this world last for ever ?"

FIG. 700.—A pilaster enriched with carved and gilded decoration in the same manner as the cornice and ceiling. The wall panels are large and the mouldings slight. Such walls were often hung with tapestries. The development of this decoration towards the pure Italian will be appreciated if compared with the wall treatment in Fig. 701. Reference should be made also to the view looking up in Fig. 743.

FIG. 701.—The simple sunk square panel such as is found in humble manor-houses is here associated with richly carved pilasters and frieze, the ornament of which is of unusually refined character, and shows Italian influence modified by that of the Low Countries. The cabochon in the centre of the pedestal panel anticipates a feature of mature Jacobean work. The extremities of the door hinges are supposed to represent cocks' heads.

c. 1664.

King: Charles II.

FIGS. 702, 703.—An interior window and its panelling at ELTHAM LODGE, KENT.

FIG. 702.—This general view of a window and adjacent woodwork is shown in greater detail in the next figure.

FIG. 703.—Here are shown details of the window architrave, panel moulding, dado capping, wainscot, and the frame for a tapestry panel. The panel is recessed from the general wall surface or, as in this case, from the wainscot. Other wall treatments embodying tapestry are shown in Figs. 416, 789.

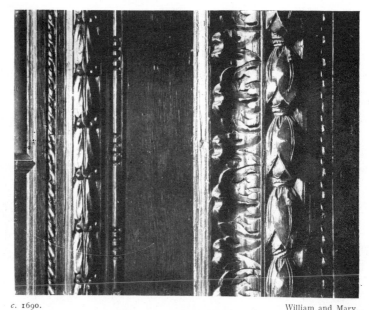

c. 1690   William and Mary

c. 1690.   William and Mary.

FIG. 704.—WILSLEY HOUSE, CRAN-
BROOK, KENT.

FIG. 705.—DENHAM PLACE, BUCKINGHAMSHIRE.

FIG. 704.—Although pictorial paintings on panels were less usual, it was a common practice to paint panelling in flat tints of green, stone, brown, etc. Here is an illustration of bolection-moulded panelling. The framing is painted in an imitation of grey-green marble, the panels with representations of scriptural subjects (painted on the wood), that illustrated being the *Legion* miracle. The paintings appear to be the work of a Fleming or German.

FIG. 705.—Detail of a door architrave in oak-panelled room (see Fig. 423). The mouldings are enriched with carving which is crisp and direct as it came from the tool, but may be compared with the more highly finished work at Hampton Court (Fig. 709).

1670.   *King:* Charles II.
FIG. 706.—HONINGTON HALL, WARWICKSHIRE.

c. 1694.   William and Mary.   c. 1694.   William and Mary   c. 1690.   William and Mary.
FIGS. 707 AND 708.—TRINITY COLLEGE CHAPEL, OXFORD.   FIG. 709.—In the King's Dressing-Room at HAMPTON
                                                                              COURT PALACE.

Reproduced by gracious permission of His Majesty the King.

c. 1690.   William and Mary.   *c.* 1694.   William and Mary.

FIG. 710.—HAMPTON COURT PALACE, MIDDLESEX.   FIG. 711.

FIG. 706.—Leather panels painted with Chinese scenes in colours, the panelling made to fit the leather-work. The use of leather for wall hangings continued in England for another century. Probably most of the material was imported from Spain and Holland, it being a favourite wall decoration in Holland, where it was used not only in panels but as a complete wall covering.

FIG. 707.—Details of bolection mouldings with raised and fielded panels, all in walnut veneers, cross-banded with an inlaid border to the panel. Cross-banding of mouldings (the grain being across the moulding and not parallel with it) is a treatment by which effects of great beauty combined with simplicity are produced. The sash window is of an early type.

FIG. 708.—Details of bolection mouldings with raised and fielded panels, almost identical with those illustrated in Fig. 707, which they adjoin; but in this example they are in oak and are neither cross-banded nor inlaid.

FIG. 709.—Details of an oak door architrave with enriched mouldings in the king's dressing-room. The depth of carving is well suited to the hard wood (oak) to be worked. Although Gibbons achieved remarkable effects in reliefs and undercuttings in oak, these seem better suited to softer woods like pear and lime (Fig. 711).

FIG. 710.—The naturalistic treatment of decorations which is marked in plasterwork extended also to wood. An entirely new treatment of surrounding panels with elaborately carved foliage, flowers, arms, birds, animals, trophies—in fact with almost every conceivable object—was introduced. Although sometimes the carving was in oak, it was more frequently done in some soft wood such as lime or pear and was of extraordinary delicacy and beauty. Such work is associated with the name of Grinling Gibbons, who worked for Hugh May at Cassiobury and at Windsor Castle, and for Wren at St. Paul's Cathedral and at Hampton Court Palace, as did other carvers like William Emmett, who produced similar work; but Grinling Gibbons was pre-eminent. The picture illustrates an example of Grinling Gibbons's carving applied outside the picture-frame moulding.

FIG. 711.—A detail of carving in limewood in the manner of—and probably by—Grinling Gibbons, a native of Rotterdam. Evelyn, who introduced Gibbons to May and to Wren, describes (1683) Gibbons's work at Windsor as " stupendous, and beyond all description the incomparable carving of our Gibbons, who is without controversie the greatest master both for invention and rarenesse of work that the world ever had in any age." In this example in limewood, the boy's hair is remarkably represented, as also are the feathers below the head. Such realism has never been surpassed.

c. 1701-30.   William and Mary.
FIG. 712.—CHICHELEY HALL, BUCKINGHAMSHIRE.

FIG. 712.—The door-case and panelling are in a manner current twenty-five years after the date attributed to the house. The panelling is inlaid with mahogany, cedar, etc. The panels are recessed, but their fields are raised; there are no bolection mouldings as usually seen in panelling of the Wren period. The mirror is a fine example of the late eighteenth century.

FIG. 713.—The large panels have small mouldings, which anticipate abandonment of bolection mouldings hitherto in fashion. The chimney breast is flanked by fluted Corinthian pilasters without pedestals. The oblong panel over the mantelpiece should be filled with a picture. All the workmanship is of the finest character. The marble fireplace is not original. In the panel moulds and the great oval of the ceiling one can trace reversion to the Inigo Jones school by Palladians.

c. 1701.
FIG. 713.—CHICHELEY HALL, BUCKINGHAMSHIRE.

1702-11.

FIG. 714.—The substitution of stucco decoration for panelling was developed by importation of highly skilled Italian stuccoists, and this example is probably the work of Artari or Bagutti. Here stucco is employed as frames to pictorial paintings. At Honington Hall (Fig. 654) the pictorial subjects are of stucco also. The centre panel of the ceiling of this room is illustrated in Fig. 756.

FIG. 714.—EASTON NESTON, TOWCESTER, NORTHAMPTONSHIRE.
Nicholas Hawksmoor, *Architect*.

c. 1702-11.

FIG. 715.—EASTON NESTON, TOWCESTER, NORTHAMPTONSHIRE.
Nicholas Hawksmoor *Architect*.

FIG. 715.—The walls of the staircase well are treated in the Grand Manner, which is evidence of the development of Vanbrugh's influence upon the architect. The walls are designed with a large Corinthian Order, and the spaces between the pilasters are furnished, alternately, with niches containing plaster casts of celebrated statues and with panels "ornamented" by subjects from the life of King Cyrus in chiaroscuro. These were painted by Sir James Thornhill, who was paid 25s. a yard for such work at Blenheim, but only 20s. at Greenwich, though there he received 60s. for painting ceilings.

HAMPTON COURT PALACE
1700

KING'S DRESSING ROOM

HALF FULL SIZE

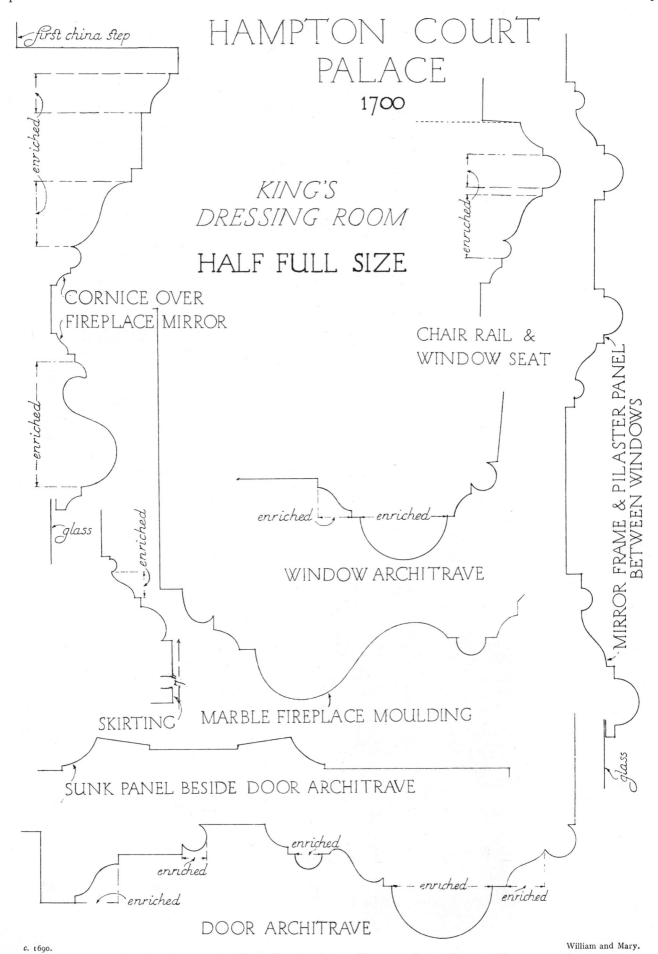

first china step

enriched

CORNICE OVER FIREPLACE MIRROR

CHAIR RAIL & WINDOW SEAT

enriched

enriched

enriched

glass

enriched

WINDOW ARCHITRAVE

MIRROR FRAME & PILASTER PANEL BETWEEN WINDOWS

SKIRTING MARBLE FIREPLACE MOULDING

glass

SUNK PANEL BESIDE DOOR ARCHITRAVE

enriched

enriched

enriched

enriched

enriched

DOOR ARCHITRAVE

c. 1690. William and Mary.

FIG. 716.—Mouldings in the King's Dressing-Room, HAMPTON COURT PALACE (Figs. 709, 792).
Sir Christopher Wren, *Architect.*

Photo : Bedford Lemere and Co.

1723-25.   *King :* George I.   1749.   *King :* George II.
FIG. 717.—MEREWORTH CASTLE, KENT.   FIG. 718.—CHESTERFIELD HOUSE, LONDON, W.
Colen Campbell, *Architect.*   Isaac Ware, *Architect.*

FIG. 717.—Although wainscot was no longer in favour with fashionable Palladian architects, skirtings, dados, and shutters of wood were still in vogue. The egg-and-tongue moulding, like most Palladian mouldings, is large in scale.

FIG. 718.—Detail of rococo wall decoration which the architect unwillingly designed to meet Lord Chesterfield's fancy for the French fashion. The fact was that the impulse of Palladianism was becoming exhausted, as also was the taste for wall decoration by Italian artists, as at Easton Neston (Figs. 650, 714), at Honington Hall (Figs. 654, 851), and at 15, Queen Square, Bath (Fig. 848). Clients seeking novelty found this in the French rococo ornament, although these designs had no rational foundation, either natural, conventional, or geometrical, but consisted of mere scrolls and curves fantastically disposed. Revulsion was inevitable, and the Adam classic revival came so opportunely as immediately to become the fashion.

c. 1777.   *King :* George III.
FIG. 719.—STOWE PARK.
Signor Borra, *Architect.*

FIG. 719.—The panels of the folding doors are on the left, and moulded and carved panels of the wainscot are on the right.

1774.   *King:* George III.

FIG. 720.—BRADBOURNE, LARKFIELD, KENT.

Carved window shutter panels and window architrave in
the drawing-room (the carving of dado and skirting
also in soft wood).

Photo: Bedford Lemere & Co.

c. 1770.   *King:* George III.

FIG. 721.—DRAYTON HOUSE, THRAPSTON,
NORTHAMPTONSHIRE.

c. 1775-76.   *King:* George III.

FIG. 722.—21, PORTLAND PLACE, LONDON.

FIG. 720.—Rich carving (subject to
a host of minor variations) is perhaps
the most excellent production of this
period. The decoration is well placed,
its design has character, and its execution is firm, clear, and sharp. See,
also, the door and panel (Figs. 465,
474, and 476). Although notable
examples of carving exist which were
carried out at this time, as a rule wood
carving was restricted to shutters,
architraves, door casings, and doors.
For wall panelling, stucco usually had
been substituted, for this could be cast
from moulds at little cost, and when
finished was practically indistinguishable from carved and painted wood.

FIG. 721.—Detail of wall panels of
the dining-room (Fig. 660). A fairly
early example of the delicate ornament
in slight relief, but more naturalistic
than most of the Adam ornament. The
stuccoist was William Rhodes.

FIG. 722.—The detail of the stucco
plaque on chimney breast (Fig. 812)
is a typical example of the use of
tablets bearing in relief representations of classic figures. Often these
were ill-placed as spots on a sea of
bare plaster, indicating decadence in
designing.

c. 1777.   *King :* George III.

FIG. 723.—STOWE PARK, BUCKINGHAM.

Signor Borra, *Architect.*

FIG. 723.—The interior decoration in colours and gold was the work of Valdré. For detail of the reverse of door-case see Fig. 719.

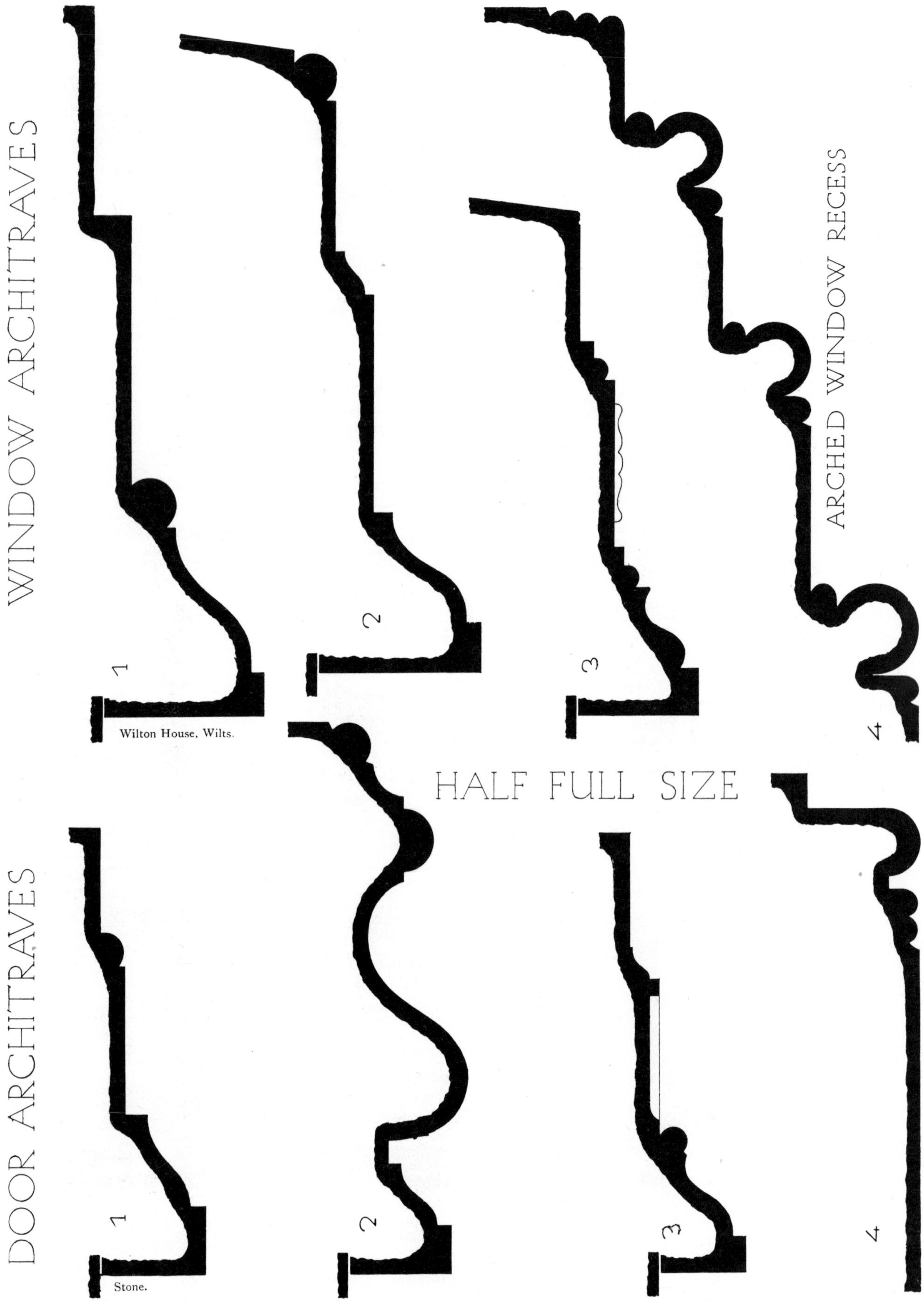
WINDOW ARCHITRAVES
ARCHED WINDOW RECESS
1
2
3
4
Wilton House, Wilts.
HALF FULL SIZE
DOOR ARCHITRAVES
1
2
3
4
Stone.

Fig. 724.—Comparative mouldings by four architects.
(1) Inigo Jones, *c.* 1630; (2) Sir Christopher Wren, *c.* 1690; (3) Robert Adam, *c.* 1770; (4) Sir John Soane, *c.* 1812.

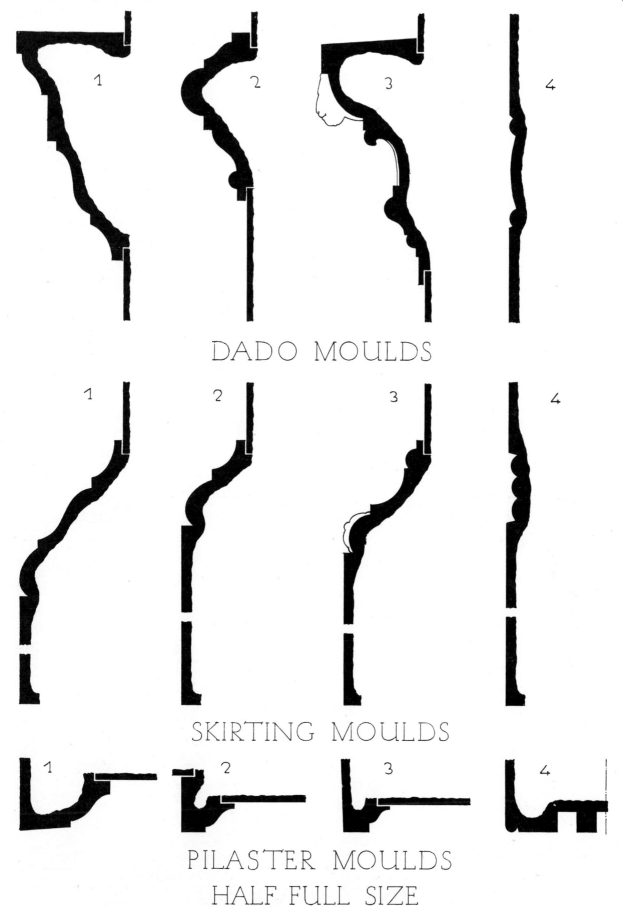

DADO MOULDS

SKIRTING MOULDS

PILASTER MOULDS
HALF FULL SIZE

FIG. 725.—Comparative mouldings by four architects.
(1) The Queen's House, Greenwich; (2) Hampton Court Palace; (3) 20, St. James's Square, S.W.; (4) 13, Lincoln's Inn
Fields, W.C.

No. 20, ST. JAMES'S SQUARE
1772

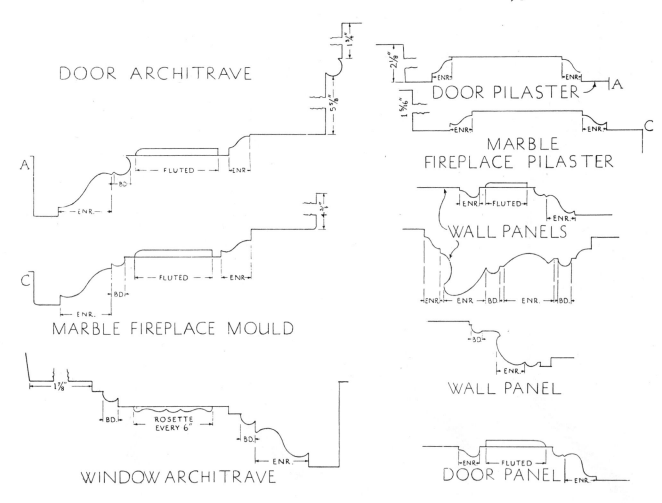

SOANE MUSEUM
1812

MOULDINGS HALF FULL SIZE

FIG. 726.—Various mouldings from 20, ST. JAMES'S SQUARE and 13, LINCOLN'S INN FIELDS, LONDON.

By courtesy of the Director of the Victoria and Albert Museum.

c. 1550-75.   *Queen : Elizabeth.*

FIG. 727.—From a house at BESFORD, WORCESTERSHIRE.

FIG. 727.—An Elizabethan wallpaper, which was pasted to the original wattle and daub plaster panels. Panels, repeated, of the arms of England, Tudor roses, vases of flowers, etc. The similarity of the work to that stencilled or painted direct to plaster is notable (see Figs. 695, 699).

First half of eighteenth century.

FIG. 728.—A hand-painted Chinese wallpaper at RAMSBURY MANOR, WILTSHIRE.

FIG. 728.—The wallpaper and border show Chinese scenery and recreations ; other Chinese papers displayed trees and foliage and birds. Often imported papers were not pasted on the walls, but to canvas mounted on a wooden framework which was fixed to wood plugs in the brick or stone.

By courtesy of the Director of the Victoria and Albert Museum.

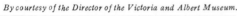

FIG. 729.—Flock wallpaper of large, conventional foliage design. A similar paper covered Verrio's mural paintings in the queen's drawing - room, Hampton Court Palace. The rapid change in fashion indicated is remarkable.

FIG. 730.—Although wallpapers superseded stucco and other relief treatments of walls, classic wall-designs may still be traced, as in this example.

By courtesy of the Director of the Victoria and Albert Museum.

c. 1735.

FIG. 729.—Flock paper from OFFICES OF H.M. PRIVY COUNCIL, LONDON.

Early nineteenth century.

FIG. 730.—SHELSEY BANK, STANFORD BRIDGE, WORCESTERSHIRE.

CEILINGS

For examples of OPEN ROOFS, also for other illustrations of CEILINGS, see—
INTERIORS, pages 352 to 392

Late fifteenth or early sixteenth century. *King:* Henry VII.
FIG. 731.—PAYCOCKE'S HOUSE, COGGES-
HALL, ESSEX.

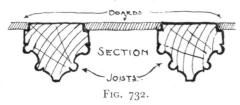

FIG. 732.

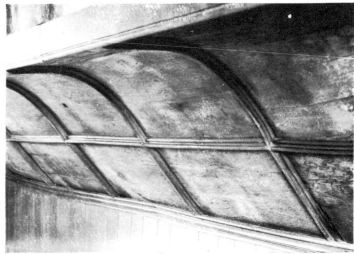

Early sixteenth century.   *King:* Henry VIII.
FIG. 733.—COMPTON WYNYATES, WARWICKSHIRE.

FIG. 731.—The rich carving of the beam soffits
has parallels in other East Anglian houses.   As
in contemporary floors, the spaces between the
joists are about the same as their widths.
Where the beams and joists are not square in
section, they are laid flat, and not on edge as in
modern practice.   These details are sure indications of medieval work.

FIG. 732.—Sometimes joists are rebated for
floorboards as in this section.   In East Anglian
cottages are instances of reeds and plaster
having been used between joists instead of floor
boards.

FIG. 733.—Another ceiling treatment (also
applied to flat ceilings) consisted of thin boarding tongued and grooved, upon which moulded
strips were applied dividing the area into
panels, also shown in Fig. 614.   In this treatment can be seen the forerunner of later
decoration in plaster.   Sometimes carved
wood bosses were introduced at the intersections of the ribs.

c. 1525.   *King:* Henry VIII.
FIG. 734.—Cardinal Wolsey's closet at HAMPTON COURT PALACE.

FIG. 734.—The design of the ceiling and frieze is
Italian in character and is an early example
of this kind of ceiling treatment in England.
The moulded papier-mâché panels are divided
by moulded wood ribs.   The bosses at the
intersections are also of wood, but the leaves
at these angles are of lead.

FIG. 735.—An example of fan vaulting of stone
in the porch at Cowdray House, similar to
that found in fifteenth-century churches.

c. 1525.   *King:* Henry VIII.
FIG. 735.—COWDRAY HOUSE, MIDHURST, SUSSEX.

By courtesy of J. R. Wigfull, F.R.I.B.A.

c. 1530. *King:* Henry VIII.

FIG. 736.—THE ABBOT'S LODGINGS, THAME PARK, OXFORDSHIRE.

c. 1570–90. *Queen:* Elizabeth.

FIG. 737.—HADDON HALL, DERBYSHIRE.

FIG. 736.—Instead of being cut out of the solid oak like the soffit carving of the beams in Fig. 731, the decoration of the beams and frieze in the abbot's chamber is fretted and applied. The character of the design and of the workmanship is Italian. The upper range of wall panels (now whitened) is of oak, carved with roundels and ornament in the manner introduced early in the sixteenth century (see also Fig. 686).

FIG. 737.—Ceiling of the long gallery, showing method of introducing heraldic devices into panels formed by slight ribs. The coat of arms is Manners impaling Vernon.

Photo: George Hepworth, Brighouse.

1580. *Queen:* Elizabeth.

FIG. 738.—THE OLD HOUSE, SANDWICH, KENT.

c. 1575.

FIG. 739.—GILLING CASTLE, YORKSHIRE.

Queen: Elizabeth.

FIG. 738.—The ceiling is divided into three by beams encased in plaster which is moulded and decorated with floral ornament. The intermediate spaces are divided into geometrical panels by slight mouldings, and contain floral and heraldic decorations in high relief. Other ceilings were enriched solely with scrolls, from which branched leaves and fruits.

FIG. 739.—The plaster ceiling is divided into panels, the ribs of which converge to form pendants. In many ceilings the pendants are less pronounced than here.

2D

Early seventeenth century.   *King:* James I.

FIG. 740.—OLD CHARLTON, KENT.

FIG. 740.—Transition ceiling design. The geometrical panels are formed by flat ribs enriched with fruits and flowers in relief and at certain points of intersection converge as pendants. Other ceilings of similar form have no pendants (see Fig. 628). The fields of the panels are filled with strapwork ornament in low relief—a type more fully developed in Fig. 742, where there are no pendants.

d. 1620.   *King:* James I.   First quarter of seventeenth century.   *King:* James I.

FIG. 741.—Ceiling from "THE GOLDEN LION," BARNSTAPLE, DEVON.   FIG. 742.—COMPTON WYNYATES, WARWICKSHIRE.

FIG. 741.—The ceiling in section is, approximately, a semi-hexagon. It is divided up into panels, each containing the representation of an animal. On each side are two cartouches enclosed by strapwork, in each of which a Biblical story is represented—Abraham sacrificing Isaac, The Annunciation, The Adoration, The Temptation. There are three pendants formed of iron, covered with plaster.

FIG. 742.—One revulsion from the prominent detail of Elizabethan ceilings took the form of geometrical panels enclosing strapwork ornament in very low relief, in which were planted rosettes, pellets, and pyramids from a variety of moulds (see Fig. 629).

c. 1618-35.

King : Charles I.

FIG. 743.—THE QUEEN'S HOUSE, GREENWICH.
Inigo Jones, *Architect*.

FIG. 743.—The ceiling of the queen's drawing-room is modelled, carved and gilded ; many of the joints are visible. This illustration also shows the pilaster (another illustration of which is given in Fig. 700) similarly enriched.

Photo from H.M Com. Ancient Mon., Vol. V, London, by courtesy H.M. Stationery Office.

c. 1631.   *King :* Charles I.

Fig. 744.—The Queen's House, Greenwich.
Inigo Jones, *Architect.*

Fig. 744.—Ceiling in the queen's bedroom. Painted (possibly by Gentileschi) in natural colouring. The centre subject is Aurora dispersing the shades of night. In the small panels is the monogram H.M.C.R. In the cove are the arms of France and Stuart impaling France.

Photo from H.M. Com. Ancient Mon., Vol. V, London, by courtesy H.M. Stationery Office.

c. 1631.   *King :* Charles I.

FIG. 745.—THE QUEEN'S HOUSE, GREENWICH.
Inigo Jones, *Architect.*

FIG. 745.—The ceiling of the main room, first floor (like the modillioned cornice), is of plaster. The cornice mouldings are used also round the quatrefoil. The paintings are modern. The fruit and flower enrichments of the trabeations may be compared with those in Fig. 743 in the same house.

c. 1631.   *King:* Charles I.   1656.   Commonwealth.
FIG. 746.—The Queen's boudoir at KEW PALACE.   FIG. 747.—THORPE HALL, near PETERBOROUGH.

FIG. 746.—In this ceiling there are five roundels, each containing an illustration of one of the Senses. The centre one (Hearing) is that illustrated. The ribs dividing the ceiling into geometrical shapes are thin, and the deterioration in the quality of design is apparent.

FIG. 747.—Instead of being divided only into rectangular compartments, as Fig. 743, one rectangle encloses a great ellipse, the enrichment of which is in the form of fruits closely packed together. The double volutes on each side of the rectangle are separated by masks set in drapery.

c. 1662.   *King:* Charles II.
FIG. 748.—COLESHILL, BERKSHIRE.

FIG. 748.—The hall ceiling shown here is more severe in design than that of the saloon (Fig. 634), but its plan is similar. A comparison of the four ceilings of this school illustrated in Figs. 743, 745, 747, 748, with Elizabethan and Jacobean ceilings, will show how utterly the Italian influence differed from them.

c. 1664. *King:* Charles II.

FIG. 749.—Detail of a plaster ceiling at ELTHAM LODGE, KENT.

FIG. 749.—The flowers in the elliptical wreath are tightly packed, as customary at this time, but the foliated scroll border of the great rectangle is treated more loosely and naturally, so anticipating work done later in the century.

c. 1685. William and Mary.

FIG. 750.—BRICKWALL, NORTHIAM, SUSSEX.

c. 1699. William and Mary.

FIG. 751.—RAMPYNDENE, BURWASH, SUSSEX.

FIG. 750.—The tendrils in the plaster ceiling over the staircase are modelled upon lead with plaster whilst still soft, and twined into position before the plaster set; the lead may now be seen where the plaster has broken away. This is an extreme example of the naturalistic forms given to plaster towards the end of the seventeenth century. Sometimes amorini were actually suspended clear from ceilings by wire. Isaac Ware (*Complete Body of Architecture*, published 1756, p. 496) wrote of this treatment: "We see boys hung up whole by the back in some coarse old ceilings; and this the architects thought bold and fine: but they always look clumsy, and seem in danger of falling."

FIG. 751.—The plaster ceiling of the entrance hall is the work of a country plasterer. The free and natural treatment of fruit, flowers, and foliage current at this period may be compared with the closely packed handling of those in Figs. 743, 747.

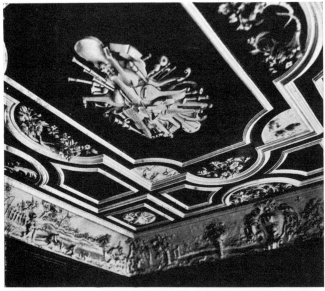

c. 1693. William and Mary. Built 1694. Painted ceiling and walls by Verrio, 1704.
FIG. 752.—DENHAM PLACE, BUCKINGHAMSHIRE. FIG. 753.—The Queen's Drawing-Room, HAMPTON COURT
PALACE.

FIG. 752.—Plaster ceiling divided into many compartments. The centre contains a trophy of musical instruments ; each angle, game-birds ; and the four squares in the corners, representations of the seasons. The coving is filled with sporting and fishing scenes in relief, with shells bearing armorial charges in the centre of each side. The ceiling and some armorials are coloured ; the scenes in the cove are white.

FIG. 753.—Painted ceilings—allegorical subjects combined with current scenes (of the British Navy) and scenes in which the patron (in this case, Queen Anne) appeared—are found in many houses of the first third of the eighteenth century. Other decorations and pictorial paintings in the palace were by Sir James Thornhill and by Robert Streater the sergeant painter, who also undertook ordinary painters' work. This practice of painting ceilings with scenes and life-size figures did not escape contemporary criticisms, of which the following are typical instances : " Great Verrio's hand hath drawn the gods in dwellings brighter than their own."—THOMAS TICKELL. And, less complimentary, " On painted ceilings you devoutly stare where sprawl the saints of Verrio and Laguerre."—ALEXANDER POPE.

1723–5. *King : George I.* 1723–5. *King : George I.*
FIG. 754.—MEREWORTH CASTLE, KENT. FIG. 755.—MEREWORTH CASTLE, KENT.

FIG. 754.—The interior of the dome shows the aperture of one of the circular windows (see Figs. 221, 222).
FIG. 755.—The ceiling of the gallery which occupies the whole of the south front. The frieze is decorated with stucco ornament, the cove is painted to represent ornament in relief, and the ceiling has panels containing paintings.

1730.   *King:* George II.

FIG. 756.—EASTON NESTON, TOWCESTER,
NORTHAMPTONSHIRE.

Photo by courtesy of Hampton and Sons.

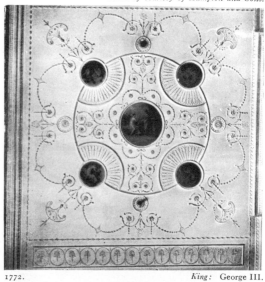

1772.   *King:* George III.

FIG. 757.—20, ST. JAMES'S SQUARE, LONDON.
Robert Adam, *Architect.*

FIG. 756.—The elliptic plaster panel in the centre of the ceiling (after Titian's *Venus and Adonis*) in the south-east room, now the dining-room, is probably by Artari or Bagutti. The spandrels are decorated with sporting accessories, and so are in keeping with the subjects of the pictures employed for the decoration of the walls (see Fig. 650).

FIG. 757.—Not only were ceiling panels furnished with paintings (as these are, in the manner of Angelica Kauffmann), but similar panels were also incorporated in schemes of wall decoration (Figs. 655, 660).

c. 1763.   *King:* George III.

FIG. 758.—MOOR PARK, HERTFORDSHIRE.

FIG. 758.—A ceiling with paintings by Cipriani. The late eighteenth-century division into compartments compares unfavourably with division of earlier ceilings (Figs. 745, 751, 752).

Photo by courtesy of the London County Council.

c. 1760.   King : George III.

FIG. 759.—PEMBROKE HOUSE, No. 7, WHITEHALL GARDENS, LONDON, S.W. 1.
Sir William Chambers, *Architect.*

FIG. 759.—The ceiling of the salon (the original coloured design for which by
Chambers is in the Victoria and Albert Museum) is a combination of formal and
floral ornaments geometrically disposed in compartments picked out in gold.

Reproduced from " The Works of Architecture of Robert and James Adam."

c. 1773.   King : George III.

FIG. 760.—No. 26, GROSVENOR SQUARE, W. 1.   (Since destroyed.)
R. and J. Adam, *Architects.*

FIG. 760.—An example of " Etruscan decoration," which was usually carried out
in yellow, red, brown, and black on a white ground.

FIREPLACES

For other examples of FIREPLACES see—
INTERIORS, pages 352 to 392

Photo: W. Lee, Grantham.

c. 1130.   *King:* Henry I.

FIG. 761.—A fireplace at ROCHESTER CASTLE, KENT.

c. 1180.   *King:* Henry II.

FIG. 762.—BOOTHBY PAGNELL MANOR HOUSE, LINCOLNSHIRE.

FIG. 761.—The fireplaces at Rochester (Fig. 761) and Castle Hedingham (Figs. 579 and 580) were semicircular in plan and had semicircular moulded arches. FIG. 762.—The stone hood has a joggled lintel carried on corbels.

Photo: W. J. Vasey, Abingdon.

c. 1240.   *King:* Henry III.

FIG. 763.—STOKESAY CASTLE, SHROP-SHIRE.

c. 1250.   *King:* Henry III.

FIG. 764.—LUDDESDOWN MANOR, KENT.

Late thirteenth century.   *King:* Edward I.

FIG. 765.—ABINGDON ABBEY, BERK-SHIRE.

FIGS. 763 AND 765.—In the thirteenth century, when the hall was on the ground floor as at Winchester and Stokesay Castles, the fire was usually on an open hearth near the centre of the floor, as at Penshurst (Fig. 769), and smoke found its way out through a louvre in the roof. But first-floor chambers had wall fireplaces and flues similar to those in Figs. 763, 764, 765. In the fireplace in a first-floor room at the lower end of the Great Hall of Stokesay Castle (Fig. 763), the Early English columns and corbels support a wooden frame from which sprung the semi-pyramidal hood which contracted into the square flue. This hood was probably made of timber and lined with clay or plaster. The short flue terminates in a stone chimney, open at the top, and is one of the pair which can be seen in Fig. 53. The fireplace in the Abbot's Parlour, Abingdon Abbey (Fig. 765) had a stone lintel and hood, after the fashion of that at Boothby Pagnell Manor House (Fig. 762). The shaft capitals have leaf ornament of Early English character like some Norman castle fireplaces; the hearth is very small and suggests that the wood fuel must have been piled up high on end. The use of timber and clay or plaster for fireplace hoods and for flues was common practice in the Middle Ages. Henry III ordered one to be made in his wardrobe at Windsor.[1]

FIG. 764.—Stone fireplace. The joggled lintel has not collapsed, although the mortar has perished.

[1] Rot. Pip. 20, Henry III.

Photo: G. H.Tyndall, Ely.

c. 1320.   King: Edward II.   c. 1325.   King: Edward II.

FIG. 766.—THE ABBOT'S KITCHEN, GLASTONBURY,   FIG. 767.—THE PRIOR'S HOUSE,
                    SOMERSET.   ELY, CAMBRIDGESHIRE.

FIG. 766.—One of the four fireplaces which occupy four sides of an octagonal plan; the other four sides contain the windows.   The kitchen is now used as a storehouse for architectural details.

FIG. 767.—The illustration of exceptionally elaborate work is apt to be misleading in such a history as this, where the object is to present typical everyday examples, but this chimneypiece in Prior Crauden's room is so characteristic in its form and construction that these cannot be veiled by the elaborate decoration.   The corbelling out from the jambs for the support of the hood which was shown at Stokesay Castle (Fig. 763) and at Luddesdown (Fig. 764) is here developed into figures, and a supporting mask bears the angle shelf.   Crenellations applied ornamentally to details came in with the Decorated period to which the geometrical tracery also belongs.

c. 1340.   King: Edward III.   c. 1341 and later.   King: Edward III.

FIG. 768.—THE MANOR HOUSE,   FIG. 769.—PENSHURST PLACE, KENT.
        MEARE, SOMERSET.

FIG. 768.—The fine stone hood of the hall fireplace is reminiscent of Continental work, but, unlike these, has no armorials painted on its surface.   The stone lintel is in one piece, not built up, as are those at Boothby Pagnell and Luddesdown (Figs. 762 and 764).   The angle bracket almost always found in medieval fireplaces may have been used to support a light.

FIG. 769.—The central hearth was a survival from primitive times continued during the medieval period in those halls which had no fireplaces or chimneys, as was generally the case when the halls were on the ground-floor level.   That at Penshurst continued in use up to recent times.   The andirons are of sixteenth-century design, but may be regarded as replacing earlier ones which served the same purpose.   This is almost the only surviving example of what was the commonest type of hearth during the medieval period.

FIG. 770.—THE FISH HOUSE, MEARE, SOMERSET.

FIG. 770.—The type of fireplace having a four-centred arch became general in the fifteenth century.

FIG. 771:—An instance of a hall on ground level which had a wall fireplace and not a central hearth.

c. 1465.   *King:* Edward IV
FIG. 771.—The fireplace in the hall at OCKWELLS MANOR. BRAY. BERKSHIRE.

FIG. 772.—A fireplace at THORNBURY CASTLE, GLOUCESTERSHIRE.

FIG. 772.—A typical fifteenth-century example built early in the sixteenth century, the only development being the flattening of the four-centred arch. Most of these mantels lack the quatrefoils and armorials with which this one is enriched.

c. 1589.   *Queen: Elizabeth.*   c. 1550.   *Queen: Elizabeth.*   c. 1580.   *Queen: Elizabeth.*

FIG. 773.—MORETON OLD HALL,   FIG. 774.—THE OLD HOUSE, SANDWICH,   FIG. 775.—THE OLD HOUSE, SANDWICH,
CHESHIRE.   KENT.   KENT.

FIG. 773.—This fireplace is a typical example of ill-proportioned Low Country design, as interpreted in plaster by an ill-instructed English craftsman.

FIG. 774.—The Elizabethan oak mantelpiece frequently consisted of columns or pilasters designed in one or other of the Orders, with a lintel over the opening. The overmantel was divided into two or three panels by columns or pilasters, and surmounted by a frieze and cornice (see Fig. 688). The panelling with which this room is lined has small squares, but is divided at intervals by fluted pilasters, and completed by a frieze and cornice. It should be noted that the horizontal divisions of the panelling bear no relation to those of the pilasters.

FIG. 775.—The country workman, who obtained ideas for designs from Flemish pattern books, often included human figures, the carving of which proved beyond his abilities. Adam and Eve, and other scriptural and allegorical characters, were favourite themes, while now and then the employer's effigy, or even that of the carver himself, was introduced.

c. 1580.   *Queen: Elizabeth.*

FIG. 776.—LITTLE DIXTER, NORTHIAM, SUSSEX.

FIG. 776.—Open fireplace with oak chimneybeam (the hood later), and cupboard in the brickwork for storage of tinder and kindling. When (early in the seventeenth century) open-roofed halls had floors inserted and the floors divided up into chambers, such chimneys and fireplaces were built at the same time, usually with oak lintels, plain as this or moulded and carved as Fig. 782.

c. 1599.   *Queen :* Elizabeth.   *c.* 1599   *Queen :* Elizabeth.   Late sixteenth or early seventeenth century.

FIG. 777.—MONTACUTE HOUSE,   FIG. 778.—COBHAM HALL,   FIG. 779.—UPPER SWELL MANOR,
        SOMERSET.   KENT.   GLOUCESTERSHIRE.

FIG. 777.—Although the arch and its mouldings are still of the Tudor type, the mantelpiece is of classic design. The small panelling with which the room is lined varies in the sizes of its squares, which are not yet disposed in orderly fashion. Whether the armorial treatment in the centre of the overmantel is part of the original scheme or not, like most heraldic design, it is effective.

FIG. 778.—An instance of the ability of an imported foreign artist is illustrated in the mantelpieces at Cobham Hall, carved by Ghiles de Witt. Incised work similar to that in the lower frieze and in the large panel is found locally in mantels of other houses in Kent. See also Fig. 787.

FIG. 779.—The fireplace and the plasterwork of the ceiling belong to the period of the house. The fireplace, which is Flemish in the character of its design and detail, is of a type uncommon in England. The plaster ceiling is divided into panels by slightly raised framing, the spaces between the borders of which are filled with vine pattern. The framing has not assumed the character and projection of beams, and the panels contain small ornamental and heraldic devices symmetrically arranged.

Photo : George Hepworth, Brighouse.   *Photo : Gibson, Hexham.*

d. 1595.   *Queen :* Elizabeth.   Late sixteenth century   *Queen :* Elizabeth.
FIG. 780.—BORWICK HALL, CARNFORTH, LANCASHIRE.   FIG. 781.—LUMLEY CASTLE, DURHAM.

FIG. 780.—Although the form of the fireplace is of the preceding century, the details show its later date.

FIG. 781.—The general design of this hall fireplace is classic as interpreted by north country crafts-men, and provides yet another variation of the column, lintel and pediment *motif*. All the carving is shallow, probably due to the hardness of the local stone.

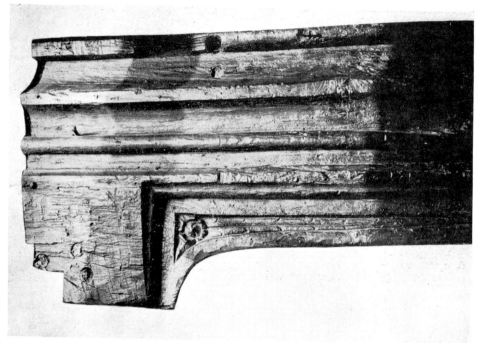

End of the sixteenth century.   *Queen:* Elizabeth.
FIG. 782.—STRAWBERRY HOLE FARM, NORTHIAM, SUSSEX.

FIG. 782.—End of oak chimney beam over open fireplace of same type as in Fig. 776. The mouldings are of the same character as found on large beams in halls of the fifteenth and early sixteenth centuries, as that in the end wall in Fig. 608, where the crenellations have been cut in the uppermost member.

c. 1625.   *King:* James I.
FIG. 783.—LITTLE WOLFORD MANOR, WARWICKSHIRE. Fireplace, jambs and lintel sixteenth century; overmantel *c.* 1625, Jacobean manner; panelling *c.* 1625, Jacobean manner.

c. 1636.   *King:* Charles I.
FIG. 784.—HOUSE AT GREAT WELDON, NORTHANTS.

FIG. 783.—An instance of two periods in one detail.

FIG. 784.—In this fireplace (from a small house of good design) the use of the Tudor arch and stops to the moulds is continued. The mantel has crudely moulded corbels, fluted frieze, and crude cornice, which show that the native craftsman had only an imperfect acquaintance with the new manner. The duck's-nest grate is of late eighteenth-century type, of which it is a good example.

c. 1605.   *King:* James I.

FIG. 785.—KNOLE, SEVENOAKS, KENT.

c. 1607.   *King:* James I.

FIG. 786.—CHARLTON HOUSE, KENT.

FIG. 785.—Skilled foreign workmen were brought to England to produce magnificent marble chimneypieces. One is illustrated in Fig. 778. There is a fine one in the solar at Knole (Fig. 628). The pair of andirons (boys carrying baskets on their heads) are of silver and dated 1696.

FIG. 786.—A plaster mantel in which are incorporated designs from Flemish pattern books. The scene in the elliptical panel— Perseus holding Medusa's head—is taken from a design by Abraham de Bruyn, while the other details are typical Flemish features.

FIG. 787.—A mantel in black marble, decorated with incised strapwork. Floral and geometrical designs are frequently found both in the full dress of an Order and in its more simple forms.

c. 1607.   *King:* James I.

FIG. 787.—CHARLTON HOUSE, KENT.

Photo by courtesy of Director of Victoria and Albert Museum.

c. 1620. *King :* James I.

FIG. 788.—Mantel from a house in LIME STREET, LONDON, W.C.

c. 1664. *King :* Charles II.

FIG. 789.—ELTHAM LODGE, KENT.
Hugh May, *Architect.*

c. 1656. Commonwealth.

FIG. 790.—THORPE HALL, near PETERBOROUGH.

FIG. 788.—The heavy profuseness of Elizabethan decoration (Figs. 775, 786), which reached its greatest development in the early seventeenth century, gave place to more simple ornaments, characterised by application of strapwork, split balusters, pendants, and cabochon to woodwork and representations of the same worked on stone. For jambs, caryatides and atlantes have been simplified into pilasters.

FIG. 789.—The mouldings and carvings of the frame to the picture and of the cornice are contemporary with the house. The bolection moulding of the fireplace is of a type which became universal during the latter part of the seventeenth century. Such panelling was often painted and grained.

FIG. 790.—The hall fireplace and overmantel are treated as one composition, the display of the owner's arms being the chief feature.

c. 1685.   *King:* Charles II.
FIG. 791.—BRICKWALL, NORTHIAM,
SUSSEX.

c. 1690.   William and Mary.
FIG. 792.—HAMPTON COURT
PALACE.

c. 1700.   William and Mary.
FIG. 793.—DRAYTON HOUSE,
NORTHANTS.

FIG. 791.—With bold bolection mouldings of marble, stone, or wood, came a reaction from the elaborate overmantel of pre-Restoration fashion. Sometimes there was a narrow shelf over the lintel, as in Fig. 640, or steps for the display of china, as in Figs. 792, 793, but often neither. Sometimes there was an oblong panel which might contain a mirror or picture, as Fig. 789, but wide mirrors of little height in carved and gilded frames were fashionable. These were usually made up of three pieces of glass, as that illustrated (Fig. 791), though the objects reflected confuse the divisions. The rococo fireback is in later style than the fire-basket.

FIG. 792.—The treatment of the panel moulds shows that this corner fireplace with china steps over, in the King's Dressing-room, was designed for the position in which it stands. Corner fireplaces afforded opportunities for overmantel designs, including china steps. (For details of the mouldings in this room, see Figs. 709, 716.)

FIG. 793.—The corner fireplace in the Duchess of Norfolk's closet has a marble bolection moulding, and the wainscot is decorated with the sunk panels which both preceded and superseded the raised and fielded panels, but one panel (that with the shield hung on it) has a bolection moulding. The ceiling decoration is contemporary, and all the woodwork is painted. The floor is inlaid with parquetry

FIG. 794.—The chimneypiece in the gallery is of the type described by Ware as a " Continued chimneypiece suited to a Drawing Room " (*A Complete Body of Architecture*, by Isaac Ware, London, 1756, p. 555), because the composition is continued up to the ceiling as distinguished from a " simple chimneypiece " which ends at the shelf (Fig. 801) or pediment at shelf level (Fig. 799). The simple treatment of the marble mantel is notable in this richly decorated room.

FIG. 795.—This corner fireplace, of wood, in the west bedchamber, is painted and the enrichments are gilded.

1723–25.   *King:* George I.
FIG. 794.—MEREWORTH CASTLE, KENT.
Colen Campbell *Architect.*

c. 1723–25.   *King:* George I.
FIG. 795.—MEREWORTH CASTLE.
Colen Campbell, *Architect.*

Photo by courtesy of F. R. Yerbury.

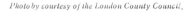

c. 1714.   *Queen: Anne.*

FIG. 796.—CASTLE HOWARD, YORKSHIRE.
Sir John Vanbrugh, *Architect.*

1725.   *King: George I.*

FIG. 797.—CADOGAN HOUSE, WHITEHALL
YARD, LONDON, S.W. 1.
Attributed to William Kent, *Architect.*

FIG. 796.—Fireplace in the great hall, the decoration of which is by an Italian stucco worker and is carried out in stucco. The marble architrave has the big bolection moulding of seventeenth-century mantels, but varied in having a serpentine curve to the lintel.

FIG. 797.—Chimneypiece of white statuary marble, having egg and leaf moulded architrave. The moulded shelf is supported by sculptured thermæ or "Termini" as Ware calls them. The continuation is in the form of a carved wood frame enclosing a painting of the Toilet of Venus. Other chimneypieces have complete male or female figures as supporters.

FIG. 798.—Such monumental fireplaces as the marble fireplace in the Cube Room are characteristic of interior details of the palatial houses built for peers (as at Houghton, in Norfolk, Fig. 649, and elsewhere) in which coloured marbles were used; special prominence was also given to white statuary marble, the working of which reached a high level of excellence.

1726.   *King: George I.*

FIG. 798.—SUDBROOKE PARK, RICHMOND, SURREY.
James Gibbs, *Architect.*

FIG. 799.—EASTON NESTON, TOWCESTER.

FIG. 800.—ST. SWITHIN'S HOUSE, LEWES,
SUSSEX.

FIG. 799.—The marble mantelpiece in the south-east room is designed in the manner of William Kent and is constructed of Carrara and " black and gold " marbles.

FIG. 800.—The fireplace and panelling are painted. Such frames as that over the mantelpiece often enclosed a picture of fruit, flowers, or other " still life " subjects, or of a landscape.

FIG. 801.—HONINGTON HALL, WARWICKSHIRE.

FIG. 802.—THAME PARK, OXFORD-
SHIRE.

FIG. 801.—The drawing-room mantelpiece. About the middle of the eighteenth century we find a rectangular tablet impaled upon the friezes of fireplaces. Such a tablet projects slightly, and the shelf cornice breaks round it. Often the field of the tablet is carved with fruit, flowers, game, or trophies in high relief.

FIG. 802.—A " continued " mantelpiece in a bedroom. The early nineteenth-century grate is " in the Gothic taste." Architects paid careful attention to the selection of materials and designs for these chimneypieces. For a wide mantel in a stateroom they were lavish, as at Mereworth (Fig. 794), at Castle Howard (Fig. 796), and at Thame Park (Fig. 803). When, however, the mantel was narrow and in an unimportant apartment, they used painted wood and simplified the design and enrichments. Ware lays stress upon these distinctions.

By courtesy of the Director of the Victoria and Albert Museum.

1745.   *King : George II.*

FIG. 803.—THAME PARK, OXFORDSHIRE.

c. 1750.   *King : George II.*

FIG. 804.—Continued chimneypiece from
WINCHESTER HOUSE, PUTNEY, S.W.

FIG. 803.—The illustration shows the hall fireplace and the decoration of stucco ornament applied to the walls, which are divided into large shallow panels with enriched mouldings. Although the treatment is distinctly baroque, it has not yet passed into the fantasies of the French rococo, as in Fig. 804. Architects designed chimneypieces with relation to the doorcases and to the decorations of the rooms, thereby ensuring unity which contributed to the satisfactory results they achieved, of which no better instance could be found than this hall. Isaac Ware, in *The Complete Body of Architecture*, p. 587, instructs young architects who design continued chimneypieces " to raise an ornament like that of other parts of the room from the chimney-piece to the cieling ; and in such manner to adapt this to the chimney-piece itself, that it shall seem naturally to rise from it, and to be connected with it, that it shall be a regular and proportioned part of the chimney-work, at the same time that it is also a regular part of the ornament of the room."

FIG. 804.—Carved pine and marble in the French taste. An illustration of the extreme to which rococo design was carried. In this taste we see revulsion from the formality of Palladianism before it, in its turn, was superseded by novelties introduced by the brothers Adam.

FIG. 805.—Carved wood or marble mantelpieces frequently had a head of Aurora carved on the tablet in the centre of the frieze. Such woodwork was intended to be painted, not stripped and waxed as is often seen now. The interior is modern.

c. 1755.   *King : George II.*

FIG. 805.

Photo by courtesy of Hampton and Sons.

Before 1774.

1772.   King: George III.

FIG. 806.

From "The Practical Builder or Workman's General Assistant," by William Pain, Architect and Joiner,1774.

FIG. 807.—No. 20, St. James's Square, London.
Robert Adam, *Architect.*

FIG. 806.—Two designs for " Continued chimney Pieces," here termed " Chimney Piece with open pediment, Glass or Picture frames ornamented." Carpenter-architects (of whom William Pain was the most important) furnished designs both in the Palladian manner and in the lighter style in fashion in 1774. This illustration might have come from Isaac Ware's *Complete Body of Architecture*, 1756, and, no doubt, was inspired by it. Earlier writers, as Thomas Rawlins, Architect, whose *Familiar Architecture* was published in 1768, illustrated only the Palladian chimneypieces.

FIG. 807.—Many marble mantels at this time had pictorial tablets. The example illustrated is genuine, but often they have been added by modern fakers.

Photo by courtesy of Hampton and Sons.   *Photo by courtesy of Hampton and Sons.*

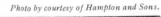

1772.   King: George III.   1772.   King: George III

FIG. 808.—No. 20, St. James's Square.
Robert Adam, *Architect.*

FIG. 809.—No. 20, St. James's Square.
Robert Adam, *Architect.*

FIG. 808.—A white marble mantel, the pilasters and frieze of which are panelled and filled with sculpture.

FIG. 809.—The ram's head was a favourite form of enrichment for consoles. It is similarly used on those of the doorways (Figs. 461, 465). By this date the mantel-shelf had been made wide enough for a mirror to stand on it and for ornaments to stand in front of the mirror. The sculpture and inlays were characterized by delicacy of design and the workmanship was never crude, as was much Jacobean work.

Photo: Bedford Lemere & Co.

c. 1775.   *King:* George III.

FIG. 810.—BRADBOURNE, LARK-FIELD, KENT.

Late eighteenth century.   *King:* George III.

FIG. 811.—No. 13, DEVONSHIRE PLACE, LONDON.

1775–76.   *King:* George III.

FIG. 812.—No. 21, PORTLAND PLACE, LONDON, W.

FIG. 810.—A coloured marble mantel in the Adam manner, with its original mirror frame over, which is also characteristic of his work. The iron firegrate is of nineteenth-century date.

FIG. 811.—A fireplace in the entrance hall, of white statuary marble, with a "duck's nest" grate of contemporary design.

FIG. 812.—One treatment of walls was to form stucco panels on them and to fill the panel over the mantelpiece (often others also, see Figs. 655, 660, 665) with pictorial or floral stucco ornament. This form of decoration had superseded the "continued" mantelpiece beloved of the Palladians. The flutes of the marble mantel (by James or Robert Adam) were filled with coloured marble or with composition. The tile lining round the grate is modern.

1780.   *King:* George III.

FIG. 813.—"The Marine Chimneypiece."

1812.   *King:* George III.

FIG. 814.—No. 13, LINCOLN'S INN FIELDS, LONDON, W.C. 2.

Sir John Soane, *Architect.*

FIG. 813.—A mantelpiece of wood, carved and painted. The sea-trophies ornament of the frieze was usually modelled in gesso and applied. Repetitive ornament, such as swags or festoons of husk pattern, paterae, etc., were sometimes cast in pewter or other soft metal, applied to the wood and then painted. Grate c. 1830, but the pierced apron is added.

FIG. 814.—Mantelpiece of white marble. The shallow incised lines, square paterae at angles, and severe rectangular treatment, are characteristic of Soane's ornament. The grate is contemporary.

STAIRCASES

For other examples of STAIRCASES see—
INTERIORS, pages 352 to 392

c. 1130.　　　　　　*King:* Henry I.

FIG. 815.—ROCHESTER CASTLE, KENT.

c. 1260-80.　　　*Kings:* Henry III, Edward I.

FIG. 816.—LITTLE WENHAM HALL, SUFFOLK.

c. 1300.　　　　　*King:* Edward I.

FIG. 817.—OLD SOAR, PLAXTOL, KENT.

FIG. 815.—The winding stairs in the Keep at Rochester Castle.

FIG. 816.—An internal newel staircase of stone at Little Wenham Hall, which starts in the ground-floor chamber and rises to the roof. Most internal stairs of this period were circular, and those outside, whether of stone or wood, usually were straight, or had one turn.

FIG. 817.—The stairs up to the hall at Old Soar (housed in a semicircular turret, see Figs. 59, 60) are here seen through the ground-floor doorway, which has outer and inner arches. The door is shown opened back into a recess. The door and metal work are ancient.

c. 1300.　　　　　　*King:* Edward I.

FIG. 818.—OLD SOAR.

c. 1341.　　　　　*King:* Edward III.

FIG. 819.—PENSHURST PLACE, KENT.

FIG. 818.—The stairway down from the hall has the first four steps in the hall itself (see plan, Fig. 60), then continues within the semicircular turret. It is lighted by a crossloop. The door (shown partially closed) actually opens back into a recess in the wall made to fit it and to leave the stairway clear. It shuts towards the hall, so that anyone wishing to force a way in could not open it towards the hall, but must destroy the door to pass it.

FIG. 819.—The stairway from the great hall to the solar is octagonal in plan, and rises from the south end of the dais. The small doorway leads down to the vaulted basement.

From " A History of English Brickwork."

c. 1494.   *King :* Henry VII.

FIG. 820.—FAULKBOURNE HALL, ESSEX.

Early sixteenth century.   *King :* Henry VIII.

FIG. 821.—ST. CROSS HOSPITAL, WINCHESTER.

Mid-sixteenth century.   *Queen :* Mary.

FIG. 822.—LITTLE WOLFORD MANOR.

FIG. 820.—Fifteenth-century stairs were still of the newel type, sometimes being built of brick, which called for considerable skill in setting out the vaulting. Moulded handrails in brick (as in this illustration) or of stone were common. In extensive buildings like Bodiam Castle there were many of these circular stairs, for planning had not reached the development of linking up apartments by passages.

FIG. 821.—Stairs still were contrived in restricted spaces, partitioned by rudely framed panelling; the mitres of the framing being mason's mitres (see Fig. 20, page 26). Many of the stairs are solid blocks of oak.

FIG. 822.—Doorway and stairs from hall to solar. The doorway mouldings are large and coarse. The new stairs of stone are more spacious than earlier ones, but generally had been superseded by wood. The ample, decorative staircases belong to the end of this century.

Photo : George Hepworth, Brighouse.

Late sixteenth century.   *Queen :* Elizabeth.

FIG. 823.—CHURCH HOUSE, NORTHIAM, SUSSEX.

End of sixteenth century.   *Queen :* Elizabeth.

FIG. 824.—OCKWELLS MANOR, BRAY, BERKSHIRE.

c. 1595.   *Queen :* Elizabeth.

FIG. 825.—BORWICK HALL, CARNFORTH. LANCS.

FIG. 823.—The stair balustrade in a farmhouse shown here is the work of a country workman; it has characteristic terminals to the newels. Many variations of its double baluster were current at this period.

FIG. 824.—A late Elizabethan addition to the fifteenth-century house. Although an early example of the spacious staircase, its simplicity contrasts with the greater elaboration of seventeenth-century examples (Figs. 828, 831)

FIG. 825.—Although it is doubtful how much of this external stair and gallery are of the same date as the house, such external access is typical of contemporary buildings. Familiar instances are the galleried court-yards of old inns, mostly destroyed, but of which many illustrations exist.

c. 1634. King : Charles I.

FIG. 826.—BATEMANS, BURWASH, SUSSEX.

c. 1641. King : Charles I.

FIG. 827.—GREAT WIGSELL, BODIAM, SUSSEX.

FIG. 826.—A staircase of Elizabethan character, which is shown in its balusters, handrail, and newel post; the latter is carved out of the solid with strapwork in relief.

FIG. 827.—In small country houses changes in style came slowly. This fine staircase has the Elizabethan type of baluster and handrail; some newels, which serve as posts carrying the floor above, are ingenious adaptations of the Ionic Order. The door and doorway are contemporary, although the door has applied mouldings forming panels.

FIG. 828.—The stairs and arcading are painted in colours; greys predominate, but warmth is introduced by the free use of yellow and by the heraldic devices which are in their proper colours; imitation of marble is also included in the colour-scheme. The balustrade on the wall and the strapwork over it are painted simulations. Whilst the balusters and handrail (finished with a $\frac{3}{4}$-roll moulding) are Elizabethan in their design, the newel posts decorated with strapwork and terminating in Sackville leopards are in the new fashion. Little extensive painting of this character has survived, though it was fashionable in the early seventeenth century.

c. 1605. King : James I.

FIG. 828.—KNOLE, SEVENOAKS, KENT.

c. 1605.   *King:* James I.

FIG. 829.—KNOLE, KENT.

FIG. 829.—The early seventeenth century brought full development of the Elizabethan grand staircase, features of which were the tall, carved newel posts having heraldic animals as finials (see Fig. 828).

Fig. 830.—The staircase in straight flights and square landings, as that illustrated in the sixteenth century (Fig. 824), was soon developed by shortening the flights and increasing the number of landings, the effect of which was that the stairs, in plan, enclosed an open space or well. Finials were in the form of heraldic beasts taken from the owner's coat of arms, or were pierced and carved and had responding pendants from the newel of the floor above. The handrail became flatter. The wall decoration is not contemporary.

c. 1607.   King: James I

FIG. 830.—CHARLTON HOUSE, KENT.

Photo: Valentine, Dundee.

1607-11.   King: James I.

FIG. 831.—HATFIELD HOUSE, HERTFORDSHIRE.
Robert Lyminge, Architect.

Fig. 831.—One of the most important staircases of a period when the staircase had become fully developed. Characteristics are the carved ornament on the newel posts, the figures by which they are surmounted, and the balusters, rectangular in section but raking with the handrail and string. In all respects a more finished and developed design than the principal staircase at Knole (Figs. 828 and 829).

1618-35. *King:* Charles I.
FIG. 832.—The " Round " Staircase, the QUEEN'S HOUSE, GREENWICH.
Inigo Jones, *Architect.*

FIG. 832.—Notwithstanding the completely Italian character of the house and its details, Inigo Jones did not adopt the important type of staircase which was soon to become a feature of the English house. The stairs were still in a confined space, though no longer winding around a central newel, as shown in Fig. 835 and others which have been illustrated. This was probably the first staircase in an English house the steps of which were tailed into the wall of the well. Attention may be drawn to the simple but graceful treatment of the stair ends (see further development in Fig. 840) and to the iron balustrade, also an innovation both in its form and in the details of its design of scrolls and flowers.

FIG. 833.—The stairs (which were once squeezed into a small space even in the most important houses), now designed in the full Italian manner, assume such prominence that the largest room in the house with a height of two storeys is devoted to them. The illustration shows the right-hand flight of stairs at Coleshill (see plans in Fig. 171). The progress in a few years from the confined, winding stairs in Fig. 832 to this spacious staircase-entrance-hall is remarkable.

c. 1662. *King:* Charles II
FIG. 833.—COLESHILL, BERKSHIRE.

Commonwealth. *c. 1656.*

FIG. 834.—THORPE HALL, near PETERBOROUGH.

Commonwealth.

FIG. 835.—THORPE HALL, near PETERBOROUGH.

c. 1690. William and Mary.

FIG. 836.—DRAYTON HOUSE, NORTHANTS.

c. 1685. *King: Charles II.*

FIG. 837.—BRICKWALL, NORTHIAM, SUSSEX.

c. 1701.   William and Mary.   c. 1714.   King: George I.

FIG. 838.—MOMPESSON HOUSE, SALISBURY.   FIG. 839.—BRADBOURNE, LARKFIELD, KENT.

FIG. 834.—The substitution of panels for balusters, pierced and carved, is of Dutch origin. The wood used was usually pine (though oak was also employed), and was intended to be painted. At Eltham Lodge, at Tyttenhanger Park, at Tredegar Castle, and in other houses built shortly before or shortly after the Restoration, this type of staircase is to be found. There is also an earlier one at Cromwell House, Highgate Hill, c. 1638, which has panels pierced and carved in formal—not floral—scrolls.

FIG. 835.—These circular stairs are unusual in form but of typical constructional detail in respect of the newels, balusters, etc. Whereas the balusters of the ascent are an Italianized variation of the

c. 1714.   King: George I.

FIG. 840.—BRADBOURNE, LARKFIELD, KENT.

double baluster, as at Burwash (Fig. 826), those of the landing are of the later vase shape, still more fully developed at Coleshill (Fig. 833). They retain their interesting painting in brown, which imitates oak.

FIG. 836 shows a walnutwood staircase with stout twisted balusters standing on the stairs—there is no string (as at Brickwall, Fig. 837) except for the balustrade on the wall side, which looks clumsy by comparison. The handrail is narrow, and there are no newel posts.

FIG. 837.—The staircase and panelling are of fir, painted. The stairs have square newels with flat cappings. The handrail has become wide and flat, and as the balusters are all the same length the spandrels of the ramp are filled with triangular panels. The balusters are sturdily substantial, with " barley-sugar " twists, and stand on a closed string.

FIG. 838.—In the eighteenth century there was a change in the design of stair balustrades. Newels were slighter, being often only twice as thick as a baluster. Balusters, too, were more slender, and two or three stood on each stair ; there was no closed string. The handrail was still flat and fairly wide.

FIG. 839.—The newel posts are slight ; the balusters are all " barley-sugar " twists, but are not carved, and there is an open string. The handrail is flat and still fairly broad.

FIG. 840.—Details of stairs in Fig. 839. The finest staircases of this period had the outlines of the carved scrolls of the stair ends projected on the soffits and carved with acanthus leaf ornament.

1702–11.   *Queen:* Anne.

FIG. 841.—EASTON NESTON, TOWCESTER,
NORTHANTS.

Photo by courtesy of H. W. Fincham, F.S.A.

1702–11.   *Queen:* Anne.

FIG. 842.—EASTON NESTON, NORTHANTS.
Nicholas Hawksmoor, *Architect.*

FIGS. 841, 842.—In the great staircase
at Easton Neston the iron balustrade,
in the Tijou manner, is combined with
the wood handrail, as it was at
Hampton Court. The **L** cypher is
that of the owner of the house, the
first Lord Lempster.

1723.   *King:* George I.

FIG. 843.—ARGYLL HOUSE, CHELSEA,
LONDON.
Giacomo Leoni, *Architect.*

FIG. 843 illustrates the entrance hall
and staircase, in which the panelling
is contemporary. The balusters are
neither vase-shaped nor spiral, but
are treated as diminishing columns.

Photo: Bedford Lemere and Co.

1749. *Ironwork c. 1730.*

FIG. 844.—CHESTERFIELD HOUSE, LONDON.
Isaac Ware, *Architect.*

FIG. 844. — The staircase balustrade (brought with the marble steps from the Duke of Chandos's house, Canons) was made *c.* 1730 and was probably the work of a French smith. Of the staircase the owner, Lord Chesterfield, wrote: " The staircase, particularly, will form such a scene as is not in England." In smaller houses the slender baluster (two or three on each stair) continued in favour. The wall decoration is in the Palladian manner, affecting that of Inigo Jones (see Figs. 700, 743).

FIG. 845.—Detail of the stair balustrade (see Fig. 844). It is regarded as one of the finest examples of wrought ironwork in England and vies with the work of Tijou at Hampton Court (Fig. 868). The design, in the French manner, is bolder and more developed than Tijou's. The naturalistic treatment of the acanthus leafage is admirable in its form, and has none of the thinness from which such ornament often suffers.

FIG. 845.—CHESTERFIELD HOUSE, LONDON.

c. 1730.

King : George II

c. 1720.   *King:* George I.

FIG. 846.—THE RED HOUSE, SAW-
BRIDGEWORTH, HERTFORDSHIRE.

c. 1725.   *King:* George I.

FIG. 847.—FINCHCOCKS, GOUDHURST, KENT.

Photo by courtesy of Mallett and Son, Bath.

1727-30.   *King:* George II.

FIG. 848.—NO. 15, QUEEN SQUARE, BATH.   John Wood the elder, *Architect.*

FIG. 846.—An interesting handling of a staircase in a limited space. The newel, balusters, and handrail are of designs common to the period, but have been cleverly adapted to the position, the ramping of the handrail being ingenious if not altogether successful. The two-panel door with fielded panels is also characteristic.

FIG. 847.—The square entrance-hall is the full depth (front to back) of the main building (Fig. 228), the stairs rising from one corner. This is essentially a country-man's work : the design of the wainscoting is crude, and its author has been unable entirely to break away from the Gothic wide, open fireplace, though he has furnished it with a classic architrave instead of the ponderous oak lintel.

FIG. 848.—The dado panelling and stair-case are in mahogany, with the exception of the treads, which are of oak inlaid with bands of mahogany. The wall decoration is in stucco and is probably the work of one of the Francini from the chapel of St. Mary near by. The reduction in the size of the newels made possible a narrower handrail than those seen in staircases of the Wren period (see Fig. 837). The collapsible dog gate is contemporary.

Photo by courtesy of The Burlington Hotel Company, Limited.

c. 1745.   *King: George II.*

FIG. 849.—MONTROSE HOUSE, PETERSHAM, SURREY.

c. 1730.   *King: George II.*

FIG. 850.—NO. 30, OLD BURLINGTON STREET.

c. 1744.   *King: George II.*

FIG. 851.—HONINGTON HALL, WARWICKSHIRE.

Mid-eighteenth century.

FIG. 852.—KEW PALACE.

FIG. 849.—A typical square entrance hall and staircase. The semi-elliptic arches over the doorways and entrances to the passages were often features of these halls, and were sometimes executed in oak, sometimes in painted pine. The bolection mouldings to the panels had long been out of fashion, but the raised panel still persisted; the sunk panel, with a small ovolo moulding, however, was the more fashionable. The soffit of the upper flight of stairs is treated as one panel—a much more economical finish than that of moulding each stair soffit, as shown in Fig. 840.

FIG. 850.—The reversion to Italian design of the Inigo Jones school by Palladian architects is apparent in the large balusters and wide handrail of this staircase, which should be compared with that at Coleshill (Fig. 833). Both are constructed of wood, but their design properly belongs to stone construction as the balustrade to the stairway up to the Queen's House, Greenwich (Fig. 165). The decoration of the staircase well and of the landing with its columns and doorcase is of excellent workmanship after designs in the full Palladian manner.

FIG. 851.—The ironwork of the stair balustrade to the staircase of the inner hall at Honington is somewhat slight, although well designed. The decoration of the arch spandrels is of stucco like that of the outer hall (Fig 654).

FIG. 852.—There was great variety of baluster designs: spiral, fluted, and attenuated-vase form, as this example, where the newels are Doric columns and the handrail is still of fairly wide and flat section.

Photo by courtesy of the London County Council.

c. 1777.

FIG. 853.—STOWE, BUCKS.

c. 1755.
                                                        King: George II.

FIG. 854.—No. 43, PARLIAMENT STREET, LONDON.

1768-9.   King: George III.

FIG. 855.—No. 3, THE TERRACE, RICHMOND HILL, SURREY.

FIG. 853.—A stone staircase with wrought-iron balustrade and mahogany handrail. The scrolled balustrade has vertical members forming panels : this tendency towards verticality is characteristic of the period. The handrail is narrow and of simple section.

FIG. 854.—A staircase balustrade of wood in the " *Chinese Chippendale* " manner.

FIG. 855.—The design of the ironwork is more straggly than that in Fig. 853, and also is more wiry.

Photo by courtesy of Hampton & Sons.   Photo by courtesy of the Curator, Soane Museum.   Photo by courtesy of the London County Council.

1768-9.

FIG. 856.—No. 20, ST. JAMES'S SQUARE, LONDON.

1794.   King: George III.

FIG. 857.—BUCKINGHAM HOUSE. Sir John Soane, *Architect.*

c. 1795.

FIG. 858.—The staircase at No. 1, HORSE GUARDS AVENUE, LONDON.

FIG. 856.—The stairs occupy one side of the hall, opposite is the niche shown in Fig. 657.

FIG. 857.—The staircase well is cold and uninteresting, notwithstanding its architectural treatment and the introduction of decorative tablets and statuary. In one of his lectures Sir John Soane said: " Staircases, vestibules, saloons, and galleries offer a wide field for the exercise of talent in Sculpture, Painting, and Architecture," and proceeds to deprecate the current " fashion of crowding on to flat monotonous ceilings in our Public and Private Buildings, plaster ornaments and small compartments, spotted occasionally with an unimportant picture." In this relation the illustration may be compared with that of Adam decoration (Fig. 657).

FIG. 858.—Graceful staircases, having a semicircular or curved sweep on plan, also economized space. The staircase illustrated here has a delicate iron balustrade with a narrow mahogany handrail. The stone steps have moulded nosings and soffits. Hereafter balustrades became plainer until they consisted only of square wood bars, $1\frac{1}{4}$ inches in diameter, with a plain mahogany handrail of elliptic section.

METALWORK

For other examples of METALWORK—

c. 1100.

FIG. 859.—A wrought-iron grille at WINCHESTER.

FIG. 859.—Medieval smith's work consisting of thin strips of iron twisted into whorls springing from a stem of square section and fixed to each other and to the frame by metal straps.

FIG. 860.—Spur knocker at Great Wigsell, Bodiam, Sussex.

c. 1640.　　　　　　　　　　　*King:* Charles I.

FIG. 860.—Iron spur knocker.

c. sixteenth and seventeenth centuries.

FIG. 861.

FIG. 861.—Iron latch, guide, and catch of type current until superseded by rim locks as in Fig. 869. For type of handle see Fig. 862.

FIG. 862.—Iron ring handle.

FIG. 863.—Iron hinges.

FIG. 862.—Ring handle and pierced rose plate of iron. For type of latch used with this see Fig. 861.

FIG. 863.—A variation of **H** pattern iron hinges. The terminals are said to represent cocks' heads.

FIG. 864.—End of Iron strap.

FIG. 864.—Until the seventeenth century door hinges usually were of **H** pattern or strap and hook type. The ends of straps often were ornamental. Here the strap has been split and twisted into two whorls.

Seventeenth century.

FIG. 865.—A wrought-iron casement hinge, handle, and stay.

FIG. 865.—Until *c.* 1685 (when sashes were becoming established) casements were used. The illustration shows the lower part of one, with the wrought-iron handle for opening and closing, the hinge, and stay for holding open. Types of turnils and spring catch are illustrated in Figs. 866, 867.

Seventeenth century.

FIG. 866.—Turnil.

Seventeenth century.

FIG. 867.—Spring catch.

FIGS. 866 AND 867.—Smiths wrought casement fastenings in great variety, introducing pierced, cut, and twisted ornaments. The two types of fastening illustrated were those most used.

c. 1698.   William and Mary.

FIG. 868.—A panel from a wrought-iron entrance gate at HAMPTON COURT PALACE.

FIG. 868.—A panel of the iron gate to the east entrance under the pediment (Fig. 182), by the French smith, Jean Tijou, who revolutionized such smithing in England. Until his advent, smithing retained its medieval character and simplicity. A detail of more elaborate work of the same character is given in Fig. 845. These illustrations may be compared with those of medieval smiths' work in Figs. 859, 865.

c. 1700.   William and Mary.

FIG. 869.—A brass rim lock from a door to the first presence chamber at HAMPTON COURT PALACE.

FIG. 869.—A brass rim lock in the first presence chamber, enriched with pierced, applied ornaments. In the building accounts is an estimate *d.* 1700 which includes the item "Two guilt Locks at £7 each." (*Wren Society*, vol. iv., p. 62.)

c. 1714.   *Queen: Anne.*

FIG. 870.—Fanlight at BRADBOURNE, LARKFIELD, KENT.

Early nineteenth century.

FIG. 871.—WENT HOUSE, WEST MALLING, KENT.

FIG. 870.—The variety of fan-lights (of which the semicircular was the favourite shape) over eighteenth-century doors was infinite. The fine example here illustrated is made of metal—both iron and lead were used for such lights—but many were of wood. Each material gave opportunity for display of taste and ingenuity in design (see Doorways, Figs. 434 to 469).

FIG. 871.—A sheet-iron hood on wrought-iron brackets. When the jalousies are open the window is perfectly shaded from oblique sun rays.

FIG. 872.—A balconette with a canopy and door hood in metal (see also the balcony in Fig. 292).

Early nineteenth century.

FIG. 872.—In OXFORD STREET, CHELTENHAM.

Early nineteenth century.   *King:* George III.

FIG. 873.—Balcony in BERKELEY PLACE, CHELTENHAM.

FIG. 873.—A verandah-balcony, of which a variety of designs remain in London and in the provinces. Iron and lead were used for the ornament, and balustrades were greatly developed from the simple rails of which they were formed in the seventeenth century.

FIG. 874.—Georgian door knockers.

VARIOUS DETAILS

c. 1240.   *King:* Henry III.   Early 14th century.   *King:* Edward I.
FIGS. 875 AND 876.—STOKESAY CASTLE, SHROPSHIRE.   FIG. 877.—OLD SOAR, PLAXTOL,
                                                                            KENT.

FIGS. 875 AND 876.—Though the hut and booth were without sanitary contrivances, houses of any importance were provided with garderobes in chambers having doorways. The shafts from these were often contrived in the thickness of the walls, and discharged into the moat below water level. One at Amberley Castle had its outlet 3 ft. above ground level, and must have been most offensive. The opening to the shaft of that at Stokesay Castle is now boarded over inside. The shaft passes down into the moat through a buttress (Fig. 876), in the upper part of which are openings to light and ventilate the garderobe chamber. As recently as fifty years ago a fourteenth-century castle in Yorkshire (Markenfield Hall, Figs. 69-73) was used as a farmhouse. It stood in one corner of a square court around which were the stables, cow shippons, and similar buildings. The whole was surrounded by a moat. The farmhouse drew all its water for domestic use from the moat at its corner, and all the drainage of the buildings and from a heap of manure piled up in the court flowed into the moat from the other sides.

FIG. 877.—A decorated piscina in the domestic chapel.

c. 1482.   *King:* Edward IV   Fifteenth century.   Late fifteenth and early sixteenth centuries.
FIG. 878.—OXBURGH HALL, NORFOLK.   FIG. 879.   FIG. 880.

FIG. 878.—The secret opening in the *solid* brick floor leads to the hiding chamber.
FIG. 879.—Ceiling beam moulded and stopped by the mouldings converging at the square of the timber. FIG. 880.—Intersecting ceiling beams moulded; the joist mouldings stopped by dividing and splaying the lowest member out to the square. A carved leaf covers the ends of the other mouldings on each side.

Late fifteenth century.   *King:* Henry VII.

FIG. 881.—THE GUILDHALL, LAVENHAM, SUFFOLK.

FIG. 881.—In some counties, and particularly in East Anglia, angle posts of half-timbered houses often were elaborately carved out of the solid. The branching head of the post may be compared with the simple one shown in Fig. 99.

Sixteenth century.   *Queen :* Elizabeth.   *c.* 1620.   *King :* James I.

FIG. 882.—TURK FARM, SMARDEN,   FIG. 883.—SOCKNERSH MANOR,
KENT.   BRIGHTLING, SUSSEX.

FIG. 882.—Moulded doorpost having four-leaf ornament, which is unusual, and base stop of characteristic sixteenth-century type (see Fig. 405).

FIG. 883.—Grotesque corbels to door hood, which is of later date. The figures are chained round the waist. That on the left has leg shackles also. That on the right holds a doll or other small figure in his hands.

Early eighteenth century.

FIG. 884.—HALES PLACE, TENTERDEN, KENT.

FIG. 884.—Grotesque corbels to door hood.

Eighteenth century.

FIGS. 885 AND 886.—WYE, KENT.

FIGS. 885 AND 886.—Grotesque corbels supporting door hoods or projecting upper storeys are found in counties where there are other traces of Low Country immigrants. Some are as early as the first quarter of the seventeenth century. A curious feature of many is the shackling of the feet by loops, as the gryphons in Fig. 885 and as the figures in Fig. 883. Some corbels of men's figures are represented also chained round the waist to the doorpost as in Fig. 883.

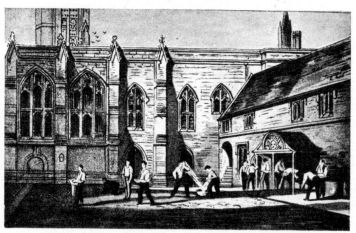

1723-25.   *King :* George I.

FIG. 887.—MEREWORTH CASTLE, KENT.   FIG. 888.—WINCHESTER COLLEGE, HAMPSHIRE.

From an old print republished in "School Life at Winchester College," by R. B. Mansfield.

FIG. 887.—A detail of the parquetry floor of the east dressing-room, a rare surviving example of this work.

FIG. 888.—Until about 1860, scholars had to wash at the old conduit in Chamber Court at all seasons of the year—in the dark, in rain, snow, and frost. "Conduit" was the name given to half a dozen brass cocks fitted on the wall; these often froze and had to be thawed with fire before water would flow.

INDEX